RESEARCH TO PRACTICE IN MENTAL RETARDATION

U.S. Capitol Building, Washington, D.C.

RESEARCH TO PRACTICE
IN
MENTAL RETARDATION

Fourth Congress
of the International Association
for the Scientific Study of Mental Deficiency (IASSMD)

Volume III

BIOMEDICAL
ASPECTS

Edited by

Peter Mittler, Ph.D.

Technical Editor

Jean M. de Jong

University Park Press
Baltimore • London • Tokyo

UNIVERSITY PARK PRESS
International Publishers in Science and Medicine
233 East Redwood Street
Baltimore, Maryland 21202

Typeset by The Composing Room of Michigan, Inc.
Manufactured in the United States of America by Universal Lithographers, Inc., and The Optic Bindery Incorporated.

Library of Congress Cataloging in Publication Data
International Association for the Scientific Study of
Mental Deficiency.
Research to practice in mental retardation.

Includes bibliographies and indexes.
CONTENTS: v. 1. Care and intervention.—v. 2. Education and training.—v. 3. Biomedical aspects.
1. Mental deficiency—Congresses. 2. Mentally handicapped—Care and treatment—Congresses. 3. Mentally handicapped—Education—Congresses. I. Mittler, Peter J. II. Title. [DNLM: 1. Mental retardation—Congresses. 2. Education of mentally retarded—Congresses. W3 IN12U 1976r/ WS107 I61r 1976]
RC569.9.I57   1977   616.8′588   77-5455
ISBN 0-8391-1122-3 (v. 1)
ISBN 0-8391-1123-1 (v. 2)
ISBN 0-8391-1124-x (v. 3)

Contents

DIAGNOSIS AND SCREENING

GENETIC DISORDERS

INBORN ERRORS OF METABOLISM

PREVENTION AND TREATMENT

ENVIRONMENTAL HAZARDS

PRENATAL INFECTIONS

NEUROPSYCHOLOGICAL ASPECTS

Contents of Volume I

PSYCHIATRIC SERVICES

COSTS

Contents of Volume II

Preface

The Fourth Congress of the International Association for the Scientific Study of Mental Deficiency was held in Washington, D.C., in August, 1976, in a year celebrating not only the bicentennial of the United States but also the hundredth anniversary of the American Association on Mental Deficiency, who acted as hosts to the conference. The event was attended by 1,152 registered participants with spouses and associates representing 63 different countries; there were about 500 speakers.

The conference theme "Research to Practice" reflects the expressed needs both of research workers and of practitioners to come to a closer understanding of each others' work and skills, and to take steps to reduce what has in the past been too large a gap between them. Because the conference was attended both by full-time research workers and by practitioners working daily with mentally retarded people, ample opportunities were available both during and between sessions for them to discuss mutual problems and to realise how much they had in common.

We look forward to renewal of acquaintance and meeting newcomers in the field at the Fifth Congress of IASSMD to be held in Israel in 1979.

In bringing together the principal papers presented at the conference, we have tried to identify the main themes of the presentations and to group these under separate headings. In doing so, we have on occasion regrouped papers under one heading that were presented in different sections or symposia. Our aim in arranging the material into themes was to provide more coherence and unity to the volumes as a whole, particularly for readers who were not themselves present at the congress.

The material is presented in three volumes: *Care and Intervention, Education and Training,* and *Biomedical Aspects.* The first volume focuses on developments in service provision, and reflects a particularly strong emphasis on the theme of early intervention and multidisciplinary treatment, on the provision of community and residential services, and on questions concerned with the evaluation of such services to ensure that the needs of mentally handicapped people are met. The second volume is devoted to the theme of education and training, and is largely concerned with questions of what and how to teach, with methods of assessing the individual's abilities and needs, and with methods of determining outcome. The third volume encompasses a wide range of biomedical studies, including prevention, detection, and early treatment, as well as a consideration of the many environmental factors related to intervention, particularly those that lend themselves to treatment. The number of pages devoted to questions concerned with the effects of malnutrition was a marked feature of this congress.

Despite a generous allocation of space, we have been able to find room for only a selection of the many papers presented at the congress. We have been guided in the selection of papers by members of our editorial board, to whom the editor owes a profound debt for their immediate response to his many requests for assistance, particularly in areas outside his own competence. We also gratefully acknowledge similar valuable help from other referees, namely Professor Schneiden and Drs. G. Claridge, T. Ingram, B. H. Kirman, B. W. Richards, N. de M. Rudolph, and J. Stern.

This is the first time that the proceedings of an IASSMD congress have been printed and published commercially. We are therefore grateful for an opportunity to express our appreciation to University Park Press, whose cooperation and efficiency have been exemplary.

But the chief credit for the prompt appearance of these volumes goes to our technical editor, Mrs. Jean de Jong, who has worked tirelessly and enthusiastically to bring order out of chaos and who has brought to the task of editing these volumes her wisdom and experience gained from assisting with the proceedings of previous congresses. Readers will be in her debt to a greater extent than they can possibly realise.

P. M.

Officers of the
International Association
for the Scientific Study
of Mental Deficiency:
1973–1976

President: **Alan D. B. Clarke**, Department of Psychology, The University, Hull, Yorkshire, England.

President-Elect: **Michael J. Begab**, NIH/NICHD/MRP, Landow Building, Room C-708, 7910 Woodmont Avenue, Bethesda, Maryland 20014, United States.

Honorary Vice-President: **Harvey A. Stevens**, Waisman Center on Mental Retardation and Human Development, University of Wisconsin, 2605 Marsh Lane, Madison, Wisconsin 53706, United States.

Vice-Presidents: **Bernard E. Cohen**, Department of Pediatrics 'B', The Chaim Sheba Medical Center, Tel Hashomer, Israel.
Annalise Dupont, Demographic-Genetic Research Department, Aarhus Psychiatric Hospital, DK-8240, Risskov, Denmark.

Past Presidents: **Harvey A. Stevens, Alexander Shapiro, Stanislau Krynski.**

Secretary: **David A. A. Primrose**, The Royal Scottish National Hospital, Larbert, Stirlingshire, Scotland FK5 4EJ.

Treasurer: **Jan B. Meiresonne**, N.O.Z., Postbus 415, Utrecht, The Netherlands.

Officers of the
International Association
for the Scientific
Study of Mental Deficiency:
1976–1979

President: **Michael J. Begab**, NIH/NICHD/MRP, Landow Building, Room C-708, 7910 Woodmont Avenue, Bethesda, Maryland 20014, United States.

President-Elect: **H. O. Åkesson**, Psychiatric Department III, Lillhagen's Hospital, S-422 03 Hisings Backa 3, Sweden.

Honorary Vice-Presidents: **Harvey A. Stevens**, Waisman Center on Mental Retardation and Human Development, University of Wisconsin, 2605 Marsh Lane, Madison, Wisconsin 53706, United States.
Alan D. B. Clarke, Department of Psychology, The University, Hull, Yorkshire, England.

Vice-Presidents: **Bernard E. Cohen**, Department of Pediatrics 'B', The Chaim Sheba Medical Center, Tel Hashomer, Israel.
Ignacy Wald, Instytut Psychoneurologiczny, Al. Sobieskiego 1/9, 02-957 Warsaw, Poland.

Honorary Officers: **Stanislau Krynski, Alexander Shapiro.**

Secretary: **David A. A. Primrose**, The Royal Scottish National Hospital, Larbert, Stirlingshire, Scotland, FK5 4EJ.

Treasurer: **Jan B. Meiresonne**, N.O.Z., Postbus 415, Utrecht, The Netherlands.

Acknowledgments

The International Association for the Scientific Study of Mental Deficiency gratefully acknowledges support for this publication from the President's Committee on Mental Retardation, the National Institute of Child Health and Human Development, the Bureau for the Education of the Handicapped, the Office for Handicapped Individuals, and the Rehabilitation Services Administration.

Congress Organized by the
International Association
for the Scientific Study
of Mental Deficiency
in Association with the
Local Organizing Committee

Host Organization: **American Association on Mental Deficiency**

President: **Burton Blatt** (1976–1977)
*Executive
Secretariat:* **George Soloyanis
Ellen Horn
Carolyn A. Bardwell
Susan J. Annis
John E. Loth, Jr.
Valerie Ducker**

Local Organizing Committee

James D. Clements
David Rosen
George Soloyanis
Robert Erdman
Mortimer Garrison

Local Arrangements Committee

Chairperson: George 'Bud' deHaven

Ruth Adams	William McCahill
Emily Baker	James Melton
Pat Nuse Carlson	Mitzi Parks
Joseph Fenton	Stan Phillips
Hilda Fishback	Muriel Rose
Iris Gordon	Stella Gore Lansing
Darryl Hagy	Raymond Terry
Elaine Hollander	Bathrus Williams
Roma Kaplan	Janice Williams
	Dennis Wyant

Scientific Program Committee

Chairperson: Michael J. Begab
Members: H. Olof Åkesson
Joseph M. Berg
Alan D. B. Clarke
H. A. A. Gresnigt
Stanislau Krynski
Jan B. Meiresonne
David A. Primrose
Harvey A. Stevens
Ignacy Wald

Proceedings Editor:
Peter Mittler

Film Review Committee

Co-Chairpersons:
Molly Gorelick
David A. Primrose

Members:
Neil Goldstein
James Magary

IASSMD Congress Publications

Editor and *Distributor* of the Proceedings of the *First* Congress:
Barry W. Richards, St. Lawrence's Hospital, Caterham, Surrey, CR3 5YA, England
Publication date: October, 1968
Price: $23.00 or £8.00 (inclusive)
Pages: xliv + 982; 175 figures, 155 tables
(supplies still available)

Editor of the Proceedings of the *Second* Congress:
David A. A. Primrose, The Royal Scottish National Hospital, Larbert, Stirlingshire FK5 4EJ, Scotland.
Publication date: December, 1971
Price: 115 guilders
Pages: xxiii + 774; 136 figures, 155 tables
Distributed by: Swets & Zeitlinger, B.V., Heereweg 347B, Lisse, The Netherlands.

Editor and *Distributor* of the Proceedings of the *Third* Congress:
David A. A. Primrose, The Royal Scottish National Hospital, Larbert, Stirlingshire FK5 4EJ, Scotland.
Publication date: April, 1975
Price: $34.00 or £12.00 (inclusive) for two volumes
Pages: Volume 1 xxv + 775; 151 figures, 208 tables
Volume 2 x + 100; 22 figures, 25 tables

Editor of the Proceedings of the *Fourth* Congress:
Peter Mittler, Hester Adrian Research Centre, The University, Manchester M13 9PL, England.
Publication date: July—September, 1977
Prices: $24.50 per volume
Pages: Three volumes; 1718 pages
Published by: University Park Press, Chamber of Commerce Building, Baltimore, Maryland 21202, U.S.A.

PROCEEDINGS OF THE FOURTH CONGRESS
OF THE INTERNATIONAL ASSOCIATION
FOR THE SCIENTIFIC STUDY
OF MENTAL DEFICIENCY

Washington, D.C., U.S.A.   22–27 August, 1976
The American University

**Research to Practice
in
Mental Retardation**

Published in three volumes:
Volume I: Care and Intervention
Volume II: Education and Training
Volume III: Biomedical Aspects

Edited by
Peter Mittler, Ph.D.
Director,
Hester Adrian Research Centre
for the Study of Learning Processes
in the Mentally Handicapped
University of Manchester,
Manchester M13 9PL, England

RESEARCH TO PRACTICE
IN
MENTAL RETARDATION

DIAGNOSIS
AND SCREENING

RESEARCH TO PRACTICE IN MENTAL RETARDATION
Biomedical Aspects, Volume III
Edited by Peter Mittler
Copyright 1977 I.A.S.S.M.D.

PRENATAL DIAGNOSTIC EXPERIENCE OUTSIDE THE UNITED STATES

L. Dallaire
Section of Medical Genetics,
Hôpital Sainte-Justine,
3175 Chemin Sainte-Catherine,
Montreal, Quebec H3T 1C5, Canada

Last spring, during a workshop, interesting points of view on the actual status of prenatal diagnosis were formulated by representatives of twelve countries (Dallaire and Milunsky, 1976). This chapter elaborates on three points of major interest that may influence the development of prenatal diagnosis of genetic disease services during the coming years. They are: 1) the importance of collaborative studies, 2) the present orientation of services, 3) the long-term impact of current results and research studies.

Prenatal diagnosis programs have evolved throughout the world with the ultimate goals of circumscribing the safety and indications of the test, and finding an answer to some of the following questions: 1) Who has access to this diagnostic procedure? 2) Who defrays the cost of the amniocentesis? 3) Is the public well informed about the availability of this test? 4) Do physicians rely on the genetic services to evaluate and direct pregnant mothers throughout the different steps of the prenatal diagnosis schedule? 5) Can diagnostic errors be avoided? 6) Will there ever be a code of ethics for the prenatal diagnosis of genetic disease?

COLLABORATIVE STUDIES

In the early 1970s, three national research projects with similar objectives and methods were designed: the United States Collaborative Study, the Canadian MRC Working Group on Prenatal Diagnosis, and the British Study Group. A strict protocol that allowed meaningful statistical analysis of data in view of some eventual pooling and comparison of results was followed by those groups. The first official report emanated from the United States and was related to 1,040 amniocentesis cases. Dr. Duane Alexander has summarized those results in

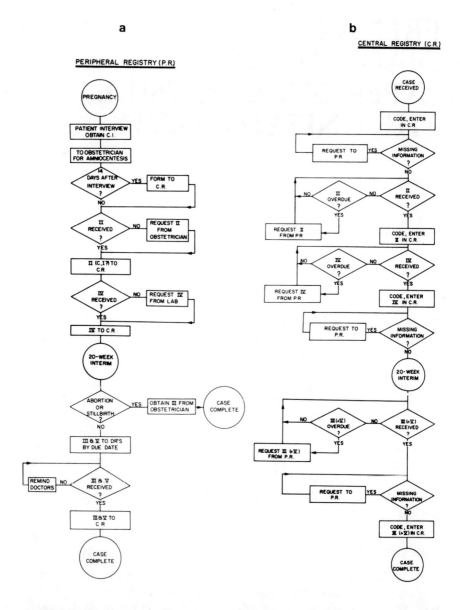

Figure 1. Figures 1a and 1b illustrate the path followed by individual charts from the Peripheral Registry to the Central Registry. P.R.–Peripheral registry; C.R.–Central registry; C–Consent Form; I–Part I: Patient interview (Nurse coordinator); II–Part II: Amniocentesis report (Obstetrician); III–Part III: Labour and delivery (Obstetrician); IV–Part IV: Laboratory report and assay form (head of laboratory); V–Part V: Neonatal physical examination (attending physician).

his presentation to this Congress. Results of a study of the same order of magnitude were communicated by the Canadian Group more recently (Canadian Registry, 1976), and a report from Great Britain should be released within the next few months (Leading article, *The Lancet,* 1977).

The two diagrams in Figure 1 illustrate the intake and processing of data in the Canadian Amniocentesis Registry. Each centre coordinated its own data on a five-part questionnaire. The first part contained personal data, identifying information, a pregnancy history, and details of the indication for amniocentesis, e.g., the karyotype if the indication were a previous chromosomal abnormality. Once an amniocentesis has been registered, it must be followed by a detailed description of the pregnancy outcome, in order to avoid bias created by an undesirable selection of patients. The second part contains information regarding the actual technical procedure, such as the size of the needle and gestational age; this is filled out by the obstetrician. The third part consists of the test results: the karyotype for chromosomal analysis, enzyme levels, and alpha$_1$-foetoprotein, and is completed by the principal investigator in the laboratory concerned. The fourth part, filled out by the obstetrician, contains information regarding the abortion or delivery, and part five consists of information regarding the outcome of the pregnancy, infant's sex, birth weight, and any abnormalities. This is filled out by the attending physician or paediatrician when the birth was a live one or went to term. The data are fed into the central registry and are punched on IBM cards and set up for data analysis by computer.

Periodically, since 1970, several reports have been published involving mainly regional centres or compiled data from several laboratories, particularly in Europe, where scientists met frequently, exchanged information on the procedure, and participated in the publication of proceedings from these general conferences. European reports were based on more than 8,000 cases, a fact pointing to the importance of prenatal diagnosis in medical practice today and also to the availability of this test outside of the United States.

Very few reports from Australia, Eastern European countries, India, Japan, New Zealand, and South Africa are found in the literature; there is no indication that what reports there are represent surveys of collaborative studies.

SERVICE AND LABORATORY FACILITIES

Canada has a population of 22 million, and 13 centres are available across the country to assure a distribution of services to each of the ten provinces. Basically, all of these centres have facilities for cytogenetic studies, and several can perform determinations of alpha$_1$-foetoprotein for the detection of neural tube defects, while evaluation of rare enzymatic problems are being carried out in three or four specialized centres. A "Prenatal Diagnosis Newsletter" was published twice a year from 1971 to 1976. During the same period, members of the Working Group met at least four times a year to evaluate the intake of cases, and all participating centers were invited once a year to a general meeting.

In West Germany, a country of 60 million individuals, 25 centres are available, but not all of these satellite centres have facilities to complete the initial cytogenetic, biochemical, or enzymatic studies. Patients may be referred from evaluation satellite centres to one of the few main centres once the case has been accepted as a high risk pregnancy and the amniocentesis justified. There is excellent exchange of information between all of these centres: a newsletter "Informationsblatt: Prenatale Diagnostik Genetisch Bedingter Defekte," edited by J. D. Murken and S. Stengel-Rutkowski from Munich, is distributed periodically and its front page cover indicates the location of participating groups.

In Denmark, there are three prenatal diagnosis centres; two are located in Copenhagen and one in Aarhus. Denmark can be compared to the province of Quebec (Canada), where, for a population of 6 million, two centres located in Montreal have up to now been able to render needed services to the at risk maternal population. A similar program exists in the Netherlands, where a population of less than 15 million inhabitants can rely on the expertise of three major laboratories. In France (population: 50 million) the main centre is located in Paris at the Centre International de l'Enfance, under Professor Boué's direction. Satellite as well as major centres are now being developed throughout the country and two or more major centres are being planned in the Paris region. Several laboratories have been established throughout the British Isles, some of which are well-known for their outstanding contribution to the development of screening methods for the detection of neural tube defects.

In other countries, such as Belgium, Finland, Greece, Norway, Sweden, and Switzerland, prenatal diagnosis facilities exist, and if these are inadequate for a particular area of expertise, they often rely on more specialized facilities available in not too distant larger European centres.

At the present time, most European and North American genetic units have access to a network of laboratories specializing in some aspects of prenatal diagnosis. The number of tests done in each of those laboratories is relatively the same at the moment (maximum 400/year) if one excepts larger service laboratories, mentioned by Jacobson (1976), where close to 1,000 cases are processed per year. It is estimated that during the last five years 10,000 cases have been studied in various European laboratories. This number is probably comparable to the number of amniocenteses done up to now for prenatal diagnosis of genetic disease in United States, if one includes data from all centres providing this service since 1970 and not included in the Registry project.

Most centres have access to ultrasound, and strong efforts are being made to screen all amniotic fluid samples, irrespective of the amniocentesis indication, for neural tube defect by the study of alpha$_1$-foetoprotein. As a rule, foetoscopy is not used for diagnostic purposes, but Professor Philip and his Danish colleagues are trying to develop a safe and useful instrument. The overall indications for prenatal diagnosis differ from one country to another, mostly because of the variable gene frequency of rare metabolic diseases, the "écart" in maternal age distribution, and the variable emphasis put on the history of a previous aneuploid birth. For instance, in Greece there is much emphasis on the study of thalassemia, and in Great Britain the detection of neural tube defects is a priority. In the Netherlands, for social reasons relatively few women aged 40 or more request an amniocentesis. In France, an excellent network of cytogenetic laboratories has focused the prenatal diagnosis services on familial reciprocal translocations and much less on the previous aneuploid birth histories. Women age 35 and over are generally accepted in the advanced maternal age group in most countries, but because of the rapid increase in referrals, several laboratories are now refusing patients under 40 years of age. In Beograd, a noncompulsory screening program was established two years ago for pregnant women over 40 (Moric-Petrovic, 1976).

Genetic centres are usually responsible for handling cases, although obstetric departments are also very closely involved. One major point of interest is the financing and the development of prenatal diagnosis programs in 1976; most laboratories have some difficulty in developing and financing this new service. France is probably ahead of most countries in planning, because public funds are now being made available for this service, while elsewhere, for instance in Denmark and the Netherlands, the respective governments are studying the long-term implications of this new service and will likely offer continuing financial support in the very near future. In Denmark a cost-benefit analysis (Mikkelsen and Nielsen, 1976) has shown a clear benefit for the age group over 40 and a small deficit for the 35–40 age group. In Canada, medicare is the responsibility of each province, and although the national research study has just been completed and results released, we do not expect a national form of support to be implemented. It is generally accepted that prenatal diagnosis of genetic disease must be completed in specialized referral centres. Public funds must be made available to assure this service and research must be supported to improve technical facilities to circumscribe the high risk group and to discover other conditions for which prenatal diagnosis could be applied with benefit.

RESULTS AND RESEARCH STUDIES

The data collection and preliminary results of the Canadian study on prenatal diagnosis of genetic disease are now completed and were released on June 10, 1976, at the annual meeting of the Society of Obstetricians and Gynaecologists of Canada, held in Toronto, Ontario. The results of the study have been published (Simpson et al., 1976), and full details of the study will appear in a monograph in 1977.

The number of pregnancies monitored was 1,020, requiring 1,220 amniocenteses. These represented 990 women, of whom 30 had two amniocenteses in different pregnancies. Approximately half of the amniocenteses were done for maternal age, with the next most common indication being a chromosome

Table 1. Number of women per 1,000 giving birth[a] who underwent amniocentesis in 1973 and 1974

	1973 Mother's age (yr)		1974 Mother's age (yr)	
Region	35–39	≥ 40	35–39	≥ 40
Maritimes	6.0	2.6	8.6	18.9
Quebec	1.5	8.3	5.6	17.2
Ontario	6.1	12.7	9.5	38.1
Manitoba	9.0	28.6	1.4	24.9
Saskatchewan	0.0	10.9	1.5	8.4
Alberta	13.0	26.6	20.6	59.9
British Columbia	17.7	56.7	10.6	106.2
All provinces[b]	5.9	15.2	8.4	34.1

[a]Statistics Canada data for 1973 and 1974; includes live births and stillbirths.
[b]Excluding Newfoundland.

abnormality in a previous child. The number of cases by indications as they were taken into the Registry show a threefold increase from 1972 to 1975, and, as expected, a rising percentage of patients at risk for a neural tube defect has been observed since 1974.

The women entering the study, as in other specialized health services and for a variety of sociological reasons, were likely to be educated, professional, and Protestant, rather than less well-educated, nonprofessional, and Catholic. The overall frequencies of foetal loss and neonatal deaths in the study were no different from those in controls taken from the Vital Statistics of Canada, several comparable hospital populations selected to match the sample, and from the United States study of 1,040 pregnancies. There were 33 foetal losses and 10 neonatal deaths from the 1,020 pregnancies in the Canadian study. There were, however, two cases of amnionitis that resulted in a foetal loss and that may have

Table 2. Interval between final amniocentesis and diagnosis

	Diagnostic test[a]	
Interval (days)	Enzyme assay	Chromosome analysis
1–7	1 (2.9)	14 (1.4)
8–14	1 (2.9)	401 (39.3)
15–21	6 (17.1)	288 (28.2)
22–28	11 (31.4)	94 (9.2)
29–35	6 (17.1)	14 (1.4)
≥ 36	6 (17.1)	10 (1.0)
No information	4 (11.4)	199 (19.5)
Total	35 (100.0)	1,020 (100.0)

[a]Number of amniocenteses and percent of total.

Table 3. Erroneous diagnoses (Canadian study – 1,020 amniocenteses)

Indication for amniocentesis	Diagnosis	Outcome	Type of error	Probable reason for erroneous diagnosis
Down's syndrome	Normal female	Spontaneous abortion; male	Sexing	Maternal contamination or erroneous pathology report
Mother's age, 40 years	Normal female	Normal male	Sexing	Maternal contamination
Down's syndrome	Neural tube defect	No neural tube defect	False +	Test limitation
Trisomy 18	Neural tube defect	No neural tube defect	False +	Test limitation
Neural tube defect	Normal female	Closed neural tube defect	False −	Test limitation
Neural tube defect	Normal female	Closed neural tube defect	False −	Test limitation
Maternal age, 45 years	Death	Stillbirth; open neural tube defect	? False −	Incorrect interpretation

Table 4. Risk of recurrence (%) of genetic disease (from selected reports mentioned in this chapter)

Indication	Canada	Denmark	France	Scotland	West Germany
Previous T/21	1.1 (348)	1.0 (75)	0 (137)	0.9 (112)	0.8 (254)
Advanced maternal age 35–39 years	1.6 (249)	1.4 (148)	–	1.0 (105)	1.2 (332)
AMA ≥ 40 years	5.5 (217)	8.8 (68)	3.4 (349)	5.4 (147)	5.2 (328)
History of neural tube defect	4.4 (90)	10.0 (10)	0 (20)	5.6 (357)	–

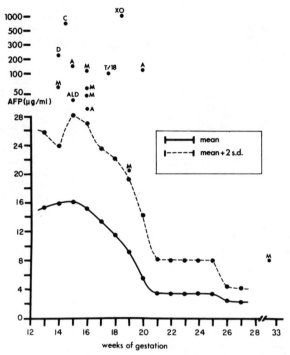

Figure 2. Patients with elevated amniotic fluid alpha₁-foetoprotein levels. The normal levels are based on the study of 400 normal AF samples. A: anencephaly; ALD: Aldrich syndrome; C: chromosomal aberration and foetal death; D: syphilis followed by foetal death; M: meningomyelocele; T/18: trisomy 18; XO: Turner syndrome. (From the prenatal diagnostic center, Hôpital Ste-Justine, Montreal).

been a result of the procedure. Generally speaking, very few pregnant women ≥ 35 years of age received amniocentesis (Table 1).

Ninety-four percent of the pregnancies had an amniocentesis that resulted in a diagnosis; the failures to produce a diagnosis were primarily due to culture failure, inability to obtain amniotic fluid, and a few tests that were inconclusive.

The time intervals that elapsed between the amniocentesis and diagnosis are given in Table 2. Patients had a longer wait if the diagnosis was dependent on an enzyme assay rather than on a chromosome analysis. Of the 62 abnormal fetuses (including 23 males for X-linked conditions), 51 were electively aborted. The errors in diagnosis are given in Table 3. Four of the seven errors were due to difficulties with the alpha₁-foetoprotein test. Two errors were in sexing; one was definitely maternal contamination and the other was possibly an erroneous reporting of the sex on the pathology report of a spontaneous abortion. As pointed out by Dreyfus and Poenaru from Paris (1976) other sources of errors could be low enzyme activities (hexosaminidase AB, arylsulfatase) found in normal individuals, dizygotic twins, and incomplete evaluation of index cases.

It is difficult to compare data from the Canadian study with reports from other countries and complete a statistical analysis of pooled results. However, several points (Table 4) are worth mentioning because they show a definite pattern. They are: 1) the risk of recurrence of random aneuploidy in family history of nondisjunction (1%), 2) the high frequency (5%) of chromosomal aberrations in the advanced maternal age group ($\geqslant 40$), particularly if there is a history of trisomy 21 in a previous pregnancy (14%) (Simpson et al., 1976). It is too early yet to conclude on the observed recurrence risk (5%) of neural tube defects because of our inability to ascertain all of those anomalies and the rather recent use of amniotic fluid and maternal serum AFP determinations for NTD screening. In our experience (Figure 2), several foetal pathologies are linked to increased amniotic fluid AFP levels, a finding pointing to the necessity of simultaneously performing ultrasonography, total alpha-foetoprotein determination, and cytogenetic studies to delineate the diagnosis in pregnancies at risk.

CONCLUSION

In a world in which family planning and the quality of life are important, the expectant mother has to be assured, within limits, that she will deliver a healthy child. It is not surprising today that a risk of 1 to 5% becomes unacceptable to parents if one considers all the socioeconomic implications associated with the birth of a severely handicapped infant. Other positive aspects of prenatal testing will arise from the reassurance of worried parents. Furthermore, medical knowledge gained while doing amniocentesis may lead to the understanding of still unsolved problems during fetal growth and development. It may eventually permit the treatment in utero of genetic diseases.

Responsibility for maintaining the actual program and for offering prenatal diagnosis of genetic disease as a service to the population belongs equally to the laboratories that have developed the techniques permitting the analysis of foetal cells and amniotic fluid and to government authorities, who have the obligation to support existing centres and to develop others when needed. Prenatal diagnosis of genetic disease is a working tool, subject to errors in diagnosis. Technical accidents and medical complications will increase as this procedure is being developed and is offered to a greater number of patients at risk. It has to be realized that if only advanced maternal age patients and neural tube defects cases at risk were to be tested, the number of patients seen for prenatal diagnosis in Canada, for instance, would be ten times greater than the actual figure and would amount to nearly 10,000 per year. In the United States this number could easily reach 50,000 per year. Fortunately, the conservative approach of the physicians and the families at risk in accepting this procedure may give enough time to elaborate satisfactory service programs and provide adequate laboratory facilities. The financial investment would be more than justified by the decrease in the incidence of major malformations with their destructive consequences on family life and morale. Major advances in the prevention of birth defects and therapy are feasible if research programs are in close association with service aspects of prenatal diagnosis. Research studies must be oriented toward the development of accelerated techniques for the diagnosis of inborn errors of metabolism, a safe and reliable method to detect neural tube defects, and the treatment of some metabolic diseases in utero.

SUMMARY

Prenatal diagnosis of genetic disease is a procedure commonly used in several countries. Canadian and European Centres have recently completed evaluation projects on the efficiency of this new diagnostic tool. Geographical and socioeconomic factors intervene in the establishment of services. Research programs, mainly in the diagnostic approach to inborn errors of metabolism and neural tube defects, should be realized in close association with genetic services and prenatal diagnostic units.

REFERENCES

Alexander, D. (1976) The safety and accuracy of mid-trimester amniocentesis: The United States Amniocentesis Registry. Paper presented at the 4th Congress of the I.A.S.S.M.D., Washington.

Canadian Registry for Prenatal Diagnosis of Genetic Disease (1976) Report from the Working Group, Annual meeting of the Society for Obstetricians and Gynaecologists of Canada, Toronto, June.

Dallaire, L., and Milunsky, A. (1976) Chairmen: Workshop: Update in prenatal diagnosis of genetic disease. Annual Meeting of the European Society of Human Genetics, Athens, Greece, May.

Dreyfus, J. D., and Poenaru, L. (1976) Difficulties and problems of antenatal diagnosis. Colloque on Prenatal Diagnosis, Institut National de la Santé et de la Recherche Médicale 61:155.

Jacobson, C. (1976) Community utilization of amniocentesis. Paper presented at the 4th Congress of the I.A.S.S.M.D., Washington.

Leading Article (1977) U.K. collaborative study. Maternal serum-alpha-foetoprotein measurements in antenatal screening for anencephaly and spina bifida in early pregnancy. Lancet 1:1323.

Moris-Petrovic, S. (1976) Psychological and ethical concerns of doctors and patients. Colloque on Prenatal Diagnosis, Institut National de la Santé et de la Recherche Médicale 61:299.

Mikkelsen, M., and Nielsen, G. (1976) Cost-benefit analysis of prevention of Down's syndrome. Colloque on Prenatal Diagnosis, Institut National de la Santé et de la Recherche Médicale 61:283.

Simpson, N. E., Dallaire, L., Miller, J. R., Siminovich, L., Hamerton, J. L., Miller, J., and McKeen, C. (1976) Prenatal diagnosis of genetic disease in Canada: report of a collaborative study. Canad. Med. Ass. J. 115:739.

RESEARCH TO PRACTICE IN MENTAL RETARDATION
Biomedical Aspects, Volume III
Edited by Peter Mittler
Copyright 1977 I.A.S.S.M.D.

CURRENT AND NEWER ASPECTS OF NEWBORN SCREENING

R. Guthrie
Bell Facility, State University of New York at Buffalo,
P.O. Box U, Station B. Buffalo, New York, 14207, United States

Phenylketonuria (PKU) was first discovered by Fölling (1934), when he tested the urine of two severely retarded siblings with ferric chloride reagent to reveal the presence of large amounts of phenylpyruvic acid, or phenylketone. It was then quickly shown that about 1% of severe retardation was due to PKU. Later, Jervis (1953), in New York, showed that the disease was due to a defect in conversion of the amino acid phenylalanine to tyrosine by the liver enzyme phenylalanine hydroxylase.

The most important practical discovery came with Bickel's demonstration (1953) that the effects of PKU could be significantly prevented by use of an artificial diet that controlled phenylalanine intake. Thus, the blood level of phenylalanine could be normalized. The remaining challenge was to find a practical method of testing every infant for the presence of PKU.

Centerwall (1957), in California, developed the first newborn screening test for PKU. He simply modified the urine test for phenylpyruvic acid, first used by Fölling, by dropping a little ferric chloride solution onto the infant's wet diaper. This is the well known "diaper test," which depends on the reaction between ferric chloride and the phenylpyruvic acid in the urine of an affected infant. With the aid of this procedure, a number of cases of PKU were detected. These were treated by means of a low-phenylalanine diet, with results that were somewhat equivocal but encouraging. However, this test was unsuitable in many ways. First, it gave positive results, at best, no earlier than about one month after birth because of the delay in rise of serum levels of phenylalanine to the point where its metabolic product would show up in the urine; thus, there was reason to suspect that by the time treatment could be initiated, the infant might already have suffered irreversible brain damage. Second, its success as a mass screening device depended heavily on the cooperation of untrained or inexperienced individuals—parents, public health nurses, etc.—who would have only the most general notion of what to look for, since their chances of having seen another case of this rare condition were remote.

In the late 1950s, I was asked by Dr. Robert Warner, in Buffalo, to run tests on serum phenylalanine levels to monitor the dietary treatment of two PKU patients. Dissatisfied with existing procedures, we devised the bacterial inhibition test. This procedure employs cultures of *Bacillus subtilis* in an agar medium. Normally, this organism is capable of synthesizing phenylalanine (which it requires for growth), but if the medium contains β-2-thienylalanine, an analogue of phenylalanine, some essential metabolic process is blocked, so that the bacterium cannot reproduce. When a filter paper disc, impregnated with blood from an affected individual, is placed on the medium, however, the exogenous phenylalanine diffuses into the medium, producing a zone of growth surrounding the disc. By appropriate adjustment of the concentration of inhibitor the test can be made sensitive over the entire range of expected phenylalanine concentrations, the width of the growth zone being proportional to the amount of phenylalanine present.

With this test, we were able to monitor Dr. Warner's PKU patients in his treatment program from 1957–61. In 1960, my niece was discovered to be retarded at the age of 13 months because of PKU. This inspired me to try a modification of our monitoring test for use as a screening test. The essential difference was finding that a disc punched from a dried blood spot could be used as a substitute for the previously used serum-impregnated filter paper (Guthrie and Susi, 1963).

This initial use of dried spots of blood was the most valuable part of the first PKU screening test. Since 1961, many different kinds of tests have been developed for use with these blood spots. Despite a long history of the use of dried blood specimens in other fields, our PKU test seems to mark the beginning of wide use of this simple blood specimen in medicine.

This test became the basis of widespread screening for PKU in the United States in the 1960s (Guthrie, 1969). Laws were passed in 43 states requiring a PKU test, so that by 1970, over 90% of infants were being tested. Many European countries, plus Australia, New Zealand, and Israel, started programs. As a result, hundreds of infants were placed on the diet before one month of age. The largest attempt to study the effects of dietary treatment is the United States National Collaborative Study, under the leadership of Dr. Richard Koch. In this study, the oldest children under treatment are now eight years of age and the youngest are four years old. There are 170 children who have been followed and treated since they were in the first month of life. The most important finding is that, of these 170 children, only three are retarded. Also, there is little significant difference in development between the PKU children and their non-PKU siblings. This illustrates that, when adequately treated, these children grow up almost normally.

PKU is a rare condition, discovered in about 1 out of 10,000 newborns. In spite of its rarity, PKU has become a model for how mental retardation can be prevented. PKU is only one of many environmental and genetic causes of mental retardation, but it has served to symbolize what can be accomplished; for that reason, it has a much broader significance for the prevention of mental retardation than the number of cases detected.

Starting in 1963, we began to develop other bacterial screening tests for inborn errors of metabolism using the same dried spots of blood (Guthrie, 1968; Guthrie, 1972), while other laboratories tried such methods as paper and thin-layer chromatography, chemical, or enzyme tests. However, some type of automation was needed to use these tests. A device called a template, developed in Glasgow by Mr. Robert Kennedy, is now being used in a number of different screening laboratories in England to facilitate placing blood discs on several different types of agar test plates.

A different type of device for automating use of the blood spots is a foot-operated quadratic punch, developed in Vienna by Professor Otto Thalhammer. He is able to test nearly every baby born in Austria, using six different tests that we have developed, for about 25 cents per baby. Three students come in every afternoon to the small screening laboratory to punch out six discs from every blood specimen, of which 100,000 are received annually.

An American attempt at automation is the Phillips' quadratic punch-index. It is more elaborate and costs more, but it pays for itself by enabling one technician to do the work of several in processing the dried blood spots.

Four laboratories in the United States work closely with us: one in the state of Oregon, one in the state of Massachusetts, one in western New York, and one in an area in metropolitan Los Angeles. A fifth laboratory in New Zealand, began working with us in 1968 (Houston and Veale, 1971). This is actually a Pacific Island program, not confined to New Zealand, and is geographically the biggest in the world; it covers more than half the Pacific Ocean. Of course, the population in many of these islands is very small. Specimens from the islands outside New Zealand are sent by airmail, and follow-up screening results can be done by short-wave radio.

Screening tests developed in our laboratory are listed in Table 1. The four tests listed as "EA" or "FST" were developed by Dr. William Murphey (Murphey, Patchen, and Guthrie, 1972), and the hemoglobin test by Dr. Michael Garrick (Garrick, Dembure, and Guthrie, 1973) in our laboratory. As previously mentioned, several screening methods using the dried spots of blood have been developed by other laboratories.

During the past five years, the screening laboratories collaborating with us have demonstrated that, with automation, six to eight of the tests listed in the table can be carried out at little increase in cost over the single PKU test, provided a sufficient volume of specimens is available. The minimum is approximately 25,000 per year; increasing volume further reduces the cost and produces other advantages. For these reasons, we have recently been proposing development of "regional" screening centers (Brandon, 1976). By "regional" program, I mean one in which a sufficient number of newborn specimens are screened daily

Table 1. Newborn screening tests[a] for inherited abnormalities

Disease	Test substance	Test	Automated	Treatable
Phenylketonuria	Phenylalanine	BIA[b]	✓	✓
Maple Syrup Urine Disease	Leucine	BIA	✓	✓
Tyrosinemia (transient and permanent)	Tyrosine	BIA	✓	✓
Homocystinuria	Methionine	BIA	✓	✓
Histidinemia	Histidine	BIA	✓	✓
Valinemia	Valine	MBIA[c]	✓	✓
Galactosemia	Galactose	MBIA or Coliphage	✓	✓
Transferase or Kinase Deficiency	Galactose Uridyltransferase	Beutler	Partly	✓
Transferase Deficiency only	Argininosuccinic Acid Lyase	EA[d]	✓	✓
Argininosuccinic Aciduria	Orotidine-1'-phosphate Decarboxylase	EA	✓	✓
Orotic Aciduria	Cl Esterase Inhibitor	FST[e]	Partly	✓
Hereditary Angioneurotic Edema	α-Trypsin Inhibitor	FST	Partly	✓
Emphysema (adult)		FST	Partly	No
Liver Disease (infant)	Haemoglobin	Electrophoresis	Partly	Palliative only
Sickle Cell Anaemia				

Reprinted with permission from Guthrie, R., "Mass Screening for Genetic Disease," *Hospital Practice*, Vol. 7, No. 6, and from "Medical Genetics," (Victor McKusick and Robert Claiborne, eds.) HP Publishing Co., Inc., New York, 1973.

[a]Using dried blood spot filter paper specimens.
[b]Bacterial inhibition assay.
[c]Metabolite bacterial inhibition assay.
[d]Enzyme-auxotroph bacterial assay.
[e]Fluorescent spot test.

to permit application of those methods of automation already routine in a number of laboratories for the purpose of carrying out at least eight of the thirteen tests available.

Even more important for such a program is close and continuous liaison between the screening center and the medical follow-up and management of the cases detected (Veale and Houston, 1976). Several programs with these features have been developed in Europe and the United States. Approximately thirty multiple-test laboratories, using four or more of our tests on dried spots of blood collected for PKU screening, have come into existence since 1964. Japan is the most recent country to develop a multiple-test screening program, and, recently, multiple-test programs have been started in Mexico and Venezuela.

In the United States, several other states have expanded their use of the PKU blood spots to include other tests; the states include Ohio, Maryland, Georgia, South Carolina, and Minnesota. New York has recently established a state-wide program for a battery of six tests, in addition to the PKU test. Several other states are planning similar programs.

The principal problems in the United States that have impeded expansion of PKU test programs to include tests for other conditions are: 1) lack of liaison between screening centers and medical centers, 2) restrictions of screening areas by state boundaries (many states have too few newborn infants per year for efficient PKU screening, let alone screening for more rare conditions), and 3) fragmentation of screening—even within large states—when private facilities are used. An outstanding example is California, where newborn tests for PKU are carried out by 150 different private laboratories at a charge that varies from $1 to $15 per test! With the same funds, two or three regional centers could test all infants for several conditions and have money left over to assist with medical follow-up and management.

Fortunately, California has just passed a bill authorizing establishment of a state-wide "centralized screening program." As a result, it is my hope that a screening program based in university departments of pediatrics will be developed in partnership with the State Health Department. Such a program would be without precedent in the United States. In my opinion, basing screening in medical schools will accomplish three goals: 1) better medical service for the infants and families identified through screening, 2) use of the screening test program for teaching, and 3) use of screening for research. The last has already been amply demonstrated during the past ten years.

This past year, Oregon began to receive filter paper blood specimens from Alaska and Montana, to begin formation of the first multi-state region. Only in this way can states with small populations have access to a large battery of tests for newborn screening. More recently, some of the small New England states have begun sending specimens to the Massachusetts Health Department Laboratory.

Finally, I must mention the most important new test available for use with dried spots of blood. This is the application of radioimmunoassay for mass screening for hypothyroidism. The pioneering efforts of Dussault and Laberge (Dussault, Coulombe, Laberge, Letarte, Guyda, and Khoury, 1975) in Quebec have been amply confirmed in Toronto, Pittsburgh, and Oregon; at present, many other centers are beginning to screen for hypothyroidism. Results so far indicate a frequency of one case in 5,000 newborn infants. In Oregon, Dr. William Murphey has found four cases in the first 12,000 infants, using Reed Larsen's (Larsen and Broskin, 1975) recent modification of the Quebec T_4 method, followed by confirmation with Foley's (Klein, Agustin, and Foley, 1974) method for thyroid stimulating hormone (TSH) or Larsen's (Larsen, Merker, and Parlow, 1976) recent method for TSH.

It is apparent that in the future, in all probability, an increasing number of rare, inherited causes of mental retardation will be discovered and that ways of preventing their damaging effects through treatment or genetic counseling will be applied. However, there is another exciting possibility that may develop from such efforts, a possibility that was predicted over seventy years ago by Sir Archibald Garrod in his classic paper, "The Incidence of Alkaptonuria: A Study in Chemical Individuality" (Garrod, 1902). Garrod originated the term "inborn errors of metabolism," and was the first to describe an inherited chemical defect in man, many years before such discoveries were made in experimental animals, plants, or even microbes. Garrod predicted that each individual person would be found to have a unique biochemical profile, or fingerprint, that would explain "normal" as well as "abnormal" individual behavior. He felt that diseases caused by "inborn errors of metabolism" are simply the more obvious manifestations of such differences. Recent advances in biochemistry and genetics have demonstrated that Garrod was fifty years ahead of his time. Screening programs for PKU as a public health measure to prevent the tragedy of mental retardation in one infant among 10,000 are forerunners of the time when every newborn infant's metabolic machinery will be tested for a long list of "errors" in order to institute any one of an equally long list of remedial measures. Equally important will be the opportunity for new knowledge of the metabolic nature of the human organism afforded from a study of these "mistakes" produced during the course of human evolution.

SUMMARY

Collection of dried spots of blood on filter paper from newborn infants for early detection and treatment of phenylketonuria has become routine in many countries since development of the bacterial inhibition assay screening method 15 years ago. Unfortunately, although many other tests have been developed for use with this convenient specimen at marginal increase in cost, their use has been limited. With the recent availability of a practical test for hypothyroidism, it is extremely important to organize regional screening programs for multiple testing, including clinical follow-up.

REFERENCES

Bickel, H. et al. (1953) Influence of phenylalanine intake on phenylketonuria. Lancet 2:812.

Brandon, G. R. (1976) Regionalization of public health metabolic laboratories. Public Health Labs. 34:56.

Centerwall, W. R. (1957) Phenylketonuria. JAMA 165:392.

Dussault, J. H., Coulombe, P., Laberge, C., Letarte, J., Guyda, H., and Khoury, K. (1975) Preliminary report on a mass screening program for neonatal hypothyroidism. J. Pediat. 86:670.

Fölling, A. (1934) Excretion of urinary phenypyruvic acid as a metabolic anomaly in connection with imbecility. Hoppe Seyler Z. Physiol. Chem. 227:169.

Garrod, A. (1902) The incidence of alkaptonuria: a study in chemical individuality. Lancet 2:1616.

Garrick, M. D., Dembure, P., and Guthrie, R. (1973) Sickle-cell anemia and other hemoglobinopathies: procedures and strategy for screening employing spots of blood on filter paper as specimens. New Engl. J. Med. 288:1265.

Guthrie, R. (1968) Screening for "Inborn Errors of Metabolism" in the newborn infant—a multiple test program. Birth Defects Original Article Series 4:92.

Guthrie, R. (1969) Screening for phenylketonuria. Triangle 9:104.

Guthrie, R. (1972) Mass screening for genetic disease. Hospital Practice 93.

Guthrie, R., and Susi, A. (1963) A simple phenylalanine method for detecting phenylketonuria in large populations of newborn infants. Pediatrics 32:338.

Houston, I. B., and Veale, A. M. O. (1971) Screening for inborn errors of metabolism. Laboratory Management 9:30.

Jervis, G. A. (1953) Phenylpyruvic oligophrenia deficiency of phenylalanine-oxidizing system. Proc. Soc. Exp. Biol. Med. 82:514.

Klein, A. H., Agustin, A. V., and Foley, T. P. (1974) Successful laboratory screening for congenital hypothyroidism. Lancet 2:77.

Larsen, P., and Broskin, K. (1975) Thyroxin (T_4) immunoassay using filter paper blood sample for screening of neonates for hypothyroidism. Pediat. Res. 9:604.

Larsen, P. R., Merker, A., and Parlow, A. F. (1976) Immunoassay of human TSH using dried blood samples. J. Clin. Endocrinol. 42:987.

Murphey, W. H., Patchen, L., and Guthrie, R. (1973) Screening tests for argininosuccinic aciduria, orotic aciduria and other inherited enzyme deficiencies using dried blood specimens. Biochem. Genet. 6:51.

Veale, A. M. O., and Houston, I. B. (1976) Mass screening for inborn errors of metabolism. Patient Management, January, p. 20.

RESEARCH TO PRACTICE IN MENTAL RETARDATION
Biomedical Aspects, Volume III
Edited by Peter Mittler
Copyright 1977 I.A.S.S.M.D.

CHROMOSOME DETERMINATION FROM AMNIOTIC FLUID CELLS
Observation of 800 Cases

J. Wahlström
Psychiatric Department III,
Lillhagen's Hospital,
S-422 03 Hisings Backa,
Sweden

Prenatal determination can reveal the chromosome constitution of an expected child during pregnancy. The investigation is based on the fact that all cells in the amniotic fluid are of fetal origin. Through amniocentesis, samples are taken of these cells that are then cultured and subjected to cytogenetic analysis. If this shows that the child has a deviant chromosome constitution, the pregnancy can be terminated. A prenatal determination of this sort makes it possible to prevent children with disabling chromosomal diseases from being born. The sample should be taken early enough during pregnancy to allow a legal abortion to be carried out if necessary.

The purpose of this article is to describe the experience gained from the first 800 consecutive prenatal chromosome determinations carried out at the cytogenetic laboratory at St. Jörgen's Hospital in Gothenburg.

PRACTICAL PROCEDURE

All the amniocenteses reported were carried out at the Women's Department of the Eastern Hospital, Gothenburg. According to our practice, each expectant mother was given appropriate information by a geneticist and a gynecologist, as follows:

1. An explanation of how amniocentesis is performed and when the result of the cytogenic analysis can be expected
2. A warning that only diseases of chromosomal origin can be revealed. For the last six months, alpha-fetoprotein tests have also been done as a routine, primarily to discover neural tube defects.

3. An explanation that, so far, the only "treatment" that can be offered a woman whose fetus has a chromosomal defect is a legal abortion.
4. Information about the risks involved in taking a sample and the risk that the woman in question may have a child with a chromosomal aberration.

Samples are usually taken during the fifteenth to seventeenth week of pregnancy. Before the amniocentesis, an ultrasound examination is made to determine the duration of the pregnancy, the position of the placenta, and whether or not twin fetuses are present. If a chromosomal aberration is found in the fetus, the parents return for further genetic advice before finally deciding whether or not the pregnancy should be terminated.

INDICATIONS

The indications for sampling are set out in Table 1. Of the 800 women, 480 underwent prenatal chromosome determination because of their "advanced age." "Advanced age" in this study meant that the woman would have reached the age of 35 before the estimated delivery date. This age limit was chosen because the risk of having a child with Down's syndrome begins to grow more pronounced after the age of 35 (see Collmann and Stoller, 1962; Lindsjö, 1974). The determination was performed for 100 women because they previously had a child with an aneuploidy. For a woman who has already had a child with Down's syndrome, the risk is placed at about 1% (Milunsky et al., 1973; Pfeiffer et al., 1973). Compared with the frequency of chromosomal deviations in newborn children, given as 0.5%, this implies twice the overall risk from this single cause. In addition, however, we also have an important psychological factor. These families, in fact, have already been faced with the problem of taking care of a child with a chromosomal aberration and have gained practical experience of what it involves. The fear of having yet another such child is therefore often very great.

Table 1. Indications for investigation of amniotic fluid cells

Indication	No. of patients
Mother's age 35–39 years	295
Mother's age 40 years and over	185
Previous child: aneuploidy	100
Previous child: structural chromosome aberration	1
Balanced translocation in one of the parents	8
Mosaicism for trisomy-21 in the mother	2
X-linked recessive disease	5
Increased risk of neural tube defect	34
Previous child: metabolic heredity disease	12
Anxiety about chromosomal abnormalities in the fetus	158
	800

In eight cases, chromosome analysis was performed because one of the parents carried a balanced translocation. Five of these cases showed a D-D translocation, while in the other three cases there was a reciprocal translocation between two autosomes. The risk of an individual with a balanced translocation transmitting the translocation in an unbalanced form to the offspring varies in accordance with the chromosomes involved. In most cases, however, this risk is considerably larger than the 0.5% given as the frequency of chromosomal aberrations in the newborn. Many persons with balanced translocations have not dared to have children before, because they knew of the greater risk of bearing a child with a chromosomal aberration. When these people have become aware of the possibility of a prenatal chromosome analysis, they may risk beginning a pregnancy.

Five women were examined because they were carriers of an X-linked recessive disease. In these cases, the purpose was merely to determine the sex of the fetus, because only half of the sons would be affected, whereas all the daughters would be healthy. Determination of the sex in these five cases was based on chromosome analyses because sex-chromatin and Y-chromatin analyses, even if they take less time to carry out, may give rise to errors.

For 158 of the women examined, there were only psychological indications for sampling. This group was composed of parents who previously had had children with various types of deformity, which, however, were not due to chromosome aberrations. This group also included parents who had relatives with some form of aneuploidy and parents who, for various reasons, had been in close contact with malformed children in other ways. In all of these cases, the parents' wish was to exclude all possibility of the expected child having a disease. The worry and anxiety of these parents were often so great that they intended to seek an abortion if they were not given a prenatal chromosome analysis.

In the two remaining indication groups, the reason for amniocentesis was not a prenatal chromosome analysis in the first place but some other form of prenatal investigation. When the indication was a previous child with neural tube defect, the purpose was to perform an alpha-fetoprotein examination, and when there was a previous child with a hereditary metabolic disease, amniocentesis was performed in view of a biochemical analysis. Even in these cases, however, I did a chromosome analysis after consultation with the parents. In my opinion, it would be unfortunate if the doctor made a prenatal analysis that showed normal conditions, only to find out later that the fetus had a chromosomal change.

RESULTS

Prenatal chromosome analysis was offered to 800 pregnant women. Two refused further amniocentesis after a first attempt at sampling failed. In five cases, the women did not learn the fetus's chromosome constitution because no more samples were taken after a first unsuccessful attempt at culturing. In one case, the chromosome determination did not succeed because the fetus was already dead at the time of sampling, as verified by the ultrasound examination. The rest of the women (99%) received information about the expected child's chromosome constitution. Chromosome analysis was done by means of the banding technique.

Table 2 shows the 18 chromosome aberrations we found among the 792 analyses undertaken. In 13 cases, the chromosome constitution was unbalanced and a legal abortion was performed. In five cases, a balanced chromosome aberration was found and there was no legal abortion. In three other cases, a high alpha-fetoprotein value was found, and this led to a legal abortion in all three. The chromosome determination from these last three samples was normal.

One of the aberrations was discovered by investigation of a twin pregnancy, revealed by ultrasound. By instilling a small quantity of methylene blue with the first puncture, we could be fairly certain that two amniotic sacs were punctured when samples were taken. Analysis showed that one of the twins was healthy, while the other had a trisomy 21. The parents elected to have an abortion performed.

Efforts were made on two other occasions to take samples in a twin pregnancy. On the first occasion, methylene blue was not used. The prenatal chromosome determination showed that two healthy boys would be born. On delivery, however, one of the twins was found to be a girl, and a chromosome analysis showed that she had an extra chromosome in the 21st pair. In the other twin pregnancy, methylene blue was used when puncturing; the prenatal determination was correct, and two healthy children were born.

If the analysis findings are related to the indication groups shown, it will be seen that in the 35–39 age group six chromosomal changes were discovered among 295 women examined, or in 2.0%. The frequency among women age 40 or over was 2.1% (4/185). For two of the remaining cases, the indications were that one of the parents carried a reciprocal balanced translocation, and in a third case, anxiety about chromosomal abnormalities in the fetus was the indication. (For a more detailed account of this last case, see Wahlström, 1974.)

Risks

What risks does sample-taking involve? Previously, the risks in this type of amniocentesis have been estimated at 1 to 2%. In an earlier compilation, however, we were able to show that taking samples of amniotic fluid during the sixteenth to eighteenth week of pregnancy did not entail any greater risk of miscarriage (Wahlström et al., 1974). We have now been able to follow-up 600 pregnancies, and have found among them six miscarriages after sampling. (For details of these miscarriages, see Table 3.) The 1% frequency of miscarriages after the sixteenth week is not higher than the corresponding frequency of abortion in women not undergoing amniocentesis (Pettersson, 1968).

Table 2. Abnormal fetal karyotypes in 800 pregnancies

No.	Abnormal karyotypes	Maternal age	Comments
1	47,XX,+21	39	Legal termination
2	47,XX,+21	35	Legal termination
3	47,XX,+21	38	Legal termination
4	47,XY,+21	41	Legal termination
5	47,XX,+21	43	Legal termination
6	47,XY,+21	40	Legal termination
7	47,XX,+21	35	Legal termination
8	47,XY,+21	38	Legal termination (twin pregnancy)
9	47,XXY	38	Legal termination
10	47,XXX	42	Legal termination
11	46,XXY, (Unbalanced translocation with partial trisomy-14)	28	Two previous perinatal deaths due to congenital malformation; legal termination
12	46,XX, (Unbalanced translocation with partial trisomy-8)	27	Legal termination
13	46,XX, (Unbalanced translocation with partial trisomy-6)	27	Legal termination
14	45,XY, (Balanced D/D translocation)	26	Delivery of a healthy child
15	45,XX, (Balanced D/D translocation)	23	Delivery of a healthy child
16	45,XX, (Balanced D/D translocation)	20	Delivery of a healthy child
17	45,XX, (Balanced D/D translocation)	34	Delivery of a healthy child
18	46,XX, (Balanced reciprocal translocation between chromosomes 14 and 22)	22	Delivery of a healthy child

Table 3. Details of six miscarriages following amniocentesis (600 cases)

	Weeks of gestation		
No.	At amniocentesis	At miscarriage	Comments
1	16	24	Twins, not detected by ultrasound, one fetus with meningocele.
2	16	25	A 42-year-old primigravida with previous infertility, submucous fibroids, and a threatened abortion at eight weeks.
3	16	26	Missed abortion.
4	15	27	Gravida 3 with two previous spontaneous abortions.
5	18+20	22	Incompetent cervix.
6	14+17	27	No fetal movements and no fetal heart sound after 24 weeks.

Another conceivable risk with sample-taking is the risk of injuring the child. Among the 600 pregnancies followed up in which a child was born after amniocentesis, however, we have not found any case with a deformity of a type that could be suspected to be attributable to the amniocentesis.

Sources of Error

Two sources of error should be considered in connection with prenatal chromosome determination: 1) "maternal overgrowth," and 2) chromosome aberrations arising in vitro.

"Maternal overgrowth" means that cells from the mother get into the sample and grow during culture. If the fetal cells do not grow at the same time, the prenatal diagnosis may be incorrect. If the chromosome analysis shows that the expected child is a boy, there is no problem. Only in the cases in which the analysis shows the fetus to be female is there a risk of confusion. Chromosomally healthy mothers and healthy female fetuses have the same chromosome constitution. If the expected child has a chromosomal aberration and the mother's healthy cells are analyzed instead, the result will naturally be misleading. To avoid errors of this type, at least two different methods have been suggested. One is to start parallel cultures simultaneously, while another is to use the "in-situ technique." The latter involves analyzing the amniotic fluid cells directly where they are being cultured, without any intervening transplantation. My routine is to use the first method.

Among the 600 cases I have followed up so far, there was one with maternal overgrowth, involving a risk of a wrong conclusion concerning the chromosome constitution. By studying several parallel cultures, I was able to establish the probability of maternal overgrowth. Because only those cases in which a difference exists between the chromosome constitution of the expected child and that of the mother show up, it can be reckoned that only half of all the cases of maternal overgrowth will be revealed. This implies that, among these 600 prenatal chromosome determinations, there were probably two cases of maternal overgrowth, or about 0.3%.

A source of error of another type, which may cause trouble, is the chromosome aberration that arises in vitro. I observed such changes in four cases. In two of the cases, the changes were numerical, with an extra No. 7 chromosome and an extra X chromosome. In the other two cases, they were structural changes, a deletion of a No. 11 chromosome and a translocation between a chromosome in pair 2 and a chromosome in pair 10. However, by studying the various parallel cultures I had started and, in three of the cases, by repeating the amniocentesis, I was able to decide that the changes found probably had occurred in vitro. All of these four cases have now been delivered, the children are healthy, and the follow-up chromosome analyses are normal.

Thus, among the 600 prenatal determinations followed up so far, there were four cases of chromosome changes occurring in vitro, a frequency of 0.7%.

DISCUSSION

Prenatal chromosome determination can be regarded today as a reliable method. Women who wish to undergo this kind of examination can be given correct information about their expected children's karyotypes. The risks to the pregnancy and to the fetus connected with sample-taking are very small, as are the risks of error in the prenatal chromosome determination. By starting several parallel cultures at the same time, I was able to discover five cases in which there were probably risks of error. The risk of chromosomal changes arising in vitro is at least as great as that of maternal overgrowth. The reasons for chromosomal changes in vitro are so far not known, but various types of infection or changes in pH may occasion chromosomal disorders, either structural or numerical.

When the question arises whether or not a woman should undergo a prenatal chromosome analysis, there are two types of risk to consider. On the one hand, there is the risk that the woman may have a child with a chromosomal aberration, and on the other, there are the risks of sampling. In my opinion, the risks of sampling are so small that even women with little likelihood of having a child with a chromosomal aberration should have the examination. However, we have to think not only of the statistical risk figures, but also of a long list of other factors. A family that has seen at close quarters what it means to have a child with a chromosomal aberration is likely to feel the risk to be much greater than will a family without this experience. It is important, therefore, that all women who wish to undergo a prenatal examination should have the opportunity to discuss it with some person well versed in prenatal diagnosis.

SUMMARY

Eight hundred amniocenteses have been done, and results from the chromosome determinations are presented. In most cases, the indications for the investigation were that the pregnant women were 35 years of age or older. Thirteen fetuses had abnormal karyotypes. All thirteen women decided to have abortions. Risks of amniocentesis are discussed.

REFERENCES

Collmann, R. D., and Stoller, A. (1962) A survey of mongoloid births in Victoria, Australia 1942—1957. Amer. J. Publ. Health 52:813.

Lindsjö, A. (1974) Down's syndrome in Sweden. Acta Paediat. Scan. 63:571.

Milunsky, A. (1973) The Prenatal Diagnosis of Hereditary Disorders. Springfield, Illinois: Charles C Thomas.

Pettersson, F. (1968) Epidemiology of Early Pregnancy Wastage. Stockholm: Scandinavian University Books.

Pfeiffer, R. A., Dhadial, R., and Michelis, K. (1973) Das wiederholungsrisiko in Familien mit einem mongoloiden Kind. Mschr. Kinderheilk. 121:312.

Wahlström, J. (1974) A prenatally discovered unbalanced translocation t (14;22) (q22 or 23; q13). Heriditas 78:251.

Wahlström, J., Bartsch, F., and Lundberg, J. (1974) Prenatal chromosome determination: a study of 219 cases. Clin. Genet. 6:184.

RESEARCH TO PRACTICE IN MENTAL RETARDATION
Biomedical Aspects, Volume III
Edited by Peter Mittler
Copyright 1977 I.A.S.S.M.D.

CONGENITAL MALFORMATIONS OF THE CENTRAL NERVOUS SYSTEM AND MENTAL RETARDATION

J. Warkany
The Children's Hospital Research Foundation,
Mental Retardation Research Center, University of Cincinnati,
Cincinnati, Ohio 45229, United States

It is obvious to everyone who works with mentally retarded patients that somatic malformations are somehow connected with the mental problems of the retarded. It is particularly the severely retarded who often show physical signs of deformity that suggest that the visible defects are paralleled by malformations of the brain. Microcephaly, hydrocephaly, cranio-facial malformations, eye and ear anomalies, or abnormal extremities are frequently seen in patients of institutions and clinics that deal with the mentally retarded. Various inappropriate terms have been used for the physical signs that accompany the mental problems. In the older literature, authors spoke of "stigmata of degeneration," and the present generation speak of "funny looking children." Such derogatory and meaningless terms must not be used in serious discussions and scientific writings. What we need are careful analyses and interpretations of visible abnormal features, which can be very useful for classification of disease pictures that include mental impairment. Somatic anomalies are also helpful in studies of etiology and pathogenesis. To give one example, the physical signs of Down's syndrome indicate not only an infant's future mentality but also, since 1959, details of the chromosomal anomalies contained in every cell, and that any thoughts of prevention must be directed toward cytogenetic principles (Lejeune et al., 1959). Thus, malformations associated with mental retardation deserve careful observation, recording, and interpretation.

In present classifications of cases of mental retardation, "malformations" play an important, although variable, role. In 1964, Malamud analyzed 1,410 consecutive necropsies performed in three hospitals for the mentally retarded in California. He attributed 61% of the cases to "malformations." In 1966, Palo et al., in Finland, found almost identical results in autopsied cases. In patients living in an institution in Australia, about 40% showed mental retardation associated with malformations (Pitt and Roboz, 1964), but, in a hospital in England, only 26% of retarded children had associated congenital anomalies (Illingworth, 1959). In some statistics malformations are not listed at all. How can these discrepancies be explained?

In spite of serious efforts, classifications of mental retardation leave much to be desired. Some of the categories are etiologic, others are descriptive. Some represent a single malformation, others a syndrome of anomalies. As research progresses, one category may be replaced by another.

Malformations are of sufficient importance to those working in the field of mental retardation to ask for clear definition of the terms used and for interpretation of their meaning for clinical, etiologic, and preventive research.

One should distinguish, if possible, *congenital* malformations from malformations that developed after birth. Pathologists and clinicians who examine adults or older children may have difficulty deciding whether a malformation is of prenatal or postnatal origin. Microcephaly (and micrencephaly) can be caused by diseases after birth, or it can be present at birth and be recognized as congenital by the neonatologist or pediatrician. Congenital microcephaly may be determined at the time of conception if it is caused by an abnormal gene or by a chromosomal anomaly. It can also be caused by interference with early embryonic development, e.g., rubella, or, it can be due to secondary destruction of a fetal brain that was originally well-designed but mutilated in late stages of gestation by, for instance, cytomegalic inclusion disease or toxoplasmosis. It is clear that there are many "critical" periods for microcephaly and the mental retardation associated with it. Its time of origin cannot be ascertained without supplementary data derived from family and pregnancy histories, postnatal records, associated malformations, and various laboratory findings.

History-taking is a science and an art that has to be learned, like laboratory work. Even the best history needs prudent interpretation. The interrogator must win the confidence of the historian and must know how to elicit pertinent facts. "Negative" family histories do not exclude genetic determination; "positive" family histories can indicate a genetic origin but familial recurrence may also be caused by continued adverse environmental conditions. An old example of the latter situation is endemic cretinism, which often was observed in more than one sibling because of persisting maternal iodine deficiency and goiter. A recent example is Minamata disease, caused by organic mercury poisoning, which may affect more than one child. Improvement of the environment can prevent such familial cases, irrespective of their genetic background (Warkany, 1971; Harada, 1968).

Pregnancy histories can be very valuable because they may bring to light causative teratogens brought about by maternal disease or medication. However, sometimes such teratogens can take a subclinical course and not be known to the mother. On the other hand, histories are often so complex that it is impossible to discern "guilty" from "innocent" events.

Perinatal and postnatal incidents sometimes help to exclude a prenatal origin of a mental disorder or a malformation. However, in some instances such late events can be superimposed upon anomalies determined long before birth. Birth traumas or neonatal infections may occur in infants with defects of prenatal origin. This can result in overemphasis on late accidents in attempts to establish causes of physical and mental retardation.

Associated malformations are often valuable in explanations of mental impairment, but they too require discriminatory interpretation. Some associated anomalies, such as cataract or high palate, can arise at any time before or after birth, whereas others, e.g., spina bifida, congenital heart disease, or cleft lip, point to damage during the first two months of gestation.

Laboratory findings can be of great importance for explanations of congenital defects. Infectious teratogens may leave their traces long after the disease process has passed. The most remarkable contributions to elucidation of multiple congenital malformations associated with mental defects have been made by cytogenetics, particularly in recent years. Findings of an extra chromosome or absence of a chromosome in patients with several well-defined disease pictures have become general knowledge during the last 15 years, but the discoveries in recent years of minor chromosomal anomalies in patients with unspecific disease pictures or multiple anomalies are still unappreciated. Partial trisomies, translocations, inversions, deletions, and mosaicisms are being discovered continually in patients whose karyotypes were considered normal before the newer cytogenetic methods were available. It will take some time before these recent cytogenetic findings can be coordinated with clinical findings, but there can be no doubt that many cases considered "unspecific" until recently will become classifiable in the near future (Lewandowski and Yunis, 1975).

Most important, many congenital malformations of the brain can be recognized intra vitam by transillumination, pneumoencephalography, x-ray scanning, and computerized axial tomography. Although these methods still are not applied routinely to neonates and infants, technical improvements probably will make it possible in the near future to recognize gross malformations of the brain soon after birth. This is important for the individual case because by absolving secondary perinatal or postnatal factors, errors in diagnosis, parental counseling, and genetic prognosis can be avoided. Correct diagnosis and classification of these types of mental retardation will also direct etiological research into proper channels and thus aid in the search for preventive measures.

SUMMARY

Much progress has been made in research on congenital malformations. Abnormal genes, abnormal chromosomes, and injurious environmental agents have been identified as causes, and, as byproducts, etiologies have been found for many forms of mental retardation. This progress has been almost imperceptible and accidental in the case of many important congenital anomalies. If more directed and concerted efforts were encouraged in the fields of clinical teratology, mental retardation research would greatly benefit from this approach.

REFERENCES

Harada, Y. (1968) Congenital Minamata disease. *In* Minamata Disease. Study Group of Minamata Disease, Kumamoto University, Japan.

Illingworth, R. S. (1959) Congenital anomalies associated with cerebral palsy and mental retardation. Arch. Dis Child. 34:228.

Lejeune, J., Gautier, M., and Turpin, R. (1959) Étude des chromosomes somatiques de neuf enfants mongoliens. C. R. Acad. Sci. 248:1721.

Lewandowski, R. C., Jr., and Yunis, J. J. (1975) New chromosomal syndromes. Amer. J. Dis. Child. 129:515.

Malamud, N. (1964) Neuropathology. *In* Mental Retardation: A Review of Research, (Eds. Stevens, H. A., and Heber, R.) Chicago: University of Chicago Press, p. 429.

Palo, J., Lydecken, K., and Kivalo, E. (1966) Etiological aspects of mental deficiency in autopsied patients. Amer. J. Ment. Defic. 71:401.

Pitt, D., and Roboz, P. (1964) A survey of 782 cases of mental deficiency. *In* Proceedings of the International Copenhagen Congress on Scientific Study of Mental Retardation Vol. II (Eds. Oster, J., and Sletved, H. V.) Copenhagen: Det Berlingske Bogtrykkeri, p. 557.

Warkany, J. (1971) Congenital Malformations. Notes and Comments. Chicago: Year Book Medical Publishers, Inc.

RESEARCH TO PRACTICE IN MENTAL RETARDATION
Biomedical Aspects, Volume III
Edited by Peter Mittler
Copyright 1977 I.A.S.S.M.D.

FETAL TECHNIQUES FOR DIAGNOSING BRAIN DAMAGE
Prenatal
Electroencephalography

M. G. Rosen, R. J. Sokol, and L. Chik
*Department of Obstetrics and Gynecology and the
Perinatal Clinical Research Center, Cleveland
Metropolitan General Hospital, 3395 Scranton Road,
Cleveland, Ohio 44109, United States*

During the past 100 years, little new information has been developed that clearly describes those prenatal events that may result in central nervous system injury and that appear later in infant development as what might be broadly described as brain damage. While it is not the purpose of this chapter to explore this entire complex problem, we do discuss the use of a single technique, the fetal electroencephalogram (FEEG) during labor, as a method of studying prenatally incurred brain damage. Specifically, this chapter directs attention to the results of programmed pattern recognition of FEEG and to discriminant function analysis of intrapartum FEEG variables for the classification of infants for neurological normality and abnormality at one year of age.

BACKGROUND

In our laboratories, practical techniques for recording FEEG during labor were introduced in 1969 (Rosen and Scibetta, 1969a). By using these techniques up to the present, we have been able to make a series of original intrapartum observations of the electrical activity of the fetal brain. It was found to be possible to obtain continuous FEEG with minimal artifacts during labor, at times, for many hours prior to birth. Visual interpretations of FEEG before birth did not appear to differ from the electroencephalogram of the normal

This work was supported by NIH Grant HD-05566–1A1 and 5 M01-RR00210 and The Grant Foundation, Inc.

newborn (Rosen and Scibetta, 1969b, 1970). Stated differently, in normal infants the electrical activity of the brain was not altered by the birth process.

The electroencephalogram of the newborn infant in its isolette had been previously described by others to be related to maturity. We could now observe that FEEG recorded in utero correlated grossly with fetal age. A 1,300-g baby at 32 weeks of gestation had the same EEG findings before and after birth (Rosen and Scibetta, 1969a, 1970), i.e., the EEG was the same for the fetus and the neonate several months after birth. In addition, the morphology of the FEEG of the mature infant could be easily distinguished from that of the premature.

In a similar manner, patterns of EEG activity associated with behavioral states in the adult and then clearly identified by investigators in the neonate could be seen in the EEG of the fetus prior to birth. Thus, EEG patterns similar to those described in the neonate, such as trace alternant (T/A), high voltage slow activity (HVS), mixed activity (MIX), and low voltage irregular activity (LVI) (Anders, et al., 1971), were recorded from the fetus.

Transient FEEG Changes

A number of short-term, i.e., transient, changes were identified in the FEEG (Rosen et al., 1970, 1972, 1973). For example, FEEG recordings were seen to change when maternal medications, such as meperidine and mepivicaine, were used for analgesia during labor. While the amount of drug present in the fetal brain could not be quantified, the rapidity of drug transfer from mother to fetus could be measured in seconds and minutes.

Another transient change that was documented was the rapid alteration of FEEG when forceps were applied with traction on the fetal vertex during birth (Rosen et al., 1972 and 1973a). The FEEG returned to its pre-existing state after removal of the forceps and after birth. It did not change during spontaneous birth.

Still another transient FEEG change was associated with periodic decelerations of the fetal heart fate during labor. Obstetricians generally recognize late fetal heart rate decelerations (late in relation to onset of a maternal uterine contraction) as being associated with fetal distress, i.e., fetal asphyxia. The fall in fetal heart rate in such deceleration patterns was often seen to be accompanied by transient slowing and flattening of the fetal brain wave that could easily be discerned visually. As the heart rate deceleration disappeared, the FEEG returned to its original state (Rosen et al., 1970).

Nontransient FEEG Changes

Findings more germane to this discussion were categorized as nontransient changes. These included prolonged voltage suppression (Rosen and Scibetta, 1973) and the presence of persistent sharp wave activity (Sokol and Rosen, 1974). Sharp waves, as visually described, were repetitive in frequency and amplitude and tended to persist throughout a tracing. They were first found to be present in the FEEGs of several infants who later convulsed early in the neonatal period and then in the FEEGs of a larger number of infants found to be brain-damaged at one year of age (Borgstedt et al., 1975).

As noted here, the visual descriptions of fetal sharp waves and low voltage were associated with clinical infant abnormalities after birth. On the basis of these early findings, attention was directed to a computer-based pattern recognition system to document more easily and carefully these parameters. Thus, the pattern recognition systems and the discriminant function analysis of these variables are presented here.

METHODS

These studies were performed on a laboratory mini-computer in disc operating system configuration (PDP 11/40, 28K Core, 16 bit memory). The programs were written in Fortran IV and are basically system-independent. Our technique of programmed FEEG analysis and data reduction is based on a method of self-adjoint differential system analysis by which FEEG is characterized in terms of amplitude and frequency time series. Program output mimics visual interpretation of EEG by classifying each 10-second epoch as one of seven patterns, based on the classification for neonatal EEG of Anders et al. (1971). Criteria for the visual interpretation of the four dominant patterns (LVI, MIX, HVS and T/A) are shown in Table 1. Details of programmed pattern recognition have been previously described (Chik et al., 1975). The relative frequencies of the four dominant FEEG patterns were used as random variables in a data set for statistical analysis.

Programmed pattern recognition of sharp waves (S/W) in FEEG was also developed for these studies and has been described (Chik et al., 1977). In short, the approach was based on visual FEEG S/W classification using discriminant function analysis. The average number of sharp waves detected per 10-second epoch of artifact-free FEEG data was used as a random variable for statistical analysis.

We chose discriminant function analysis as an analytic procedure suitable for the classification of infants for neurologic outcome at age one year.

Table 1. Criteria for visual pattern recognition of four dominant patterns in EEG

Pattern	Dominant voltage range (μV)	Dominant frequency (CPS)
Low Voltage Irregular (LVI)	10–25	5–10
Mixed (MIX)	10–50	2.5–10
High Voltage Slow (HVS)	50–100	< 5
Trace Alternant (T/A)	20–100/5–25	2.5/10–2.5–15

Adapted from Anders et al., 1971.

Table 2. The relative frequencies of program recognized FEEG patterns of infants found to be neurologically normal and abnormal at one year of age (in percent)

Pattern	LVI	MIX	HVS	T/A
Normal infants (N = 42)	11.62	38.37	14.76	30.33
Abnormal infants (N = 19)	16.95	34.20	14.88	33.17
All infants (N = 61)	13.28	37.07	14.79	31.21

RESULTS

Programmed detection of the four dominant FEEG patterns (LVI, MIX, HVS and T/A) and of S/W produced outcomes that were 85 to 95% consistent with visual FEEG interpretations (Chik et al., 1975). The relative frequencies of the four dominant FEEG patterns in 219 hours of FEEG monitoring data from 61 infants with known neurological outcomes at age one year are shown in Table 2. Of these 61 infants, 42 were normal and 19 were abnormal at age one year. The relative frequency of LVI was found to be greater in the abnormal than in the normal infants.

In the FEEG records of the 61 patients, 16 were visually identified to have persistent sharp waves present and 45 were not. In the 16 files with persistent visually detected sharp waves, there was an average of 3.16 program-detected sharp waves per 10-second epoch. In the 45 files without persistent visually detected sharp waves, there was an average of 1.47 program-detected S/W per 10-second epoch. Using discriminant function analysis, a decision threshold of 2.3 program-detected sharp waves per 10-second epoch of FEEG was derived for a classification for persistent S/W activity. As shown in Table 3, this threshold produced an overall consistency of 78%, comparing programmed with visual analysis of FEEG for sharp waves ($p < 0.005$).

The program-recognized FEEG findings were then related to infant neurologic outcome at age one year using discriminant function analysis. As shown in

Table 3. The relationship of programmed S/W recognition to visually recognized S/W in 61 FEEGs. The threshold of 2.3 S/W per 10-second epoch was derived by discriminant function analysis. The overall consistency rate is 78% ($\chi^2 = 17.4236$, $p < 0.005$).

	Programmed Analysis	
Visual analysis	S/W < 2.3	S/W > 2.3
No S/W	39	6
S/W	7	9

Table 4. Summary of discriminant function analysis of program recognized FEEG variables for the classification of 42 neurologically normal infants and 19 neurologically abnormal infants at one year of age

FEEG variables used for classification		Infant outcome at one year		Overall consistency
S/W LVI HVS T/A MIX		Normal (%) (N = 42)	Abnormal (%) (N = 19)	
X		73.8%	47.3%	65.5%
	X	64.3%	63.2%	63.9%
X	X	73.8%	73.1%	73.8%

Table 4, using the frequency of S/W alone, 73.8% of the normal infants and 47.3% of the abnormal infants were correctly classified, with an overall consistency of 65.5%. Using the relative frequencies of the four dominant FEEG patterns alone, 64.3% of the normal infants and 63.2% of the abnormal infants at age one year were correctly classified, for an overall consistency of 63.9%. Combining both sets of variables, as is done in the last line of Table 4, reveals that 73.8% of the normal infants and 73.1% of the abnormal infants were correctly classified for one year neurologic outcome, for an overall consistency of 73.8%.

DISCUSSION

Several general statements may be made concerning the results obtained by monitoring the brain during the intrapartum period. The relative frequencies of the four dominant FEEG patterns, i.e., LVI, MIX, HVS and T/A, appear to be different in those infants who are later found to be neurologically abnormal at age one year from the relative frequencies of these patterns in the FEEG of normal infants. Particularly apparent is the higher relative frequency of the low voltage irregular pattern. Although the data are not presented here, in the computer analysis of these patterns no significant change was found when the relative frequencies of these patterns in the first half-hour of monitoring were compared with the relative frequencies of the patterns in the last half-hour of monitoring (Chik et al., 1976). Described differently, it appears that the relative frequencies of the dominant patterns are often consistent during the course of labor. Specifically, an increased relative frequency of LVI present early in labor is often present later in labor. We also suspect that this is the case for sharp waves. Although at this time we consider our data with respect to sharp waves preliminary, we strongly suspect, on the basis of visual analysis, that sharp waves are not generally altered by, or associated with, intrapartum events (Chik et al., 1977; and Rosen et al., 1973).

These data would appear to suggest, then, that early in labor the FEEG is already "predictive" of brain damage in some children (Chik et al., 1977a). Several important pieces of information are not yet available and remain to be described. Still not clear is what additional morbidity may occur in association with specific intrapartum events, such as periodic fetal heart rate decelerations that are also associated with brain wave changes, as well as other intrapartum variables, such as when an abnormal course of labor, the use of medications, and the use of forceps are added to the already stressed infant. Moreover, we must turn our attention towards specific etiological events that may lead to described clinical pathology. We may ask, for example, "What is the effect of specific antenatal events, such as maternal illness, fetal dysmaturity, or fetal distress prior to the onset of labor?"

A larger population is now being studied. We are looking at discrete groups of obstetrical events and the time in fetal development during which these illnesses occur in an attempt to relate prenatal illness to single expressions of abnormality and infant development at one year of age.

Early detection of brain damage is an important first step in the treatment of the damaged infant. At the present time, it is clear that the FEEG allows one to make preliminary observations relevant to this problem. More important, however, is that with the use of FEEG we begin to discriminate some forms of damage that may already be present before birth, and, in some cases, before labor. This becomes important in limiting the search to a smaller number of potential factors during the antenatal period that may be associated with the development of the brain damaged infant.

SUMMARY

The technique of fetal electroencephalography (FEEG) has been studied as a method of diagnosing brain damage which may take place prior to birth. The visual findings of the human FEEG are described, as well as the construction of a pattern recognition system for the computer recognition of FEEG variables. The incorporation of these FEEG variables into a discriminant function analysis to predict infant morbidity at one year of age is discussed.

REFERENCES

Anders, T., Emde, R., and Parmelee, A. (1971) A Manual of Standardized Terminology, Techniques and Criteria for Scoring States of Sleep and Wakefulness in Newborn Infants. UCLA Brain Information Service/BRI Publication Office, NIMDS Neurological Information Network, pp. 1–11.

Borgstedt, A. D., Rosen, M. G., Chik, L., Sokol, R. J., Bachelder, L., Steinbrecher, M., and Leon, P. (1975) Fetal electroencephalography: relationship to neonatal and one year developmental-neurologic examinations in high risk infants. Amer. J. Dis. Child. 129:35.

Chik, L., Rosen, M. G., and Sokol, R. J. (1975) An interactive computer program for studying fetal electroencephalograms. J. Reprod. Med. 14:154.

Chik, L., Sokol, R. J., and Rosen, M. G. (1977) Computer interpreted fetal electroencephalogram. Sharp wave detection and classification of infants for one year neurological outcome. Electroencephalogr. Clin. Neurophysiol. 42:745.

Chik, L., Sokol, R. J., Rosen, M. G., and Borgstedt, A. (1976) Computer interpreted fetal electroencephalogram. I. Relative frequency of patterns. Amer. J. Obstet. Gynecol. 125:537.

Chik, L., Sokol, R. J., Rosen, M. G., Regula, G. A., and Borgstedt, A. D. (1977a) Computer interpreted fetal monitoring data: discriminant function analysis of perinatal data for the classification of infants for one year neurological outcome. J. Pediatr. 90:985.

Rosen, M. G., and Scibetta, J. J. (1969a) The human fetal electroencephalogram. I. An electrode for continuous recording during labor. Amer. J. Obstet. Gynecol. 104:1057.

Rosen, M. G., and Scibetta, J. J. (1969b) Documenting the human fetal EEG during birth. Electroencephalogr. Clin. Neurophysiol. 27:661.

Rosen, M. G., and Scibetta, J. J. (1970) The human fetal electroencephalogram. II. Characterizing the EEG during labor. Neuropaediatrie 2:17.

Rosen, M. G., and Scibetta, J. J. (1973) On the fetal EEG during parturition. In: Publication of papers from the Sir Joseph Barcroft Centenary Symposium, 1972) Cambridge University Press, p. 71.

Rosen, M. G., Scibetta, J. J., Chik, L., and Borgstedt, A. D. (1973) An approach to the study of brain damage: the principles of fetal electroencephalography. Amer. J. Obstet. Gynecol. 115:37.

Rosen, M. G., Scibetta, J. J., and Devroude, P. J. (1972) Fetal electroencephalography during birth: a review of research and clinical applications. Davis' Gynec. Obstet. Hagerstown: Harper & Row.

Rosen, M. G., Scibetta, J. J., and Hochberg, C. J. (1970) The human fetal electroencephalogram. III. A discussion of EEG pattern changes in the presence of fetal heart rate alterations and after the use of maternal medications. Obstet. Gynecol. 36:132.

Rosen, M. G., Scibetta, J. J., and Hochberg, C. J. (1973a) Fetal electroencephalography. IV. The FEEG during spontaneous and forceps births. Amer. J. Obstet. Gynecol. 42:283.

Sokol, R. J., and Rosen, M. G. (1974) The fetal electroencephalogram. Clinics in obstet. gynec. W. B. Saunders Philadelphia/London 1:123.

GENETIC DISORDERS

RESEARCH TO PRACTICE IN MENTAL RETARDATION
Biomedical Aspects, Volume III
Edited by Peter Mittler
Copyright 1977 I.A.S.S.M.D.

GENETIC DISORDERS IN MENTAL RETARDATION

F. de la Cruz
Mental Retardation and Developmental Disabilities Branch,
National Institute of Child Health and Human Development,
National Institutes of Health,
Bethesda, Maryland, United States

Diseases with a genetic etiology impose a great health burden on our population. The agony suffered by the affected individual and his family is incalculable, while its impact on the nation's economy is considerable. Social progress, medical and technological advances, and emphasis on preventive health care have resulted in improvements in nutrition, sanitation, and better community and family health standards. Improved treatment of infectious diseases and availability of vaccines and chemotherapeutic agents have created a shift in the pattern of diseases affecting both the young and the old. These changing patterns of disease have resulted in the increasing proportion of surviving children with genetic conditions and congenital anomalies and a growing pool of adult patients with chronic debilitating disorders associated with hereditary components. Consequently, patients with genetic problems constitute an increasing proportion of cases in a physician's practice.

Approximately 12 million persons in the United States have some genetic disorder, and it is estimated that total life-years lost from birth defects due to genetic causes is 3.5 times that due to cancer, 6.5 times that due to heart disease, and 8 times that due to stroke (Desforges, 1976).

Genetic disorders can be classified into three groups: Mendelian or single-gene disorders, chromosome disorders, and the multifactorial or polygenic disorders. Table 1 compares the relative frequency, in percent, of causes of diseases among hospitalized children in three cities (Childs and Simopoulos, 1975). A review of admissions to a pediatric hospital in Montreal covering a 12-month period in 1969 to 1970 showed that about 30% of admissions resulted from abnormal gene-environment interaction.

This article was written by the author in his private capacity. No official support or endorsement by the National Institute of Child Health and Human Development, National Institutes of Health, is intended or should be inferred.

Table 1. Frequency of genetic and nongenetic causes of diseases among hospitalized children

Study	Single gene	Chromosomal	Gene-influenced	Unknown	Nongenetic
Montreal[a]	6.8%	0.4%	22.3%	6.7%	63.7%
Baltimore[b]	6.4%	0.7%	31.5%	8.2%	53.2%
Newcastle[c]	8.5%	2.5%	31.0%	17.0%	41.0%

[a]Scriver (1973).
[b]Childs (1972).
[c]Roberts (1970).

REFERENCES

Deforges, J. F. (1976) Current Concepts in Genetics. New Engl. J. Med. 294: 393.

Childs, B., Miller, S. M., and Bearn, A. G. (1972) Gene mutation as a cause of human disease. *In* Mutagenic Effects of Environmental Contaminants (Eds. Sutton, H. E., and Harris, M. I.) New York: Academic Press, p.3.

Childs, B., and Simopoulos, A. (1975) Genetic Screening Programs, Principles, and Research. Washington, D.C.: Assembly of Life Sciences, National Research Council, National Academy of Sciences, p. 10.

Roberts, D. F., Chavez, J., and Court, S. D. (1970) The genetic component in child mortality. Arch. Dis. Child. 45:33.

Scriver, G. R., Neal, J. L., Saginur, R., and Clow, A. (1973) The frequency of genetic disease and congenital malformation among patients in a pediatric hospital. Canad. Med. Assoc. J. 108:1111.

RESEARCH TO PRACTICE IN MENTAL RETARDATION
Biomedical Aspects, Volume III
Edited by Peter Mittler
Copyright 1977 I.A.S.S.M.D.

RECENT TRENDS IN DOWN'S SYNDROME

Z. A. Stein and M. Susser
Departments of Epidemiology and Mental Retardation Research,
School of Public Health, Columbia University, and N. Y. Psychiatric Institute,
600 West 168th Street, New York, N.Y. 10032, United States

When considering Down's syndrome, there are two seeming paradoxes that come to mind, especially when discussing preventability. First, measures of disease frequency have moved in opposite directions. The prevalence of Down's syndrome has gone up, while the incidence has gone down. Second, there has been a marked change in the chances of survival for trisomy 21 individuals in the postnatal period, but probably a negligible change if any in the intrauterine period.

There has been a decline in incidence rates of Down's syndrome at birth, from an estimated one in 600 earlier in the century to an estimated one in 900 at present. The risk of bearing a child with Down's syndrome is higher in older mothers, and the decline in incidence at birth has followed directly from a relative change in the proportion of older age groups among maternities. For instance, Figure 1 shows the changes in child-bearing age that have occurred in the United States over the past thirty years.

The most important factors influencing women's age at childbirth have been: age at marriage, opinions on optimal family size, use and reliability of contraceptive measures, and the legalization of induced abortion.

Over the same period there has been a rise in the prevalence of Down's syndrome among children, and especially among adults. This rise appears remarkable at first in view of the decline in incidence. Prevalence, however, is a cross-sectional rate based on a census of a population taken at one point in time. Prevalence may therefore rise, even if incidence is declining, when more of the affected infants who are born manage to survive (Figure 2). Surgery for congenital defects, immunization, and antibiotics against respiratory infections have dramatically prolonged the expectation of life in Down's syndrome. If Down's syndrome infants are given all the health care they need, including surgery and nursing care, many will survive to be adults.

Let us now turn to incidence at birth and our estimates for different maternal age groups. We have estimates based mainly on three sources:

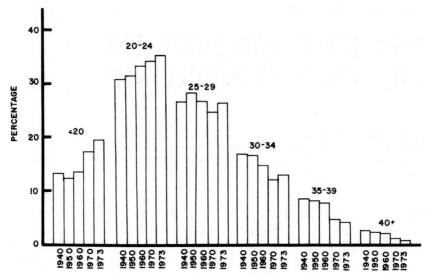

Figure 1. Percentage distribution of live births by maternal age groups in the United States, 1940–1973.

1. large, careful surveys from hospitals, agencies and services carried out up to two decades ago
2. more recent prospective studies on a smaller scale
3. amniocentesis.

There are considerable differences between estimates from these sources: the early surveys give the lowest rates, amniocentesis the highest.

Among the most-used earlier estimates of maternal age-specific incidence rates for Down's syndrome births are those from the State of Michigan, and from Victoria, Australia (Collmann and Stoller, 1962), both based on infants and children identified through various health agencies. As estimates of the probability of conceiving a trisomy 21, there are two intrinsic difficulties with these otherwise excellent studies. Both these studies precede the era of diagnosis based on karyotype. Even so, Down's syndrome is a fairly distinct and recognizable condition for the experienced clinician, and children so deviant in appearance and performance tend to be recognized. Consequently imprecision of diagnosis is not a major problem for the epidemiologist.

Changing patterns of survival are far more serious difficulties. The stillbirths and neonatal and infant deaths are likely to have been lost to enumeration (many would have escaped recognition) and these older estimates would not hold at this time if perinatal survival has changed. At best, one may interpret the older figures as representing "the incidence of Down's syndrome births which survived the neonatal period."

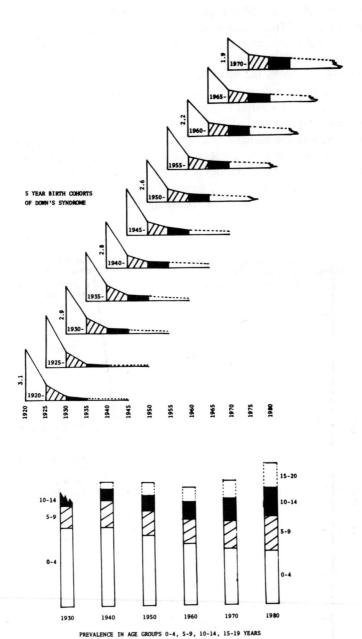

Figure 2. The incidence and prevalence of Down's syndrome.

More recently, maternal-age–specific incidence figures published from Israel (Harlap, 1973) and from Sweden (Lindsjo, 1974) do include karyotype confirmation of the diagnosis, and are based on newborn infants and children followed from maternity hospitals. The similarity between the earlier and later series at younger ages confirms the view that karyotyping has not made a dramatic difference to estimates based on clinical diagnosis alone, and, more surprisingly, neither has neonatal survival (Figure 3). (We will comment later on the raised risk in much older women.)

However, like the earlier series, neither of these later series includes stillbirths. We know from other sources that a considerable loss does take place at this stage. More recent probabilities of trisomic conception, which are now being quoted from amniocentesis series, seem to be considerably higher than appears from Figure 3. The amniocentesis figures apply particularly to rates in older

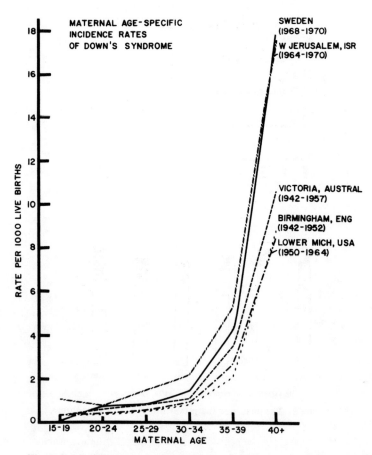

Figure 3. Maternal age–specific incidence rates of Down's syndrome.

women. We should, however, take into account whether or not the rates of practical interest apply to all conceptions or only to those that result in a live birth.

The two later series show higher rates for births in older women, compared to the earlier series (although there is less difference in rates for younger women). Some of the reasons we might advance are:

1. The changes in older women may reflect increased survival in the neonatal period over recent years. (As noted above, losses in the perinatal period could affect enumeration of cases, thus the estimates of incidence at birth.) But if this were so, why is the effect confined to older women? We know of no evidence to suggest that Down's syndrome infants born to older women are any different in clinical characteristics from those born to younger women, so why should there have been a differential rate of survival?

2. The differences are attributable to chance: the probability that this is so is $p < 0.005$.

3. There has been a real rise in the incidence of Down's syndrome in older women, associated perhaps with some environmental change of exposure. Such exposures must be of a kind that will be reflected more clearly in a raised rate of Down's syndrome in older women but not in younger women.

One set of observations bears on this possibility, namely irradiation exposure. Against several negative studies (all unsatisfactory for their purpose), there are three positive studies, one from Winnipeg (Uchida et al., 1968), one from Baltimore (Sigler et al., 1965), and one from London (Alberman et al., 1972). Each showed that increased preconceptional exposure to x-rays in the mother raised her risk of a Down's syndrome birth. In the Baltimore series, the effect was found for women who had had therapeutic irradiation, and, in the Winnipeg series, abdominal irradiation. However, the London study showed a raised risk of a Down's syndrome birth in women who, more than ten years prior to that conception, had been exposed to diagnostic irradiation. What is especially important to the present argument is that in each of the three positive studies, the raised risk that was found was present mainly in older women.

It is possible that a change in the risk of a trisomic conception could be evidence of some environmental factor that would effect mainly older women and then only after a latent period following the exposure.

Some support for such a supposition can be adduced from a report at a recent conference made by Stark and White (N.Y. State Birth Defects 1976). They showed that, whereas in the United States Black women and White women had similar rates of Down's syndrome births at younger ages, at older ages the rates for Black women were lower than those for White women. These differences could reflect different exposures to environmental factors between Black and White women.

One might see the differences in the rates of Down's syndrome between the later and earlier series, between irradiated women and others, and between White and Black women as coherent with the following argument: that environmental factors operate mainly on older women because the ovaries are sensitive to certain environmental stimuli, whose effects are recognizable only after a long latency period.

We open up this possibility as a conjecture to be explored. Certainly, none of the changes that have been shown is large, and irradiation, whether diagnostic or therapeutic, can be held responsible for only slight effects. We might want, however, to reconsider Penrose's division of Down's syndrome births into those that are maternal age–dependent and those that are maternal age–independent. Penrose's (1951) classification preceded recognition of the trisomy 21 karyotype, and he correctly guessed that there would be karyotypic forms that were special to younger women, and especially to those younger women who produced repeated Down's syndrome births. We now know that, in fact, over 90% of Down's syndrome infants born to younger women are standard trisomy 21, indistinguishable in terms of karyotype from those born to older women. If we exclude translocation Down's syndrome births entirely, it is still possible to draw distribution curves as Penrose did, dividing Down's syndrome births into maternal age–dependent and maternal age–independent groups (Penrose and Smith, 1966). However, as Moran showed, it is not necessary to divide them thus, and our argument here is that it may be in fact deceptive. Standard trisomy 21 births may be affected by similar influences at all maternal ages, but the influences could be summative, or exponential, in effects over time. We have recently used New York City notification of Down's syndrome at birth (1966–1974) to show the conformity of a rising age-incidence with an essentially linear increase by maternal age.

The increase by maternal age, however, is much more marked than are any effects associated with irradiation. Theories that have been put forward to explain the phenomenon of a raised risk of Down's syndrome in older women have had to take into consideration the fact that all the oocytes that will eventually mature into ova seem to be present already in the ovary of a newborn infant girl and to remain in a resting phase until shortly before ovulation. There are some who consider that the oocytes are so arranged in the ovary that they ripen in the order that they were laid down and that the last to be laid down (and they are last to ripen) are inferior (the production line theory); there are others who consider that the maternal age effect is through some alteration of the chromatids that could take place over the long resting phase of maturation (the deterioration theory). Although an epidemiological test of these competing theories is difficult, it should not be impossible. The assumption of a latency of effect seems to support a deterioration hypothesis. Latency is not uncommonly observed in occupational hazards and cancers, for instance with asbestos cancer and mesotheliomata.

The world-wide distribution of Down's syndrome, always showing a greater risk for older mothers, suggests that if there are such environmental influences they should be fairly ubiquitous, or that the effect of each will be small.

Apart from latency, or summated exposures, another possibility is that other, common, age-related attributes of the mother might underlie the association, for instance, diabetes or disorders of the thyroid.

Another possibility that could relate to a changed risk over time might be the changing age of menarche, which has been occurring at younger ages over this century. If an effect on the oocyte related not to duration of exposure but to duration of the fecund period, then a rise in rates at older ages would reflect an earlier age at menarche.

Recently, paternal transmission of the extra chromosome has been shown in selected cases of Down's syndrome. However, the age of the father seems not to be influential in the epidemiology when the age of the mother is controlled. This was shown in earlier studies, and recently confirmed by ourselves.

There are two other possibilities to which we shall now turn. The first concerns the possibility that it is not the conception of trisomy 21 but rather the failure to abort such conceptions that is commoner in older women. The second concerns the possibility that there is a general tendency to anomalous conceptions with senescence, which is reflected in declining fecundability, and an increase in twinning and in trisomic conceptions, and that the rather rare phenomenon of a Down's syndrome term birth is but a chance survivor of this general tendency. Such a possibility is in no way incompatible with an environmental influence on the ovary, discussed above, but it makes the effect less specific.

We will discuss both these possibilities in the context of the second paradox to be discussed, that is, the contrasting effects of the environment on the survival of trisomy 21 conception in the prenatal as opposed to the postnatal period.

In general, changes in the intrauterine environment of trisomy 21 individuals have probably been on a lesser and indeterminate scale, when compared to changes in the postnatal environment, which are dramatic.

The great majority of recognized conceptuses with trisomy 21 do not survive the intrauterine period (Figure 4).

While social factors and advances in medical knowledge and application have undoubtedly profoundly influenced the survival of Down's syndrome infants in the postnatal period, by contrast we believe they have not much changed survival of trisomy 21 individuals in the prenatal period.

We can now examine the possibility previously suggested, that trisomy 21 births are not more common in the conceptions of older women, but only among term births. This can be ruled out on the evidence. Trisomy 21 is very much more common in the spontaneous abortion fetuses as well as in the term births of older women.

Spontaneous abortion seems to be a maternal mechanism for rejecting anomalous fetuses. Two-thirds of trisomy 21 fetuses never come to term, as is shown in Figure 4. There is in fact a 100-fold increase of anomalies in spontane-

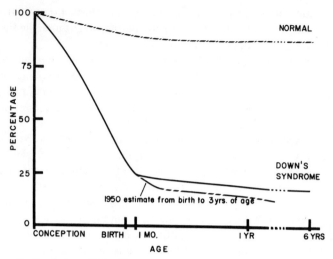

Figure 4. Survival model for Down's syndrome: conception through childhood.

ous abortions compared to term births. Older women do abort trisomy 21 fetuses, perhaps even as efficiently as do younger women.

I would like to emphasize here that we cannot be absolutely certain that the Down's syndrome child who survives a pregnancy to term is biologically identical in early life to the trisomy 21 fetus that aborts. It is better to use the term trisomy 21 fetus quite specifically and separately from Down's syndrome birth, which signifies a conception that has gone to term. However, there are two epidemiological observations on Down's syndrome that would suggest that trisomy 21 fetuses and term births with Down's syndrome are similar in some ways:

1. a raised risk with advanced maternal age
2. a raised risk with prolonged pelvic irradiation of the mother.

These factors are common to abortions with trisomy 21 and to births with Down's syndrome.

If we return to the second possibility previously suggested, that there is a general tendency to anomalous conceptions with senescence, such evidence that we have from spontaneous abortions does lend some support to this view. As far as other trisomies are concerned, the trisomic forms of other chromosomes resemble trisomy 21 in being maternal age–related (Figure 5), and in being more common in older women who have been irradiated years before. There is also the extraordinarily provocative report of Alberman et al. (1975), which states that of 250 women who had trisomic chromosomes (not 21) in spontaneous abortions, no less than five had previously given birth to infants with Down's syndrome.

Taken together, these three observations do suggest that there may be a common underlying process for trisomic conceptions in general, and that this process may not be specific to Down's syndrome.

We have opened up the possibility in this paper that conceptions of trisomy 21 could have been influenced by environmental factors acting on the mother over the long period of maturity. However, it is clear that at this time only a small proportion of individuals with trisomy 21 survive the screening mechanism of spontaneous abortion. Previously, few also survived the rigors of the germ-ridden extrauterine world, but there is now a divergence between the relative stability of the environment in the prenatal period and the remarkable changes in the environment after birth.

The only measures we presently have for reducing prevalence is to reduce the prevalence of trisomy 21 individuals among term births and to modify the disabilities in those who are born.

The benefits of such measures are likely to be considerable. There is one benefit that I believe could be of special importance to the present generation of young women. Modern obstetrics has greatly reduced the risk of childbearing to

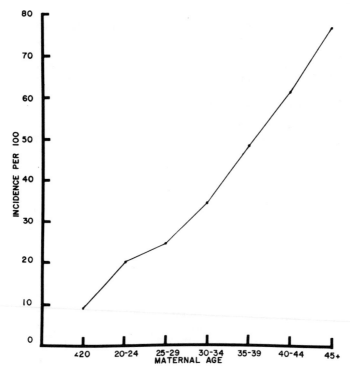

Figure 5. Incidence per 100 of autosomal trisomies (exclusive of 21) in a series of 1,349 spontaneous abortions by maternal age (Boué, personal communication).

both mother and infant, and prenatal screening now reduces the risk of a Down's syndrome birth. Many women will see this as an opportunity to delay childbearing instead of interrupting their education or their training, and procreation will be deferred. Fertility control now includes, besides contraception and induced abortion, the monitoring of the high risk pregnancy through the prenatal period.

REFERENCES

Alberman, E., Elliott, M., Creasy, M., et al. (1975) Previous reproductive history in mothers presenting with spontaneous abortions. Brit. J. Obstet. Gynaec. 82:366.

Alberman, E., Polani, P. E., Roberts, J. A., et al. (1972) Parental exposure to x-irradiation and Down's syndrome. Ann. Hum. Genet. 36:195.

Collmann, R. D., and Stoller, A. (1962) A survey of mongoloid births in Victoria, Australia, 1942–1957. Amer. J. Publ. Health 52:813.

Harlap, S. (1973) Down's syndrome in west Jerusalem. Amer. J. Epidemiol. 97:225.

Lindsjo, A. (1974) Down's syndrome in Sweden. Acta Paediat. Scand. 63:571.

Penrose, L. S. (1951) Maternal age in familial mongolism. J. Ment. Sci. 97:738.

Penrose, L. S., and Smith, G. F. (1966) Down's Anomaly. London: J. & A. Churchill.

Penrose, L. S. (1967) The effects of change in maternal age distribution upon the incidence of mongolism. J. Ment. Defic. Res. 11:54.

Sigler, A. T., Lilienfeld, A. M., Cohen, B. H., and Westlake, J. E. (1965) Radiation exposure in parents of children with mongolism (Down's syndrome). Bull. Johns Hopkins Hosp. 117:374.

Uchida, I. A., Holunger, R., and Lawler, C. (1968) Maternal radiation and chromosomal aberrations. Lancet 2:1045.

RESEARCH TO PRACTICE IN MENTAL RETARDATION
Biomedical Aspects, Volume III
Edited by Peter Mittler
Copyright 1977 I.A.S.S.M.D.

NEW CHROMOSOMAL SYNDROMES AND MENTAL RETARDATION

H. A. Lubs[1,2] **and J. Walknowska**[1]
[1]*Department of Pediatrics*
[2]*Department of Biophysics and Genetics,*
University of Colorado Medical Center,
Denver, Colorado 80220, United States

The development of the banding techniques, which began in 1970 with Caspersson's report of Q banding, brought about a major revolution in the field of human genetics. These many techniques, including Q, G, and R banding, permit identification of each chromosome in man and other species because of the variations and the intensity of staining along the chromosomes (bands), and the detection of relatively small abnormalities in each chromosome. An R banded karyotype is shown in Figure 1. The uniqueness of each pair is readily apparent.

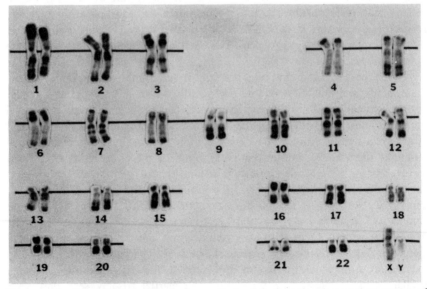

Figure 1. An R banded karyotype is shown. Each of the homologs has a unique pattern of staining.

A useful genetic map of human chromosomes is now being developed as another offshoot of this work.

One of the most predictable results of the use of these techniques was the recognition of many new chromosomal syndromes, as is seen in Figure 2. Only autosomal syndromes are shown in the figure. The number of syndromes described each year is shown to the left and the total number along the top. Prior to the introduction of these techniques, only 12 autosomal syndromes, either trisomies or deletions, were known, and few new syndromes were being added each year. It has taken several years for the various laboratories to perfect these techniques for daily use and to have screened enough children with mental retardation and congenital anomalies to have permitted the recognition of sizable numbers of new syndromes, but this is now occurring very rapidly, as the figure shows. In the past year, 18 new syndromes were described and a total of at least 41 are now known.

A dual definition of the term "syndrome" is used in this discussion: both the cytogenetic abnormality and the clinical features must be similar. Many other instances where there are one or two case reports could have been included, and the number of syndromes shown in Figure 2 would have been much greater. We felt, however, that at least a few cases were necessary to permit the official designation of "syndrome" even though it is very likely that most of these case reports will shortly be part of recognized syndromes.

Few of these syndromes have quite as unique an appearance as Down's syndrome, or trisomy 21. As we get more information and see more pictures of patients with these syndromes, there is often the feeling of déjà vu. We do believe that it is possible to make a tentative diagnosis of many of these syndromes by looking at the child, or at least that we will be able to do so after a few more years of experience. The final answer will always rest in the cytogenetic findings.

It can be predicted that the number of syndromes will continue to rise dramatically and that these will be associated with the still smaller and smaller cytogenetic abnormalities. Ultimately, it may be shown that certain autosomal dominant disorders with anomalies and mental retardation are in fact small cytogenetic abnormalities rather than point mutations. Already there are several trisomies involving 9p, in addition to trisomy for the entire short arm. These involve one or more bands rather than the entire arm, and the clinical features are slightly different. These were not included in Table 1 for the sake of simplicity. Moreover, it should also be pointed out that the majority of cases summarized in Table 1 are secondary to a parental translocation. Thus, in most cases there is both a partial trisomy (duplication) and partial monosomy (deficiency or deletion). However, in cases where a pure partial trisomy, such as an extra short arm and centromere of 9p is present, the clinical features are quite similar to those present in the comparable partial trisomy secondary to a translocation. It seems, therefore, that most of the clinical manifestations are attributable to the duplication part of the "duplication" deficiency syndromes. This limitation in methodology in deriving the information in Table 1 should be understood, as well as the possibility that when several hundred cases are available for analysis a more exact definition of syndromes will probably result. In the interim, such a compilation is still of great use in recognizing affected children.

In many ways, the most convincing evidence that these are indeed syndromes comes from the appearance of the children. It is impossible to reprint here a sufficient number of appropriate photographs to make this apparent, so

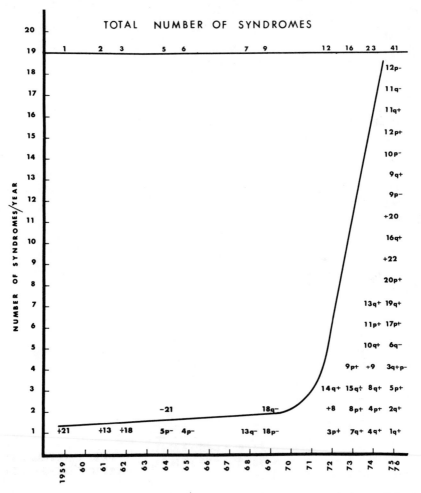

Figure 2. The increase in total number of syndromes due to autosomal abnormalities is shown here. The rapid rise followed the introduction of the banding technics and the total number of syndromes, shown at the top, is now at least 41.

Table 1. New autosomal syndromes

Chromosome abnormality	No. cases	Typical facies	Clinical features	
			Unusual and especially helpful findings	Common but nonspecific findings
	4	yes	elfin-like face, thymic abnormality, hirsutism, (absence of gall bladder)	low birth weight, wide-set eyes, cleft palate, micrognathia, cardiac anomalies, undescended testes, long fingers (Ref. 12)
	6	yes	upper lip in form of "chapeaux de gendarme"	mental and growth retardation, low set ears, prominent forehead, micrognathia, depressed nasal bridge, flat philtrum (Refs. 10, 47)

continued

			facies	clinical features
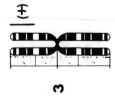 3	3	yes	square-shaped face with large down-turned mouth, short nose	mental retardation, microcephaly, hypertelorism, high forehead, macrostomia, hypotonia, small penis, high frequency of whorls (Ref. 30)
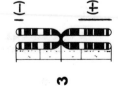 3	18	yes	Potter Syndrome facies	mental retardation, growth retardation, skeletal anomalies, extremely short palpebral fissures, omphalocele, no speech (Ref. 2)
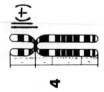 4	19	yes	characteristic, lower facial region, bulbous nose, bushy eyebrows, dysplastic ears, hirsutism on side of face, low frontal hair line, upper jaw prominent, large mouth	psychomotor and growth retardation, microcephaly, prominent glabella, large depressed nasal bridge, large tongue, low set ears with broad concha, wide spread nipples, joint flexions, hip dislocation (Refs. 13, 31)

Table 1. New autosomal syndromes *continued*

Chromosome abnormality	No. cases	Typical facies	Clinical features	
			Unusual and especially helpful findings	Common but nonspecific findings
4	11	yes	straight, prominent nose (Roman nose) short and protruding philtrum, over hanging upper lip	mental retardation, microcephaly, prominent forehead, prominent eyes, large ears with hypoplastic lobule, short neck, wide set nipples, undescended testes, abnormal extremities, renal anomalies (Ref. 9)
4	40	yes	coloboma of the iris, preauricular tags or pits, square-tipped nose	mental and growth retardation, cleft palate, prominent glabella, short philtrum with down turned mouth, small chin, hypospadias, hypoplastic dermal ridges, retarded bone age (Ref. 7)
5	6	yes	pupillary constriction, short first toes	mental retardation, large head, dolichocephaly, hypotonia, respiratory difficulties, renal anomalies (Ref. 24)

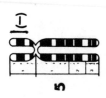 **5**	40	yes	"moon-like" facies, characteristic "cat cry"	mental and growth retardation, hypertelorism, oblique palperbral fissures, epicanthus, low set ears, abnormal palmar dermatoglyphics (Ref. 15)
 **6**	2	yes	never talked or walked, small and slender extremities, peculiar face	mental and growth retardation, nipples widely spread, trunk obese, small penis, no testes in scrotum, abnormal kidney, atrophic pancreas (Refs. 22, 23)
 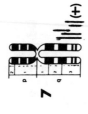 **7**	9	?	abnormal shaped head	mental and growth retardation, low set and malformed ears, hypertelorism, hypertonia, flat nose bridge, small nose, micrognathia, rocker bottom feet, fifth finger and thumb were clenched over other fingers (Refs. 40, 42)
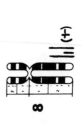 **8**	5	?	abnormal or extra vertebrae	mental retardation, microcephaly, dysplastic ears, micrognathy, long slender trunk, arched palate, short fifth fingers, malposition of the toes (Refs. 11, 34)

continued

Table 1. New autosomal syndromes *continued*

Chromosome abnormality	No. cases	Typical facies	Clinical features	
			Unusual and especially helpful findings	Common but nonspecific findings
8	5	yes	long slender trunk, slender pelvis, deformed skull, restricted articular function, macrocephaly	mild or moderate mental retardation, strabismus, high-arched palate, low set or dysplastic ears, micrognathia, long and slender trunk, anomalies of vertebrae and ribs, bulging skin with deep furrows, koilosternia (Ref. 19)
8	11	?		microcephaly, short neck, koilosternia, extra rib, abnormal vertebrae, narrow pelvis, club foot, joint stiffness (Ref. 20)
9	50	yes	prominent nose with inverted nostrils, short upper lip with the corners of mouth slanting downwards, protuberant ears, decreased number digital triradii	mild or moderate mental retardation, microcephaly, brachycephaly, flat forehead, enophthalmos, hypoplasia of phalanges, decreased number of whorls on the fingers, small penis (Refs. 5, 21, 36, 44, 48)

7	yes	trigonocephaly, abnormal ear lobule	psychomotor retardation, mongoloid eyes, flat nasal bridge, anteverted nostrils, long philtrum, low set ears, high arched palate, micrognathia, low hair line, short neck, wide set nipples, long fingers, square nails (Ref. 1)
8	yes	high and bulky forehead, polycystic kidney, bones and joint abnormalities	mental retardation, low set ears, hypoplastic helix, broad nasal bridge, retrognathia, cleft lip and palate, low origin line of hair growth, dolichocephaly, club feet (Refs. 5, 14, 35, 46)
12	yes	severe growth retardation, flat and round face, small nose and depressed nasal bridge, arched and wide-set eyebrows	severe mental retardation, hypotrophy, hypotonia, ptosis, micropthalmia, microcephaly, retrognathia, agenesis of palate, low implantation of ears, short neck, heart defects, decreased renal function (Refs. 29, 45)

9 (−)

10 (+)

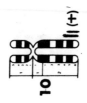

10 (+)

continued

Table 1. New autosomal syndromes *continued*

Chromosome abnormality	No. cases	Typical facies	Clinical features	
			Unusual and especially helpful findings	Common but nonspecific findings
11 (+)	12	yes	old-looking wrinkled face, long beaked nose	mental retardation, microretrognathia, malformation of the palate, low set ears, prominent anterior helix, short neck, narrow chest with nipples set widely, micropenis, hypertonia of the limbs, congenital heart disease, renal agenesis or malformation of the urinary tract, agenesis of thoracic girdle (Ref. 4)
11 (+)	3	?	unable to speak and unable to sit	mental and growth retardation, prominent frontal bossing, strabismus, epicanthal folds, high arched palate, weak suck and cry, spasticity of extremities, broad fingers and toes (Refs. 26, 33)
11 (−)	5	yes	trigonocephaly, round small nose, philtrum poorly developed, large mouth	mental and growth retardation, microcephaly, epicanthus, hypertelorism, low implantation of ears, retrognathia (Ref. 39)

			Clinical features	
12 (+)	5	yes	peculiar flat and round facies with prominent cheeks, broad and irregular implantation of eye-brows, broad and flat nasal bridge with short and narrow nose, broad and prominent lower lip, spade-shaped fingers	severe mental and growth retardation, low set ears with folded helix, increased space between first and second toes, hypotonia, hyporeflexia of knees and ankles, nystagmus (Refs. 3, 32)
12 (−)	3	yes	dysmorphia and asymmetry of facies, bilateral atrophy of the nervous opticus, high forehead, peculiar dry hair, high hair line	mental retardation, craniostenosis, hypertelorism, large nose bridge, elongated philtrum, low set ears, receding chin (Refs. 25, 38)
17 (+)	2	?	?	mental and motor retardation, hypertelorism, receding chin, small mouth, low set ears, high arched palate, hypertonia, flat occiput, foot deformities, deformity of the thumbs, large joints, widely set nipples, congenital heart disease (Refs. 18, 27)
19 (+)	2	yes	hypoplastic gall bladder, abnormality of lungs, multicystic lesions of kidneys double right thumb, flat face	microcephaly, palpebral fissures were slanted downwards, hypertelorism, small upturned nose, fishshaped mouth, cleft palate, short neck, widely spaced nipples, hypoplastic genitalia, clinodactyly (Ref. 17)

continued

Table 1. New autosomal syndromes *continued*

Chromosome abnormality	No. cases	Typical facies	Clinical features	
			Unusual and especially helpful findings	Common but nonspecific findings
20 (+-)	6	yes	unable to sit, walk, or talk, peculiar face, "half-moon" shaped eyes, small beaked nose, open mouth	mental retardation, micrognathia, depressed nasal bridge, hypertelorism, colobomata, wide spaced nipples, hypotonia, clinodactyly, dislocation of hips (Refs. 8, 37)
20 (+)	2	yes	prominent nose, deep-set eyes, small jaw, lank hair, typical "cat cry"	psychomotor retardation, low set ears, micrognathia, cleft palate, hypertelorism, short neck, cystic duplication of the esophagus and stomach and other internal abnormalities (Refs. 16, 28, 43)
22 (+)	4	yes	preauricular skin tags	mental and growth retardation, microcephaly, hypertelorism, antimongoloid slant, beaked nose, increased philtrum length, cleft palate, micrognathia, low set ears, heart disease, dislocation of hips (Refs. 41, 49)

+ = Extra chromosomal material, either partial or complete trisomy, as shown by adjacent lines.
− = Deleted or absent chromosomal material, as shown by adjacent lines.

the reader must be referred to the bibliography given at the end of this chapter, where at least one current reference for each syndrome is included. Table 1 is not intended as a complete description of each of these syndromes. Rather, there is emphasis on the unusual and most diagnostically helpful features of each syndrome (shown in the left-hand column). Other common features that are less specific are shown to the right. (A special compliment should be given to the French cytogeneticists, who have done more than any other group to delineate these new syndromes.)

DISCUSSION AND SUMMARY

The introduction of the chromosomal banding techniques has resulted in a startlingly rapid rise in the number of known syndromes resulting from chromosome abnormalities. At least 41 autosomal syndromes are now known, and 18 of these have been described in the last year. This figure does not include abnormalities of the sex chromosomes or individual case reports. Very likely these will be supplemented in the next few years by similar reports and quickly become recognized syndromes. There will likely be at least 100 well-described syndromes within the year.

The facial appearance of the great majority of these syndromes is quite characteristic. Although the facies are not as striking as that in trisomy 21 (Down's syndrome) it does appear possible in many instances to make a tentative diagnosis based on appearance. Most of these new syndromes are due to a partial trisomy, although some are due to deletions (partial monosomies). The cytogenetics of many of these abnormalities is clearly more complex than was the case in the recent past. Simple partial trisomy or an unbalanced translocation account for the majority of these abnormalities, but complex segregations during meiosis, local duplications or deletions, insertions, etc., play a significant role in their etiology.

The indications for chromosome study in children with mental retardation can be quite clearly stated: any child with mental retardation in whom there is no evident etiology but who has some evidence of physical abnormality, such as an unusual face or several minor anomalies, should be studied. Two cells are generally sufficient; thus it is possible to screen in institutions and in diagnostic operation centers without great cost. A positive chromosomal finding may be anticipated in about 5–10% of such children. It is absolutely essential, however, that good cytogenetic techniques be employed (either R or G banding). This does not cost more than conventional unbanded methodology.

The benefits of such screening or diagnosis are considerable. The establishment of the diagnosis in the child always is helpful in the management of the child, in his prognosis, and in providing an explanation to the family. Of greater importance, probably, are the benefits to the family. Since most syndromes result from an abnormal set of chromosomes in one parent, many other family members are at risk and are often unaware of this. Thus, by combining family cytogenetic studies and genetic counseling, and by making available antenatal diagnosis to the family members who are at risk, a number of cases may be prevented in the majority of these families. For this same reason, however, it is important to carry out the cytogenetic study early, while the parents and close relatives are still planning their families.

BIBLIOGRAPHY

1. Alfi, O. S., Donnell, G. N., Allderdice, P. W., and Derencseny, A. (1976) The 9p-syndrome. Ann. Genet. 19:11.
2. Allderdice, P. W., and Browne, N. Chromosome 3 duplication q21-qtr deletion p25-pter syndrome in children of carriers of a pericentric inversion (3)(p35q21). Personal communication.
3. Armendares, S., Salamanca, F., Nava, S., Ramiriz, S., and Cantu, J. M. (1975) The 12p trisomy syndrome. Ann. Genet. 18:89.
4. Aurias, A., and Laurent, C. (1975) Trisomie 11q. Individualization d'un nouveau syndrome. Ann. Genet. 18:189.
5. Blank, C. E., Colver, D., Potter, A. M., McHugh, J., and Lorber, J. (1975) Physical and mental defect of chromosomal origin in four individuals of the same family. Trisomy for the short arm of 9. Clin. Genet. 7:261.
6. Cantu, J., Salamanca, F., Buentello, L., Carnevale, A., and Armendares, S. (1975) Trisomy 10p. A report of two cases due to a familial translocation rcp (10;21)(p11;p11). Ann. Genet. 18:5.
7. Centerwall, W., Thompson, W., Allen, I., and Fobes, C.: Translocation 4p-syndrome. Amer. J. Dis. Child. 129:366.
8. Cohen, M., Davidson, R., and Brown, J. (1975) A familial F/G transloca-tion[t(20p-; 22q+)] observed in three generations. Clin. Genet. 7:120.
9. Dutrillaux, B., Laurent, C., Forabosco, A., Noel, B., Suerinc, E., Biemont, M., and Cotton, J. (1975) La trisomie 4q partielle. A propos de trois observations. Ann. Genet. 18:21.
10. Forabosco, A., Dutrillaux, B., Toni, G., Tamborino, G., and Cavazzuti, G. (1973) Translocation equilibrée t(2;13)(q32;q33) familiale et trisomie 2q partielle. Ann. Genet. 16:255.
11. Fryns, J., Verresen, H., Van den Berghe, H., Van Kerckvoorde, J., and Cassiman, J. (1974) Partial trisomy 8: trisomy of the distal part of the long arm of chromosome number 8+(8q2) in a severely retarded and malformed girl. Humangenetik 24:241.
12. Garrett, J., Finley, S., and Finley, W. (1975) Fetal loss and familial chromosome 1 translocations. Clin. Genet. 8:341.
13. Giraud, F., Mattei, J., Mattei, M., Ayme, S., and Bernard, R. (1975) La trisomie 4p. A propos de 3 observations. Humangenetik 30:99.
14. Grosse, K., Schwanitz, G., Singer, H., and Wieczorek, V. (1975) Partial trisomy 10p. Humangenetik 29:141.
15. James, A., Jr., Atkins, L., Feingold, M., and Janower, M. (1969) The Cri du Chat Syndrome. Radiology 92:50.
16. Krmpotic, E., Rosenthal, I., Szego, K., and Bocian, M. (1971) Trisomy F(?20). Report of a 14q/F(?20) familial translocation. Ann. Genet. 14:291.

17. Lange, M., and Alfi, O. (1975) Trisomy 19q. Ann. Genet. 19:17.
18. Latta, E., and Hoo, J. (1974) Trisomy of the short arm of chromosome 17. Humangenetik 23:213.
19. Lejeune, J., and Rethore, M. (1973) Trisomies of chromosome no. 8. *In* Chromosome Identification—Technique and Applications in Biology and Medicine. Nobel Symposium 23. (Eds. Caspersson T. and Zech L.). New York: Academic Press.
20. Lewandowski, R., and Yunis, J. (1975) New chromosomal syndromes. Amer. J. Dis. Child. 129:515.
21. Lurie, I., Lazjuk, G., Gurevich, D., and Usoev, S. (1976) Genetics of the +p9 syndrome. Hum. Genet. 32:23.
22. Mikkelsen, M., Dyggve, H., and Poulsen, H. (1973) (6;15) translocation with loss of chromosome material in the patient and various chromosome aberrations in family members. Humangenetik 18:195.
23. Milosevic, J., and Kalicanin, P. (1975) Long arm deletion of chromosome No. 6 in a mentally retarded boy with multiple physical malformations. J. Ment. Defic. Res. 19:139.
24. Opitz, J., and Patau, K. (1975) A partial trisomy 5p syndrome. *In* New Chromosomal and Malformation Syndromes. (Ed. Bergsma, D.) Birth Defects Original Article Series Vol. XI(5) p. 191.
25. Orye, E., and Craen, M. (1975) Short arm deletion of chromosome 12. Humangenetik 28:335.
26. Palmer, C., Poland, C., Reed, Terry, and Kojetin, J. (1976) Partial trisomy 11, 46,XX,−3,−20,+der3,+der20,t(3:11:20), resulting from a complex maternal rearrangement of chromosomes 3, 11, 20. Humangenetik 31:219.
27. Palutke, W., Chen, H., Woolley, P., Espiritu, C., Vogel, H., Gohle, N., and Tyrkus, M. (1976) An extra small metacentric chromosome identified as a deleted chromosome no. 17. Clin. Genet. 9:454.
28. Pan, S., Fatora, S., Haas, J., and Steele, M. (1976) Trisomy of chromosome 20. Clin. Genet. 9:449.
29. Prieur, M., Forabosco, A., Dutrillaux, B., Laurent, C., Bernasconi, S., and Lejenue, J. (1975) La trisomie 10q24→10qter. Ann. Genet. 18:217.
30. Rethore, M., Lejeune, J., Carpentier, S., Prieur, M., Dutrillaux, B., Seringe, P., Rossier, A., and Job. J. (1972) Trisomie pour la partie distale du bras court du chromosome 3 chez trois Germains. Premier exemple d'insertion chromosomique: ins (7;3)(q31;p21;26). Ann. Genet. 15:159.
31. Rethore, M., Dutrillaux, B., Giovannelli, G., Forabosco, A., Dallapiccola, B., and Lejeune, J. (1974) La trisomie 4p. Ann. Genet. 17:125.
32. Rethore, M., Kaplan, J., Junien, C., Cruveiller, J., Dutrillaux, B., Aurias, A., Carpentier, S., Lafourcade, J., and Lejeune, J. (1975) Augmentation de l'activité de la LDH-B chez un garçon trisomique 12p par malsegregation d'une translocation maternelle t(12;14)(q12;p11). Ann. Genet. 18:81.
33. Sanchez, O., Yunis, J., and Escobar, J. (1974) Partial trisomy 11 in a child resulting from a complex maternal rearrangement of chromosomes 11, 12 and 13. Humangenetik 22:59.
34. Sanchez, O., and Yunis, J. (1974) Partial trisomy 8 (8q24) and the trisomy 8 syndrome. Humangenetik 23:297.
35. Scheiermacher, E., Schliebitz, U., and Steffens, C. (1974) Brother and sister with trisomy 10p: A new syndrome. Humangenetik 23:163.
36. Stoll, C., Levy, J., and Gardea, A. (1975) Trisomy 9p in a girl whose mother has a translocation t(9;20)(q12;p13). Humangenetik 27:269.

37. Subrt, I., and Brychnac, V. (1974) Trisomy for short arm of chromosome 20. Humangenetik 23:219.
38. Tenconi, R., Baccichetti, C., Anglani, F., Pellegrino, P., Kaplan, J., and Junien, C. (1975) Partial deletion of the short arm of chromosome 12(p11; p13). Ann. Genet. 18:95.
39. Turleau, C., Chavin-Colin, F., Roubin, M., Thomas, D., and de Grouchy, J. (1975) Monosomie partielle 11q et trigonocephalie un nouveau syndrome. Ann. Genet. 18:357.
40. Turleau, C., Rossier, A., de Montis, G., Roubin, M., Chavin-Colin, F., and de Grouchy, J. (1976) Trisomie partielle 7q. Un ou deux syndromes? A propos d'une nouvelle observation. Ann. Genet. 19:37.
41. Vianello, M., and Bonioli, E. (1973) Trisomy 22. J. Hum. Genet. 23:239.
42. Vogel, W., Siebers, J., and Reinwein, H. (1973) Partial trisomy 7q. Ann. Genet. 16:277.
43. Wahlström, J., Borsgard, J., and Sabel, K. (1976) A case of trisomy 20? Clin. Genet. 9:187.
44. Weber, F., Muller, H., and Sparkes, R. (1975) The 9p trisomy syndrome due to inherited translocation. In New Chromosomal Malformation Syndromes. Birth Defects Original Article Series Vol. XI, No. 5. (Ed. Bergsma, D.) p. 201.
45. Yunis, J., and Sanchez, O. (1974) A new syndrome resulting from partial trisomy for the distal third of the long arm of chromosome 10. J. Pediatr. 84:567.
46. Yunis, E., Silva, R., and Giraldo, A. (1976) Trisomy 10p. Ann. Genet. 19:57.
47. Zabel, B., Hansen, S., and Hartmann, W. (1976) Partial trisomy 2q and familial translocation t(2;12)(q31;q24). Hum. Genet. 32:101.
48. Zaremba, J., Zdzienicka, E., Glogowska, I., Abramowicz, T., and Taracha, B. (1974) Four cases of 9p trisomy resulting from a balanced familial translocation (9;15)(q13;q11). Clinical picture and cytogenetic findings. J. Ment. Defic. Res. 18:153.
49. Zellweger, H., Ionasescu, V., and Simpson, J. (1975) Trisomy 22. J. Hum. Genet. 23:65.

RESEARCH TO PRACTICE IN MENTAL RETARDATION
Biomedical Aspects, Volume III
Edited by Peter Mittler
Copyright 1977 I.A.S.S.M.D.

CLINICAL PROFILES OF ATYPICAL CHROMOSOME-G ANOMALIES

J. Dey
Illawarra Region,
Health Commission of New South Wales,
Wollongong, N.S.W., Australia, 2500

Since the establishment of Grosvenor Hospital in 1965 as a central diagnostic and assessment clinic for the intellectually handicapped of New South Wales, 5,460 new cases have been assessed, of whom 950 had Down's syndrome, an incidence of 17.4%, or approximately one in 5.75 patients referred. The criteria for confirming the clinical diagnosis of Down's syndrome by chromosome analysis have been:

1. mothers were under 35 years of age at the time of their birth
2. a positive family history
3. chromosome analysis particularly requested by parents
4. any diagnostic doubt.

Using these criteria, chromosome analyses were done for 485 cases, and of these 10.31% had atypical karyotypes, the remaining 89.69% were standard trisomy-G karyotypes with parents with normal karyotypes or with parents who have not had chromosome analyses. In view of reports in the literature of balanced chromosome anomalies in parents of children with standard trisomy-G karyotypes, we have, over the past 5½ years, arranged chromosome analysis for both parents of mongols born to mothers under 35 years of age. In the atypical group of fifty cases, thirteen are G/G translocations, thirteen are D/G translocations, thirteen are mosaics, nine are standard trisomy-G with one parent with an abnormal chromosome pattern, one is a trisomy-G with a D/D translocation, and one is a trisomy-G with Klinefelter mosaicism (Table 1). Our survey findings are compared to those of other similar surveys published recently in Table 2.

Table 1. Chromosome karyotypes for 485 Down's syndrome cases

Result	Number		Percentage	
Trisomy G	435		89.69	
G/G translocation	13 ⎞		2.68 ⎞	
D/G translocation	13 ⎟		2.68 ⎟	
Mosaic	13 ⎬ 50		2.68 ⎬ 10.31	
Parental anomaly	9 ⎟		1.86 ⎟	
Other	2 ⎠		0.41 ⎠	
Total	485		100.00	

G/G TRANSLOCATION

Of these thirteen cases, seven are males and six are females, and at the time of their births their mothers ranged in age from 18–34 years. Five of the thirteen are the first-born child (three being only children); only four are the youngest. Of the 26 parents, chromosomes were examined in all except four; 21 had normal karyotypes and one mother had a G/G translocation. The failure to examine parental chromosomes occurred in the oldest of this group and in the

Table 2. Comparison with similar surveys

Survey	No. of cases	Regular Trisomy 21 (%)	D/G Translocation (%)	G/G Translocation (%)	Mosaic (%)	Other (%)
Mikkelsen, 1967 Denmark	100	89	5	4	2	
Cowie, 1966 U.K.	65	93.9	1.5	4.6		
Unnamed	Not stated	94.7	1.5	1.4	2.4	
Edgren, 1966 Finland	73	97.2			1.4	1.4
Petersen, 1965 U.S.A.	227	92.1	5.7	2.2		
Stevenson, 1969	161	94.4	3.1		2.5	
Moric-Petrovic, 1971	180	93.9	1.7	3.3	1.1	
Richards, 1965 U.K.	225	94.2	0.9	1.3	2.7	0.9
Huang, 1967 China	77	94.8	2.6	1.3	1.3	
Wright, 1967 U.S.A.	1382	Not stated	2.9	2.8	Not stated	
Dey, 1976 Australia	485	91.5	2.7	2.7	2.7	0.4

child who was a state ward and whose parents could not be traced. In one family there had been a subsequent stillborn unaffected child, in another a prior miscarriage, and in another two prior miscarriages. This group's present age range is from 2¼ to 32 years.

D/G TRANSLOCATION

Of these thirteen cases, ten are females and three are males, and at the time of their births their mothers ranged in age from 21 to 32 years. Five are first-born (four of whom are only children), seven are the youngest in two- or three-child families, and one is the only child of this union, but has four maternal half-siblings and three paternal half-siblings. Chromosomes were analysed for all parents except two fathers, who refuse so far to have this done, but whose wives' karyotypes are normal. Of the remaining eleven couples, only four husbands and wives both have normal karyotypes, four mothers and three fathers have a D/G translocation, while their respective spouses have normal karyotypes. Chromosomes of close relatives were examined, and in six families at least another D/G balanced translocation was identified: one maternal aunt, one paternal uncle, one paternal grandfather and brother, one maternal grandfather, one paternal grandfather and two paternal uncles, and, in the sixth family, a maternal grandmother and sister. Four of the mothers had had one miscarriage and another a stillborn child. This group's present age range is from two years to six years, three months.

MOSAIC

Of these thirteen cases, ten are males and three are females, and at the time of their births, their mothers ranged in age from 25 to 45 years. None is first-born, but nine are the youngest of the family. Parental chromosomes were examined for only three couples, and all had normal karyotypes. Two mothers had had two miscarriages, one had had four, and one had had a stillborn child. The group's present age range is from 2½ years to 20 years.

PARENTAL ANOMALY

Of the nine cases, six are males and three are females, and all have standard trisomy-21 karyotypes. At the time of their births, their mothers ranged in age from 15 to 34 years. Two are brothers. Three are only children and three the elder of two. Parental chromosomes were analysed for all except one father and one male donor (artificial insemination). Two fathers and two mothers were mosaic mongols of normal intelligence with 69% to 95% normal cells. One father had a constant additional chromosomal fragment. One father had an XXY karyotype, with three of the 26 analysed cells also having an extra G chromosome. One father has three out of the 29 cells studied with XXY, and one mother had a balanced D/B translocation. One mother had had one miscarriage. The present age range of this group is 13 months to 7¼ years.

PARENTAL SEX CHROMOSOME ANOMALY

In addition to the fathers just mentioned with the XXY sex chromosome patterns, one of the D/G translocation mongols has a most interesting mixed chromosome pattern in her female maternal relatives:

M. Grandmother	39 cells with D/G translocation and normal XX sex pattern
	1 cell with a D/G translocation and XXX sex pattern
	2 cells with 46 chromosomes
Mother	31 cells with D/G translocation and XX sex pattern
	1 cell with D/G translocation and XXX sex pattern
1st sister	constant D/G translocation with XX sex pattern
2nd sister	17 cells with XXX sex pattern
	7 cells with XX sex pattern
Propositus	25 cells with Trisomy G and D/G translocation and XX sex pattern
	2 cells with XXX sex patterns

There are no boys in this family. The father, maternal grandfather and maternal uncle all have normal male karyotypes.

D/D TRANSLOCATION/TRISOMY G

This girl was born when her mother was 23 years old, and is the middle child in a family of three. Her mother has had no miscarriages and no stillborn children. She is now just eight years old. Her mother has a normal karyotype, as does her brother. Both her father and paternal grandmother have a balanced D/D translocation. The incidence of D/D translocation in the general population is 1:800. Ridler et al. (1969) reported four cases of trisomy-21 with D/D translocation, and gave an incidence of one in every 552 mongols with this double chromosomal anomaly.

TRISOMY G/KLINEFELTER MOSAIC

This boy was born when his mother was 21 years old, and is the elder of two children, his mother having had one miscarriage. He is now two years and nine months of age. His chromosome analysis showed 80 cells with trisomy G, 6 cells with trisomy G plus XXY sex chromosomal pattern, and 9 cells with normal karyotypes. Chromosome studies have not yet been done on his parents or sibling. He is severely retarded.

MATERNAL AGE

For the total 950 cases under review, the maternal age at the time of the birth of the Down's syndrome child ranged from a fourteen-year-old girl to two women of fifty years. Table 3 shows the maternal age range distribution, which reflects the clinic's policy of karyotyping those cases born to mothers under 35 years of age. In all the atypical subgroups except mosaicism, all the mothers were under 35 years of age. In the parental anomaly group there is a significant increase in first-born affected offspring.

The normal distribution curve for maternal age at birth in New South Wales is contrasted with that of the 924 cases, where maternal age was recorded, in Figure 1.

Table 4A shows the percentage distribution of chromosomal types at each maternal age group, and Table 4B again shows this percentage distribution, but only for those cases where chromosome analysis was done, i.e., excluding the "karyotype unknown" cases.

DEGREE OF RETARDATION

The small number of mosaic and D/G translocation mongols described function slightly above the expected level of intellect for the total group (Table 5).

CONCLUSIONS

This study reinforces the need to have the results of chromosome analyses of both the child and his young parents, and, in the translocation and parent anomaly groups, those of siblings and other close relatives, before giving genetic counselling. It also underlines the need for chromosome analyses for first-born mongols, and those with a family history of Down's syndrome. Monitoring of future pregnancies by amniocentesis and chromosome analysis of the cells so obtained should be made available to those high risk families who wish to have further children.

SUMMARY

This study analyses Down's syndrome patients attending the central diagnostic and assessment clinic for the intellectually handicapped in the state of New South Wales over the past eleven years. 10% of these had either a mosaic or translocation karyotype, or one parent also had a chromosomal abnormality— these groups are discussed in depth.

ACKNOWLEDGMENTS

I should like to thank my colleagues at Grosvenor Hospital for their cooperation in this study, the referring doctors, and the Director and staff of the Oliver

Table 3. Maternal age range

Maternal age group	Trisomy 21	G/G translocation	D/G translocation	Mosaic	Parental anomaly	Other	Karyotype not known	Totals	%
14–19	26	3			1		10	40	4.2
20–24	86	2	6		4	2	28	128	13.5
25–29	116	3	5	3	2		50	179	18.8
30–34	75	5	2	3	2		61	148	15.6
35–39	71			2			134	207	21.8
40–44	53			4			130	187	19.7
45–50	8			1			26	35	3.7
M.A. not known							26	26	2.7
Totals	435	13	13	13	9	2	465	950	100.0

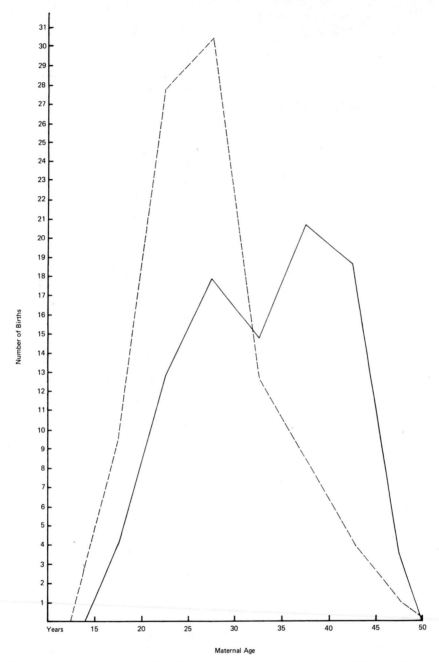

Figure 1. Comparison of the distribution curve for maternal age at birth in New South Wales, Australia, with that of births of Down's syndrome. Key: All births in N.S.W. for year 1974, in thousands = *dotted line;* Down's syndrome births (924) in tens = *solid line.*

Table 4A. Percentage distribution of chromosomal types at each maternal age group

Maternal age group	Trisomy 21	G/G translocation	D/G translocation	Mosaicism	Parental anomaly	Other	Karyotype not known	Total
14–19	65.0	7.5	0.0	0.0	2.5	0.0	25.0	100.0
20–24	67.2	1.6	4.7	0.0	3.1	1.6	21.8	100.0
25–29	64.8	1.7	2.8	1.7	1.1	0.0	27.9	100.0
30–34	50.7	3.4	1.4	2.0	1.4	0.0	41.1	100.0
35–39	34.3	0.0	0.0	1.0	0.0	0.0	64.7	100.0
40–44	28.3	0.0	0.0	2.2	0.0	0.0	69.5	100.0
45–50	22.9	0.0	0.0	2.8	0.0	0.0	74.3	100.0

Table 4B. Percentage distribution of chromosomal types at each maternal age group excluding "karyotype not known" group

Maternal age group	Trisomy 21	G/G translocation	D/G translocation	Mosaicism	Parental anomaly	Trisomy-21 + additional chromosome anomaly
14–19	86.7	10.0	0.0	0.0	3.3	0.0
20–24	86.0	2.0	6.0	0.0	4.0	2.0
25–29	89.9	2.3	3.9	2.3	1.6	0.0
30–34	86.2	5.7	2.3	3.5	2.3	0.0
35–39	97.3	0.0	0.0	2.7	0.0	0.0
40–44	93.0	0.0	0.0	7.0	0.0	0.0
45–50	88.9	0.0	0.0	11.1	0.0	0.0

Table 5. Degree of retardation

Incidence of characteristic	IQ 69–90 (%)	IQ 52–67 (%)	IQ 36–51 (%)	IQ 20–35 (%)	IQ <20 (%)	Too young for testing (%)
Survey of 500 cases	1.2	14.4	50.7	26.3	7.3	
G/G translocation		7.7	38.5	30.8	15.4	7.7
D/G translocation	7.7	38.5	15.4	23.1		15.4
Mosaic	7.7	23.1	38.5	23.1		7.7
Parental anomaly			55.6	22.2		22.2

Latham Laboratory, who performed the majority of the chromosomal analyses. I should also like to thank my Regional Director of Health and the Health Commission of New South Wales for the opportunity to present this report. I am grateful to the Editor of the *Australian Paediatric Journal* for his permission to use some material that he first published in April, 1974.

REFERENCES

Cowie, V. (1966) Sixty-five infants with Down's syndrome. Ala. J. Med. Sci. 3:493.

Dey, J. (1971) Survey of 500 cases of Down's syndrome. Austr. J. Ment. Retard. 1:154.

Edgren, J. et al. (1966) Cytogenetic study of seventy-three patients with Down's syndrome. J. Ment. Defic. Res. 10:47.

Huang, S. W. et al. (1967) A cytogenetic study of 77 Chinese children with Down's syndrome. J. Ment. Defic. Res. 11:147.

Mikkelsen, M. (1967) Down's syndrome at young maternal age. Ann. Hum. Genet. 31:51.

Moric-Petrovic, S. et al. (1971) Cytogenetic survey of Down's syndrome in Serbia (Yugoslavia). Incidence of numerical and structural abnormalities. J. Ment. Defic. Res. 15:102.

Petersen, C. D., and Luzzati, L. (1965) The role of chromosome translocation in the recurrence risk of Down's syndrome. Paediatrics 35:463.

Richards, B. W. et al. (1965) Cytogenetic survey of 225 patients diagnosed clinically as mongols. J. Ment. Defic. Res. 9:245.

Ridler, M. A. C. et al. (1969) Association of D/D translocation with mongolism. J. Ment. Defic. Res. 13:89.

Stevenson, A. C. et al. (1969) Down's syndrome in families referred for advice. J. Ment. Defic. Res. 13:206.

Wright, S. W. et al. (1967) Frequency of trisomy 21 translocation in Down's syndrome. J. Pediatr. 70:420.

RESEARCH TO PRACTICE IN MENTAL RETARDATION
Biomedical Aspects, Volume III
Edited by Peter Mittler
Copyright 1977 I.A.S.S.M.D.

SEVERE MENTAL RETARDATION IN SWEDEN
Karyotypes, Associated Physical Handicaps, and Social Functioning

L. Wallin
Psychiatric Research Centre,
St. Jörgen's Hospital,
S-422 03 Hisings backa,
Sweden

At the congress of this association at the Hague in 1973 I reported prevalence figures for severe mental retardation in a Swedish industrial town of medium size. Severe mental retardation was operationally defined as corresponding to an intelligence level with IQ lower than three times the standard deviation below the mean on the Swedish version of the revised Stanford-Binet Scale, Form L. In the case of persons over 18 years of age, conclusive evidence was required that this grade of handicap was already present before that age.

The population numbered 33,400, and the mean prevalence for severe mental retardation was 0.24%. Table 1 shows the prevalence figures, divided by

Table 1. Severe mental retardation (IQ under 52)[a]

Age in years	Number of males	Number of females	Both sexes	%
0–9	7	9	16	0.31
10–19	10	11	21	0.46
20–29	10	8	18	0.30
30–39	3	3	6	0.14
40–49	2	5	7	0.15
50–59	2	5	7	0.18
60 +	1	5	6	0.13
All ages	35	46	81	0.24

[a]Prevalence (percent) in the population of Mölndal November 1, 1969, by age.

Table 2. Sex distribution in relation to grade of retardation in 81 severely mentally retarded in Mölndal November 1, 1969

Level	Males		Females		Both sexes	
	number	%	number	%	number	%
Medium grade	27	0.16	36	0.21	63	0.19
Low grade	8	0.05	10	0.06	18	0.05

age and sex, for the population of Mölndal on the census day, November 1, 1969. The sex distribution in relation to grade of mental retardation is shown in Table 2. There are no significant differences in sex distribution.

This population study used an intensive search method. By use of a complete register of the population, every single inhabitant was assessed. All those for whom the available information from schools, hospitals, and social registers was not sufficient to preclude all suspicion of mental retardation were contacted and personally assessed by psychometric and other methods. This comprehensive approach was deemed essential for the tracing of all cases in the anonymous society of an industrial town, and its necessity was shown by the fact that 24 of the 81 cases traced were not under the supervision of the care authority. Ten of them had previously attended special schools but had been deregistered after leaving school. The remaining 14 (16%) had never been registered with the care authority.

Thus, in this investigation there are good grounds for considering that the mentally retarded persons traced constitute the total number of medium- and low-grade mentally retarded individuals in the population of Mölndal. Studies of completely unselected samples of mentally retarded are still very few in number, and despite the limited size of this sample it appears of interest to present results from the clinical and social investigations that were made.

In the clinical part of the study, apart from psychiatric and psychological assessment, the investigation included general physical and neurological examination, laboratory tests on blood and urine, and determination of the karyotype. All these investigations were successfully carried out on the majority of the 81 mentally retarded. The aetiological classification used was that suggested by Heber (1961). Table 3 shows the distribution in the different diagnostic groups.

Symptoms of organic disease or injury that could be related to the mental retardation were present in 63% (corresponding to Categories I–VII in Table 3). Thirty-two percent corresponded to what are usually termed "aclinical cases" and 5% could not be classified because of incomplete information. The chromosomal aberrations are shown in Category VI. Eighteen cases, or 22.2%, of those examined had trisomy 21, two other cases had some other deviant karyotype. The total number with chromosomal aberrations amounted to 24.7%. The type and number of observed aberrations are shown in Table 4.

Table 3. Classification of 81 mentally retarded cases in aetiological categories

Categories	Number of cases	%
Mental retardation due to:		
1 Infection	7	8.6
2 Toxic agents	2	2.5
3 Injury	3	3.7
4 Metabolic disorder	0	0.0
5 Tumour	0	0.0
6 Prenatal influence	25	30.9
7 Unknown cause with neurological signs	14	17.3
8 Unknown cause without neurological signs	26	32.1
Cases not classifiable	4	4.9
Total	81	100

In round numbers, therefore, one in four of the mentally retarded in my sample showed a chromosomal aberration. As one might expect, the majority of the chromosomal abnormalities involved the G-group. Two further cases had a deviant karyotype. One woman had an X chromosome missing in one-fifth of the mitoses analysed. However, she showed no clinical features of Turner's syndrome. Finally, one case was encountered with what was interpreted as a selective endoreduplication of chromosome 2. The biochemical tests on blood and urine failed to reveal any case of aminoaciduria or any other metabolic disorder.

In a series of publications (Pitt and Roboz, 1965; Roboz and Pitt, 1968, 1969a, 1969b, 1970, 1971), Pitt and Roboz made intensive investigations of 782 mentally retarded inmates of institutions, the great majority being described as medium- or low-grade mentally retarded. In their study, organic disease or injury that could be related to the mental retardation was found in 78%, as compared with 63% in my investigation. The aclinical cases, 31% in my sample, constituted only 10% in their study. These differences are probably explained by the fact that those investigated by Pitt and Roboz were all inmates of institutions and also that they were considerably younger than those I examined. Institutional

Table 4. Chromosomal deviants by karyotype

Karyotype	Number
47,XY, +G	7
47,XX, +G	9
46,XY/47,XY, +G	1
46,XX/47,XX, +G	1
45,X/46,XX	1
46,XY, ? end (2q)	1
Total	20

cases are likely to show a higher proportion with severe injury than unselected cases. Young persons offer the best opportunities for obtaining information of relevance for aetiological assessment. For a more detailed account of the epidemiological and clinical findings, see Wallin (1974).

The social part of the study sought to give a picture of the life situation of the severely mentally retarded, their degree of independence and the conditions necessary for this. Types of residential accommodation in the 81 cases, divided into two age groups, are shown in Table 5. Of the 18 cases with low-grade mental retardation, two were being cared for at home. One of them was in the fifties, the other was a preschool child. Of the 63 cases with medium-grade mental retardation, 36 were living outside institutions. There are no statistically significant differences in sex distribution between the two main groups, institutional and noninstitutional. The 18 cases with the diagnosis of Down's syndrome did not differ from the others with respect to living conditions.

Table 5. Distribution of 81 cases by age group

Residential accommodation	0–19 years	20+ years	All ages
Living in institutions	19	24	43
Living at home	17	18	35
Other	1	2	3

Turning to work capacity and employment, I found that of the 54 over 16 years of age, 16 (seven men and nine women) were in regular work. Three of them were self-supporting. The other 13 were in sheltered workshops, training centres, etc., and none of them was in any significant degree self-supporting.

The only one in the series who had married was a woman; she is childless. The other mentally retarded woman of medium grade has borne a child. Another woman with medium-grade mental retardation had had a pregnancy terminated. As far as is known, none of the men in the series has fathered a child.

Only one of the 81 cases in my series has been indicted for crime; this was for persistent thieving. He was granted penal exemption and was admitted to a special hospital.

My findings as to residential accommodation, occupation, and earning capacity agree well with those of Åkesson five years earlier in an adjacent country area (Åkesson, 1968). No statistically significant differences can be shown.

In a large proportion of the severely mentally retarded, the intellectual defect is not the only handicap suffered. Other handicaps are very frequent, and these account for much of the dependency and need for help in mentally retarded persons. To illustrate how common multiple handicaps are, I have made the following calculation (I have considered seven main groups of handicapping conditions, every one of them involving some function important for the achievement of social independence):

1. disturbed motor function: confined to wheel-chair or otherwise affected by severe motor disability
2. defective vision: blind or suffering severely impaired vision
3. defective hearing: deaf or suffering severely impaired hearing
4. epilepsy: convulsive attacks under inadequate control
5. behaviour disturbance: very defective power of concentration, serious difficulty in contact
6. inadequate speech: incapable of speech or suffering serious speech disorder
7. other conditions: diabetes, pronounced kyphoscoliosis, severe organic heart disease etc.

If we exclude those with low-grade mental retardation, in whom functional capacity is usually so gravely impaired that it can be difficult to assess the importance of individual handicapping conditions, there remain 63 mentally retarded persons of medium grade. The following scheme shows the numbers with one or more separate handicaps in addition to the mental retardation among these 63:

Number of separate handicaps (in addition to mental retardation)	Number examined
0	17
1	17
2	15
3	10
4	4

Forty-six of the 63 medium-grade mentally retarded suffered one or more handicapping conditions in addition to mental retardation.

The frequency of handicapping conditions can also be illustrated in other ways. In a study on the population of Wessex in England, Kushlick and Cox (1973) classified those with medium- and low-grade mental retardation in the following four categories:

NA = nonambulant (unable to walk)
All SB = all severely behaviour-disordered (able to walk but presenting seriously disruptive behaviour)
SI = severely incontinent (not in NA or All SB categories, but severely incontinent)
CAN = continent, ambulant, and without severe behaviour disorders

Table 6 shows the distribution of my mentally retarded cases within these categories. It can be seen that 31 of the 81 cases are particularly in need of care. My results do not differ in any material respect from those reported by Kushlick and Cox in Wessex.

The purpose of my report is not merely to present figures. The collection of data must lead us to certain conclusions. In Sweden and in many other parts of the world there is a movement that asserts, in effect, that "The mentally retarded are people, like everyone else. They should not be segregated in

Table 6. Behavioural category by age groups for 81 severely mentally retarded in Mölndal

Age group	NA	SB	SI	CAN	Nonclassifiable	Total
0–19	3	4	3	27	1	38
20 + years	8	10	2	23		43
All ages	11	14	5	50	1	81

institutions, they should live among the rest of us." I have no objection to this ideology, but it presents us with enormous demands. The assertion that the mentally retarded are like the rest of us is in itself something of an idealization, in a way a prejudiced point of view. They differ from others in that they have a definite handicap. My figures show, however, that in fact they are very often burdened not only by one but by two and sometimes by three or more handicaps. Their needs are far greater than those of the average population and this does not apply only to social and pedagogic services. We must be quite clear that the integration idea is not feasible unless at the same time we provide them with richly differentiated medical services.

SUMMARY

An account is given of a sample consisting of the total number of medium- and low-grade mentally retarded persons in a medium-sized Swedish industrial town. The distribution of aetiologically relevant diagnoses was studied by intensive clinical analysis, including among other things, karyotype determination. To illuminate the life situation and the requirements for social independence of the severely mentally retarded, information is presented on employment, living conditions, and the frequency of multiple handicaps. The implications of the findings are discussed, with emphasis on the need for a richly differentiated medical service.

REFERENCES

Åkesson, H. O. (1968) Severe Mental Deficiency in Sweden. Göteborg, Sweden: Akademiförlaget.

Heber, R. (1961) A manual on terminology and classification in mental retardation. Amer. J. Ment. Defic. Monogr. Suppl. 2.

Kushlick, A., and Cox, G. R. (1973) The epidemiology of mental handicap. Develop. Med. Child. Neurol. 15:748.

Pitt, D., and Roboz, P. (1965) A survey of 782 cases of mental deficiency. J. Ment. Defic. Res. 9:4.

Roboz, P., and Pitt, D. (1968) Studies on 782 cases of mental deficiency. Part II. Aust. Paed. J. 4:260.

Roboz, P., and Pitt, D. (1969a) Studies on 782 cases of mental deficiency. Part III. Aust. Paed. J. 5:38.

Roboz, P., and Pitt, D. (1969b) Studies on 782 cases of mental deficiency. Part IV. Aust. Paed. J. 5:137.

Roboz, P., and Pitt, D. (1970) Studies on 782 cases of mental deficiency. Part V. Aust. Paed. J. 6:185.

Roboz, P., and Pitt, D. (1971) Studies on 782 cases of mental deficiency. Part VI. Aust. Paed. J. 7:12.

Wallin, L. (1974) Severe Mental Retardation in a Swedish Industrial Town. Göteborg, Sweden: Diss. Akademiförlaget.

Wallin, L. (1975) A study of mental retardation in a Swedish urban community. Proc. 3rd Congr. IASSMD, The Hague, 1973, p. 189.

RESEARCH TO PRACTICE IN MENTAL RETARDATION
Biomedical Aspects, Volume III
Edited by Peter Mittler
Copyright 1977 I.A.S.S.M.D.

CLINICAL, GENETIC, AND PSYCHOLOGICAL FINDINGS IN 600 FAMILIES WITH MORE THAN ONE MENTALLY RETARDED CHILD

A. Rett
*Ludwig Boltzmann Institute for Research on Brain
Damaged Children, Vienna,
Riedelgasse 5,
1130 Wien, Austria*

The presence of one mentally retarded (MR) child causes enormous physical, psychological, social, and economic hardship for the family. This fact is rarely disputed today and need not be emphasized here.

A large patient population of about 14,000 children and juveniles contains, of course, families who care for more than one MR child. We have observed 600 families burdened in this manner who care for a total of 1,300 handicapped children, which amounts to 9.28% of the patient population examined. (Tables 1, 2, and 3 show the characteristics of the families.)

It is, therefore, of great interest to consider these special patients in detail. The question why multiple incidences occur in these families is of paramount importance. Only a satisfactory answer can form the basis for preventive measures. In order to find such an answer, investigations are necessary in the following fields:

1. neurological, psychiatric, and pediatric status of the children, as well as anamneses
2. cytology and biochemistry of the children, their parents, and their healthy brothers and sisters
3. anthropology and morphometrics of the whole family
4. psychosocial analyses of the family structure.

Table 1. Families with more than one MR child

Number of MR children per family	Families		Children	
	N	%	N	%
2	551	91.83	1102	84.76
3	29	4.83	87	6.69
4	7	1.16	28	2.15
5	6	1.00	30	2.30
6	2	0.33	12	0.92
7	2	0.33	14	1.07
8	1	0.16	8	0.61
9	1	0.16	9	0.69
10	1	0.16	10	0.76
Total	600		1300	

The rapidly increasing efforts expended on behalf of the MR child during the past few decades have yielded the description of a variety of syndromes. These were sufficiently well analyzed and defined in their neurological, psychiatric, psychological, cytological, and biochemical aspects. Difficulties are, however, encountered with anamneses that allow the description of clearly recognizable etiological factors for relatively few syndromes only. An overview of etiological factors is given in Table 4.

The largest group is made up of patients with etiologically unclarified mental disorders. It is interesting to note that in this group families with more than two MR children are overrepresented. The proportion of determinable chromosomal aberrations (7.9%) is rather small. Epilepsy with mental retardation shows a

Table 2. MR children in single and multiple births[a]

Type of Birth	N	%
Single births	1,095	84.23
Twin births (both MR)	87	6.69
Twin births (one MR)	112	8.61
Triple births (one MR)	1	0.07
Triple births (two MR)	2	0.15
Triple births (three MR)	3	0.23
Total	1,300	

[a]One family had two twin births with both children MR each time. Three families had a three-time occurrence of twin births, of which two families had one MR child at each birth. The other family had one MR child at one birth.

Table 3. Structure of the family

Type of family	N	%
Families with MR children only	318	53
Families with both MR children and healthy children	282	47
Total	600	

relatively high incidence (14.6%). Cytological investigations show a preponderance of mosaicism, ring-chromosomes, trisomy 13, 18 and 14, as well as the cri du chat syndrome in autosomal, and the Turner and Klinefelter syndromes in gonosomal aberrations. Phenylketonuria is predominant among the metabolic disorders and was found in 12 families. Hypothyroidism is notably frequent (6.6%).

Clinical examinations alone are simply not sufficient if one deals with families burdened in this manner, especially since typical lines of inheritance are often assumed but rarely proven. Therefore, we believe anthropological studies (including the use of morphometric methods), such as we have been using for several years, are indispensable. Only through intensive studies of deviations from normal attribute distributions (intensity) in the general population, as well as from their occurrences in the family of our individual patients, can we find out about cause and effect relationships, linkings, and genetic transmissions. A detailed knowledge of the variations of all relevant attributes and characteristics in the healthy (normal) comparison population is, of course, a necessary prerequisite for such studies. The concentration of certain attribute variants would

Table 4. Etiology of MR in family

	Etiological factors	N	%
1.	Trisomy 21	11	1.8
2.	Other chromosomal aberrations	37	6.1
3.	Dominant hereditary disease	23	3.8
4.	Recessive hereditary disease	39	6.5
5.	Perinatal injuries	26	4.3
6.	Epilepsy	88	14.6
7.	Cerebral-atrophy syndrome	12	2.0
8.	Prenatal injuries	24	4.0
9.	Metabolic oligophrenia	19	3.1
10.	Deformation of the CNS	21	3.5
11.	Postencephalitis syndrome	11	1.8
12.	Autism (Kanner)	4	0.66
13.	Hypothyroidism	20	3.3
14.	Etiologically unclarified mental disorders	160	26.6
15.	Combinations of 1,2,5,6,10,11,13	105	17.5
	Total	600	

lead one to suspect a genetically determined predisposition. Such micromanifestations were already mentioned by Zellweger and Abbo (1964) in connection with Down's syndrome.

We are currently trying to investigate a variety of syndromes along these lines, especially in families with multiple factors, and we believe that we have found clear indications for the presence of micromanifestations, particularly for trisomy 21, for a series of metabolically conditioned disturbances and for dominant and recessive syndromes. The frequency of occurrence of micromanifestations is remarkably high (65%) in the group of etiologically unclarified families of our patient population. These micromanifestations occur mainly in the areas of ear, eye, and lines of the hand, (Rett, 1977; Seidler, 1977).

Psychological investigations were conducted that included measures of intelligence and the assessment of socioeconomic and educational data for the parents (Tables 5 through 8). The main results show a greater frequency of attendance at special schools and an earlier termination of the educational process among the parents with more than one MR child as compared to parents of the total patient population. This could be interpreted to mean that the coming to terms with an incidence of mental retardation within the family depends on the intelligence level of the parents and thereby on the availability

Table 5. Educational attainment of parents with multiple incidence of MR as compared to that of parents of total patient population

Parents	Multiple MRs		Total Patients (%)
	N	%	
Fathers			
Special education	57	9.5	5.3
Basic education			
(Volksschule)	179	29.8	28.2
(Hauptschule)	244	40.6	48.7
Highschool–College	76	12.6	14.3
University	44	7.3	2.9
Total	600		
Mothers			
Special education	72	12.0	6.3
Basic education			
(Volksschule)	204	34.0	28.0
(Hauptschule)	268	44.6	58.4
Highschool–College	47	7.8	6.7
University	9	1.5	0.7
Total	600		

Table 6. Stratification by income of families with multiple incidences of MR as compared with that of parents of total patient population

Income of families	Multiple MRs		Total patients (%)
	N	%	
Minimal and small	216	36.0	23.1
Medium	315	52.5	61.0
Higher	67	11.1	14.7
Highest	2	0.3	0.9
Total	600		

and possession of information. Such parents frequently remark: "We did not notice anything for a long time." Particularly prominent was the lack of information about the possibilities of birth control. It should be noted, however, that the incidence of more than one MR child in the family has been decreasing in recent years, probably due to more and better information about biological mechanisms. (Annual statistical analyses of first examinations in our clinic shows a decrease of 36% in families with more than one handicapped child between the years 1965–1975. Also, comparing families who already have one handicapped

Table 7. Combination of intellectual level of retarded children within families with two and more than two MR children

Intellectual levels[a]	*N*	%
Families with two MR children		
Debility and debility	157	28.49
Debility and imbecility	159	28.85
Debility and idiocy	49	8.89
Imbecility and imbecility	78	14.15
Imbecility and idiocy	51	9.20
Idiocy and idiocy	57	10.30
Total	551	
Families with three to ten MR children		
Debility and debility	8	16.00
Debility and imbecility	3	6.12
Debility and idiocy	3	6.12
Debility, imbecility and idiocy	7	14.28
Imbecility and imbecility	17	34.69
Imbecility and idiocy	10	20.40
Idiocy and idiocy	1	2.04
Total	49	

[a]Debility refers to an IQ range of 46–80. All tests were performed using the German versions of WAIS or WISC.

Table 8. Means and point values of IQ of parents with more than two MR children[a]

Incidence in family (N)	Children (N)	IQ values	
		Fathers	Mothers
3	29	108.10	105.44
4	7	104.42	99.32
5	6	98.00	85.00
6	2	84.00	82.00
7	2	92.50	86.50
8	1	86	66
9	1	97	84
10	1	83	72
Total	49		

[a]An incidental sample of 100 parents with two MR children yielded the following mean IQ values: fathers, 111.98; mothers, 107.65. IQ was assessed by HAWIE, the German version of the Wechsler Adult Intelligence Scale.

child in our care and whose later children are always examined by us, we find a 64% decrease in the incidence. Since the total intake of new patients did not greatly differ between 1965 and 1975, we think that the percentages observed support the assertion that the incidence of more than one mentally retarded child in the family has been decreasing in recent years.)

Among the families discussed in the present study, abortions were performed in 108 cases. Sterilizations were performed on 93 women and five men.

SUMMARY AND CONCLUSIONS

From our experiences so far, we can list the following tentative conclusions:

1. The incidence of more than one MR child per family is relatively high in our patient population.
2. The analysis of probable causes shows a high percentage of etiologically unclarified cases. Only a small portion of the cases could be determined on a cytological—chromosomal or biochemical—metabolic basis.
3. Clinical examinations of the mentally retarded child and his family have to be supplemented by anthropological—morphometric methods if we are to develop reproducible qualitative and, especially, quantitative norms and standards that are the basis of nosography. In the future it will be necessary to go beyond the current usage of symptomatic accounting methods (Leiber, 1975).
4. Cytological, biochemical, and metabolic investigations are indispensible for such families. All members of the families must be examined, i.e., father, mother and even seemingly healthy siblings.

5. Only intensive investigations of etiology and recurrence risks make an effective human genetics counseling system possible. Abortions and sterilizations are occasionally the only and necessary means.
6. The statistics presented show that the intellectual level of the parents, as seen from their educational and social position, is lower than that of the parent population with only one MR child.
7. The conclusion can be drawn that these families are less informed about birth control and recognize disturbances in their children less frequently and mainly at a later stage.
8. Austria has had a screening system in operation for about three years that makes possible the assessment of 99% of all births (including the pregnancies) and infants up to the completion of the first year of life. The chances of early detection and treatment as well as prevention have thus substantially increased.

REFERENCES

Leiber, B. (1975) Zur Klinik der chromosomalen Aberration—Probleme der Semiotik und Nosographie. Pädiatrie und Pädologie, Suppl. 4:32.

Rett, A. (1977) Down Syndrome: Biological, Educational and Social Problems. Bern, Switzerland: H. Huber.

Seidler, H. (1977) Anthropometrical Studies on Patients with Down Syndrome and their Parents. Infant cerebropolliscus. Horn, Austria: F. Berger.

Zellweger, H., and Abbo, G. (1964) Moderne Mongolismus-Probleme. Mongolismus, Paramongolismus und mongoloide Stigmatisierung in klinischer und zytogenetischer Betrachtung. Dt. med. Wschr. 89:405.

RESEARCH TO PRACTICE IN MENTAL RETARDATION
Biomedical Aspects, Volume III
Edited by Peter Mittler
Copyright 1977 I.A.S.S.M.D.

THE GENETIC CONTRIBUTION OF MENTAL SUBNORMALITY IN SINGAPORE CHILDREN

F.M. Paul
Department of Pediatrics,
Faculty of Medicine,
University of Singapore,
Sepoy Lines, Singapore, 3

In Singapore, during the ten-year period from 1963 to 1973, in a survey of 2,982 mentally subnormal children (Paul, 1971) it was found that genetically determined diseases contributed considerably to the familial occurrence of disease. It was therefore necessary to give genetic counselling, to conduct biochemical tests, and to improve the environment where genetic diseases occurred. In Singapore it has been shown that, of all genetic diseases, diseases of large mutant effect formed 15%, (Wong, 1972), diseases due to maternofoetal incompatibility formed 5%, chromosomal diseases formed 5%, and multifactorial diseases formed as high as 55% (Wong, 1972).

NEONATAL JAUNDICE AND BRAIN DAMAGE (KERNICTERUS)

Neonatal jaundice in Singapore is not usually caused by Rh incompatibility (Wong, 1966), but nearly half the affected children had glucose-6-phosphate dehydrogenase (G6PD) deficiency. The trigger factors responsible for intra-vascular haemolysis were the various cultural habits of the population, e.g., feeding herbal mixtures to newborns; pregnant mothers taking herbs post-partum, believing themselves strengthened thereby, and then breast feeding their babies; and by keeping diapers in naphthalene mothballs. Liver immaturity was also known to be a more important cause of kernicterus in Chinese, Malay, and Indian babies than in British babies born in Singapore (Brown and Wong, 1965). Liver immaturity, which is not an uncommon cause of kernicterus (although not genetic insofar as local customs of feeding and clothing impair hepatic function), behaves like a genetic disease in its familial tendency because parents continue the same habits with each child.

The incidence of G6PD deficiency is 3–4% among Chinese and Malays. It is type B (similar to the Hong Kong type) and is controlled by a sex-linked gene. Since 1962, all newborn cord bloods of babies are screened for G6PD using a modification of Bernstein's (1962) method with dichlorophenol as a colour indicator. About 90% of all Singapore babies are delivered at the maternity hospitals, and with this rapid method of screening over a quarter million of the Singapore population and a total of 4,540 families are known to be G6PD deficient. All siblings, parents, and grandparents are screened once a baby is found glucose-6-phosphate deficient. All the families, including those with G6PD babies, are given two cyclostyled handouts.

1. One is to the obstetrician delivering the next baby stating that the family is at risk, directing him to refer the baby for observation.
2. The other is a list of drugs and chemicals to be avoided, and it is directed to any doctor treating the G6PD baby for other, later illnesses in order to prevent drug-induced haemoglobinuria.

EFFECTS OF SCREENING FOR G6PD

With the help of the Singapore Ministry of Health, an intensive medical and lay public educational campaign was organised, notifying the public about the dangers of kernicterus. The fall in kernicterus deaths since the establishment of this surveillance system is seen in Figure 1 (Wong, 1974). Not only has the

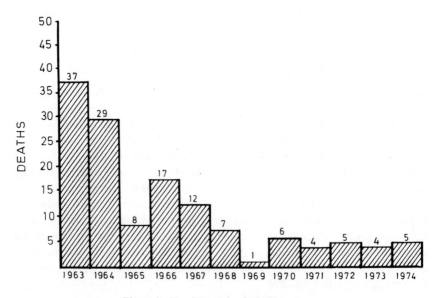

Figure 1. Kernicterus deaths in Singapore.

mortality rate been reduced, but also, far more important, is the reduction in morbidity, namely spasticity and severe mental subnormality in survivors.

CHROMOSOMAL DISORDERS

In a survey of mental subnormality in Singapore children, 16.7% of all the known cases were associated with chromosomal disorders, 14.8% were due to mongolism, and 1.9% were due to other chromosomal abnormalities (Paul, 1974).

MONGOLISM

The incidence of mongolism, based on the total number of live births, is 1 in 700 births in Singapore. In spite of active family planning measures, there does not seem to be a significant drop in the incidence of mongolism, although the number of births has dropped. Table 1 shows the number of mongol babies born at the major maternity hospital in Singapore (Kandang Kerbau Hospital). The sudden drop in live births from 1970 onwards is attributable to other government hospitals sharing deliveries (Alexandra Hospital and Thomson Road Hospital).

Among 178 mongols studied from 1963 to 1968 in Singapore (Paul, 1971) all were born to mothers in the age group of 40 to 44 years, while the range of the most common child-bearing ages among Singapore mothers is from 25 to 29 years. Among 146 mongols studied from 1969 to 1973, 67% had mothers from 40 to 44 years old, while in 1971 the more popular child-bearing age of Singapore mothers dropped to 20 to 24 years. This would explain why there has been no dramatic drop in the incidence of mongolism—the older mothers are still producing children, and it is not uncommon to find sibships of 13—16.

With the Singapore Government offering sterilisation in the form of ligation of the Fallopian tubes after delivery of the second child, one would expect the incidence of mongolism to go down in the next five years.

Table 1. Incidence of mongolism in Singapore children based on live births

Year	Live births	Newborn mongols	Incidence
1965	39,207	52	1/754
1966	39,085	55	1/710
1967	38,456	34	1/1130
1968	39,816	52	1/765
1969	31,174	37	1/802
1970	29,307	27	1/1085
1971	29,956	40	1/748
1972	30,245	47	1/641
1973	28,913	34	1/850

FAMILIAL MONGOLISM

A study of 324 mongol children in Singapore (Paul, 1974) revealed seven families with familial mongolism; the first family was reported in 1963 (Paul, 1963). Although the incidence of dual mongolism in the same family is rare, the risk of a mother having a second mongol child is high. Figure 2 shows seven pedigrees with familial mongolism.

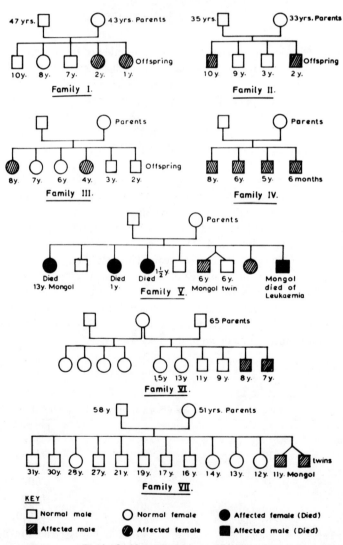

Figure 2. Mongolism in seven families.

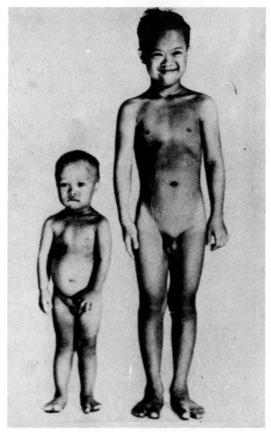

Figure 3. Two Chinese mongol brothers in Family II.

The fifth family, reported by Tan and Chua (1969), was a unique family in which there were five mongols, three of whom had had chromosome analysis. All three had classical trisomy 21. The close association between mongolism and leukaemia is seen in the last child, who died of leukaemia.

Figure 3 illustrates the facial characteristics of two Chinese mongol brothers in the same family (Family 2). In all seven families the mongols were a regular trisomy 21 and the underlying mechanism was nondisjunction due to failure of homologous chromosomes to go to opposite poles during gametogenesis.

TRANSLOCATION MONGOLISM

Mongolism can be inherited from parents who themselves are balanced translocation carriers D/G or G/G translocations being the most common. Under these circumstances the risk of another mongol offspring is high and approaches that of diseases due to an autosomal recessive gene (Figure 4).

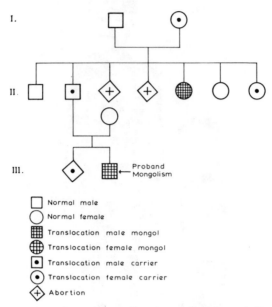

Figure 4. Pedigree with translocation mongolism 13–15/21.

The baby mongol had a 13–15/21 translocation karyotype, while his father and the grandmother were carriers, balanced with a modal number of 45. The father's sister was also a mongol.

We have also encountered families with 21/21 or G/G translocation.

PRENATAL DIAGNOSIS OF MONGOLISM

In Singapore we are now able to prevent multiple mongols occurring in the same family by prenatal diagnosis using amniocentesis and chromosome culture. In the case of a translocation mongol we notify the mother that the risk of the foetus being a translocation mongol is 25%, and a therapeutic abortion can be done on eugenic grounds.

OTHER CHROMOSOMAL DISORDERS OF GENETIC SIGNIFICANCE

Cri-du-chat Syndrome in Singapore

Out of nine children with cri-du-chat syndrome seen in Singapore, there were five patients seen in two Chinese families (Wong and Chua, 1968). The parents were phenotypically normal, but genotypically the father revealed a partial deletion of the short arm of chromosome No. 5, and there was an abnormally long chromosome of group 3, believed to be a translocation of chromosome No. 5 onto chromosome No. 3, i.e., a 3–5 translocation, so that the father was chromosomally balanced and was otherwise normal.

Edward's Trisomy 17–18 Syndrome

There was yet another family with two members affected with Edward's 17–18 trisomy syndrome, one of whom died as a baby, while the other is alive and is a mosaic Edward's trisomy syndrome.

All of these chromosomal abnormalities point to the importance of amniocentesis in women above the age of 30 years and in those who have produced one child with a chromosomal abnormality.

GENES OF LARGE MUTANT EFFECT

Mutant genes form 15% of all genetically determined diseases in Singapore, including children with mental subnormality due to a Mendelian inheritance.

AUTOSOMAL RECESSIVE
INHERITANCE CAUSING MENTAL SUBNORMALITY

Microcephaly

In a study of 198 children with microcephaly it was found that 51.6% of children were associated with primary microcephaly (Paul, 1973) with a high

FAMILIAL   MICROCEPHALY

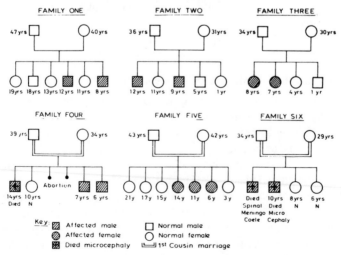

Figure 5. Familial microcephaly. Of six families, three had consanguineous marriages.

FAMILIAL MICROCEPHALY

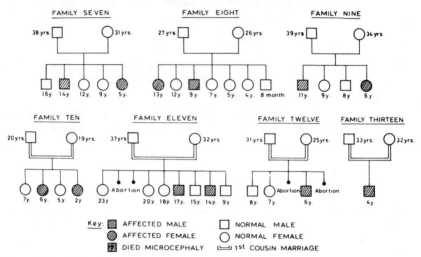

Figure 6. Familial microcephaly. Seven more affected families, showing four with consanguineous marriages.

risk figure of 25% of the offspring being affected. Familial incidence and a high degree of parental consanguinity has been reported in Japan by Komati, Kishimoto, and Oxaki (1955). There were 13 cases in this series, giving an incidence of 6% microcephalics (Figures 5 and 6).

Because little can be done for microcephalics from a therapeutic point of view, prevention is more important. Genetic counselling is still emphasized, but now, with advent of the use of ultrasound, the biparietal diameter of the foetal head can be measured. Anencephalics, microcephalics, and hydrocephalics can be detected, and we hope to reduce our incidence of cranial anomalies.

Mucopolysaccharidosis in Multiple Members of Families

Among the mucopolysaccharidoses were two families with Hurler type I abnormality that affected many members in the same family (Paul, 1964). The first family (Figure 7) was interesting because there were six gargoyles, one female and five males in a family of eight children. Both parents were healthy and not consanguineous. All affected siblings had classical features of gargoylism with corneal opacities (Figure 8). The peripheral blood film showed inclusion bodies and the urine was positive for mucopolysaccharides. All the children with corneal opacities were treated by corneal grafts. In the second family, with two affected children, the bony abnormalities were so severe that they were unable to walk. Both these families were reported by Paul (1964) at a time when amniocentesis and intrauterine diagnosis were not possible.

In Singapore we have not reached the stage of qualitative analysis of the different mucopolysaccharides in the amniotic fluid, but specific enzymes are now known in Hurler, Hunter, Sanfilippo, and Schie's syndromes. It is now possible for different enzymatic determinations of the amniotic fluid to contribute to antenatal diagnosis of these conditions.

Multiple Members Affected with Laurence-Moon-Biedl Syndrome

Laurence-Moon-Biedl syndrome is characterised by six cardinal features, namely obesity, retinitis pigmentosa, mental retardation, hypogonadism, polydactyly, and a familial incidence. The mode of inheritance is autosomal recessive.

The first family (Figure 9) reported by Paul (1965) was referred because of an 11-year-old boy who was unable to cope with his lessons at school. He had the classic features of pathological obesity, polydactyly of fingers and toes, retinitis pigmentosa, hypogonadism, and mental subnormality.

The second family had three affected members, aged three years, two years, and one year, respectively (Figures 10, 11, 12 a and b). In both the families with Laurence-Moon-Biedl syndrome, the repeated abnormality had occurred several times before the families sought any form of medical advice. Unfortunately, there is no biochemical test that would establish the diagnosis before birth.

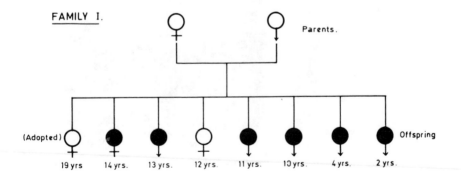

GENETIC   TREE   OF   A   FAMILY   WITH

HURLER – HUNTER'S   SYNDROME.

Figure 7. Family 1. Family with Hunter-Hurler syndrome. ♀ = normal female; ♀ = normal male; ♀ = affected female; ♀ = affected male.

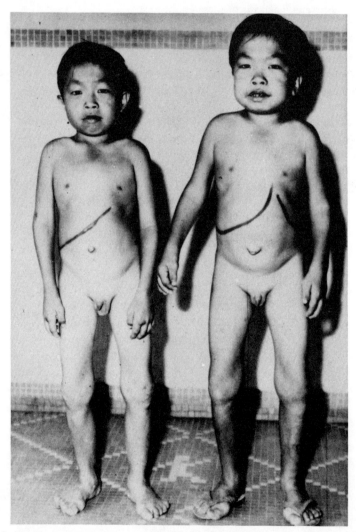

Figure 8. Family 1. Note the ugly facies, hepatosplenomegaly, and bony abnormalities of Hurler type I.

GENETIC TREE OF FAMILY I WITH LAURENCE MOON BIEDL SYNDROME.

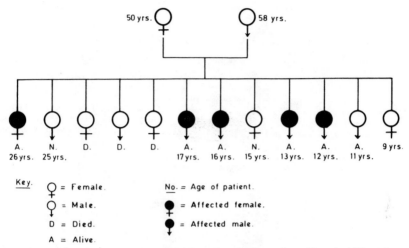

Figure 9. Family 1. Laurence-Moon-Biedl syndrome. Note five affected children in one family.

GENETIC TREE OF FAMILY II WITH LAURENCE MOON BIEDL SYNDROME.

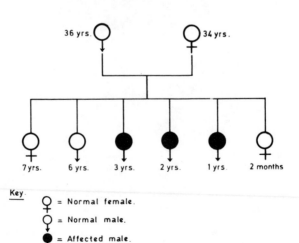

Figure 10. Family 2. Laurence-Moon-Biedl syndrome.

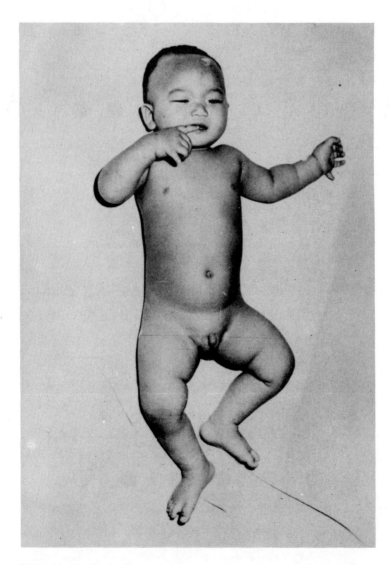

Figure 11. Family 2, obese youngest member, Laurence-Moon-Biedl syndrome.

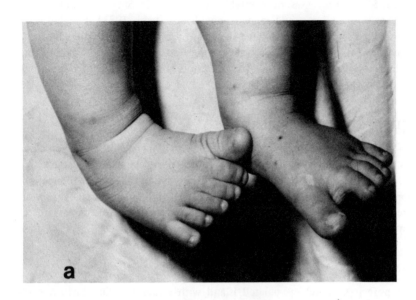

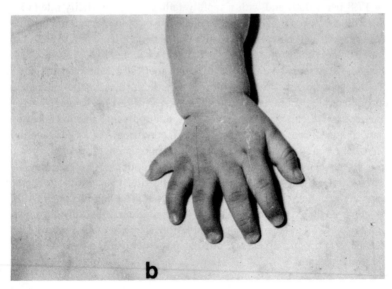

Figure 12. Note polydactyly of toes (a) and uniform polydactyly of fingers (b) in child with Laurence-Moon-Biedl syndrome.

EPILEPSY AND RELATED CONDITIONS

About 5% of the cases of mental subnormality in Singapore children occur together with epilepsy and related convulsions (Paul, 1971). Familial cases of epilepsy with mental defect have occurred; febrile convulsions occur very frequently in Singapore, and in a survey done by Chan (1974) a high incidence of familial cases was found. However, the mode of inheritance of febrile convulsions is not clear.

ROLE OF POLYGENIC INHERITANCE

The extent to which polygenic or multifactorial inheritance has played a part in this survey of mental subnormality has yet to be ascertained in Singapore. In our survey here a high percentage of familial cases among ESN (mildly educationally subnormal) level children was seen, and the children of mentally subnormal parents will have a higher mean IQ than the parents (regression towards community mean), a feature common to multifactorial inheritance.

CONCLUSION

Singapore is a densely populated island with a rapidly falling birth rate (birth rate = 17.8 per 1,000) and with a rapidly falling infant mortality rate (13.6 per 1,000). The intensive family planning policies of the Government are designed so that each family will have the ideal number of two children and so that families will have the best chance for babies free of genetic disease.

Japanese-style small families have been genetically beneficial because they reduce the frequency of Down's syndrome by one third, and other miscellaneous genetic defects by about one tenth (Matsunaga, 1966). In some cases, genetic diseases express themselves in a favourable environment, and manipulation of the environment can prevent the diseased condition, e.g., G6PD deficiency states, where genetic counselling before embarking on pregnancy, or amniocentesis after pregnancy, has solved the problem in our cases in Singapore.

Amniocentesis followed by therapeutic abortion of abnormal foetuses will increase the prenatal selection of good phenotypes. The trend to small families is also eugenic in that it minimises the level of mutations, especially chromosomal ones. Hence, with a reduction in population size and with improved health conditions, the genetic aspects of population structuring become an important problem in Singapore.

REFERENCES

Brown, W. R., and Wong, H. B. (1965) Ethnic group differences in hyperbilirubinaemia in newborns in Singapore. Paediatrics 36:745.

Chan, K. Y. (1974) A study of febrile convulsions in Singapore children. M.D. thesis, University of Singapore.

Komati, T., Kishimoto, K., and Oxaki, Y. (1955) Genetic study of microcephaly based on Japanese material. Amer. J. Hum. Genet. 7:51.

Matsunaga, E. (1966) Population Problems and Genetics in Heredity and Society. New York: MacMillan.

Paul, F. M. (1963) Familial mongolism. J. Singapore Paediat. Soc. 3:81.

Paul, F. M. (1964) Gargoylism in multiple members of two Chinese families. J. Singapore Paediat. Soc. 6:65.

Paul, F. M. (1965) Laurence-Moon-Biedl syndrome in multiple members of two Chinese families in Singapore. J. Singapore Paediat. Soc. 7:17.

Paul, F. M. (1971) A survey of mental subnormality in Singapore children. M.D. thesis, University of Singapore.

Paul, F. M. (1974) A study of mongolism in Singapore children. J. Singapore Paediat. Soc. 16:70.

Paul, F. M. (1975) A survey of microcephaly in Singapore children. J. Singapore Paediat. Soc. 17:10.

Tan, G., and Chua, T. S. (1969) Cytogenetic studies in mongols in Singapore. J. Singapore Paediat. Soc. 8:90.

Wong, H. B. (1966) Singapore Kernicterus. A review and the present position. Bull. K. K. Hosp. Singapore. 5:1.

Wong, H. B. (1972) Science and genetics in Singapore and the technical age. Singapore: Chopman Enterprises.

Wong, H. B. (1974) Prevention and management of genetic diseases in newborn. J. Singapore Paediat. Soc. 16:1.

Wong, H. B., and Chua, T. S. (1968) Cri-du-chat syndrome in Singapore. J. Singapore Paediat. Soc. 10:104.

Wong, H. B., and Chua, T. S. (1969) Cytogenetic studies in mongols in Singapore. J. Singapore Paediat. Soc. 11:8.

INBORN ERRORS
OF METABOLISM

RESEARCH TO PRACTICE IN MENTAL RETARDATION
Biomedical Aspects, Volume III
Edited by Peter Mittler
Copyright 1977 I.A.S.S.M.D.

SPECIFICITY OF PHENYLKETONURIA SCREENING TESTS IN NEWBORNS

H. Hansen
Epidemiology of Mental Retardation Research Unit,
Psychiatric Institute,
New York State Department of Mental Hygiene, and
Division of Epidemiology,
Columbia University School of Public Health,
New York, N.Y. 10032, United States

The selection of the threshold level that defines negative and positive screening test results determines the effectiveness and efficiency of case detection for a given prevalence of cases. Effectiveness is high if the chosen threshold level produces a high proportion of positives among the cases, i.e., if sensitivity is optimized. Efficiency of case detection is a function of the predictive value, i.e., the proportion of true positives among the positives, all of whom require diagnostic follow-up.

Neonatal screening for phenylketonuria (PKU) has generated high proportions of false positives, resulting in low efficiency of case detection. The field trial of the bacterial inhibition assay (BIA) in 400,000 infants, now the most widely used screening method, gave the first indication of a low predictive value in unselected newborn populations. Approximately 86% of the newborns with positive screening test results were false positive (Guthrie and Whitney, 1967). In New York state, nearly two million newborns were screened for PKU from 1965 to 1970, and about 94% of the 2,000 positive infants were false positive (Bush et al., 1973).

This chapter examines opportunities for improving the efficiency of case detection in PKU screening without compromising its effectiveness. The proposed strategy is predicated on three characteristics that are considerably more frequent in false positives than in true positives: low birth weight, nonWhite ethnicity, and moderate phenylalanine (PA) elevation. The extent to which the

This work was supported by Grant U-2233 from the Health Research Council of the City of New York.

relationship of these three variables discriminates between true and false positives is estimated from the experience of the New York City program. The analysis suggests that selective follow-up according to birth weight, ethnicity, and PA level can greatly reduce the proportion of false positives without reducing sensitivity. The proposed criteria would cut the follow-up load of screening programs similar to the New York City experience by 84%.

MATERIAL AND METHODS

Data Sources

Coverage of the newborn population by the New York City PKU screening program is virtually complete. Our observations represent all children with positive screening test results born in New York City from 1966 through 1970. The data were derived from three sources. The Bureau of Laboratories of the New York City Health Department provided the results of screening and follow-up tests. The New York City PKU Center at Bellevue Hospital provided diagnostic classifications of the children referred for evaluation. The Division of Research and Biostatistics of the New York City Health Department provided birth certificate information on magnetic tape.

Screening and Follow-up

Laboratory records were available for 1,094 infants with positive screening test results. Up to the end of 1966, a screening test result of 6 mg/100 ml or higher was considered positive, i.e., in need of follow-up. In 1967, the level requiring follow-up was lowered to 4 mg/100 ml or higher. Infants who had been positive on screening were judged normal if the PA value was 5.6 mg/100 ml or lower on a follow-up test. The screening test was the BIA on dried filter-paper blood spots, and follow-up tests were done by fluorometry on microcapillary blood samples.

Referral for Evaluation

Children with follow-up test results of 5.7 mg/100 ml or higher were usually referred to the designated PKU Center for New York City. A very high screening test value usually resulted in immediate referral. Of the 1,094 positive infants, 59 had a record of referral. The diagnoses were obtained from the New York City PKU Center for 56 of these children, and from other sources for the remaining three children. The three outcome categories of evaluation were classic PKU, hyperphenylalaninemic variants (HPA), and normal. PKU children had persisting PA values above 20 mg/100 ml; HPA children with values between 15 and 20 mg/100 ml were usually treated, while HPA children with values below 15 mg/100 ml usually went untreated.

Diagnostic Classification

For the purpose of this analysis, all 1,094 infants with positive screening test results were classified according to three categories: true, false, and unclassified positive. The true positives consist of all children who were treated, 39 for PKU and seven for HPA. The false positives include the 704 infants with a follow-up test result below 5.7 mg/100 ml and the infants not thought to require treatment upon evaluation, ten of whom were diagnosed as HPA and three as normal. The unclassified positives consist of the 269 infants with no record of follow-up and the 62 infants with a last follow-up result recorded as 5.7 mg/100 ml or higher.

Record Linkage

Ethnicity was not stated in the laboratory records, and information on birth weight was incomplete. These two variables were obtained from the birth certificate tapes. The 1,094 infants with positive screening test results were matched against the 736,473 birth certificate records available for the five-year period. Matching succeeded for 1,040, or 95%, of all laboratory records. The success rates were 98, 96, and 93%, respectively, for the true, false, and unclassified positives.

RESULTS

Over the five-year period, the number of annual live births averaged around 147,000, ranging from 142,000 to 153,000. Table 1 presents the 1,094 positive infants by screening test result and final classification for each of the five years. The annual frequencies of moderately elevated screening test results of 4 and 6 mg/100 ml showed large variations. Together, they varied considerably more than the annual number of live births. This suggests a lack of reliability at the levels of 4 and 6 mg/100 ml, because population changes during this short period are unlikely. In contrast, the annual frequencies of the higher PA elevations combined showed little variation. At these levels, the screening test results appear to be more reliable.

Moderately elevated screening test results contributed 983 infants, or 90%, to the follow-up load. The only infant identified as true positive in this group was diagnosed as PKU in the first year of the period, after a screening test result of 6 mg/100 ml. The convention to diagnose PKU relatively more frequently than HPA in the early program period may have contributed to this rare event. The PKU:HPA ratio was 16:5 in the first two years, and 13:11 in the last two years. Similar diagnostic trends have occurred in other PKU screening programs (Hansen, 1975).

Higher screening test results, 8 to 20 mg/100 ml, contributed 111 infants, or 10%, to the follow-up load, but accounted for 98%, all but one, of the true

Table 1. Classification of positive screening test results, New York City PKU Program

Screening test result	Classification	Year of screening					
		1966	1967	1968	1969	1970	1966–1970
4 mg/100 ml	true positive		0	0	0	0	0
	false positive		71	105	115	88	379
	unclassified		24	43	69	58	194
6 mg/100 ml	true positive	1	0	0	0	0	1
	false positive	155	58	36	27	13	289
	unclassified	49	16	23	21	11	120
8 mg/100 ml	true positive	0	1	0	0	0	1
	false positive	10	11	6	3	6	36
	unclassified	1	3	5	2	2	13
12 mg/100 ml	true positive	2	2	1	3	4	12
	false positive	2	1	0	4	3	10
	unclassified	1	0	0	3	0	4
20 mg/100 ml	true positive	5	7	9	8	3	32
	false positive	1	0	2	0	0	3
	unclassified	0	0	0	0	0	0
Total		227	194	230	255	188	1,094

positives. Only two of the 45 true positives had screening test results below 12 mg/100 ml.

Attainment of follow-up was lower for moderately elevated screening test results, 68%, than for the higher screening test results, 85%. Thus, incomplete follow-up was concentrated among those infants who were virtually at no risk of being true positive. The overall proportion of unclassified positives rose from 22% in the first year to 38% in the last year. Either attainment of follow-up has become more difficult in New York City or the absence of true positives among the moderately elevated screening test results has diminished the interest in follow-up.

Table 2 presents the distribution of 1,038 positive infants for whom birth weight and ethnicity could be obtained from their birth certificates, by screening test result. Each cell shows the total number of positives and the ratio of true positives over true positives and false positives combined, i.e., the predictive value.

Premature infants with birth weights of 2,500 g or lower contributed 35% of the follow-up load. The predictive value in this birth weight group was 0.7% for the two ethnic groups combined. Higher birth weight groups showed increasing predictive values: 5% for 2,501–3,000 g, and 12% for 3,001 g or higher. No true

Table 2. Number of positives and predictive value (true positives over true and false positives), by birthweight (g), ethnicity, and screening test result (mg/100 ml)

Birthweight	White						Non-White					
	4	6	8	12	20	Total	4	6	8	12	20	Total
≤2,000	28 / 0:23	37 / 0:33	3 / 0:1	1 / 0:1	0 / 0:0	69 / 0:58	36 / 0:25	29 / 0:24	5 / 0:5	1 / 0:1	0 / 0:0	71 / 0:55
2,001–2,500	55 / 0:38	59 / 0:43	7 / 0:7	2 / 1:1	3 / 1:3	126 / 2:92	59 / 0:40	35 / 0:26	5 / 0:3	2 / 0:1	0 / 0:0	101 / 0:70
2,501–3,000	70 / 0:44	55 / 0:36	7 / 1:4	4 / 2:3	5 / 5:5	141 / 8:92	76 / 0:48	40 / 0:26	6 / 0:4	2 / 1:2	0 / 0:0	124 / 1:80
3,001–3,500	76 / 0:57	69 / 1:43	5 / 0:4	9 / 4:7	10 / 10:10	169 / 15:121	68 / 0:42	37 / 0:24	3 / 0:2	0 / 0:0	1 / 1:1	109 / 1:69
3,501+	41 / 0:30	22 / 0:14	5 / 0:3	5 / 4:5	14 / 14:14	87 / 18:66	30 / 0:17	8 / 0:7	1 / 0:1	1 / 0:1	1 / 1:1	41 / 0:27
Total	270 / 0:192	242 / 1:169	27 / 1:19	21 / 11:17	32 / 30:32	592 / 43:429	269 / 0:172	149 / 0:107	20 / 0:15	6 / 1:5	2 / 1:2	446 / 2:301

positives were found among the infants with birth weights below 3,001 g and moderately elevated screening test results.

Non-White infants contributed 43% of the follow-up load, and no case of PKU was found among them. The two true positives were treated for HPA. The predictive value in the non-White group was 0.7%. There were no true positives among nonWhites with screening test results below 12 mg/100 ml. Among White infants the predictive value was 10%. No true positives were found among White infants with a screening test result of 4 mg/100 ml, and only one each at levels of 6 and 8 mg/100 ml.

The distribution of predictive values by screening test result, birth weight, and ethnicity identifies a large section of positives, framed in Table 2, which did not yield true positives during the five years of observation. The infants in these categories accounted for 87% of the follow-up load. In retrospect, they were not at risk of being true positive, and exclusion from follow-up appears to be appropriate for at least some of these categories.

DISCUSSION

Threshold values that define negative and positive screening test results have been lowered in some programs (Levy et al., 1970) and raised in others (Wainer and Sideman, 1974). The New York City experience suggests that a return to a level of 6 mg/100 ml or higher designating positives would double the predictive value without compromising sensitivity. Efficiency of case detection could be improved further if the differentiation of risk by birthweight and ethnicity is taken into account. The effect of a selective designation of threshold values on the infants shown in Table 2 is demonstrated in Table 3. All infants with screening test results of 12 or 20 mg/100 ml are retained as positive. In addition, white infants with screening test results of 8 mg/100 and birthweights above 2,500 g and white infants with screening test results of 6 mg/100 ml and birthweights above 3,000 g are retained as positive. The remaining 869 infants, among whom no true positives were found, are designated negative. The retained

Table 3. Selective follow-up: number of positives and predictive value, based on data from the New York City PKU Screening Program

Birthweight	6 mg/100 ml	8 mg/100 ml	12+ mg/100 ml	Total
≤ 2,500			9 2:7	9 2:7
2,501–3,000		7 1:4	11 8:10	18 9:14
3,501 +	91 1:57	10 0:7	41 33:39	142 34:103
Total	91 1:57	17 1:11	61 43:56	169 45:124

169 positives would represent a reduction of the follow-up load by 84%, all true positives would be included, and the predictive value would improve from 6 to 36%.

Holtzman et al. (1974b) have cautioned against raising the threshold value in PKU screening. Their survey of cases known to state health departments and PKU clinics in the United States and Canada revealed 23 cases who had been missed at newborn screening. Two sources of error may give rise to false negative results. The laboratory may fail to measure accurately an elevated PA level, or the infant may be screened before the PA level has risen. Holtzman et al. pointed out that the problem of laboratory error was compounded by the fact that several of the states reporting false-negatives did not have centralized screening or laboratory control (1974a). However, the authors based their argument against raising the threshold value on the possibility that early screening, in the United States at discharge from the newborn nursery, encounters minimally elevated PA levels in some PKU children (1974b).

Results of repeat screening, PA patterns in true positives, and observation on false negatives suggest that the possibility of minimal PA elevations in the first days of life may be negligible.

Repeat screening at four to six weeks of life should detect cases who had been negative at discharge from the newborn nursery, if early screening encounters PA levels too low to be detected. The two programs with the largest experience in repeat-screening now consider a second screening test unnecessary. The Massachusetts program did not detect an additional case among 435,000 repeats (Levy et al., 1970), and the Oregon Program found only two initially negative cases among 237,000 repeats at a time when the procedure was still being standardized (Buist and Penn, 1974). One of the two "cases" was later reclassified as a hyperphenylalaninemic variant (Brandon, 1975).

The distribution of PA levels in true-positive does not support the likelihood of minimal PA elevations at the age of screening. Under this hypothesis, a continuous distribution of PA levels from minimal to moderate to high elevations would be expected among the true positives. Our review of eight laboratories (four in New York State and one each in Massachusetts, Pennsylvania, Michigan and Oregon) that had screened four million infants in five states between 1962 and 1974 showed no confirmed PKU case with an initial result of 4 mg/100 ml. Confirmed cases with an initial result of 6 mg/100 ml were extremely rare: one in New York City among 735,000 screened, none in New York Upstate among 1,000,000 (Bush et al., 1972), none in Massachusetts among 800,000 (Levy et al., 1970), one in Pennsylvania among 555,000 (Wainer and Sideman, 1974), and none in Michigan among 410,000 (Read et al., 1969).

Early screening would be expected to be more frequent among those with minimal PA elevations than among those with moderate elevations. The survey of Holtzman et al. (1974b), did not support this expectation. Minimal elevations, more than 2 through 8 mg/100 ml, were found in 94 cases and 66% ($N =$

62) of them were screened before four days of age. Of the 80 cases with moderate elevations, more than 8 through 12 mg/100 ml, 76% ($N = 61$) were screened before that age.

Newborn PKU infants who had serial PA determinations have not shown PA levels too low to be detected at discharge from the nursery. A review of 22 cases reported up to 1966 (Hsia, 1967) demonstrated a minimal PA level of 5.5 mg/100 ml, observed during the first 24 hours of life. An additional 15 cases with serial PA determinations observed in the California program between 1966 and 1970 (Dontanville and Cunningham, 1973) showed a minimal PA level of 4.8 mg/100 ml, observed two hours after birth. The PA level rose rapidly in all children.

False negatives have not been documented very thoroughly. However, two observations among them conflict with the hypothesis of minimal PA elevations. False negatives would be expected to show an excess of early tests compared with true positives. None of the 23 false negatives identified in the survey by Holtzman et al. was tested before two days of age, and 17% were tested before three days of age (1974a). In contrast, of 302 true positives 4% were tested before two days of age, and 19% before three days of age (1974b). Insufficient food intake in the first days of life has been proposed as an explanation for false negative screening test results. The California experience did not support this assumption. One quarter of the true positives had low PA intake (0–199 mg) prior to testing, but none of the false-negatives was in this category (Dontanville and Cunningham, 1973).

It appears that false negative results are attributable to laboratory error rather than to insufficient elevations of PA levels. The accuracy of PKU screening test results has varied considerably between and within laboratories (Hansen, 1975). Where accuracy is low, conservative thresholds must be maintained even though they generate large follow-up loads with undue proportions of false positives.

Thus, the specificity of PKU screening test results, and consequently the efficiency of case detection, can be improved first by monitoring and upgrading the accuracy of screening test results, second by the assessment of predictive values of positive results in distinct categories of children, and third by the establishment of selective criteria for follow-up based on demographic as well as biochemical characteristics.

SUMMARY

The large proportion of false positive results encountered in screening newborn children for PKU can be reduced considerably if selective criteria for follow-up are established. The program experience in New York City suggests that certain categories of newborns, defined by birthweight, ethnicity, and screening test result, could be excluded from follow-up without compromising case detection.

As a result, the predictive value would increase sixfold, and the follow-up load would be reduced by more than 80%.

ACKNOWLEDGMENTS

The cooperation of the Bureau of Laboratories and of the Division of Research and Biostatistics of the New York City Department of Health, and of the New York City PKU Center is gratefully acknowledged. Dr. Mervyn Susser, Columbia University School of Public Health, and Dr. Zena Stein, New York State Psychiatric Institute, have made valuable contributions to this study.

REFERENCES

Buist, M. R. M., and Penn, R. L. (1974) Follow-up screening for phenyl-ketonuria. New Engl. J. Med. 290:577.

Bush, J. W., Chen, M. M., and Patrick, D. L. (1972) Unpublished report.

Bush, J. W., Chen, M. M., and Patrick, D. L. (1973) Health status index in cost effectiveness: Analysis of PKU program. *In* Health Status Indexes (Ed. Berg, R. L.) Chicago, pp. 173, 181, 182.

Brandon, G. R. (1975) Personal communication.

Dontanville, V. K., and Cunningham, G. C. (1973) Effect of feeding on screening for PKU in infants. Pediatrics. 51:531.

Guthrie, R., and Whitney, S. (1967) Phenylketonuria Detection in the Newborn Infant as a Routine Hospital Procedure. United States Dept. Health, Education, and Welfare, Children's Bureau.

Hansen, H. (1975) Prevention of mental retardation due to PKU: Selected aspects of program validity. Prevent. Med. 4:310.

Holtzman, N. A., Meek, A. G., and Mellits, E. D. (1974a) Neonatal screening for phenylketonuria: I. Effectiveness. JAMA 229:667.

Holtzman, N. A., Mellits, E. D., and Hallman, C. H. (1974b) Neonatal screening for phenylketonuria: II. Age dependence of initial phenylalanine in infants with PKU. Pediatrics 53:353.

Hsia, D. Y. Y. (1967) Screening tests for the detection of phenylketonuria. *In* Phenylketonuria and Allied Metabolic Diseases (Eds. Anderson, J. A., and Swaiman, K. F.) United States Dept. Health, Education & Welfare, Children's Bureau.

Levy, H. L., Shih, V. E., Karolkewicz, V., and MacCready, R. A. (1970) Screening for phenylketonuria. Lancet 2:522.

Read, S. S., Allen, R. J., and Haddy, T. B. (1969) Phenylketonuria in newborns. Mich. Med. 68:691.

Wainer, S. C., and Sideman, L. (1974) Nine years of PKU screening in Pennsylvania. Health Lab. Sci. 11:306.

RESEARCH TO PRACTICE IN MENTAL RETARDATION
Biomedical Aspects, Volume III
Edited by Peter Mittler
Copyright 1977 I.A.S.S.M.D.

HETEROZYGOTE DETECTION IN PHENYLKETONURIA

F. Güttler and G. Hansen
The John F. Kennedy Institute
DK-2600 Glostrup, Denmark

The enzyme deficient in phenylketonuria, phenylalanine hydroxylase (phenylalanine 4-monooxygenase; EC 1.14.16.1; L-phenylalanine, tetrahydropteridine: oxygen oxidoreductase), occurs in the liver (Kaufman, 1969). Heterozygous carriers for this deficiency are, therefore, preferably detected by indirect methods, e.g., by the administration of a loading dose of phenylalanine (Hsia et al., 1956; Rampini et al., 1969; Westwood and Raine, 1973).

In the last decade there has been a growing number of observations showing heterogeneity in phenylketonuria. Instead of a single clinical and biochemical entity, a spectrum of disorders in the hydroxylation of phenylalanine to tyrosine has been recognized (Rampini et al., 1969; Menkes and Holtzman, 1970; Blaskovics et al., 1974). The aim of the present investigation was to develop a test of heterozygosity for phenylketonuria with high discriminatory ability, in order to examine whether or not the heterogeneity among affected homozygotes mentioned above is reflected by a similar heterogeneity of the heterozygous phenotypes.

MATERIAL AND METHODS

The criteria for distinguishing classical versus mild phenylketonuria and these forms versus persistent hyperphenylalaninemia have been described in previous papers (Güttler and Wamberg, 1972; Güttler and Hansen, 1977). Briefly, to keep serum phenylalanine levels within 180–425 μmol/liter (3–7 mg/100ml) children with classical phenylketonuria tolerate 9–18% and children with the mild form of phenylketonuria 22–36% of a normal daily intake of phenylalanine. This distinction cannot be made until the child is more than 2½ years of age (Güttler

Financial support was received from the Danish Health Insurance Foundation (Grant H6/87.74), 512-6840, the Research Committee of the Danish Mental Retardation Service (project 93), and P. Carl Petersens Foundation.

and Hansen, 1977). Children with persistent hyperphenylalaninemia show serum phenylalanine values below 605 μmol/liter (10 mg/100 ml) on a normal dietary intake of phenylalanine.

After an overnight fast, a sample of venous blood was drawn from 122 parents of these children and 36 individuals with no family history of phenylketonuria. A load of a pure solution of 0.6 mmol L-phenylalanine per kg body weight was then given orally, and venous blood was sampled hourly for the next 4 hours. The serum was stored within 30 min at $-20°$ C until analyzed. Serum phenylalanine and tyrosine were determined fluorimetrically as described previously (Güttler and Wamberg, 1972; Güttler and Hansen, 1977).

RESULTS

The Response to an Oral Load of Phenylalanine

The responses to a phenylalanine load of 99 heterozygotes for phenylketonuria, 23 heterozygotes for hyperphenylalaninemia, and 36 controls are shown in Figure 1. The following discriminant based on phenylalanine loading was found to be the most powerful: the rate of tyrosine formation in μmol per liter of serum per hour (b_{tyr}, Figure 2) multiplied by the maximum value of serum tyrosine (tyr_m, Figure 2) in μmol per liter over the maximum value of serum phenylalanine in μmol per liter (phe_m', Figure 2) according to the function: $b_{tyr}(tyr_m/phe_m)$. Four successive phenylalanine loading tests of the same person showed discriminant values of 8.26, 8.82, 9.29, and 11.0. Four heterozygotes were loaded twice. The coefficient of variation was 5.0%, 5.3%, 5.7%, and 11.4%, respectively. The median value of the discriminant for 99 heterozygotes of phenylketonuria was 2.8 (range 0.1–11.8) and for 36 normal homozygotes 17.8 (range 10.8–60.8), $p < 0.001$, with an overlap of 3%. The distribution of the logarithmic transformation of the individual discriminant values is shown in Figure 3. The discriminatory power according to Penrose (1951) was 3.3 (Figure 4).

Phenotypic Combination of Parents
Related to the Phenyotype of Their Affected Offspring

The distribution of the discriminant described above revealed a heterogenous population of parents of children in whom the type of phenylalanine deficiency was verified, i.e., classical phenylketonuria, mild phenylketonuria, or hyperphenylalaninemia (see Material and Methods) (Figure 5a). In order to examine whether subpopulations of heterozygotes could be distinguished, parents of children with hyperphenylalaninemia were excluded. This operation eliminated one top and much of the tailing of the distribution (Figure 5b). Parents of children in whom the mild form of phenylketonuria could be established were subsequently excluded. A fairly symmetrical distribution of the discriminant was then obtained (Figure 5c). The remaining population of parents had children

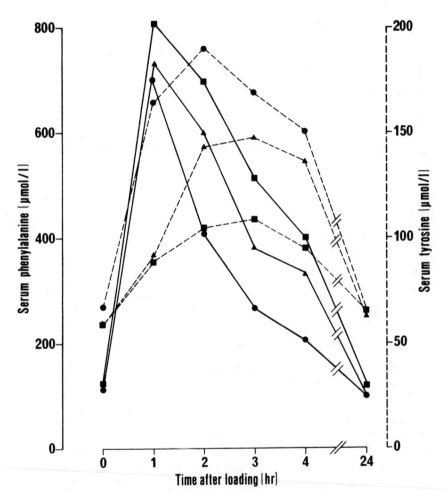

Figure 1. Median serum phenylalanine (μmol/liter) ——— and median serum tyrosine (μmol/liter) − − − response to an oral load of L-phenylalanine in 82 heterozygotes for phenylketonuria (■), 23 heterozygotes for hyperphenylalaninemia (▲), and 33 control subjects (●).

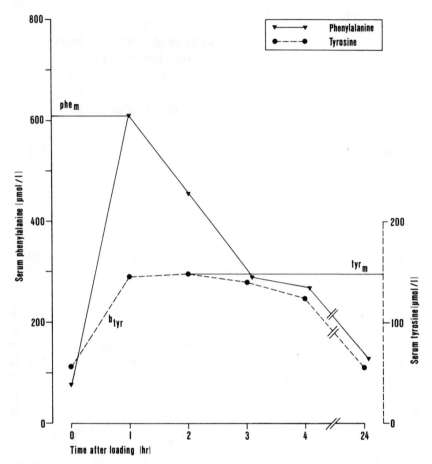

Figure 2. Serum phenylalanine (μmol/liter) (▲——▲) and serum tyrosine (μmol/liter) (●– – –●) response to an oral load of a pure solution of 0.6 mmol phenylalanine per kg of body weight. Rate of tyrosine formation, b_{tyr}; maximum value of serum phenylalanine, phe_m; maximum value of serum tyrosine, tyr_m.

with classical phenylketonuria (Figure 5c). The observation that the successive exclusion of parents of children with the mild form of phenylketonuria resulted in a symmetrical distribution of the discriminant might be explained by assuming three heterozygous phenotypes for phenylalanine hydroxylase deficiency. According to their discriminant value, the heterozygous parents were divided into three groups, and the phenotypic combination of the parents was compared with the phenotype of their affected offspring. In 22 families having children with the classical form of phenylketonuria only one parent showed a discriminant value above 6, whereas 41 parents had discriminant values below 6 (Table 1). Only half of the parents of children with the mild form of phenylketonuria had discriminant values below 6 ($p < 0.005$, Table 1). All children

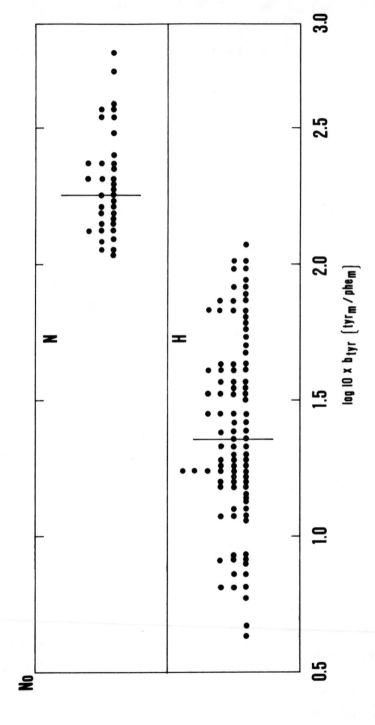

Figure 3. Distribution of individual values of the logarithm to the discriminant, $b_{tyr}(tyr_m/phe_m)$ (for explanation see Figure 2) of 36 control subjects (N) and 99 heterozygotes for phenylketonuria (H). The median value is indicated by a vertical line.

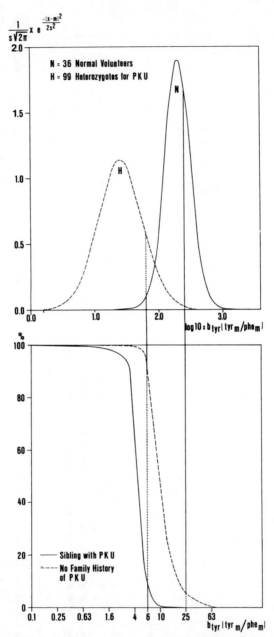

Figure 4. The distribution of the discriminant $b_{tyr}(tyr_m/phe_m)$ among 36 control subjects (N) and among 99 heterozygotes for phenylketonuria (H) (upper half of the figure). The relative probability of heterozygosity for any specific value of the discriminant is the height of the left-hand curve over the height of the right-hand curve at this point, e.g., 6 or 25. The percentage probability of being a heterozygote can be read on the curves shown in the lower half of the figure. The solid line takes account of the frequency of heterozygotes in the Danish population and the dotted line gives the probability of heterozygosity if the individual has a sibling with phenylketonuria.

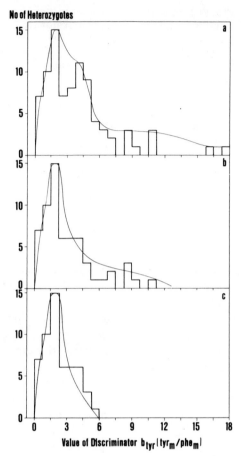

Figure 5. Distribution of the discriminant $b_{tyr}(tyr_m/phe_m)$ for 86 heterozygotes for phenylalanine hydroxylase deficiency (*a*), 63 heterozygotes for the mild and the classical form of phenylketonuria (*b*), and 41 heterozygotes for classical phenylketonuria (*c*).

with hyperphenylalaninemia had parents with discriminant values above 2 (Table 2). In seven out of 16 families with the mild form of phenylketonuria, one parent showed a discriminant value below 2 ($p < 0.05$, Table 2).

The Percentage Probability of Heterozygosity

Discrimination is the assignment of an individual to a certain class (e.g., heterozygote for phenylketonuria or normal homozygote) on the basis of a number of measured characters (e.g., based on the ability to hydroxylate phenylalanine to tyrosine). According to Smith (1969), the use of a "discriminant function," which is a combination of observed characters (e.g., $b_{tyr}(tyr_m/phe_m)$), can help us to do the classification. As a first approximation we assume the distribution

Table 1. The parental phenotypes in 21 families with classical phenylketonuria (classical PKU) and in 16 families with mild phenylketonuria (mild PKU) related to the phenotype of their affected offspring

Phenotype of both parents[a]	Family	
	Classical PKU	Mild PKU
>6	1	14
<6	41	18
χ^2 19.2 $p < 0.005$		

[a]As reflected by the discriminant b_{tyr} (tyr_m/phe_m). For explanation, see Figure 2.

of the discriminant values of the 96 heterozygotes for phenylketonuria and the distribution of the values of the 36 presumed normal homozygotes to be Gaussian (Smith, 1969). The distributions are therefore given by the formula, $f(x) = (1\sqrt{\pi 2s^2}\ \exp\ (-(x-m)^2/2s^2)$ where s^2 is the combined variance, x the discriminant value of one individual, and m the mean of the discriminant values of the population in question, i.e., heterozygous or normal (Figure 4, upper half). For a given value of the discriminant, e.g., 6 (Figure 4), the ratio of the density function of the heterozygote distribution ($f(x)_{het}$) over the density function of the normal distribution ($f(x)_{norm}$) can be calculated as follows, $f(x)_{het}/f(x)_{norm}$ = 0.61/0.11 = 5.55/1. Thus, on the basis of that discriminant

Table 2. The parental phenotypes in 12 families with hyperphenylalaninemia (HPA) and in 16 families with mild phenylketonuria (mild PKU) related to the phenotype of their affected offspring

Phenotype of both parents[a]	Family	
	HPA	Mild PKU
<2	0	7
>2	24	25
χ^2 6.00 $p < 0.05$		

[a]As reflected by the discriminant b_{tyr} (tyr_m/phe_m). For explanation, see Figure 2.

value alone, an individual with discriminant value 6 is 5.55 times as likely to be heterozygote as normal homozygote. However, this likelihood must be modified by the family history of the subjects, i.e., the a priori probability of heterozygosity (Smith, 1969). If the individual has a sibling with phenylketonuria, the ratio must be multiplied by 2; siblings of a phenylketonuric have a 66.7% chance of being a heterozygote and a 33.3% chance of being a normal homozygote. Thus, in the case of a discriminant value of 6 and a sibling with phenylketonuria the likelihood ratio of 5.55/1 must be multiplied by 2, giving a value of 11.1. Expressed in another way, his probability of being heterozygous is 11.1/(11.1 + 1) = 0.92 or 92% (cf. Figure 4, lower part, the dotted line). If the individual has no family history of phenylketonuria, the ratio must be multiplied by 1/58, as the frequency of heterozygotes for phenylketonuria in the Danish population is estimated to be 0.0168. Thus, in this case the a priori probability of heterozygosity is 5.55/1 × 1/58 = 0.10 and expressed as the percentage probability of being a heterozygote 1/(10 + 1) = 0.09 or 9% (cf. Figure 4, lower part, the solid line). It should be noted that for each new subject added to the series of either heterozygotes or normal homozygotes the mean and variance of the group have to be recalculated. Moreover, it is necessary to take account of the coefficient of variation of approximately 10%.

DISCUSSION

A complete separation of the phenotypes of heterozygotes for phenylketonuria from normal homozygotes is rarely achieved (cf. Rampini et al., 1969). When the probability of heterozygosity is estimated on the basis of the response to an oral load of phenylalanine, various variables must be taken into consideration, e.g., diurnal variations in serum phenylalanine (Güttler et al., 1969), and rate of phenylalanine absorption and stimulation of tyrosine transamination (Rose and Cramp, 1970). Accordingly, in the present study phenylalanine was fully dissolved in 0.01 N HCl (pH 3.3) and the pure solution was given orally after an overnight fast. Subjects to be loaded stayed overnight before the test and no meals nor medicine were allowed from 6 p.m. before the loading and during the first four hours of the loading test. Females were tested on days when they were not taking oral contraceptives. The subject was asked to sit down for 15 min before blood sampling.

Among the variables that theoretically might account for the shape of the phenylalanine and tyrosine curves following a load of phenylalanine is the absorption of L-phenylalanine (Goodwin, 1964). Preliminary investigations showed that the maximum serum phenylalanine concentration is obtained within 60 min after an oral load of fully disolved L-phenylalanine (cf. Figure 1). The test was repeated in individuals showing a maximum serum phenylalanine concentration later than 60 min after the load. As observed in a number of investigations, the phenylalanine values within the first four hours following oral phenylalanine loading were higher in heterozygotes for phenylketonuria than in normal homozygotes (Güttler and Wamberg, 1972; Westwood and Raine, 1973). We have observed that the slope of the rectilinear part of the tyrosine curve within 30–45 min after oral phenylalanine loading is significantly smaller in heterozygotes for phenylketonuria than in normal homozygotes (Figure 6). This observation may account for the differences in the first or second hour serum phenylalanine values in loaded heterozygotes as compared with normal homozygotes. Thus, the first hour serum phenylalanine value may reflect the rate of conversion of phenylalanine to tyrosine (cf. Figures 1 and 6). This may explain the present observation that the use of a "discriminant function" that combines the slope of the rise in serum tyrosine with the maximum serum tyrosine

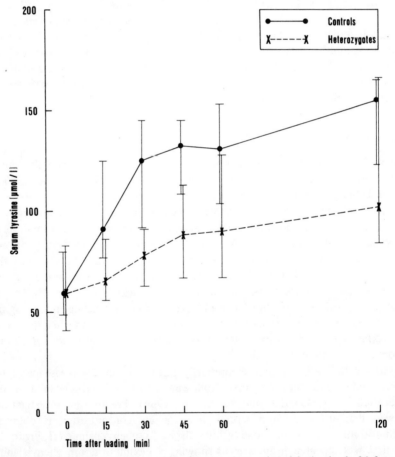

Figure 6. Course of serum tyrosine within 2 hours after a phenylalanine load of 0.6 mmol per kg body weight given orally. Normal homozygotes (No. = 4), (•); heterozygotes (No. = 15), (x). Median and range.

concentration *over* the maximum serum phenylalanine concentration improved the discriminatory ability of the phenylalanine loading test.

The distribution of the discriminant described above revealed a heterogeneous population of heterozygotes for phenylalanine hydroxylase deficiency (cf. Figure 5a). Similar observations have been published by Wang et al. (1961), and Kääriäinen and Karlsson (1973). The present study supports the observation of Rosenblatt and Scriver (1968) of a correlation between the phenotypic combination of the parents and the phenotype of their affected offspring. Studies by Berman et al. (1969), Cunningham et al. (1969), and Kang et al. (1970) revealed no differences in the phenotypes of heterozygotes for phenylketonuria and heterozygotes for the variants of phenylketonuria. One explanation for the discrepancy between these observations and the observation of Rosenblatt and Scriver (1968), Jackson et al. (1971), and the present study may be that different diagnostic criteria have been used.

The present finding of a correlation between the phenotypic combination of parents and the phenotype of their affected offspring may suggest genetic polymorphism in phenylketonuria. The genetic basis for the various phenotypes of abnormalities related to the metabolism of phenylalanine to tyrosine has been outlined by Hsia (1970). Multiple alleles at the phenylalanine hydroxylase locus or a major modifier are the most convincing possibilities.

The probability of heterozygosity at a given discriminant value was expressed as the percentage probability of being a heterozygote (Westwood and Raine, 1975). According to our experiences, this interpretation has proven to be the most meaningful way of explaining the loading test result of the person requiring genetic counselling.

SUMMARY

Phenylalanine loading was carried out on 122 parents of children with phenylalanine hydroxylase deficiency and 36 apparently normal individuals with no family history of phenylketonuria. The best discriminant was found to be the logarithmic transformation of the slope of the rise in serum tyrosine multiplied by the maximum serum tyrosine concentration over the maximum serum phenylalanine concentration obtained after an oral load with a pure solution of 0.6 mmol L-phenylalanine per kg body weight. The overlap between heterozygotes for phenylketonuria and normal homozygotes was 3%. The distribution of the discriminant values suggested three heterozygous phenotypes for phenylalanine hydroxylase deficiency, and the phenotypic combination of parents could be correlated to the phenotype of their affected offspring, i.e., classical phenylketonuria, mild phenylketonuria, or hyperphenylalaninemia. The probability of heterozygosity for phenylketonuria was determined by calculating the heterozygote likelihood ratio based on the heterozygote and normal homozygote distributions of the discriminant. The likelihood of being a heterozygote was corrected for the genetic background of the person requiring genetic counselling and was finally expressed as the percentage probability of being a heterozygote for phenylketonuria.

ACKNOWLEDGMENTS

We are indebted to Dr. Erik Wamberg for encouragement, helpful discussions and advice. We thank the staff of the John F. Kennedy Institute for their considerable help and advice.

REFERENCES

Berman, J. L., Cunningham, G. C., Day, R. W., Ford, R., and Hsia, D. Y. Y. (1969) Causes for high phenylalanine with normal tyrosine in newborn screening programs. Amer. J. Dis. Child. 117:54.

Blaskovics, M. E., Schaeffler, G. E., and Hack, S. (1974) Phenylalaninaemia. Differential diagnosis. Arch. Dis. Child. 49:835.

Cunningham, G. C., Day, R. W., Berman, J. L., and Hsia, D. Y. Y. (1969) Phenylalanine tolerance tests in families with phenylketonuria and hyperphenylalaninemia. Amer. J. Dis. Child. 117:626.

Goodwin, B. L. (1964) The metabolism of aromatic amino acids in health and disease. D. Phil. Thesis, University of Oxford.

Güttler, F., and Hansen, G. (1977) Different phenotypes for phenylalanine hydroxylase deficiency. Ann. Clin. Biochem. 14:124.

Güttler, F., Olesen, E. S., Wamberg, E. (1969) Inverse diurnal variations of serum phenylalanine and tyrosine in phenylketonuric children on low-phenylalanine diet. In Enzymopenic anaemias, Lysosomes and other papers, Proceedings of the 6th Symposium of The Society for the Study of Inborn Errors of Metabolism, (Eds. Allan, J. D., Holt, K. A., Ireland, J. T., and Pollitt, R. J.) Edinburgh and London: Livingstone, p. 149.

Güttler, F., and Wamberg, E. (1972) Persistent hyperphenylalaninemia. Acta Paediat. Scand. 61:321.

Hsia, D. Y. Y. (1970) Phenylketonuria and its variants. In Progress in Medical Genetics, Vol. VII, (Eds. Steinberg, A. G., and Bearn, A. G.) New York and London: Grune & Stratton, p. 29.

Hsia, D. Y. Y., Driscoll, K. W., Troll, W., and Knox, W. E. (1956) Detection by phenylalanine tolerance tests of heterozygous carriers of phenylketonuria. Nature 178:1239.

Jackson, S. H., Hanley, W. B., Gero, T., and Gosse, G. D. (1971) Detection of phenylketonuric heterozygotes. Clin. Chem. 17:538.

Kang, E. S., Kaufman, S., and Gerald, P. S. (1970) Clinical and biochemical observations of patients with atypical phenylketonuria. Pediatrics 45:83.

Kaufman, S. (1969) Phenylalanine hydroxylase of human liver: Assay and some properties. Arch. Biochem. Biophys. 134:249.

Kääriäinen, R., and Karlsson, R. (1973) Heterozygous carriers in the relatives of a case of phenylketonuria. Hereditas 75:109.

Menkes, J. H., and Holtzman, N. A. (1970) Neonatal hyperphenylalaninemia: A differential diagnosis. Neuropädiatrie 1:434.

Penrose, L. S. (1951) Measurement of pleiotropic effects in phenylketonuria. Ann. Eugen. 16:134.

Rampini, S., Anders, P. W., Curtius, H. CH., and Marthaler, Th. (1969) Detection of heterozygotes for phenylketonuria by column chromatography and discriminatory analysis. Pediat. Res. 3:287.

Rose, D. P., and Cramp, D. G. (1970) Reduction of plasma tyrosine by oral contraceptives and oestrogens: A possible consequence of tyrosine aminotransferase induction. Clin. Chim. Acta 29:49.

Rosenblatt, D., and Scriver, C. R. (1968) Heterogeneity in genetic control of phenylalanine metabolism in man. Nature 218:677.

Smith, C. A. B. (1969) Biomathematics, 4th Edition, Vol. 2, London: Charles Griffin, p. 467.

Wang, H. L., Morton, N. E., and Waisman, H. A. (1961) Increased reliability for the determination of the carrier state in phenylketonuria. Amer. J. Hum. Genet. 13:255.

Westwood, A., and Raine, D. N. (1973) Some problems of heterozygote recognition in inherited metabolic disease with special reference to phenylketonuria. *In* Treatment of Inborn Errors of Metabolism, (Eds. Seakins, J. W. T., Saunders, R. A., and Toothill, C.) Edinburgh and London: Churchill Livingstone, p. 63.

Westwood, A., and Raine, D. N. (1975) Heterozygote detection in phenylketonuria. J. Med. Genet. 12:327.

RESEARCH TO PRACTICE IN MENTAL RETARDATION
Biomedical Aspects, Volume III
Edited by Peter Mittler
Copyright 1977 I.A.S.S.M.D.

PHENYLKETONURIA IN JAPAN

T. Oura
Children's Medical Center of Osaka City,
Osaka, Japan

Since phenylketonuria (PKU) was first detected in Japan in 1950 by Dr. Kishimoto and his colleagues, more than 200 cases have been reported. Phenylketonuria is in fact one of the most common inborn metabolic errors associated with mental retardation in Japan as well as in the United States and Europe. Two kinds of low-phenylalanine diet, namely Lophemilk and Phenytol, appeared in Japan in 1963 under the direction of Professor Takai and myself (1967). Since then, almost all Japanese PKU patients have been treated successfully with Japanese products.

A screening program for phenylketonuria using urine with Phenistix or urine-impregnated filter paper was instituted in 1966 and has spread all over Japan. The program resulted in many false negative cases that were later found to be PKU with more or less established brain damage. Therefore, Guthrie's microbial inhibition assay has been replacing the urine tests since 1968.

It seems appropriate to discuss the actual state of PKU in Japan on this occasion, because Japan is the only country, outside Western countries, that has made a great effort in the early detection and treatment of PKU. I have been engaged in research, screening, and treatment for PKU for the past 15 years. During that time I have noticed some peculiarities of Japanese PKU in several respects.

INCIDENCE

First of all, the incidence of PKU in Japan is quite different from that in Western countries. It seems to be much lower in Japanese than in Caucasian people. This has been demonstrated by genetic statistics and by newborn screening using the blood filter paper test that has been performed as a pilot study for about 8 years.

Gamo, Kawabe, and Oura (in preparation) made a nation-wide survey on PKU in 1974 in order to elucidate the clinical picture of Japanese PKU patients and to estimate the gene frequency of PKU in Japan. We obtained 214 case histories of PKU patients from questionnaires and from the literature. In

estimating the gene frequency of PKU, we excluded tangible hyperphenylalaninemia and cases with equivocal histories. The total number of families for
estimation was 95, of which 60 parents (63.2%) were free from consanguinity
and 35 parents (36.8%) were blood-related. The gene frequency of PKU in Japan
was estimated to be 0.00310–0.00720, and the incidence of PKU patients is one
in 84,700 to one in 16,900.

These figures are derived from Dr. Fujita's formula (1965), a modification of
Dahlberg's, with special consideration of the gradual decrease in consanguinity
rate in recent years in Japan. The PKU incidence in Europe and the United
States is nearly one in ten thousand. Even in Japan it had been calculated by a
Japanese geneticist to be one in ten thousand to one in fifteen thousand. Our
figure is considerably lower.

The second evidence of low incidence of PKU in Japan comes from direct
newborn screening, with a total of approximately 300,000 tests by the end of
January 1976. Ten laboratories have been working in a collaborative study using
the Guthrie method. Two PKU patients were detected among general newborn
infants and eight PKU patients were detected from high risk families—this means
that the families of these newborn patients already had a known history of PKU,
mostly in siblings.

Because the high risk families are scattered throughout the country beyond
the area covered by our screening program, it is too early to come to a definite
conclusion about PKU incidence in Japan. Nevertheless, it is reasonable to
assume that PKU in Japan is considerably less than expected before. I tentatively
postulate it to be one in 40,000 to 60,000.

PHENYLALANINE LEVEL

The second point which I would like to emphasize is the low serum phenylalanine level of our patients as compared to that of Caucasian patients. Table 1
depicts the serum phenylalanine values of untreated patients plotted against age.
It shows the gradual decline of serum phenylalanine with age within a wide
range. The mean serum phenylalanine level of the patients under one year of age
was 35.99 mg/dl, and this high level lasts until the third year, followed by
gradual decrease thereafter. The mean serum phenylalanine level of the patients
over five years of age was 22.07 mg/dl and in about half of them it was below 20
mg/dl. This seems to us quite interesting.

One of the criteria of hyperphenylalaninemia is that the serum phenylalanine
concentration is below 20 mg/dl on a normal diet. According to that criteria,
half of our patients over five years of age would belong to hyperphenylalaninemia, which is incredible.

Although protein intake per kilogram body weight decreases with age in
every country, we Japanese used to take less protein than Occidental people did,
and breast feeding was more common until about ten years ago. The Japanese

Table 1. Serum phenylalanine level and age at first diagnosis

Phenylalanine level (mg/dl)	Number of patients Age in months						Total
	0–12	13–24	25–36	37–60	61–120	121+	
>30	13	10	7	2	2	3	37
30–20	6	7	2	7	7	2	32
<20	2	1	3	0	9	5	19
Total	21	18	12	9	18	10	88
Mean[a]	33.92	35.35	28.11	27.88	20.86		29.03
S.D.[b]	±10.68	±13.73	±10.28	±6.35	±7.06		±11.82
Mean[c]	35.99	36.27	32.20			24.24	30.10
S.D.[b]	±8.98	±13.57	±5.72			±11.41	±11.49

[a]Including "HPA."
[b]Standard deviation.
[c]Excluding "HPA."

took approximately 70 g protein daily about ten years ago, and Western people took roughly 90 g protein per day at that time. This might explain why we have such a great many PKU patients with low phenylalanine concentration. It is absolutely definite that we do have hyperphenylalaninemia in Japan. However, we have to be very careful to differentiate classical PKU from hyperphenylala-ninemia in Japan, especially when the patient is over five years of age. We found three families in our survey that have at least two siblings with PKU in which the younger siblings had the typical PKU phenylalanine level of over 20 mg/dl, while the older siblings had serum phenylalanine of below 20. Two out of the three pairs of parents were first cousins, and one of the fathers was in other respects phenylketonuric but with serum phenylalanine of only 11.1 mg/dl. These facts demonstrate the age-dependency of serum phenylalanine very clearly.

IQ

The third point I would like to mention concerns the intelligence quotient of Japanese PKU patients. Dr. Jervis (1963) reports on 500 PKU patients over three years of age classified into different IQ groups. We had 68 Japanese PKU patients over three years of age. When we compare the IQ distribution of these two groups, we immediately notice that Japanese patients have a relatively high IQ. An IQ below 30 is seen in nearly 80% of Dr. Jervis's series but in only 40% of ours. On the contrary, a relatively high IQ of over 70 is seen in only 0.2% of his series but in 8.8% of ours. This difference could also be due to the relatively low protein intake in infancy and early childhood resulting in a low serum phenylalanine level in our patients (Table 2).

The nutritional status of the Japanese has been improving significantly or at least getting closer to that of Western countries in recent years. Accordingly, there may well be less difference in serum phenylalanine and IQ between Caucasian and Japanese patients in the near future.

Table 2. IQ of PKU patients more than 3 years of age[a]

Investigator	IQ				Total
	−30	31−50	51−70	71−	
Jervis (United States)	395 0.790	88 0.176	16 0.032	1 0.002	500
Oura (Japan)	27 0.397	22 0.324	13 0.191	6 0.088	68

[a]Comparison between Jervis' and Oura's data.

EYE COLOR

Another point that deserves mention is that there has been no report of blue eyes in Japanese PKU patients, which is taken for granted as one of the characteristics of PKU in Caucasians. This seems to be simply because of inherent abundant melanine pigmentation in the Japanese race. However, blond hair and fair skin are not uncommon in infancy, even in Japanese patients.

TREATMENT

With regard to the treatment of PKU, Japan is in a rather favorable situation. We have two Japanese low-phenylalanine products available on the market, and costs of hospitalization and outpatient treatment, including the diet, are paid by health insurance supplemented by the government under a program covering most congenital diseases. Approximately 50 PKU patients have been treated in our clinic and a part of the results is summarized in Table 3.

The patients whose treatment began earlier than six months after birth have a mean IQ/DQ of 100 before treatment and 94 after treatment. The duration of treatment of this group was approximately four years. The patients whose treatment began at 7 to 24 months of age have a mean IQ of 80 before treatment and 83 after treatment. The duration of treatment of this group is 5½ years. Patients whose treatment began later than 24 months of age have a mean IQ of 57 before treatment and 65 after treatment. The duration of the treatment of this group is about 7½ years.

During treatment we make every possible effort to maintain serum phenylalanine concentration between 3 and 12 mg/dl. In order to keep the serum phenylalanine within this range, our diets usually provide phenylalanine more to the young infants and less to the older children. Table 4 shows the amount of phenylalanine in our diets for various age groups, estimated from our own experience.

Table 3. Loss of DQ/IQ with age and dietary treatment

Age diagnosed (months)	No.	Mean age diagnosed		Initial DQ/IQ mean (range)	Latest DQ/IQ mean (range)	Present mean age	
		Year	Month			Year	Month
≤ 6	7	0	1.3	normal or ≐ 100	94 (80–109)	4	2
7–24	16	1	2	80 (31–114)	83 (38–127)	6	9
> 24	8	3	7	57 (23–94)	65 (14–104)	11	0

Table 4. Amounts of nutrients for children with PKU at various ages

Age (months)	Phenylalanine mg/kg/day		Protein g/kg/day		Calories	Protein from Lophemilk (%) Total protein intake	
	range	mean	range	mean	cal/kg/day	range	mean
< 3	50–70	60	3.7–4.3	4.0	110–140	68–84	78
3–6	40–60	50	3.5–3.8	3.7	110–130	84–87	86
7–12	30–50	40	3.5–3.8	3.5	100–120	77–86	81
13–24	25–50	35	2.8–4.0	3.2	100	76–93	82
>24	20–30	25	2.3–3.5	2.9	100	77–90	84

Our diets provide 50–70 mg phenylalanine per kilogram body weight per day to infants before 3 months of age, 40–60 mg/kg/day to infants 3 to 6 months old, approximately 40 mg/kg/day to infants 7 to 12 months old, 25–50 mg/kg/day to infants 1 year to 2 years old, and 20–30 mg/kg/day to young children over 2 years of age. The intake of total amino acids as protein equivalent and calories per kilogram body weight per day is also listed in the table.

One of the important problems we face is deciding when to terminate dietary treatment. Most American doctors are in favor of early termination, by four to five years of age, while European doctors, of whom Dr. Bickel is a representative, are in favor of late termination. I now agree with Dr. Bickel's opinion. I usually start to relax the dietary restriction at six years of age, when the patients enter primary schools. They begin to eat ordinary lunches provided by the schools, together with their classmates. It is a part of the training curriculum in our primary schools. Unless it elicited unfavorable clinical symptoms, I would discontinue the diet entirely between seven to ten years of age. We did not worry too much about a high serum phenylalanine or a positive ferric chloride test in urine. However, I found three patients who developed convulsive seizures at 9, 11, and 14 years, respectively, following discontinuance or relaxation of the strict dietary treatment. They were all first diagnosed later than one year of age, having IQs of 68, 77, and 54, respectively.

In retrospect, we recognized that they often demonstrated abnormal EEGs of a certain type before the appearance of seizures and we suspected that we had relaxed our diets too soon. The abnormal EEG pattern most frequently encountered in these ages was paroxysmal slow wave burst and sporadic spikes, often accentuated over the central and parietal regions. These do not necessarily imply the occurrence of clinical seizure. However, when they develop generalized spike and wave complexes, polyspikes, and marked dysrhythmia, we have to consider the reinstitution of the diet or administration of anticonvulsant medication, or both, depending upon the age and background of the patient. If the patient is older than ten years, I prefer anticonvulsant medication to reinstitution of the diet.

I am now trying to continue dietary treatment until ten years of age, as far as the parents can manage it. The higher the IQ of the patient, the easier the family can manage. We have to follow the patient at least up to puberty so as to make a final decision on the termination of the diet.

The Ministry of Health and Welfare of Japan has decided, effective in 1977, to change the screening to multiple blood tests, instead of the less sensitive urine tests. These tests done on one blood sample will include not only PKU but also homocystinuria, maple syrup urine disease, histidinemia, and galactosemia. Furthermore, a new screening program for the detection of congenital hypothyroidism by means of a radioimmunoassay of TSH is now under way in Tokyo and Osaka on a pilot study basis.

SUMMARY

Since the first Japanese PKU patient was reported in 1950, more than 200 cases have been detected. Their IQ/DQ is higher than that of Caucasian PKU reported by Dr. Jervis. Their serum phenylalanine level seems lower than Caucasians'. Newborn screening has recently revealed relatively low incidence of PKU in Japan.

REFERENCES

Bickel, H. Personal communication.

Fujita, Y. (1965) New approaches for estimation of the frequency of rare recessive genes in man. Jap. J. Hum. Genet. 10:49.

Gamo, S., Kawabe, S., and Oura, T. Clinico-genetic study of phenylketonuria in Japan. (in preparation).

Jervis, J. A. (1963) The Clinical Picture in Phenylketonuria (Ed. Lyman, F. L.) Springfield: Charles C Thomas, p. 52.

Kishimoto, K., and Hirose, N. (1950) On the biochemical genetics of the phenylpyruvic oligophrenia (Japanese). Jap. J. Genet. 25:251.

Takai, T., Harumoto, T., Araki, M., Okumura, Y., Oura, T., Isshiki, G., Tsugawa, S., and Omodaka, J. (1967) Principle and practice of low-phenylalanine diet for phenylketonuric patients (Japanese). Acta Pediat. Jap. 71:879.

RESEARCH TO PRACTICE IN MENTAL RETARDATION
Biomedical Aspects, Volume III
Edited by Peter Mittler
Copyright 1977 I.A.S.S.M.D.

PYRUVATE DEHYDROGENASE (E_1) DEFICIENCY ASSOCIATED WITH CONGENITAL LACTIC ACIDOSIS

D. F. Farrell
Division of Neurology and
The Child Development and Mental Retardation Center,
School of Medicine,
University of Washington,
Seattle, Washington 98195, United States

The clinical syndrome congenital lactic acidosis is not a single disease entity, but rather may be caused by a variety of genetically determined enzyme deficiencies. The clinical presentation is somewhat variable, but most of the infants described so far have had severe mental retardation, alterations in the level of consciousness, either muscle hypotonia or spasticity, frequent uncontrollable seizures, and hyperventilation. While the clinical presentation has not always been stereotyped, the diagnosis of the syndrome has been established on the basis of a persistent metabolic acidosis associated with elevated concentrations of lactic and pyruvic acids in the serum. It is from this heterogeneous group of patients that individuals with specific enzyme deficiencies have been recognized. To date, patients in whom a specific enzyme deficiency has been demonstrated tend to fall into two groups: 1) patients who have congenital lactic acidosis associated with hypoglycemia, and 2) patients with congenital lactic acidosis and normoglycemia. The former group have usually been shown to have deficiencies of either pyruvate carboxylase or fructose 1,6 diphosphatase, important enzymes involved in gluconeogenesis. The latter group have been shown to have a deficiency of one of the various enzymes that make up the pyruvate dehydrogenase complex, the enzyme complex responsible for the conversion of pyruvate to acetylcoenzyme A.

The pyruvate dehydrogenase complex is a multi-enzyme system that has been successfully purified and separated into at least three separate components

Table 1. Congenital lactic acidosis blood and plasma values

Factor	Affected	Normal range
Blood pH	7.30	(7.35–7.45)
pCO_2	22 mm Hg	(35–45)
Bicarbonate	11 mEq/liter	(22–30)
Pyruvate	0.65 mM	(0.03–0.1)
Lactate	14.8 mM	(0.5–2.1)
Alanine	1.4 mM	(0.24–0.41)

and then reconstituted from the individual components. The three enzymes that comprise the pyruvate dehydrogenase complex are pyruvate dehydrogenase (E_1),[1] dihydrolipoyl transacetylase, and dihydrolipoyl dehydrogenase. Pyruvate dehydrogenase (E_1) in vivo exists in an active and inactive form. The conversion from the active to the inactive form is catalyzed by the kinase pyruvate dehydrogenase:ATP transphorphorylase, with the conversion from the inactive to the active form being catalyzed by the divalent metal ion dependent phosphatase, pyruvate dehydrogenase-phosphate phosphatase. The interconversion is reversible and has been shown to be controlled by the metabolic state of the individual.

We have recently reported (Farrell et al., 1975) some of our studies of an infant who demonstrated an absence of pyruvate dehydrogenase complex activity secondary to a deficiency of pyruvate dehydrogenase (E_1) activity, the first enzyme of the pyruvate dehydrogenase complex.

The infant was born prematurely, after a 35-week gestation, and weighed 1.32 kg at birth. He was noted to have rapid respirations and a compensated metabolic acidosis (Table 1). The pH of the blood was 7.30, with a pCO_2 of 22 mm Hg and a bicarbonate of 11 meq/liter. Subsequently, he was found to have a plasma pyruvate concentration of 0.65 mM, a lactate concentration of 14.8 mM, and an alanine concentration of 1.4 mM.

A sequential series of dietary manipulations were tried in an attempt to correct the lactic and pyruvic acidosis. High doses of thiamine, biotin, and lipoic acid had no effect on the acidosis. At about 40 days of age the infant was placed on a 5% carbohydrate diet with the remainder of the dietary calories being provided as medium-chain triglycerides and proteins. There was a dramatic lowering of the plasma lactate and pyruvate to near normal concentrations. Two months later the infant was placed on a normal diet for one day, which resulted in an immediate increase in the concentration of both lactate and pyruvate. The infant continued with his low carbohydrate diet for the remainder of his short

[1] Some confusion exists in the literature as to the name of the first enzyme of the pyruvate dehydrogenase complex. The commonly used name "pyruvate decarboxylase" is technically incorrect because this name refers to a bacterial enzyme that is not part of the pyruvate dehydrogenase complex. The more accurate name for the enzyme under discussion is either pyruvate dehydrogenase (E_1) or pyruvate -$K_3Fe(CN)_6$ reductase, decarboxylating (E.C. 1.2.2.2).

Table 2. Enzyme activity in brain and liver

	PDH Complex[a]	PDH (E$_1$)[a] $\times 10^{-3}$	α KDH Complex[a] $\times 10^{-2}$
Brain			
Control	0.1 ± 0.017	4.29 ± 1.51	2.43 ± 0.35
Affected	0.005	< 0.01	2.48
Liver			
Control	0.14 ± 0.008	1.73 ± 0.37	8.26 ± 3.68
Affected	0.005	< 0.01	16.87

[a]μmol/hr/mg of protein, mean ± standard deviation.

life. While the infant's metabolic status could be improved by dietary manipulation, no observable improvement in his neurologic status was observed.

During the short life of this infant his examination showed severe muscle hypotonia, microcephalus, and continual seizures. He demonstrated no evidence of central nervous system development, was both cortically blind and deaf, and died at six months of age of bronchopneumonia.

Brain and liver tissues were obtained at autopsy and were either stored frozen at $-70°$C for later enzyme analysis or processed for histological study. Pyruvate dehydrogenase complex activity and α-ketoglutarate dehydrogenase complex activity were assayed by the method of Cremer and Teal (1974). Pyruvate dehydrogenase (E$_1$) activity was assayed by the method of Reed and Willms (1966) modified to utilize carbon-14 sodium pyruvate labeled in the 1-position (Table 2). The brain pyruvate dehydrogenase complex activity was

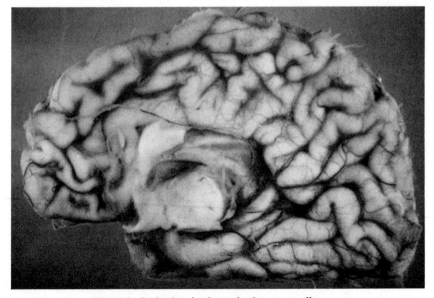

Figure 1. Brain showing hypoplastic corpus callosum.

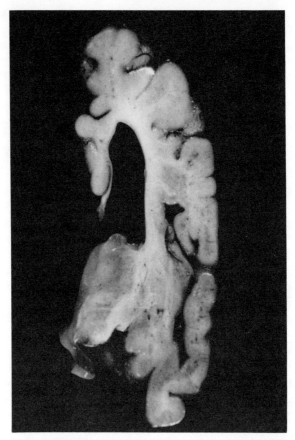

Figure 2. Brain showing hypoplastic corpus callosum and marked ventricular enlargement.

less than 0.005 μmol/hr/mg of protein in the affected infant, while the specific activity in pathological controls was 0.1 μmol/hr/mg of protein. Pyruvate dehydrogenase (E_1) specific activity was less than 0.01×10^{-3} μmol/hr/mg of protein with a control value of 4.29×10^{-3} μmol/hr/mg of protein. Alpha-ketoglutarate dehydrogenase complex was also assayed because the third enzyme of the PDH complex, dihydrolipoyl dehydrogenase is common to both complexes. The α-ketoglutarate dehydrogenase complex activity was similar for both affected and control brain. A similar deficiency of pyruvate dehydrogenase (E_1) and pyruvate dehydrogenase complex activity was found in liver tissues from the affected infant.

Anatomically, the brain demonstrated two major types of pathological changes: 1) numerous "congenital" anomalies of the brain were present and 2) severe postanoxic changes that were probably the result of both the uncontrollable seizures and the cardiopulmonary arrests that occurred during the life of the infant.

The brain was very small, weighing only 350 g, compared to the 770 g expected for that age. Structures that were normally derived embryologically from the lamina reuniens (pars crassa) were found to be quite hypoplastic. The corpus callosum was absent behind the foramen of Monro. Figure 1 demonstrates the partial absence of the corpus callosum from the medial surface of the bisected brain. Figure 2 shows the markedly hypoplastic corpus callosum ending blindly without crossing the midline. The other commisural systems were also hypoplastic. The fornices were quite small, contained no recognizable communicating fibers and the large space between the fornices was lined with pia arachnoid. The white matter was very thin and the lateral ventricles were dramatically enlarged.

In addition to these forebrain anomalies, the descending corticospinal tract was located in an aberrant location in the pons being at the junction of the tegmentum and basis pontis. The corticospinal tract was in its normal location in both the midbrain and medulla. One final anomaly was noted (Figure 3). There was an incomplete migration of a portion of the inferior olivary nucleus such that ectopic elements of that nucleus remained in the posterior part of the medulla.

It would be interesting to speculate that these "congenital" anomalies were a direct result of the pyruvate dehydrogenase deficiency and that at certain critical developmental stages defective carbohydrate metabolism was not able to provide adequate energy for normal development.

The remainder of the pathologic changes found in this infant's brain were thought to result from repeated anoxic episodes. They included perinatal teloleukoencephalopathy with microcephaly, laminar necrosis of the cerebrum, gliosis of the cerebellar cortex, and bilateral uncal herniation with gliosis.

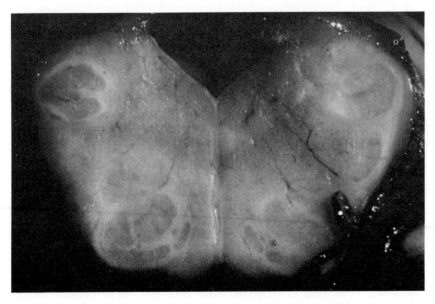

Figure 3. Medulla showing ectopic inferior olivary nuclei.

PYRUVATE DEHYDROGENASE
DEFICIENCY IN ALTERED SKIN FIBROBLASTS

A punch biopsy of the skin was obtained from the affected infant and cultured in a routine manner. The day before cell harvesting, the cells were fed fresh media. Following harvesting, the cultured cells were homogenized and the enzyme assays performed immediately. Attempts to freeze the harvested cells so that the enzyme assays could be performed at a more convenient time were unsuccessful.

The initial assay of the pyruvate dehydrogenase (E_1) and pyruvate dehydrogenase complex of the cultured cells from the affected infant demonstrated a marked deficiency of enzyme activity, as we had found in both brain and liver, but shortly we began to obtain normal or even super normal values for the pyruvate dehydrogenase (E_1) activity. At about this time we began to check routinely all of our tissue culture samples for the presence of mycoplasma contamination by the tritiated uracil uptake method of Kenny (1973). By utilizing this uptake technique Clark et al. (1976) were able to show that when there were more than 200 cpm of $[^3H]$uracil incorporated into the culture, mycoplasma contamination was present and the pyruvate dehydrogenase (E_1) activity was markedly elevated while the pyruvate dehydrogenase complex and the α-ketoglutarate dehydrogenase complex activities were only moderately elevated. Enzyme analysis of a homogenate of *Mycoplasma pneumoniae* showed this particular mycoplasma to have a pyruvate dehydrogenase (E_1) specific activity 900 times that found in mycoplasma-free fibroblasts. The pyruvate dehydrogenase complex and the α-ketoglutarate dehydrogenase complex specific activities in *Mycoplasma pneumoniae* were both elevated, but not nearly to the extent seen with the pyruvate dehydrogenase (E_1).

Once we had eliminated mycoplasma contamination as an exogenous source of enzyme activity we proceeded to investigate cultured skin fibroblasts from the parents and siblings of the affected infant. Table 3 shows a summary of our results. Control skin fibroblasts have a pyruvate dehydrogenase complex activity of 7.6×10^{-3} μmol/hr/mg of protein, while the pyruvate dehydrogenase (E_1) has an activity of 2.6×10^{-4} μmol/hr/mg of protein. The cultured skin fibroblasts from the affected infant had less than 5% of control, while the parents had intermediate values for both pyruvate dehydrogenase (E_1) and pyruvate dehydrogenase complex activity when compared to the enzyme activity of the affected infant and his two siblings. The specific activities of these two enzymes in the parents overlapped with some of our low normal controls, but we feel that within this particular family we have documented that this is a recessively inherited disorder.

Shortly after completion of the family study the mother became pregnant, and at 14 weeks gestation a percutaneous amniocentesis was performed by Dr. Larry Karp. Table 3 shows the results of the analysis of the pyruvate dehydroge-

Table 3. Pyruvate dehydrogenase complex and pyruvate dehydrogenase (E_1) in cultured skin fibroblasts and amniotic fluid cells

Cell type	Determinations	PDH Complex (μmol/hr/mg protein) X 10^{-3}	PDH(E_1) (μmol/hr/mg protein) X 10^{-4}
Fibroblasts			
controls	20	7.6	2.6
proband	2	< 0.19	< 0.07
father	2	4.2	0.88
mother	2	5.7	1.06
sister	3	7.39	1.90
brother	3	8.87	3.01
Amniotic fluid cells			
controls	5	4.6	3.3
fetus at risk	2	5.8	6.6

nase complex and pyruvate dehydrogenase (E_1) activities in controls and the fetus at risk. Normal values were obtained and we are now anxiously awaiting the birth of the child.

To date, there have been infants with congenital lactic acidosis described who are missing each of the various enzymes that make up the pyruvate dehydrogenase complex. A few years ago Blass et al. (1972)[2] reported a child who had a deficiency of the pyruvate dehydrogenase complex, but who had a normal pyruvate dehydrogenase (E_1) activity, and postulated that the child had a defect in either the dihydrolipoyl transacetylase or the dihydrolipoyl dehydrogenase. This same group (1976) has extended their work and have studied children who have defects in these last two enzymes. Stromme et al. (1976) have recently reported a patient with the same defect in pyruvate dehydrogenase (E_1) as we have studied. Robinson and Sherwood (1975) have reported an infant with congenital lactic acidosis who had an apparent defect in the pyruvate dehydrogenase phosphate phosphatase, the enzyme responsible for the activation of the pyruvate dehydrogenase (E_1) enzyme.

In summary, enzymatic defects have been documented with four of the enzymes associated with the pyruvate dehydrogenase complexes (Table 4). If an individual has a deficiency of pyruvate dehydrogenase (E_1), then both pyruvate dehydrogenase (E_1) and the pyruvate dehydrogenase complex activity will be deficient, and the α-ketoglutarate dehydrogenase activity will be normal.

---

[2] Two genetically distinct mutations of the pyruvate dehydrogenase (E_1) have so far been recognized. A partial deficiency of this particular enzyme, a residual enzyme activity of about 25%, and a clinical picture of intermittent cerebellar ataxia has been described by Blass and coworkers. A second and distinct form of pyruvate dehydrogenase (E_1) deficiency results from a mutation that causes a severe reduction of enzyme activity, less than 5% residual activity, with a clinical picture of congenital lactic acidosis.

Table 4. PDH(E_1), PDH Complex, and αKHD Complex activities resulting from specific deficiencies of the PDH Complex

Genetically deficient enzyme	Enzyme activities		
	PDH(E_1)	PDH Complex	αKDH Complex
1. Pyruvate dehydrogenase (E_1)	↓	↓	→
2. Dihydrolipoyl transacetylase (E_2)	→	↓	→
3. Dihydrolipoyl dehydrogenase (E_3)	→	↓	↓
4. PDH: Phosphate phosphatase	→[a]	→[a]	→

[a]Delay in the divalent dependent activation of the inactive PDH(E_1) and PDH complex.

If the dihydrolipoyl transacetylase activity is deficient, then the pyruvate dehydrogenase complex activity will be deficient and both the pyruvate dehydrogenase (E_1) and the α-ketoglutarate dehydrogenase complex activity will be normal. If a dihydrolipoyl dehydrogenase deficiency is responsible for the disorder, then both the pyruvate dehydrogenase complex and the α-ketoglutarate dehydrogenase complex activities will be low, because both complexes have this enzyme as a part of their activity. With a deficiency of the pyruvate dehydrogenase phosphate phosphatase all three enzyme activities are normal (standard assay techniques). It is only after the enzyme is converted to the inactive form in the presence of ATP and then activated in the presence of calcium that a defect in the activation of the pyruvate dehydrogenase (E_1) or the pyruvate dehydrogenase complex is recognized.

All of these enzymes are present in cultivated somatic cells and prevention of the severe forms of congenital lactic acidosis caused by a deficiency of one of the above enzyme activities appears to be possible through antenatal diagnosis.

SUMMARY

The genetically determined deficiencies of the various enzymes that constitute the pyruvate dehydrogenase complex may cause severe mental retardation, intractable seizures and lactic acidosis. With the recognition of specific enzyme deficiencies and their quantitative measurement in cultured skin and amniotic fluid cells, prevention through antenatal diagnosis appears possible.

REFERENCES

Blass, J. P., Kark, R. A. P., and Cederbaum, S. D. (1976) Pyruvate dehydrogenase deficiency: Summary of 25 cases. Amer. Soc. Neurochem. 7:167.

Blass, J. P., Schulman, J. D., Young, D. S., and Hom, E. (1972) An inherited defect affecting the tricarboxylic acid cycle in a patient with congenital lactic acidosis. J. Clin. Invest. 51:1845.

Clark, A. F., Farrell, D. F., Burke, W., and Scott, C. R. (1976) The effect of mycoplasma contamination on the in vitro assay for pyruvate dehydrogenase activity in cultured fibroblasts. J. Clin. Invest. 24:147A.

Cremer, J. E., and Teal, H. M. (1974) The activity of pyruvate dehydrogenase in rat brain during postnatal development. Fed. Eur. Biochem. Soc. Lett. 39:17.

Farrell, D. F., Clark, A. F., Scott, C. R., and Wennberg, R. P. (1975) Absence of pyruvate decarboxylase activity in man: A cause of congenital lactic acidosis. Science. 187:1082.

Kenny, G. E. (1975) Rapid detection of mycoplasmata and nonculturable agents in animal cell cultures by uracil incorporation. Microbiology, 1975 (Ed. Schlessinger, D.) Amer. Soc. Microbiol., p. 32.

Reed, L. J., and Willms, C. R. (1966) Purification and resolution of the pyruvate dehydrogenase complex (*E. coli*). Methods Enzymol. 9:247.

Robinson, B. H., and Sherwood, W. G. (1975) Pyruvate dehydrogenase phosphatase deficiency: A cause of congenital chronic lactic acidosis in infancy. Pediatr. Res. 9:935.

Stromme, J. H., Bound, O., and Moe, P. J. (1976) Fatal lactic acidosis in a newborn attributable to a congenital defect of pyruvate dehydrogenase. Pediatr. Res. 10:62.

RESEARCH TO PRACTICE IN MENTAL RETARDATION
Biomedical Aspects, Volume III
Edited by Peter Mittler
Copyright 1977 I.A.S.S.M.D.

MENTAL RETARDATION SYNDROMES RESULTING FROM INBORN ERRORS OF GLYCOPROTEIN CATABOLISM

G. Dawson and G. C. Tsay
Departments of Pediatrics and Biochemistry,
Joseph P. Kennedy Jr., Mental Retardation Research Center,
University of Chicago,
Chicago, Illinois 60637, United States

Interest in the metabolism of glycoproteins has increased considerably in recent years as a result of the realization that most proteins are in fact glycosylated and that the carbohydrate moiety may be involved in cell-cell interactions and in the directing of molecules, such as hormones, to their target cells (Winterburne and Phelps, 1972). Studies on human erythrocytes have shown that the carbohydrate groups of both glycosphingolipids and glycoproteins project outward from the cell surface (Steck and Dawson, 1974), and this is presumably true for all cells, including those of the central nervous system. Glycoprotein oligosaccharide units, which generally contain the sugars L-fucose (Fuc) D-mannose (Man), D-galactose (Gal), *N*-acetylglucosamine (Glc*N*Ac), *N*-acetylgalactosamine (Gal*N*Ac) and sialic acids (Neu*N*Ac) (although many, such as ovalbumin, contain only Man and Glc*N*Ac (Spiro, 1969)) (Figure 1), are believed to be assembled on the rough endoplasmic reticulum and Golgi apparatus of the cell (Spiro, 1969), although many recent studies have shown that plasma membrane lipid-bound intermediates are required for the assembly of Man and Glc*N*Ac residues in the correct stereochemical conformation (Wedgewood et al., 1974). Because glyco-proteins are probably involved in coding and decoding the intercellular messages

This work was supported in part by USPHS Grant HD-06426, HD-04583, and HD-09402 and National Foundation March of Dimes Grant I-340. Glyn Dawson is the recipient of USPHS Research Career Development Award NS-00029 and a Joseph P. Kennedy, Jr., Scholar.

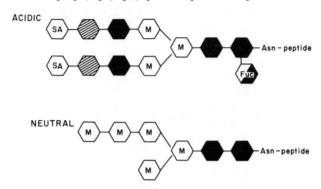

Figure 1. Schematic representation of the two major types of oligosaccharide units found in mammalian glycoproteins. The acid type contains sialic acid, ⑤ₐ; galactose, ▨; N-acetylglucosamine,●; mannose,Ⓜ; and fucose⬢. The neutral type contains only Man and GlcNAc.

required for the correct movement and assembly of cells that will eventually form the mature central nervous system, a genetic defect in biosynthesis or its regulation could account for many of the mental retardation syndromes that result from developmental impairment. However, this field remains to be explored and no definitive studies have yet been made.

The mechanism by which glycoproteins are catabolized is perhaps better understood, and with the possible exception of the removal of sialic acid residues by a plasma membrane-bound neuraminidase (Schengrund and Rosenberg, 1970; Morell et al., 1971), the carbohydrate moiety is degraded by the sequential action of a group of acid exo- and endoglycosidases located within

Table 1. Enzymes involved in glycoprotein catabolism

Exo-glycosidases	Endo-glycosidases
1. α-Neuraminidase	1. Endo-N-Acetyl-β-glucosaminidase (cleaves GlcNAc-GlcNAc chitobiose linkage)
2. α-Fucosidase	
3. β-Galactosidase	2. N-Acetylglucosaminyl asparaginase (cleaves sugar peptide bond)
4. N-Acetyl-β-hexosaminidase	
5. α-Mannosidase	
6. β-Mannosidase	

Table 2. Nature of the accumulating sphingolipid material in disorders in which both glycosphingolipid and oligosaccharide material accumulates

Sphingolipidosis	Major accumulating glycosphingolipids
SANDHOFF'S DISEASE (N-Acetyl-β-hexosaminidase deficiency)	GalNAc $\beta(1 \rightarrow 4)$ Gal-Glc-Cer $\quad$ (G_{M2}) $\qquad\mid$ $\qquad$ NeuNAc GalNAc $\beta(1 \rightarrow 4)$ Gal-Glc-Cer $\quad$ (asialo-G_{M2}) GalNAc $\beta(1 \rightarrow 3)$ Gal-Gal-Glc-Cer (Globoside)
G_{M1}-GANGLIOSIDOSIS (β-Galactosidase deficiency)	Gal $\beta(1 \rightarrow 3)$ GalNAc-Gal-Glc-Cer $\quad$ (G_{M1}) $\qquad\mid$ $\qquad$ NeuNAc
FUCOSIDOSIS (α-Fucosidase deficiency)	Fuc $\alpha(1 \rightarrow 2)$ Gal-GlcNAc-Gal-Glc-Cer (H-antigen)

lysosomes (Table 1). An examination of this list indicated at least three enzymes, namely N-acetyl-β-D-glucosaminidase, β-D-galactosidase and α-fucosidase, which could also be involved in the hydrolysis of glycosphingolipids (Table 2). We therefore decided to examine three known sphingolipidosis mental retardation syndromes, namely the Sandhoff variant of Tay-Sachs disease (G_{M2}-gangliosidosis) (Sandhoff et al., 1971), G_{M1}-gangliosidosis (O'Brien, 1972), and fucosidosis (Durand et al., 1969), for evidence of impaired glycoprotein catabolism. In two of these disorders, namely G_{M1} and G_{M2} gangliosidosis, the level of glycoprotein-derived storage material was small in the brain, but high in the liver. Thus the neurological impairment is almost certainly a secondary effect of massive glycosphingolipid accumulation and resultant membrane disruption. However, in fucosidosis and the two related disorders α-mannosidosis (Autio et al., 1973) and aspartylglucosaminuria (Palo et al., 1972) the accumulation of glycoprotein-derived storage material can be considered to be the primary cause of the observed severe mental retardation.

ISOLATION AND CHARACTERIZATION OF STORAGE MATERIAL

Water-soluble (oligosaccharide) storage material was isolated by disrupting a 1-2g fresh weight sample of autopsy brain from patients with fucosidosis, G_{M1}-gangliosidosis Type I, G_{M1}-gangliosidosis Type II (Petrelli and Blair, 1975), G_{M2}-gangliosidosis (Type A; Tay-Sachs disease), and G_{M2}-gangliosidosis (Type O; Sandhoff's disease) in 2.0 ml of water with a sonifier (Heat Systems Model W-185-E). The $5000\,g$ supernatant was then chromatographed on a column (180 $\times$ 1 cm diam) of Bio-Gel P-10 and carbohydrate-positive fractions detected by the phenol-sulfuric acid method (Dubois et al., 1956) (Figure 2). The oligosac-

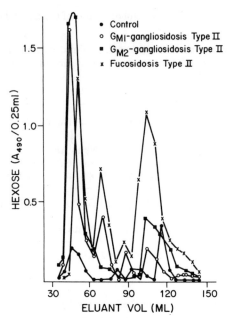

Figure 2. Fractionation of water-soluble human autopsy brain extracts on a column (180 × 1.0 cm diam.) of Bio-Gel P-10. Aliquots were assayed for the presence of carbohydrate by the phenol-sulfuric acid colorimetric method.

charide (low molecular weight, 500–3500) fraction was further fractionated on Bio-Gel P-2 (Tsay et al., 1976) and finally purified by paper chromatography in n-butanol-acetic acid-water (12:3:5 by vol.) (Dawson and Clamp, 1968). Molecular weight estimations were carried out by the Sephadex G-25 method of Bhatti and Clamp (1968).

Table 3. Low molecular weight oligosaccharide fraction isolated from brain of patients with inborn errors of glycoprotein catabolism (Bio-Gel P-10): further purified on Bio-Gel P-2

Sugar	Fucosidosis		G_{M1}-Gangliosidosis		G_{M2}-Gangliosidosis		Mannosidosis[b]
	I	II	Type I	Type II	Type A	Type O	
			(relative moles of monosaccharide)				
Fucose	2.0	1.0	0	0	Tr	0	0
Mannose	3.0	0	4.0	3.3	Tr	3.6	4.6
Galactose	2.2	0	2.0	2.0	Tr	0	0
GlcNAc	3.0	1.0	3.0	3.0	Tr	3.0	1.0
NeuNAc	0	0	0	0	Tr	0	0
Total μmol/g[a] fresh wt.	15.9	4.0	0.9	0.5	0.1	2.1	0.8

[a]Control brain contains 0.05 μmol/g fresh wt.
[b]Öckerman, P.-A. (1969). J. Pediat. 75:360–365.

The carbohydrate composition of the purified material was determined by gas-liquid chromatographic analysis of the derived trimethylsilyl ether methyl glycosides, as described previously (Dawson and Clamp, 1968; Dawson, 1976), and the results are given in Table 3. The monosaccharide sequence was determined by sequential digestion with highly purified α-fucosidase, β-galactosidase, N-acetyl-β-hexosaminidase, and α-mannosidase, as described previously (Tsay et al., 1976). Final structural assignments were derived from a combination of periodate oxidation and permethylation studies in which the derivatives were identified by a combination of gas-liquid chromatography, mass-spectrometry and mass-chromatography (Tsay et al., 1976). The results indicated that the storage material was derived from glycoproteins and that from studies on fucosidosis, G_{M1}-gangliosidosis, G_{M2}-gangliosidosis, mannosidosis, and aspartylglucosaminuria, a catabolic pathway could be constructed (Figure 3). Although the appropriate endo-N-acetylglucosaminidase has not yet been isolated from human tissues, its existence is attested to by the fact that the majority of the storage material is found in oligosaccharide rather than glycopeptide form. In G_{M1}-gangliosidosis, a similar storage material has been elegantly characterized in liver from Type 1 patients by Wolfe et al. (1974) and material structurally related to desulfated keratan sulfate linkage region isolated from the liver of a Type 1 variant patient (Feldges et al., 1973; Tsay et al., 1975), as shown in Figure 3.

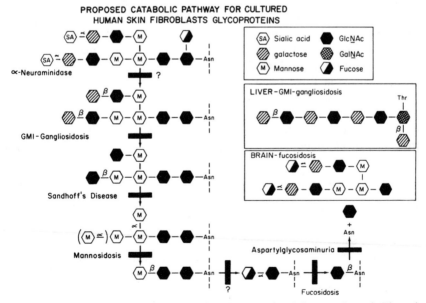

Figure 3. Proposed catabolic scheme for acidic glycoprotein of the type shown in Figure 1. showing the site of catabolic block in known inborn errors of glycoprotein catabolism.

Table 4. Carbohydrate composition of the glycopeptide isolated from cultured skin fibroblasts from patients with inborn errors of glycoprotein catabolism

Sugar	Fucosidosis	G_{M1}-gangliosidosis Type I	G_{M2}-gangliosidosis Type O	Mannosidosis
		molar ratio of sugars		
Fucose	1.0	0	0	0
Mannose	0	2.8	2.7	3.4
Galactose	0	1.8	0	0
GlcNAc	1.0	4.0	4.0	1.0
Total μmol/10^8 cells	1.4[a]	1.9	1.7	0.5

[a]Control cells contained less than 0.1 μmol/10^8 cells.

DEMONSTRATION OF THE DEFECT IN CULTURED SKIN FIBROBLASTS

All five disorders show considerable phenotypic heterogeneity, which can be explained to some degree by biochemical observations. Since therapy for lysosomal storage disease has thus far proved impracticable, it was important from the point of view of genetic counseling and prenatal diagnosis to demonstrate the defect in tissue culture. Numerous laboratories have reported that the enzymic deficiency in these and other lysosomal storage diseases can be readily demonstrated in cultured skin fibroblasts and amniotic fluid cells and in all cases studied the residual enzymatic activity was less than 5% of normal (Tsay and Dawson, 1975). In addition, we were able to demonstrate the accumulation of glycopeptide in lysosomes of fibroblasts from patients with fucosidosis, G_{M1}-gangliosidosis Type 1, G_{M2}-gangliosidosis Type O, and mannosidosis. The amount varied from 0.5–2.0 μmol of carbohydrate per 10^8 cells and the results are summarized in Table 4 and Figure 3. It can be seen that, with the exception of fucosidosis, where the storage material was a Fuc-GlcNAc-Asparaginyl-glycopeptide and we were unable to demonstrate the fucodekasaccharide found in the brain, the structure of the material corresponds closely to that isolated from the patient's brain.

TREATMENT OF INBORN ERRORS OF GLYCOPROTEIN CATABOLISM

Having demonstrated the ability of cultured human skin fibroblasts to store glycoprotein-derived material it was then possible to carry out potentially therapeutic endeavors on the cultured skin fibroblasts, i.e., attempts at enzyme replacement therapy. A number of clinical trials with purified lysosomal hydrolases have demonstrated the ability of such enzymes to remain in circulation for several hours before removal by the liver, but there are few reports of catabolism of stored material (Brady et al., 1974) and even fewer reports of lasting clinical benefit to the patient. Before attempting any clinical trials it appears to us to be a minimum requirement that the enzyme be tested for its ability to degrade material stored in cultured cells. We have previously demonstrated this for Fabry's disease and α-galactosidase (Dawson et al., 1973), and have now shown that α-fucosidase, purified by commercially-available affinity columns (Alhadeff et al., 1975) from human brain and spleen, (Figure 4) will enter cells, fuse with pre-existing lysosomes and effect the catabolism of the fucoglycopeptide. The uptake of purified α-fucosidase by fucosidosis fibroblasts GM291 is shown in Figure 5. In this particular case, maximum uptake, corresponding to 3% of the enzyme added to the medium, was achieved after 24 hours, and this level of activity was maintained in the cells for a period of 48 hours. The mechanism of this relatively low-affinity uptake is presumably pinocytosis, and we have been unable to demonstrate any high affinity uptake that could be blocked by the presence of high concentrations of sugars (0.1M) such as mannose (Hieber et al., 1976). Uptake was stimulated to 6% of added enzyme by the addition of dibutyryl cyclic AMP (optimum concentration 10^{-3}M), which is generally believed to stimulate membrane activity, and inhibited by cytochalasin B, which inhibits phagocytosis. In Figure 6 one can see that the uptake of enzyme could be related to the rate of breakdown of stored material, because the cells had been prelabeled for 48 hours with [^{3}H] fucose. It is possible that fibroblasts have a lysosomal enzyme uptake mechanism that differs from that of other types of cells (Hickman et al., 1974), but such studies would appear to offer some basis for continuing the idea of enzyme replacement therapy. Potential problems include the need to improve the efficiency of enzyme uptake, which could be solved by the ability to modify the enzyme into a high-affinity uptake form protected from rapid destruction by the liver, and

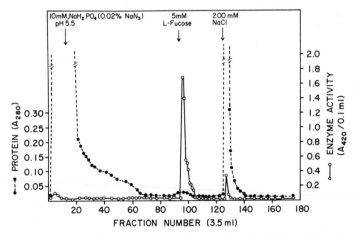

Figure 4. Purification of α-L-fucosidase from human spleen by affinity column chromatography on epsilon-amino-caproyl-fucosamine Agarose (Miles Lab Inc.). The enzyme was eluted with 5mM L-fucose and enzymatic activity measured with the 4-methylumbelliferyl α-L-fucoside substrate.

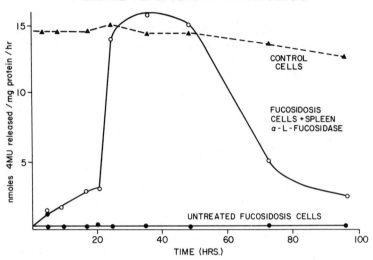

ENZYME REPLACEMENT IN FUCOSIDOSIS

Figure 5. Uptake of human spleen. α-L-fucosidase by α-fucosidase-deficient (fucosidosis) cultured human fibroblasts.

from difficulties in getting the enzyme across the blood-brain barrier. Further, the examination of fetuses afflicted with lysosomal storage disorders (Schneck et al., 1972) has shown that extensive pathology exists prior to birth and well before the onset of clinical symptoms. Such findings account for the current emphasis on genetic counseling, heterozygote detection, and amniocentesis for

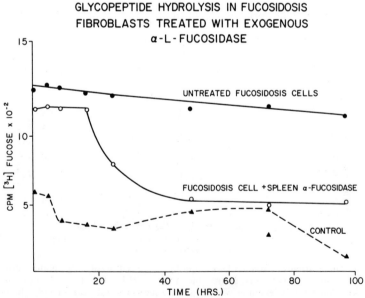

GLYCOPEPTIDE HYDROLYSIS IN FUCOSIDOSIS FIBROBLASTS TREATED WITH EXOGENOUS α-L-FUCOSIDASE

Figure 6. Catabolism of [³H]fucose-labelled lysosomal storage material in cultured fucosidosis fibroblasts by exogenously added human spleen α-L-fucosidase.

the inborn errors of glycoprotein catabolism and the related sphingolipidoses and mucopolysaccharidoses. However, basic research on lysosomal hydrolases and their properties is of potential therapeutic value in assigning these enzymes to specific human chromosomes (for future "genetic engineering" attempts) and for direct therapy (enzymatic or drug) of the later onset forms of these disorders. For example, in juvenile Tay-Sachs and G_{M1}-gangliosidosis, where the mental retardation and visceral abnormalities are not so life-threatening, the potential for remedial therapy appears to be highest.

SUMMARY

Glycoproteins are important membrane constituents that have been implicated as important factors in the modulation of neural plasticity. At least five inherited mental retardation syndromes have been attributed to the absence of a specific lysosomal enzyme involved in glycoprotein breakdown. Our biochemical findings are discussed, and we attempt to relate these to the clinical heterogeneity, including severity of neurological impairment, observed.

REFERENCES

Alhadeff, J. A., Miller, A. L., Wenaas, H., Vedvick, T., and O'Brien, J. S. (1975) Human liver α-L-fucosidase. J. Biol. Chem. 250:7106.

Autio, S., Nordén, N. E., Öckerman, P.-A., Riekkinen, P., Rapola, J., and Louhimo, T. (1973) Mannosidosis. Acta Paediatr., Scand. 62:55S.

Bhatti, T., and Clamp, J. R. (1968) Determination of the molecular weight of glycopeptides by exclusion chromatography. Biochim. Biophys. Acta 170:206.

Brady, R. O., Pentchev, P. G., Gal, A. E., Hibbert, S. R., and Dekaban, A. S. (1974) Replacement therapy for inherited enzyme deficiency: Use of purified glucocerebrosidase in Gaucher's disease. New Engl. J. Med., 291:989.

Dawson, G., and Clamp, J. R. (1968) Investigations on the oligosaccharide units of an A myeloma globulin. Biochem. J. 107:341.

Dawson, G. (1976) Gas Chromatographic Analysis of Carbohydrates in Glycolipids. 2nd edition., New York: Marcel-Dekker, Inc. p. 666.

Dawson, G., Matalon, R., and Li, Yu-Teh (1973) Correction of the enzymatic defect in cultured fibroblasts from patients with Fabry's disease: Treatment with purified α-galactosidase from ficin. Pediatr. Res. 7:684.

Dubois, M., Gilles, K. A., Hamilton, J. K., Rebers, P. A., and Smith, F. (1956) Colorimetric method for determination of sugars and related substances. Anal. Chem. 28:350.

Durand, P., Borrone, C., and Della Cella, G. (1969) Fucosidosis. J. Pediatr. 25:665.

Feldges, A., Müller, H. J., Bühler, E., and Stalder, G. (1973) Helv. Paediat. Acta 28:511.

Hickman, S., Shapiro, L. J., and Neufeld, E. F. (1974) A recognition marker required for uptake of a lysosomal enzyme by cultured fibroblasts. Biochem. Biophys. Res. Commun. 57:55.

Hieber, L., Distler, J., Schmickel, R., Myerowitz, R., and Jourdian, G. W. (1976) The role of glycosidically-bound mannose in the assimilation of β-galactosidase by skin fibroblasts. Fed. Proc. 35:89.

Morrell, A. G., Gregoriadis, G., Scheinberg, I. H., Hickman, J., and Ashwell, G. (1971) The role of sialic acid in determining the survival of glycoproteins in the circulation. J. Biol. Chem. 246:1461.

O'Brien, J. S. (1972) The Metabolic Basis of Inherited Diseases. 3rd edition. New York: McGraw-Hill, p. 639.

Palo, J., Riekkinen, P., Arstila, A. Y., Autio, S., and Kivimaki, T. (1972) Aspartylglucosaminuria. Acta Neuropath. (Berl.) 20:217.

Petrelli, M., and Blair, J. D. (1975) The liver in G_{M1}-gangliosidosis types 1 and 2. Arch. Pathol. 99:111.

Sandhoff, K., Harzer, K., Wässle, W., and Jatzkewitz, H. (1971) Enzyme alterations and lipid storage in three variants of Tay-Sachs disease. J. Neurochem. 18:2469.

Schengrund, C.-L., and Rosenberg, A. (1970) Neuraminidase in neuronal synaptosomal membrane. J. Biol. Chem. 245:6196.

Schneck, L., Adachi, M., and Volk, B. W. (1972) The fetal aspects of Tay-Sachs disease. Pediatrics 49:342.

Spiro, R. G. (1969) Glycoproteins; Their biochemistry, biology and role in human disease. New Engl. J. Med. 281:991.

Steck, T. L., and Dawson, G. (1974) Topographical distribution of complex carbohydrates in the erythrocyte membrane. J. Biol. Chem. 249:2135.

Tsay, G. C., and Dawson, G. (1975) Glycopeptide storage in fibroblasts from patients with inborn errors of glycoprotein and glycosphingolipid catabolism. Biochem. Biophys. Res. Commun. 63:807.

Tsay, G. C., Dawson, G., and Li, Y.-T. (1975) Structure of the glycopeptide storage material in G_{M1}-gangliosidosis. Biochim. Biophys. Acta. 385:305.

Tsay, G. C., Dawson, G., and Sung, S-S. J. (1976) Structure of the accumulating oligosaccharide in fucosidosis. J. Biol. Chem. 251: Sept.

Wedgewood, J. F., Warren, C. D., Jeanloz, R. W., and Strominger, J. L. (1974) Enzymatic utilization of P'-Di-N-acetylchitobiosyl P^2-dolichyl-pyrophosphase and its chemical synthesis. Proc. Nat. Acad. Sci. USA 71:5022.

Winterburne, P. J., and Phelps, C. F. (1972) Nature. 236:147.

Wolfe, L. S., Senior, R. G., and Ng Ying Kin, N. M. K. (1974) The structure of the oligosaccharide accumulating in the liver of G_{M1}-gangliosidosis Type 1 patients. J. Biol. Chem. 249:1828.

PREVENTION
AND TREATMENT

RESEARCH TO PRACTICE IN MENTAL RETARDATION
Biomedical Aspects, Volume III
Edited by Peter Mittler
Copyright 1977 I.A.S.S.M.D.

GENETIC COUNSELLING CONSIDERATIONS IN DOWN'S SYNDROME

J. M. Berg
Surrey Place Centre, Toronto,
Canada M5S 2C2

Practically from the time of the first definitive description of Down's syndrome more than a century ago (Down, 1866), attention has been focused on the question of the risks of occurrence and recurrence of this disability. Despite an enormous accumulation of observations and published findings on the syndrome, its basic aetiology remains unravelled, a consideration that has hampered the capacity to provide a precise answer to the question mentioned. Nevertheless, advances in knowledge bearing on this aspect of the syndrome are now sufficiently extensive to constitute a basis, albeit largely an empirical one, for reasonably accurate guidance to families. Furthermore, the current capacity to recognize Down's syndrome prenatally, in a convenient and safe manner, offers an effective means for preventing the birth (although not, of course, the conception) of affected individuals.

This presentation, although largely concerned with known factual data bearing on genetic counselling in Down's syndrome, reflects personal views on the interpretation and application of these data in practice.

HISTORICAL PERSPECTIVE

Early observations bearing on risks of Down's syndrome occurring or recurring were derived from erroneous opinions as to aetiology. For instance, parental syphilis (Sutherland, 1899), tuberculosis (Shuttleworth, 1906), and alcoholism (Cafferata, 1909) had their respective advocates as causes of the syndrome, and an explanation based on propositions of maternal exhaustion as a consequence of many pregnancies (Shuttleworth, 1909) also had its adherents. The last-mentioned of these notions, although invalid, may on occasion have prevented the birth of a Down's syndrome infant by discouraging late child-bearing.

The clear demonstration that maternal age, and not, by themselves, paternal age (Jenkins, 1933; Penrose, 1933) or parity (Penrose, 1934), was significantly correlated with the incidence of the syndrome provided the first rational basis for genetic counselling. It was now appropriate to collect empirical data on the incidence in different maternal age groups and to use these figures as an approximate guide to risks. These kinds of data are realistic for counselling purposes in the majority of cases (that is, where the occurrence of Down's syndrome is maternal age-dependent), but are misleading when maternal age-independent circumstances are operative.

With the recognition that Down's syndrome is directly connected with extra No. 21 chromosome material (Lejeune et al., 1959) and the subsequent detection of various anomalies in addition to standard trisomy involving this chromosome (for example, balanced and unbalanced translocations and mosaicism), many maternal age-independent cases of Down's syndrome could be accounted for and more precise risk figures for occurrence of the syndrome could be established. Improved techniques of chromosomal examination, notably banding procedures (Caspersson et al., 1971), added further sophistication to delineation of risks. Alongside these developments, a significant new component was added to the preventive armamentarium by establishing reliable methods of examining the foetal karyotype at about 16 weeks of gestation (Milunsky, 1973).

Genetic counselling in Down's syndrome thus hinges chiefly on two types of data (maternal age considerations and relevant chromosomal observations), and has taken on a distinctly practical connotation in the context of the capacity for prenatal diagnosis.

MATERNAL AGE–DEPENDENT DOWN'S SYNDROME

The most common circumstance leading to requests for genetic counselling in Down's syndrome is the previous birth of an affected child. If chromosomal examination is then undertaken, in the overwhelming majority of instances the child is found to have standard trisomy 21 while the parents have apparently normal karyotypes. Where this finding emerges, or when chromosomal data cannot be obtained for some reason, maternal age is the essential criterion on which risk estimates must be based.

The incidence of Down's syndrome among live births at different maternal ages has been determined empirically in a fair number of surveys. The results differ to some extent, but those from several studies of populations of European origin may be summarized as shown in Table 1 (Mikkelsen and Stene, 1970).

If parents who have not had a Down's syndrome child seek guidance about their risks, the figures in the table may be used as a first approximation. They can be quoted with greater confidence if the parents are known to have apparently normal karyotypes. After one affected child with standard trisomy 21 and seemingly normal parental chromosome constitutions, there is some uncertainty about recurrence risk. This risk has a distinct relationship to maternal age and is therefore not uniform. It could, however, often be of the order of one to two percent. There is no convincing evidence that parents with apparently normal chromosome appearances whose Down's syndrome child has

Table 1. Incidence of Down's syndrome at different maternal ages

Maternal age	Incidence per 1,000 live births
<30	< 1
30–34	1–2
35–39	2–5
40–44	5–10
>44	10–20

a (Dq21q) or (Gq21q) translocation have a different order of recurrence risk than such parents whose child has standard trisomy 21.

The one to two percent possibility of recurrence mentioned above is about ten times higher than the chance of a Down's syndrome child being born in the general population as a whole. However, it is still relatively low compared to many other circumstances in which genetic counselling is sought—for example, the 50% risk of an affected child if a parent carries the gene for an autosomal dominant disability, the 25% risk if the parents are heterozygotes for an autosomal recessive disorder, or even the approximately four to five percent recurrence risk for a neural tube defect.

MATERNAL AGE–INDEPENDENT DOWN'S SYNDROME

It has long been known that a proportion of cases of Down's syndrome occur for reasons essentially unconnected with maternal age. With the advent of chromosomal examination, an explanation for many, although not all, of these cases became possible. The parental chromosomal anomalies associated with an increased risk for Down's syndrome recently have been discussed in detail by Smith and Berg (1976) and the main considerations related to genetic counselling are summarized below.

Parental Balanced Translocations

Parental balanced translocations involving a No. 21 chromosome are an important basis for an elevated risk of having an affected child. These translocations are usually of the (Dq21q) or (Gq21q) type. They can be detected only by examination of the karyotype, since, in balanced form, they are not associated with recognizable phenotypic effects. With a parental balanced (Dq21q) translocation, live-born Down's syndrome children are less frequent than would be expected theoretically, and, for reasons which are uncertain, such children are produced more often by maternal than paternal carriers; empirical findings indicate that the risk is about 10% for carrier mothers and only about 2.5% for carrier fathers. With a parental balanced (Gq21q) translocation, prospects are different depending on whether the translocation is of the (22q21q) or (21q21q) type. If it is (22q21q), empirical risks for carrier mothers and carrier fathers are less well established but they may be fairly similar for each parent and in the neighbourhood of 10%; if it is (21q21q), the risk is the worst possible one, in that all live births would be expected to have Down's syndrome. The figures quoted apply to nonmosiac balanced translocation parents. If the carrier is mosaic with a normal cell line, risks would be lower, although to a variable and generally uncertain extent. Additional balanced translocations in parents, involving a No. 21 and a chromosome other than a D or G, have been described in association with Down's syndrome offspring, but each of these events has been too rare to delineate empirical risks accurately. The effect of still other balanced parental translocations not involving chromosome No. 21, for instance (DqDq), on the chances of producing a Down's syndrome infant is also not well defined, but, in general, the risk does not appear to be unduly increased in these circumstances.

Fully Affected or Mosaic Down's Syndrome Individuals

Fully affected or mosaic Down's syndrome individuals face very substantial risks that any children they may have will be affected as well. Half the offspring of 18 reported nonmosaic standard trisomy 21 mothers had Down's syndrome. The prospects would be poor also for fathers with such a karyotype. However, no such male is known to have fathered a child, so that concern is hypothetical rather than practical in these circumstances. On the other hand, males as well as females who are Down's syndrome mosaics have been parents of Down's syndrome children. Here, precise risks are difficult to determine accurately, because they would depend on the variable and uncertain chromosomal constitution of the germ cells. Another difficulty is that a parent with a seemingly normal karyotype, and hence a good prognosis for children, may be an unrecognized mosaic with a less favourable outlook.

Other Parental Chromosomal Anomalies

Other parental chromosomal anomalies may be connected with increased chances of having Down's syndrome children, but reasonably precise risk figures are difficult to compile because of the rarity of known relevant pregnancies. For example, individual parents with a 47,XXX, a 47,XYY and a 46,XX/47,XX,C+ karyotype have on occasion been reported to have had a Down's syndrome child, but the chances of this happening in such parents are unclear. Nor is it clear to what extent, if any, unrecognizable variations in parental chromosome morphology, or even visible ones such as satellite formation and secondary constrictions, increase the likelihood of nondisjunction.

Other Factors

Additional circumstances, not associated with detectable morphological changes in parental chromosomes, may be relevant in increasing risks for Down's syndrome. Genes and adverse environmental influences (such as viral infection and radiation) have been postulated as factors that might predispose to nondisjunction. However, no satisfactory data are available that enable realistic usage of such considerations in calculating or estimating risks for a given family.

PRENATAL DIAGNOSTIC AMNIOCENTESIS

It is becoming increasingly apparent that amniocentesis for purposes of foetal karyotyping is both reliable and safe for mother and foetus when undertaken in centres with appropriate provisions and experienced staff. If reliability and, in particular, safety could be assured almost invariably, there would seem to be no good reason, other than shortage of facilities, why the procedure should not be accessible to all pregnant women who might wish to avail themselves of it. Such a time may well come in the not too distant future. At present, however, it is generally the practice to restrict the test mainly to relatively high risk situations of the kinds considered above. The chief indications usually are:

1. *"Advanced" maternal age per se.* When no other indications are present, few recommend amniocentesis below the age of 35 years, some advocate it from that age onwards, and nearly all agree, in the absence of moral qualms, that it is appropriate at 40 years and beyond.
2. *Parental chromosomal anomalies.* There is general consensus that amniocentesis should be undertaken if one or other potential parent is a (Dq21q) or (Gq21q) translocation carrier or shows cytological evidence of complete or mosaic Down's syndrome. Risks with other morphological peculiarities of a No. 21 chromosome are less well defined but should be added to the list of indications if considered suspicious.
3. *Family history of Down's syndrome.* Most favour an amniocentesis if the parents have previously had a child with Down's syndrome, although, in the absence of other indications mentioned above, there is less agreement when more distant relatives are affected.

In view of the impressive evidence of safety and reliability of prenatal diagnostic amniocentesis for Down's syndrome, it seems entirely reasonable to interpret the listed indications liberally rather than restrictively. It is appropriate also to add to these what may be called a psychological indication; in other words, parental emotional stress and anxiety about having a Down's syndrome child could very well constitute suitable grounds for amniocentesis even in circumstances where risks are very low. It is perhaps hardly necessary to add that moral judgements on whether to proceed with amniocentesis, with the prospect of a subsequent termination of the pregnancy, must not be made by the counsellor but remain the unhindered prerogative of the parents.

SUMMARY AND CONCLUDING REMARKS

An increasing number of families are seeking advice and guidance in regard to chances of occurrence or recurrence of Down's syndrome and the interconnected question of prenatal diagnosis. As indicated above, the risks in particular circumstances range from less than 0.1% up to 100%. Fortunately, in the large majority of pregnancies, the prospects are favourable, with relatively few situations where the risk exceeds 1% and still rarer ones where it is greater than 10%. On the basis of family data, including maternal age, previous history of Down's syndrome and relevant chromosomal findings, the risk often can be calculated or estimated with reasonable accuracy.

Potential parents are, of course, entitled to expect a comprehensive discussion and appraisal of the nature of Down's syndrome, of the risks applicable to them, and of the related consideration of diagnostic amniocentesis. In general, these expectations are met for those attending genetic counselling centres, although all too many families who could benefit from such counselling do not receive it even in countries with well-developed medical and health-related programmes. It may be anticipated that a growing awareness of the usefulness and value of genetic services in the health care of the community will lead to a steady increase in availability and appropriate application of existing knowledge.

REFERENCES

Cafferata, J. F. (1909) Contribution à la littérature du mongolisme. Arch. Med. Enf. 12:929.

Caspersson, T., Lomakka, G., and Zech, J. (1971) The 24 fluorescent patterns of the human metaphase chromosomes—distinguishing characters and variability. Hereditas. 67:89.

Down, J. (1866) Observations on an ethnic classification of idiots. Clin. Lec. Rep., Lond. Hosp. 3:259.

Jenkins, R. L. (1933) Etiology of mongolism. Amer. J. Dis Child. 45:506.

Lejeune, J., Gautier, M., and Turpin, R. (1959) Les chromosomes humains en culture de tissus. C. R. Acad. Sci. 248:602.

Mikkelsen, M., and Stene, J. (1970) Genetic counselling in Down's syndrome. Hum. Hered. 20:457.

Milunsky, A. (1973) The Prenatal Diagnosis of Hereditary Disorders. Springfield, Ill.: Charles C Thomas.

Penrose, L. S. (1933) The relative effects of paternal and maternal age in mongolism. J. Genet. 27:219.

Penrose, L. S. (1934) A method of separating the relative aetiological effect of birth order and maternal age, with special reference to mongolian imbecility. Ann. Eugen. 6:108.

Shuttleworth, G. E. (1906) Comments on Langdon Down's paper. J. Ment. Sci. 52:189.

Shuttleworth, G. E. (1909) Mongolian imbecility. Brit. Med. J. 2:661.

Smith, G. F., and Berg, J. M. (1976) Down's Anomaly. 2nd edition. Edinburgh, London and New York: Churchill Livingstone.

Sutherland, G. A. (1899) Mongolian imbecility in infants. Practitioner. 63:632.

RESEARCH TO PRACTICE IN MENTAL RETARDATION
Biomedical Aspects, Volume III
Edited by Peter Mittler
Copyright 1977 I.A.S.S.M.D.

RECURRENCE RISK IN MENTAL RETARDATION

M.-L. E. Lubs, and J. A. Maes
Department of Pediatrics,
University of Colorado Medical Center,
4200 East 9th Avenue,
Denver, Colorado 80220, United States

Because the causes of mental retardation are so many and so varied, families with an affected child represent a particular challenge for the genetic counselor. Specific recurrence risks may be derived by separating those individuals with syndromes attributable to known genetic defects or environmental insults and establishing their recurrence risks. This can be accomplished by the aid of genetic formulas for segregation or through empirical data.

Although new entities are identified every year, the remaining group with mental retardation of unknown origin is still very large. This is the group most worrisome for the genetic counselor, who is well aware that within it are included cases with a recurrence risk of 25% or more, as well as cases with virtually zero risk, but who is unable to identify these cases. Therefore, one is left with an overall risk figure for the group of about 5%, which is based on empirically derived data.

PRESENTATION OF PUBLISHED DATA

Etiology of Mental Retardation

Since the risk estimates are more exact in those cases in which the diagnosis is known, genetic counseling becomes more precise as more syndromes are identified. However, one would also instinctively feel that over a period of time we would also change the risk estimates for the idiopathic group. In order to evaluate this, we have tried to assess the recurrence risk estimates over time. The recurrence risks are, of course, closely related to classifications of mental retardation. The etiologies of mental retardation, as determined in several studies over a 40-year period, are summarized in Table 1. The table shows that the estimate of genetically determined mental retardation has remained remarkably stable since the landmark study of Penrose in 1938, while the estimate of known "acquired" or "environmentally caused" mental retardation has proportionately

Table 1. Etiologies of mental retardation

Author	Year	Number of probands	Etiology (%)				
			Known genetic	Known environmental	Unknown	Other	Unknown and other
Penrose	1938	1,260	33.8	7.5	58.7		58.7
Yannet	1945	1,330	50.6	7.0	31.1	11.4 (cerebral palsy, epilepsy)	42.5
Berg and Kirman	1959	200	36	28	36		36
Pitt and Roboz	1965	728	48.6	18.5	24.7	8.1 (epilepsy)	32.8
McDonald	1973	507	44	24	32		35
Turner[a]	1975	1,000	45	32	22		22
Opitz	1977	1,449	38.1	13	16.1	32.9 (cerebral palsy, seizures, hypotonia)	49.0
Average		(Σ6,474)	42.5	15.6			41.8

[a]Excludes those with Down Syndrome.

increased. When one considers the medical advances during this time period, however, it is surprising that the changes in recurrence risks are so small. It should be noted that only moderate or severe forms of mental retardation are included in the table, the IQ of the cases in most of the studies being less than 50. The weighted, average proportion of retardation attributable to genetic causes in these studies was 42.5%.

If the etiology is known, the recurrence risk can usually be stated with greater accuracy. In the class with unknown etiology, however, the overall empirical recurrence risk figure will not uncommonly be quite erroneous for specific cases. For instance, if the disorder is caused by an undetected de novo chromosomal lesion, the recurrence risk would be virtually zero. On the other hand, it may be caused by a small, also undetected, translocation that is balanced in the parent and unbalanced in the child, or it could be caused by a rare recessive disorder. In both of the latter cases, the recurrence risk would be quite high. Therefore, it becomes important to subclassify this group in which the cause of the retardation is unknown in order to identify classes with different recurrence risks. Since the genetic component in mental retardation has long been known, many investigators have used the family history of retardation as one way of subclassifying the retarded. As shown in the next few tables, this subclassification can be made in several ways.

Risk When One or Both Parents are Retarded

There are two situations in particular that are common in the Genetics Clinic. The first is a couple in which one or both partners are borderline or mildly retarded and who have been referred for genetic counseling before they have any children. Studies that have investigated the risk for retarded couples with no previous retarded children are shown in Table 2. The results of the three studies

Table 2. Risk of having a retarded child when parents are retarded

| Author | Year | Retarded parents | | Total retarded parents | IQ of retarded parent | No. of offspring | Retarded offspring (%) |
		Father	Mother				
Brandon	1957	0	73	73	(mean 61.1, range 38–84)	109	9.2
Shaw and Wright	1960	120	122	242[a]	> 69 = 11% 50–69 = 76% < 50 = 13% mean 60	377	12.2
Scally	1968	32	310	342	not stated	669	10.8
Total		152	505	657		1155	11.1 (Avg.)

[a]These constituted 232 couples. In 10 couples, both partners were retarded.

are in close agreement. The pooled estimate of retardation in the offspring is 11.1%. In the largest of these three studies, the degree of mental retardation in the offspring was not stated, but, in the other two, the mean IQ was around 60.

Recurrence Risk After One Retarded Child

The second and most common situation is two normal parents who have had one retarded child and who want to know the recurrence risk. This risk has been estimated in several studies. The results of some of these are shown in Table 3. The estimates of the risk for mental retardation in a subsequent sibling are in close agreement. The average risk if the proband is moderately or more severely retarded in these seven studies was found to be around 6%.

In the two studies by Penrose in 1938 (see also Penrose, 1962) and Reed and Reed in 1965, the parents as well as the offspring were classified by degree of retardation. All parents had at least one affected child; however, the data are valid only for the second counseling situation, that of a couple with a retarded child. Table 4 summarizes the data from these studies. Although the investigations were 27 years apart, they show remarkably similar results. If the parents were both normal, the overall recurrence risk for a retarded child was found to be around 5% and the risk of having a child with an IQ of less than 85 was 10%. If one of the parents was retarded or both parents were borderline retarded, the recurrence risk for retardation rose to almost 20%, and for an IQ of less than 85 the risk was around 40%. Two retarded individuals who had already had a retarded child had a 40–45% risk for a subsequent child with an IQ of less than 70 and about a 2/3 risk of having a child with an IQ of less than 85.

Sex Differences in Mental Retardation

There is a predominance of males among the retarded. The greatest excess of males is found among the moderately retarded, among whom the sex ratio in different studies has varied between 1.2 and 1.6 (Pitt and Roboz, 1965; Reed and Reed, 1965; Angeli and Kirman, 1972; Bundey and Carter, 1974; Turner and Turner, 1974; Innes et al., 1968; Patients in Mental Institutions, 1964). X-linked recessive inheritance has been proposed to explain part of this sex difference (Turner and Turner, 1974; Lehrke, 1974; Turner et al., 1971; Davison, 1973), but there is also a predominance of males when other causes can be identified, such as prenatal infection or trauma (Patients in Mental Institutions, 1964). A lower threshold in males for polygenically determined mental retardation has been postulated. Turner et al., in 1971, evaluated the recurrence risks for siblings divided by the sex of the proband. A summary of the results of these studies is shown in Table 5. If the proband is a male with mild or moderate retardation, the recurrence risk is twice as high as it would be if he were severely retarded or if the proband were a female.

Table 3. Recurrence risk of mental retardation in sibs (proband has retardation of unknown cause)

| Author | Year | Number of probands | IQ of proband | | | Risk (%) IQ of sibs | | | |
			<50	50–69	Not specified	<50	50–69	Not specified	All retarded
Penrose[a]	1938, 1962	487	x			2.8	1.6		4.4
Pitt	1965	380			x			3.4	3.4
Reed & Reed[a]	1965	~120			x			5.7	5.7
Akesson	1961, 1967, 1968	122	x			5.1	3.4		8.5
Akesson	1961, 1967, 1968	85		x		1.5–4.8	5.2–16.1		13.9
Turner, Collins, Turner	1971	189	x					5.4	5.4
Turner, Collins, Turner	1971	740		x				5.8	5.8
Angeli and Kirman	1972	330			x	4.7	2.4		7.1
Bundey & Carter	1974	179	x			2.9	2.2		5.2

[a] Based on data where parents were known to be normal.

Table 4. Recurrence risk after one affected child

Author	Year	Mating	Number probands	Percent of matings	No. sibs	IQ in subsequent child		
						<85	<70	<50
Penrose	1938	N X N	807	68	3,135	9.6	4.1	2.2
Reed and Reed	1965				104		5.7	
Penrose	1938	N X R	309	25.9	1,229	39.1	17.1	5.4
Reed and Reed	1965				317		19.9	
Penrose	1938	R X R	78	6.5	216	64.4	44.0	13
Reed and Reed	1965				76		42.1	

Influence of Recent Research on the Recurrence Risks

Although no drastic changes in the recurrence risks for the group with unclassified mental retardation have occurred in the last decade, there are a number of new disorders that have been identified. In particular, the number of chromosomal syndromes has increased markedly as a result of new preferential staining techniques. An average of one new chromosomal syndrome was identified each year in the 1960s. After 1971, when the new techniques started to become available, the number identified each year increased rapidly, and in 1975 seventeen new syndromes were described. In those families in which a new syndrome has been identified, the recurrence risk figure quoted by the geneticist will be very different, higher or lower, than the estimate with no known diagnosis. Thus, the advances have benefited the individual families more than the remaining group of unclassified cases. Since the cost for chromosome studies is comparatively high, it becomes important to identify by clinical classification those individuals who have a higher probability of having a chromosomal syndrome. Table 6 shows the karyotype analysis in 191 pediatric patients evaluated for retardation at the JFK Center in Denver (Lubs and Lubs, unpublished data). The table shows that in the children who had mental retardation with no physical abnormalities, there were no chromosome abnormalities. Chromosome abnormalities were found most often in children who were retarded and had one or more additional problems, either major anomalies,

Table 5. Recurrence risk in the undiagnosed retarded

		Recurrence risk	
Degree of retardation in proband	Sex ratio in probands	Male proband	Female proband
Mild or Moderate ($N = 489$) (IQ 36–67)	1.5	9%	4%
Severe or Profound ($N = 367$) (IQ <36)	1.1	4%	4%

After Turner, Collins, and Turner, 1971.

Table 6. Summary of clinical and cytogenetic findings in 191 pediatric patients evaluated at the JFK Center in Denver

Clinical problem	Total estimated	Number with abnormal karyotype
Mental Retardation		
with no anomalies or seizures	40	0
with major anomalies with or without seizures	49	7 (14%)[a]
with multiple minor anomalies with or without seizures	19	1[a]
with seizure disorder	35	1[a]
atypical personality (autism)	15	0
chromosomal syndromes	11	11[b]
other syndromes	22	2[c]
Total patients	191	22

Lubs and Lubs, 1973, with unpublished data.

[a]Of these nine abnormalities, two were small duplications (involving 6q and Yq), three represented deletions (a ring 21, 9q-mosaic, and 18p-) and the remaining four were combined duplications and deficiencies (involving chromosomes 8, 10, 18p and 18q). Five of these cases have previously been published. All were small and somewhat complex abnormalities.

[b]Ten had Down's syndrome, one had 45,X (Turner's syndrome).

[c]Both had ataxia-telangiectasia.

multiple minor anomalies, or seizures. Children with autism or disorders caused by inborn errors of metabolism, or children with mental retardation as the only finding, generally had normal chromosomes.

Diagnostic Workup to Determine the Recurrence Risk

In the search for a diagnosis, therefore, the children with anomalies should have a chromosome analysis as well as a biochemical screen, and in children without anomalies or seizures biochemical screens may suffice. An attempt to summarize the diagnostic workup of a patient for purposes of obtaining a reasonable recurrence risk figure is presented in Figure 1. This chart can be used when no clear diagnosis has been established either clinically or by biochemical screening, when the parents are normal, and when no environmental cause is known. The recurrence risks for children with anomalies or seizures are generally lower than for children with "pure" mental retardation. The exceptions are the inherited structural rearrangements in which the recurrence risks generally are 10–30% when the ascertainment is made through an abnormal proband. It reaches 100% in the rare cases of 21/21 or 13/13 balanced translocation in the parent. It should be noted, however, that when the ascertainment is made from a balanced carrier, as can be done in a newborn survey, the risk for a child with an unbalanced translocation is much lower, probably less than 5%. The only exceptions are the Robertsonian translocations involving chromosomes 13 or 21.

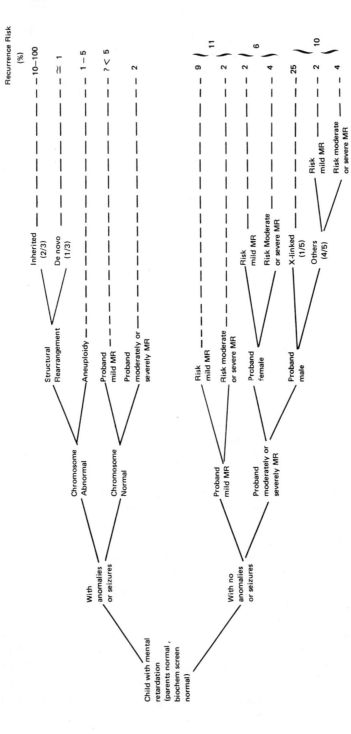

Figure 1. Subclassification of the retarded for genetic counseling purposes. MR = mental retardation.

For chromosomal aneuploidy, the recurrence risk is 1–2%, except for a woman 40 years old or older. If the child's chromosomes are normal, the recurrence risk after a retarded child with anomalies or seizures is 2–5%.

If the proband has mental retardation without any associated findings, it is more likely that he or she is simply at the low end of the normal IQ distribution. As a consequence, the risks for recurrence increase. If the proband of either sex is mildly retarded, the risk is around 10%. The proportion of the X-linked recessive cases included in the group of males with moderate retardation will make the overall recurrence risk higher if the proband is a male than if it is a female. If an X-linked pedigree can be obtained, the risk is 25%, but if the pedigree is uninformative or unknown, the recurrence risk is around 10% if the proband is a male, as opposed to about 5% if the proband is a female. If there are two moderately retarded children with a very similar degree of retardation, the recurrence risk for normal parents approaches 25%.

CONCLUSIONS

The purpose of this review was to obtain recurrence risk estimates for different subclasses of idiopathic mental retardation. Studies over the last three decades show very similar risk estimates for this group of retarded, even though a large number of syndromes have been identified and separated from it over the years. The benefit of improved laboratory methods as aids in diagnostic workup, therefore, has been to the families with newly identified syndromes rather than to the remaining group. The survey shows that, at least to some extent, it is possible to subclassify the idiopathic group and to obtain subgroups with more specific recurrence risks. Subclasses with low recurrence risks include those in which the proband has congenital anomalies or seizures in addition to the retardation.

In those circumstances, the risk is generally less than 5%. Comparatively higher risk estimates were found if the proband had "pure" mental retardation. Depending on the severity of retardation and the sex of the proband, the recurrence risks in these subclasses were found to be from 2–25%. A guide for subclassifying the retarded for the purpose of obtaining more accurate recurrence risks is presented.

SUMMARY

Improved recurrence risk estimates for mental retardation have been established for many families due to recent advances in cytogenetic and other diagnostic techniques. Even when no specific syndrome is diagnosed, further subclassification of retarded individuals on a clinical basis will lead to improved recurrence risk figures. Risk estimates for subclasses are discussed.

REFERENCES

Åkesson, H. O. (1961) Epidemiology and Genetics of Mental Deficiency in a Southern Swedish Population. Uppsala: Almqvist and Wiksell.

Åkesson, H. O. (1967) Severe mental deficiency in a population in western Sweden. Acta. Genet. Basel. 17:243.

Åkesson, H. O. (1968) Risk figures in mental deficiency. Proc. 1st Congr. IASSMD p. 19.

Angeli, E., and Kirman, B. H. (1972) Genetic counselling of the family of the mentally retarded child. Proc. 2nd Congr. IASSMD p. 692.

Berg, J. M., and Kirman, B. H. (1959) Some aetiological problems in mental deficiency. Brit. Med. J. 2:848.

Brandon, M. W. G. (1957) The intellectual and social status of children of mental defectives. J. Ment. Sci. 103:710, 725.

Bundey, S., and Carter, C. O. (1974) Recurrence risks in severe undiagnosed mental deficiency. J. Ment. Defic. Res. 18:115.

Davison, B. C. C. (1973) Familial idiopathic severe subnormality: the question of a contribution by X-linked genes. Genetic Studies in Mental Subnormality: Brit. J. Psychiat. Spec. Publ. No. 8.

Innes, G., Kidd, C., and Ross, H. S. (1968) Mental subnormality in North-East Scotland. Brit. J. Psychiat. 114:35.

Lehrke, R. G. (1974) X-linked Mental Retardation and Verbal Disability. Birth Defects Original Article Series, 10, No. 1. (Ed. Bergsma, D.) New York: Intercontinental Medical Books.

Lubs, H. A., and Lubs, M. L. (1973) New cytogenetic technic applied to a series of children with mental retardation. In Nobel Symposia XXIII, Medicine and Natural Sciences, Chromosome Identification Technique and Application in Biology and Medicine. (Eds. Caspersson, T., and Zech, L.) New York: Academic Press, p. 241.

McDonald, A. D. (1973) Severely retarded children in Quebec: prevalence, causes and care. Amer. J. Ment. Defic. 78:205.

Opitz, J. M. (1977) Diagnostic genetic studies in severe mental retardation. Genetic Counseling. (Eds. Lubs, H. A., and de la Cruz, F.) Washington: Raven Press, p. 417.

Patients in Mental Institutions (1964) Part I: Public Institutions for the Mentally Retarded, Bulletin 1452. US Public Health Service, National Institute of Mental Health, 1966.

Penrose, L. S. (1938) A Clinical and Genetic Study of 1,280 Cases of Mental Defect. (Colchester Survey) M.R.C. Spec. Rep. Ser No. 229. London: HMSO.

Penrose, L. S. (1962) The Biology of Mental Defect. 2nd ed. New York: Grune & Stratton.

Pitt, D. (1965) Recurrence risks in mental deficiency. Med. J. Austr. 2:184.

Pitt, D., and Roboz, P. (1965) A survey of 782 cases of mental deficiency. J. Ment. Defic. Res. 9:4.

Reed, E. W., and Reed, S. C. (1965) Mental Retardation: A Family Study. Philadelphia: W. B. Saunders.

Scally, B. G. (1968) The offspring of mental defectives. Proc. 1st Congr. IASSMD, p. 246.

Shaw, C. H., and Wright, C. H. (1960) The married mental defective. Lancet 1:273.

Turner, G. (1975) An aetiological study of 1,000 patients with an IQ assessment below 51. Med. J. Austr. 2:927.

Turner, G., Collins, E., and Turner, B. (1971) Recurrence risk of mental retardation in sibs. Med. J. Austr. 1:1165.

Turner, G., and Turner, B. (1974) X-linked mental retardation. J. Med. Genet. 11:109.

Turner, G., Turner, B., and Collins, E. (1971) X-linked mental retardation without physical abnormality: Renpennings syndrome. Develop. Med. Child Neurol. 13:71.

Yannet, H. (1945) Diagnostic classification of patients with mental deficiency. Amer. J. Dis. Child. 70:83.

RESEARCH TO PRACTICE IN MENTAL RETARDATION
Biomedical Aspects, Volume III
Edited by Peter Mittler
Copyright 1977 I.A.S.S.M.D.

APPROACHES TO THE THERAPY OF GENETIC DISEASES

A. Dorfman
Department of Pediatrics and the
Joseph P. Kennedy, Jr., Mental Retardation Research Center,
Pritzker School of Medicine,
University of Chicago,
Chicago, Illinois 60637, United States

During the past 25 years, the great progress in biochemical genetics and cell biology has resulted in a marked increase in the understanding of many types of human diseases. In no group has this been more true than in genetic diseases. As mechanisms of metabolic aberrations have become increasingly clear, genetic diseases can be classified in ways that may be useful for planning strategies of therapy. This chapter analyzes such a classification and summarizes approaches to therapy that may result from such an analysis.

Until recently our knowledge of mechanisms of disease stemming from genetic variation was largely restricted to those mechanisms that followed the Garrodian pattern. In such cases, a mutation causes a replacement of an amino acid in a protein that has an enzymic function. If the amino acid substitution results in diminished enzymic activity, a metabolic aberration ensues. Such a mechanism may be illustrated by the following series of reactions:

$$A \xrightarrow{\ E_1\ } B \xrightarrow{\ E_2\ } C \xrightarrow{\ E_3\ } D \xrightarrow{\ E_4\ } E$$

When a pathway for conversion of A to E exists, a mutation resulting in decreased activity of any enzyme in the series may cause the following sequelae:

1. If E is an essential metabolite, unavailable from another source, e.g., an alternate pathway or diet, such a mutation would be lethal. However, if the block is incomplete, with sufficient E to sustain life, a disease may be produced that is treatable by the administration of substance E. Such a mechanism appears to obtain in orotic aciduria.
2. If product E is available in the diet, as is tyrosine in phenylketonuria, absence of the end product produces no disease. However, if precursors such as A, B, C, or D (or some product derived from them), are toxic in increased

187

concentrations, disease may result from the accumulated precursor substances that result from enzymic deficiency. Such a mechanism is thought to be responsible for phenylketonuria. The symptoms of mental deficiency in untreated patients are caused by elevated levels of phenylalanine (or some product derived therefrom).

Diseases of this type have already been successfully treated. In the case of galactosemia, the elimination of galactose from the diet represents a highly specific and successful method of treatment. Control of phenylketonuria is more complex because phenylalanine is an essential amino acid.

3. Another mechanism, which is the consequence of a structural change of an enzyme, depends on the altered synthesis or coenzyme binding required for enzymic activity. Diseases produced by this mechanism may be treated by administration of large doses of the requisite cofactor. The increased concentration of cofactor may restore full enzyme activity and overcome the metabolic aberration responsible for disease. Examples of this type are Vitamin B_6 dependency or methylmalonic aciduria.

Genetic diseases caused by lack of, or altered production of, factors other than enzymes involved in various essential physiological functions have been known for some time. An example of this type of genetic disease is hemophilia. Therapy in such cases is most likely to be accomplished by replacement of the absent product.

The series of reactions depicted above has been considered from the point of view of synthesis of substances required for anabolism. A similar series of reactions may be written for the degradation of structural macromolecules (catabolic reactions). Genetic diseases have now been identified that are characterized by diminished activity of almost every known hydrolase concerned with degradation of glycosaminoglycans, glycosphingolipids, glycoproteins, and glycogen. In general, the involved enzymes are characterized by an acid pH optimum and localization in lysosomes. Diminution in the activity of any of the enzymes involved in the catabolic pathways causes an accumulation of partially degraded macromolecules within the lysosomes. Characteristic of such diseases is distortion of many types of cells, such as liver, spleen, bone, glia, and neurones. In those disorders, such as most of the mucopolysaccharidoses and glycosphingolipidoses in which the nervous system elements are affected, mental retardation, usually progressive in nature, is a consequence. Examples of lysosomal storage diseases are Tay-Sachs, Hurler's, Hunter's, G_{M1}-gangliosidosis, and Type II glycogen storage diseases.

With the rapid elucidation of the enzymic basis of many storage diseases, heterozygote determination and prenatal diagnosis have all become possible. Whereas these procedures contribute considerably to the control of lysosomal disease, treatment represents an unmet challenge.

For many years, no treatment of such storage diseases seemed possible, but in recent years a ray of hope has resulted from research. It was generally accepted that cells are largely impervious to enzymes of the extracellular fluid. Recent studies, particularly those of Ashwell and coworkers and Neufeld and coworkers, indicate that glycoproteins are recognized by cell surface receptors and are selectively taken up by the process of pinocytosis. The pinocytotic vacuoles fuse with primary lysosomes to form secondary lysosomes that contain enzyme and substrate. The accumulated partially degraded macromolecules may then be degraded by the administered enzyme. Such experimental studies have suggested that purified enzymes may be utilized for the treatment of storage diseases. A wide variety of techniques are being investigated to stabilize enzymes in the circulation as well as to direct them to the appropriate tissues. Some success in direct enzyme replacement has been claimed by Brady and coworkers in the treatment of Gaucher and Fabry's disease. However, it is premature to convey a great sense of optimism regarding this mode of therapy.

Although enzyme replacement therapy at this time appears to be possible, important theoretical and practical problems remain unsolved. A large number of the storage diseases, such as the mucopolysaccharidoses and glycosphingo-lipidoses, result from accumulation of incompletely degraded material in the central nervous system. There is considerable question whether or not administered enzymes (or those produced by grafted tissues) will pass the blood-brain barrier. Additionally, in certain storage diseases, there is evidence that abnormal storage occurs before birth. Finally, there is no information regarding cost of preparation of pure enzymes, length of effects, and reversibility of pathological processes. That further research is needed for a decision regarding the practicability of enzyme therapy is clear.

Transplantation has also been suggested as a mode of therapy of storage diseases. Kidney transplantation has been reported to result in improvement in Fabry's disease, although it is not clear whether or not the apparent clinical improvement was merely due to improved renal function. Recently, transplantation of skin in Hunter's disease has been reported to produce chemical alterations. Similarly, transfusion of leukocytes has been employed in Hurler's and Sanfilippo B disease with no striking clinical improvement.

Recent studies in molecular biology indicate that the processes of maintaining the fidelity of the DNA code in any individual or species are considerably more intricate than previously supposed. Among these complex mechanisms are enzymic processes that repair damage to DNA resulting from ultraviolet radiation. A number of genetic diseases, the various types of xeroderma pigmentosum (including the DeSanctis-Cacchione syndrome, which is characterized by mental retardation), result from defects in these repair mechanisms. Although rapid progress is being made in unravelling the mechanisms of these diseases, no direct approach to therapy is yet available.

Space does not permit the elaboration of the large number of mechanisms responsible for the myriad human diseases of hemoglobin structure and synthesis. Hemoglobin may be considered as a structural protein of red cells, but it carries out a unique carrier function. For the most ubiquitous of hemoglobin abnormalities, Hgb S in sickle cell anemia, the amino acid replacement results in structural change, which is the root of the pathology of the disease. Although many therapeutic modalities are employed to alleviate certain manifestations of the disease, no treatment is available that alters the physical-chemical properties of the abnormal hemoglobin in such a way as to result in a molecule that behaves like hemoglobin A. Many attempts to achieve this purpose are now underway.

A more general approach to the treatment of genetic disease has been usually termed "genetic engineering." This term has been widely used in the lay press to describe a wide variety of procedures, including such futuristic horrors as cloning and test tube babies. A more closely defined type of genetic engineering involves the possibility of producing, in the laboratory, human genes that may be converted to an appropriate form for treatment of human disease. Whereas discussion of such possibilities was in the realm of science fiction only a few years ago, technology is now advancing so rapidly that the possibility of gene therapy seems realistic.

Many questions have been raised concerning the validity of genetic engineering. Criticism of current studies has stemmed from concern about the safety of experimentation leading to the development of such procedures, and their safe clinical application. A great deal of concern is caused by the use of *E. coli* in current experiments. As a result of extensive deliberations, guidelines for such experimentation have recently been issued by the National Institutes of Health. A more general concern has been that genetic manipulation, although originally developed for treatment of human illness, may be employed to alter the genetic characteristics of the race or of particular individuals. Clearly, advances in genetics have introduced new problems, ethical, legal, and moral, into medical research.

RESEARCH TO PRACTICE IN MENTAL RETARDATION
Biomedical Aspects, Volume III
Edited by Peter Mittler
Copyright 1977 I.A.S.S.M.D.

PREMATURE INFANT REFOCUS

K. Barnard, W. Wenner, B. Weber, C. Gray, and A. Peterson
Child Development and Mental Retardation Center,
University of Washington,
Seattle, Washington 98195, United States

The care of the infant born prematurely has been a matter of significant medical and health care concern. Increasing efforts have been made to create the technology to support and improve the outcome of the premature infant. There has been a long-standing concern about the impact of the typical early environment of the premature infant, i.e., the hospital incubator. First concerns raised in the perinatal literature were related to the amount of noise produced by the motor that circulates air in the incubator. More recent concerns have focused on the inappropriateness of the stimuli available to the infant.

It is in the area of environmental support to the premature infant's developmental progress that this study focuses its major efforts. The specific concern addressed by the research presented in this chapter is the absence of a temporal patterning of stimulation that would support the organization and integration of behavior for the premature infant born prior to 34 weeks of gestational age.

The control of behavior, particularly sleep-wake, before 35 weeks of gestational age, is problematic for the young infant because central nervous system control, which allows the organization of distinct quiet and active sleep states and the periodicity of state patterns, cannot be controlled intrinsically because of the lack of development; hence, there is a need for extrinsic support. In utero, it is believed that the mother's pattern of inactivity-activity and sleep provides the kind of organizing and temporal feedback that the baby uses to organize periods of inactivity and activity. The incubator environment as it exists today provides for constant sources of stimulation with regard to light, sound, and temperature. Other stimuli to which the infant is exposed have mainly an irregular occurrence in terms of caregiving and the baby's own activity pattern.

Studies of newborn attention to varieties of stimulus targets suggest the human neonate is differentially responsive, both behaviorally and physiologi-

This project is supported by the Maternal and Child Health and Crippled Children Services, Health Service and Mental Health Administration, Public Health Service, Department of Health, Education and Welfare, Grant MC-R-530348-02-0.

cally, to stimulus patterning soon after birth (Fantz, 1963, 1965; Korner, 1970; Eisenberg, 1969; Brazelton, 1973). The infant's alertness to a variety of stimulation modalities has implications for how the infant will begin processing information about the environment as well as how he will be received by his parents. The task of the infant after birth is to develop neuronal organizations of these behaviors that will respond appropriately to the environment. The more immature infant at birth has greater difficulty developing these early organizations. One of the earliest forms of learning, demonstrable in the neonate and a basic attribute of attention, is the ability to decrease responsiveness with repeated stimulation. An important mediator of infant behavior is the infant's ongoing state and environment, which remain crucial variables in assessing infant behavior (Prechtl, 1964).

The incubator in which the premature infant is kept in controlled temperature and in which he is provided oxygen is very different from the intrauterine condition. The intrauterine world is rich in tactile, auditory, proprioceptive, and kinesthetic stimuli. In addition, this environment provides stimulation on a constant predictable schedule. There are periods of the day when the mother's activity is greater than at others, and maternal vital organs provide sounds, such as the heartbeat, on a constant, recurring, temporal pattern. In contrast, the premature infant is placed in an incubator where certain sounds, light, temperature, and humidity, remain constant and others are present irregularly. Particularly for the most immature babies, there is an irregular and virtual bombardment of stimulation in their being handled and treated. There is also an irregularity brought on by the baby's own irregular activity.

DESCRIPTION OF STIMULATION EXPERIMENT

How do these differences in extrauterine living influence the immature infant? We are not sure. But we do know from a study done by Barnard (1974) that premature infants who had a program of regular recurring stimulation (rocking and heartbeat) based on a temporal sequence, occurring every hour for 15 minutes, during their thirty-third through thirty-fifth weeks of conceptual age, developed more quiet sleep during the immediate neonatal period and had better weight gain compared to a control group. A follow-up study one and one-half years later showed more positive development in the experimental group (Barnard 1976a).

PREMATURE REFOCUS STUDY

In a current study (Barnard et al., 1976) at the University of Washington, Seattle, we are testing two temporal patterns of stimulation to support the organization and integration of behavior for the premature infant.

Treatment 1 is an exact replication of the prior study, using the rocking motion and heatbeat sound, which turns on automatically according to a predetermined schedule. Stimuli are offered on a schedule of 15 minutes every hour to coincide with the usual duration of quiet sleep and with the length of the active-quiet-active cycle duration in the term infant.

Treatment 2 is a modification of Treatment 1, in which the infant's existing neurological state organization activates the system. In this treatment group, the infant turns on the stimuli of rocking and heartbeat when he has a minute and a half of no motor activity. To accomplish this self-activated stimulation program the infant is placed on a motion-sensitizing mattress and monitor. The mattress produces a pneumatic signal generated by changes in volume of the mattress caused by the infant's movement. These pressure changes are then transmitted to a monitoring unit where pressure transducers convert the pneumatic input into an electrical signal that is then processed to control the time and the duration of the rocking bed and heart-beat program. Thus, the infant, who by our 1.5-minute criteria of inactivity seems to be in a quiet sleep state, is provided soothing stimuli to which he has learned not to attend, while at the same time he is prevented from arousal from this quiet sleep state.

The third group of infants are control subjects. They receive the regular program of nursing and medical care in the neonatal intensive care unit. The length of the stimulation in Treatment 1 or Treatment 2 is variable in accordance with our philosophy that the need for stimulation on a temporal basis to organize sleep behavior is concurrent with the infant's inability to maintain physiological homeostasis as demonstrated in such adaptive behavior as temperature control. Therefore, the treatment is discontinued when the infant is transferred to a crib. There is a minimum of eight days of treatment for all subjects.

Sample Selection

All infants eligible are admitted into the study as soon after birth as possible, and not later than two weeks after birth. Table 1 lists the selection criteria. The study uses a random block design for assigning subjects to treatment groups.

Table 1. Criteria for accepting subjects and blocking variables

---

1. Acceptance criteria
    A. Gestational age of 33.9 weeks or less as determined from reliable maternal history and Dubowitz method (1970) of scoring
    B. No evidence of central nervous system dysfunction, Down's syndrome, late pregnancy maternal drug addiction
    C. Consent of medical staff and parents
2. Blocking variables
    A. Gestational age
       Four groups equally dividing the infants into younger and older from 33.9 weeks and below
    B. Health states as high or low, determined on admission to the study by the Infant Perinatal Factor Score
       Criteria developed by Parmelee and Littman (1974)
    C. Previous caregiving of the parents: none or some

Admission to the study began in October 1975 and is expected to continue through at least August 1977. From past admission records, we had anticipated approximately eight subjects per month to meet our criteria; this assumption has not held. While the census in the University Hospital Neonatal Intensive Care Unit for infants < 33.9 weeks averages 17 infants per month, the available study population is greatly reduced by morbidity and mortality factors. The neonatologists have been supportive and almost all parents approached have agreed to have their infant in the study. As of July 1976, we had studied 32 infants.

Because of our random blocking procedure, it is too early to have any data relative to the basic hypothesis. A general statement of our experimental questions is summarized as follows. Providing regulation of sensory input to the premature infant will facilitate:

1. organization of sleep behavior
2. responses to sensory stimuli
3. ability to initiate, sustain, and elicit interactive behavior with his parent(s).

DEPENDENT MEASURES

While we have no data at this time relative to the basic hypothesis, we have a wealth of experience in selecting and developing appropriate dependent measures. It is not possible to discuss all measures used, but they are listed and referenced in Table 2. For purposes of this chapter two measures will be described: 1) the measure of sleep-wake activity, and 2) newborn behavioral responsiveness.

Considerable effort has been put into developing a measure of infant state organization, since it is both clinically important and directly related to the stimulation program. We were interested in being able to describe the frequency and duration of sleep and wakeful states (quiet, active, indeterminant sleep, awake states) as well as the presence of a sleep cycle and a circadian rhythm. Likewise, we were concerned about selecting a technique that could be used over a 24-hour period and did not require attachment of electrode discs.

The work of Sostek and Anders (1975) using time-lapse video recording to describe state of the term infant was our starting point. We have now developed a system of recording and coding premature infant activity with the use of a time-lapse video recorder that records at a time reduction of 13:1. A metal frame was designed that holds the recorder, positions the camera, and fits over and around the isolette frame, with little inconvenience to the hospital staff.

The camera is focused on the baby to allow the best view of the infant's eyes and extremities. A small nine-inch monitor gives the ongoing camera view so that staff can reposition the baby for optimal recording periodically and after intervention. We tape one 24-hour period of behavior prior to the start of treatment, one 4, 8, and 12 days after starting, one at 34 weeks of conceptual age, and one after the baby has graduated to the crib for at least 24 hours. The

Table 2. Description of dependent measures

1. Sleep-wake activity
   A. Time-lapse video recording of infant's behavior activity for 24-hour
      periods on all subjects
   B. Polygraphic sleep recording during an intrafeed interval on
      approximately 1/10 of sample population
   C. Seven-day record mother keeps of sleep-wake activity at one month post
      discharge and four and eight months post birth (Barnard, 1976b)
2. Neurological, motor and mental development
   A. Brazelton Neonatal Assessment, Premature adaptation at 34 weeks
      conceptual age, prior to discharge, and one month post hospital
      discharge
   B. Assessment of muscle tone, reflexes, state during hospital period using
      adaptation of the following schemas: St. Anne Dargassies (1969),
      Prechtl and Beintema (1964), Wenner (1975)
   C. Brain stem evolved responses to auditory stimuli at four months post
      birth (Salamy et al., 1975; Schulman-Galambos, 1975; Weber, 1976)
   D. Bayley Scales of Mental, Motor and Behavioral Development at eight
      months post birth (Bayley, 1969)
3. Parent-Infant interaction
   A. Observation and rating of interaction during a teaching and feeding
      session at four and eight months post birth (Barnard et al., 1976)
   B. Video-taping and coding of newborn, four and eight month play
      parent-infant interaction (Kogan, 1975)
   C. Interviews with parents (Gray and Williams, 1975)

resulting two hours of tape for each 24-hour period are coded every 4.6 seconds
of tape time, which equals one minute of real time. Therefore, in a 24-hour
period we have 1,440 data points, each of which describes the infant's motor
and eye movement. In addition to those behaviors, we have data about when the
infant received stimulation and was attended.

We have been doing concurrent validation studies with standard polygraphic
sleep recording during an interfeed period on a small number of subjects. While
we feel confident the data are not directly comparable with the standard sleep
scoring criteria, we are using these comparisons to develop rules for computer
scoring of the behavioral data to provide the most meaningful analysis of the
codes.

In coding the data, we have been intrigued with what seems to be almost no
state-contingent caregiving of the premature infant. This is in contrast to the
term infant, who is generally attended following a natural build-up of activity.
We are now analyzing the attending behaviors in relation to infant activity on
ten control subjects. If this pattern of noncontingent caregiving holds, it provides additional support concerning the inappropriateness of the temporal patterning of the premature infant's environment.

Another measure we have adapted is the Brazelton Newborn Behavioral
Assessment Scale. In general, we adhere to the protocol of administration and

scoring described in the Brazelton Manual (1973). At times, however, modifications in administration procedures and supplementary scores are necessary. We do not recommend that the Brazelton exam be used on infants below 34 weeks of conceptual age because the degree of handling that is necessary seems to disorganize the more immature infant, as evidenced by cardiovascular responses and their difficulty in not attending to the stimulation once they come to an alert state. It appears they have not developed the capacity to shut out stimuli. The supplementary scores that we used describe the variability of the premature infant's response, differences in self-organization, energy level, and control over

Table 3. Alertness supplementary score for Brazelton item 10 (alertness)[a]

A. Alertness summary score: examiner effort needed to elicit responsivity
    A. Despite constant manipulation the examiner is unable to elicit alerting.
    B. Examiner needed to continuously manipulate the baby to elicit alerting.
    C. Examiner needed to manipulate baby several times to elicit alerting.
    D. Examiner needed to manipulate baby only a few times to elicit alerting.
2. Baby's ability to alert
    A. Baby unable to alert, spontaneously or with manipulation.
    B. Baby demonstrated brief attention to stimuli; little if any other attempts to orient.
    C. Baby spontaneously alert at times; baby vacillates between states 3 and 4.
    D. Baby spontaneously alert and baby participates with ease.
3. Quality of alertness
    A. No response.
    B. Eyes wander and move generally independently of each other.
    C. Infant briefly alerts and orients with directional quality changes in stimuli. Infant's respirations may become labored. Infant looks fatigued though interested in stimuli.
    D. Infant may be spontaneously alert but response to stimuli is latent; infant turns to auditory stimuli after prolonged presentation of stimuli; delays in pursuit of visual stimuli.
    E. Spontaneously alert. Responsive and able to modulate orientation to stimuli.
    F. Spontaneously alert but responsivity is obligatory. Infant unable to modulate responsiveness.
    G. Spontaneously alert but infant has difficulty responding to stimulation with motor and visual pursuit. Infant mirror gazes.
4. Discrepancy of behavior to animate and inanimate stimuli
    A. Response to inanimate stimuli better than to animate stimuli.
    B. Response to animate stimuli better than to inanimate stimuli.
    C. Response to both animate and inanimate are qualitatively about the same.
5. Discrepancy of behavior to visual and auditory stimuli
    A. Response to visual stimuli better than to auditory stimuli.
    B. Response to auditory stimuli better than to visual stimuli.
    C. Response to both auditory and visual are qualitatively about the same.

[a]Developed in consultation with Dr. T. B. Brazelton, September, 1974–March, 1976.

environmental input. The premature infant will often maintain low states of consciousness throughout the examination. His response decrement is less well-defined and he has difficulty in arousing. Table 3 gives an example of the supplementary scores we have developed and use in addition to the Manual's nine-point scale for item 10 (Alertness) (Kang, 1976).

We have been interested in the finding on our repeat Brazelton exam that some infants are much more irritable and harder to alert at one month after hospital discharge than during the previous two examinations done before discharge. To us this observation has important implications for the infant-care-giver interaction.

Briefly, an introduction to the Premature Refocus Project has given the overall research plan and described two important measures: 1) sleep-wake activity, and 2) behavioral responsiveness. This research will provide important information about a crucial ecological question. How does the early environment of the infant with an immature central nervous system influence later neurological and behavioral development? While a few recent studies of premature infants would suggest a positive outcome, data such as that reported in 1975 by the State of Texas Office of Early Childhood Development emphasize the need for more systematic studies of infants born prematurely. Their findings were from a survey of all 6-year-old children. They found, in comparing those children whose birth weight was under 2,500 grams at birth with those of average birth weight, that the incidence of motor delay in the former group was 51%, compared to 5% in the term group on the Denver Development Screening Test. Likewise, twice as many were delayed on the language section. We are addressing what we judge to be a meaningful search to see how postnatal factors may contribute to that discrepancy in development.

SUMMARY

It is our position that improvement in the prognostic picture of the premature infant will come about by increased attention and study of the interaction between the infant and his postnatal environment. While we have had significant and worthwhile focus on the infant's basic physiological homeostasis in the past, we have not practiced the same rigor in research or in clinical practices related to the developing central nervous system's need for appropriate stimulation. The early period, when neuronal organizations are developing, is a sensitive and important period that demands a *refocusing* of our attention to the needs of emerging development. The study of temporal patterning cited in this chapter is indeed an example of the needed emphasis.

REFERENCES

Barnard, K. (1974) The effect of stimulation on the sleep behavior of the premature infant. Communicating Nursing Research. 6.

Barnard, K. (1976a) A program of stimulation for infants born prematurely. ERIC Document Reproduction Service, Arlington, Virginia, RD 112544.

Barnard, K. (1976b) The state of the art: nursing and early intervention with handicapped infants. *In* Intervention Strategies for High Risk Infants and Young Children. (Ed. Tjossem, T. D.) Baltimore: University Park Press.

Barnard, K., Wenner, W., Weber, B., Gray, C., and Peterson, A. (1976) Progress Report Premature Infant Refocus Project. University of Washington, unpublished manuscript.

Bayley, N. (1969) Bayley Scales of Infant Development. New York: The Psychological Corporation.

Brazelton, T. B. (1973) Neonatal Behavioral Assessment Scale. London: Spastics International Medical Publications.

Dubowitz, L. M. S., Dubowitz, V., and Goldberg, C. (1970) Clinical assessment of gestational age in the newborn infant. J. Pediatr. 77:1.

Eisenberg, R. B. (1969) Auditory behavior in the human neonate: functional properties of sound and their ontogenetic implications. International Audiology 8:34.

Fantz, R. L. (1963) Pattern vision in newborn infants. Science 140:296.

Fantz, R. L. (1965) Visual perception from birth as shown by pattern selectivity. Ann. N.Y. Acad. Sci. 118:793.

Gray, C., and Williams, K. (1975, 1976) Premature Infant Refocus Grant Proposal and Progress Report. University of Washington, unpublished manuscript.

Kang, R. (1976) Adapted form of Brazelton Neonatal Assessment Scale for Prematures. University of Washington, unpublished manuscript.

Kogan, K. L., and Gordon, B. (1975) Interpersonal behavior constructs: a revised approach to defining dyadic interaction styles. Psychological Reports 36:24.

Korner, A. F. (1970) Visual alertness in neonates: individual differences and their correlates. Percept. Mot. Skills. 31:499.

Parmelee, A., and Littman, B. (1974) Perinatal Factor Scores. University of California at Los Angeles Medical School, Dept. of Pediatrics, unpublished manuscript.

Prechtl, H., and Beintema, B. (1964) The Neurological Examination of the Full Term Newborn Infant. Spastics International Medical Publications.

Sainte-Anne Dargassies, S. (1969) Neurological maturation of the premature infant of 28–41 weeks gestational age. *In* Human Development (Ed. Falkner, F.) Philadelphia: W. B. Saunders.

Salamy, A., McKean, C. M., and Buda, F. B. (1975) Maturational changes in auditory transmission as reflected in human brainstem potentials. Brain Res. 96:361.

Schulman-Galambos, C., and Galambos, R. (1975) Brainstem auditory evoked responses in premature infants. J. Speech Hear. Res. 18:456.

Sostek, A. M., and Anders, T. F. (1975) Effect of varying laboratory conditions on behavioral-state organization in two- and eight-week-old infant. Child Dev. 46:871.

Weber, B. (1975, 1976) Premature Infant Refocus Grant Proposal and Progress Report. University of Washington, unpublished manuscript.

Wenner, W. (1975) Premature Infant Refocus Proposal. University of Washington, unpublished manuscript.

RESEARCH TO PRACTICE IN MENTAL RETARDATION
Biomedical Aspects, Volume III
Edited by Peter Mittler
Copyright 1977 I.A.S.S.M.D.

OVERVIEW OF PSYCHOPHARMACOLOGY FOR THE RETARDED IN THE UNITED STATES

R. L. Sprague
Institute for Child Behavior and Development,
University of Illinois,
Champaign, Illinois 61820, United States

A psychotropic drug is a medicine prescribed by a physician that has a primary effect of altering the person's behavior, mood, or thought processes. A primary question, often asked, is how frequently are psychotropic drugs used with the mentally retarded. Although this is a simple question, it is rather difficult to answer. First, one must define the population of the mentally retarded that is under consideration. There is information available about the frequency of usage of psychotropic drugs with the institutionalized mentally retarded, but almost no information about the use of such drugs with the mentally retarded in the community and in special education classes (Sprague and Gadow, 1977).

About ten years ago, Lipman (1967, 1970) sent a questionnaire concerning the use of psychotropic drugs to every public institution for the mentally retarded in the United States. Approximately 60% of the institutions returned useable data for his survey. The results of his survey were very revealing in at least two aspects. First, the frequency of usage of these medications was quite high; in fact, 51.1% of the institutionalized population received such medication. Second, high doses were used often, even exceeding the recommendations of the manufacturer. Instances of 3,000 mg/day for chlorpromazine and 1,800 mg/day for thioridazine were reported.

In a study less than two years old, DiMascio (1975) surveyed the use of psychotropic drugs in two institutions in Massachusetts, one facility housing 2,132 patients and the other facility housing 878 patients. In the large facility, 26% of the patients were receiving psychotropic drugs, whereas 53% were receiving psychotropic drugs in the smaller facility where the more severely disturbed patients were located. Anticonvulsant drugs also were used extensively (diphenylhydantoin 68% and phenobarbital 85% in the small institution, and 14% and 20%, respectively, in the large institution).

Table 1. Demographic data from large midwestern institution (*N* = 1,638)

Population	Drug *N* = 1100 (67.2%)	No Drug *N* = 538 (32.8%)
Mean age	27.4 years	29.6 years
Mean length of time at institution	16.4 years	18.9 years
Mean IQ	18.3	20.6
Sex: male	682 (62.0%)	386 (71.7%)
female	418 (38.0%)	152 (27.3%)

In regard to dosage, DiMascio classified 400 mg/day as a high dosage for both thioridazine and chlorpromazine and found that 7% of the patients were receiving dosages as high or higher. He classified 600 mg/day for diphenyl-hydantoin and 150 mg/day for phenobarbital as high dosages and found 43% of the patients received high doses of phenobarbital and 16% high doses of diphenylhydantoin.

In 1976 our laboratory was able to complete a drug survey of the total population of two institutions in the midwest: one was a large, older institution containing 1,638 patients and the other was a new, small institution with 286 patients. The demographic characteristics of the patients are shown in Tables 1 and 2.

Table 3 lists the most commonly used drugs by rank order for the two institutions. It should be noted that the rank order of the medication is almost the same for the two institutions in spite of major differences in facility size, newness, program, etc. In general, the mean doses are relatively high for most of the drugs, and the ranges, particularly the upper end of the dose range, are extremely high for the large institution. Lipman found that approximately 22% of the patients were receiving psychotropic drugs indefinitely, i.e., the patients who were placed on medication were given it for an indefinite or a very long period of time. Fortunately, the tendency for very long prescription periods seems to have changed somewhat in the last ten years. In our survey of the large institution, thioridazine had been given for an average of almost three years, diphenylhydantoin for an average of approximately four years, phenobarbital for somewhat over three years, chlorpromazine for about two years, and diazepam for about two years.

Table 2. Demographic data from small midwestern institution (*N* = 286)

Population	Drug *N* = 187 (65.4%)	No Drug *N* = 99 (34.6%)
Mean age	28.8 years	30.6 years
Mean length of time at institution	1.2 years	1.1 years
Mean IQ	38.4	35.7
Sex: male	113 (60.4%)	64 (64.6%)
female	74 (39.6%)	35 (35.4%)

Table 3. Drug survey results from large midwestern institution (N = 1100)

Rank	Drug	N	Daily mg dose	Mg/kg	Months administered	Weight (Kg)	Number of other drugs	Number of daily administrations
1	Melleril (thioridazine)	477 (43.4%)	Mean 229.8 Median175 Range 10–1200	Mean 4.12 Median3.07 Range .36–18.12	30.9	55.97	1.1	2.2
2	Dilantin (diphenylhydantoin)	437 (39.7%)	Mean 177.2 Median180 Range 30–400	Mean 3.88 Median3.70 Range .44–18.38	50.0	49.21	1.8	2.4
3	Phenobarbital	422 (38.4%)	Mean 112.2 Median 95 Range 15–400	Mean 2.49 Median2.04 Range .37–15.27	39.2	49.62	1.8	2.2
4	Thorazine (chlorpromazine)	92 (8.4%)	Mean 296.2 Median250 Range 25–1200	Mean 5.00 Median4.49 Range .59–20.79	22.6	59.48	2.1	2.7
5	Valium (diazepam)	89 (8.1%)	Mean 12.4 Median 10 Range 2–40	Mean .30 Median .24 Range .05–.96	38.0	43.13	1.3	2.7
Drug survey results from small midwestern institution (N = 187)								
1	Melleril (thioridazine)	97 (51.9%)	Mean 206.2 Median300 Range 25–600	Mean 3.20 Median2.76 Range .54–10.67	6.9	65.79	1.0	2.5
2	Dilantin (diphenylhydantoin)	61 (32.6%)	Mean 217.7 Median300 Range 50–400	Mean 3.50 Median3.56 Range .69–8.24	7.7	64.21	1.9	2.3
3	Phenobarbital	53 (28.3%)	Mean 117.5 Median120 Range 30–300	Mean 1.80 Median1.70 Range .38–4.56	8.0	64.65	1.9	2.0
15	Thorazine (chlorpromazine)	3 (1.6%)	325.0	3.96	3.0	70.41	1.3	2.7

In brief, our recent results show that the frequency of drug usage *has not* declined in the past ten years. If anything, it may have increased from about 50% to 65% or more of the patients in the institution.

SUMMARY

From the surveys cited, it is apparent that psychotropic drugs are used extensively—in about 65% of the institutionalized population—with mentally retarded people. There simply is no evidence in the United States concerning the frequency of usage with retarded people in community placement. This heavy usage for long periods of time has led to growing controversy that is resulting in continual re-evaluations and changes on the part of the federal agency responsible for monitoring medication, the FDA.

REFERENCES

DiMascio, A. (1975) An examination of actual medication usage in retardation institutions: A study of 2,000 cases. Paper presented at the Meeting of the American Association on Mental Deficiency, Portland, May.

Lipman, R. S. (1967) Results of a survey on psychotropic drug usage in institutions for the mentally retarded. Paper presented at the Meeting of the American Association on Mental Deficiency, Denver, May.

Lipman, R. S. (1970) The use of psychopharmacological agents in residential facilities for the retarded. *In* Psychiatric Approaches to Mental Retardation (Ed. Menolascino, F. J.) New York: Basic Books.

Sprague, R. L., and Gadow, K. (1977) The role of the teacher in drug treatment. *In* The Hyperactive Child and Stimulant Drugs (Eds. Bosco, J. J., and Robin, S. S.) Chicago: University of Chicago Press.

RESEARCH TO PRACTICE IN MENTAL RETARDATION
Biomedical Aspects, Volume III
Edited by Peter Mittler
Copyright 1977 I.A.S.S.M.D.

THE ROLE OF DRUGS IN THE PREVENTION AND TREATMENT OF MENTAL RETARDATION

M. A. Lipton, C. B. Nemeroff, G. Bissette, and A. J. Prange, Jr.
Departments of Psychiatry and Anatomy,
Biological Sciences Research Center,
University of North Carolina,
School of Medicine,
Chapel Hill, North Carolina 27514, United States

In the strictest sense of the word, pharmacological treatment involves the use of drugs. Drugs may be defined narrowly or broadly. In the narrow sense, drugs are chemicals occurring in natural products or chemicals synthesized by the organic chemist. Drugs in this sense are alien to mammals and are administered for diagnostic or therapeutic purposes. Thus digitalis, penicillin, diuretics, and anti-hypertensive agents are clearly drugs. But reference to any standard textbook of pharmacology (Goodman and Gilman, 1970) reveals that drugs also are more broadly defined as any chemicals which affect protoplasm. Thus, such books include consideration of the mode of action and therapeutic utility of elements like oxygen or iron, inorganic compounds like sodium chloride, nutrients like amino acids or glucose, and vitamins and hormones. For the purposes of this review, we have employed both the narrow and the broad definitions. We do this for several reasons. First, as is seen later, it is often difficult to determine whether a natural agent is being used physiologically or pharmacologically. Second, to date, synthetic agents that will specifically prevent or treat most forms of mental retardation directly have not been developed, nor do the prospects for development seem very bright. Rather, the history of progress in the prevention and treatment of mental retardation has shown us that, as the myriad of causes are untangled and pathogenesis is understood, prevention and

The authors are supported by the USPHS (Career Scientist Award MH-22536 to A. J. Prange, Jr., NIMH MH-11107, MH-16522, MH-15631, the Schizophrenia Research Foundation (CBN) and an Alfred P. Sloan Foundation Grant to the Neurobiology Program.

treatment of specific types of mental retardation become possible. Drugs in both the narrow and broad sense are used to prevent or to cure infection, to correct the biochemical abnormalities associated with genetic defects and endocrine disorders, and to diminish prematurity and its commonly associated hypoxia. Thus, most drugs used in prevention or treatment of mental retardation are used to combat those conditions which predispose to mental retardation, rather than the mental retardation itself. Antibiotics for the treatment of congenital and neonatal infections, nutritional additives during pregnancy and in early infancy, special diets for correction of metabolic defects, and hormones for the correction of endocrine disorders detected early in life have contributed substantially to the prevention and treatment of mental retardation of many types.

Much has already been learned, and the theme of this volume is quite appropriate, because if we properly applied what we already know, there would be a massive reduction in mental retardation. Impediments to using what we already know are of at least two sorts. The first are social, economic, and educational. The second are related to therapeutic impotence of adult conditions that we know relate to mental retardation but that we are unable to treat effectively. Alcoholism, drug abuse, and smoking are three common conditions in which therapeutic efficacy is woefully lacking. There is also need for substantial improvement in the treatment of hypertension, diabetes, and many other adult illnesses that predispose to defective or vulnerable babies.

There is a tendency to forget that mental retardation is part of a public health problem. As research improves parental and particularly maternal health, it invariably improves the health of offspring. Therefore, research in the treatment of adult conditions is essential to progress in mental retardation research. The second reason for emphasizing this is that, because so much of our drug treatment of infants is a spin-off from treatment initially designed for adults, there is a tendency initially to treat children as small adults, and to pro rate drug dosage on a weight basis. This should not be the case. Neonates and small infants have different rates of absorption and excretion of many drugs (Hanninen, 1975). Significant differences exist in the ability of children to detoxify such drugs; this includes changes in both binding to plasma proteins and rates of metabolic degradation. A very recent example has been given by Aranda and co-workers (1976). Theophylline, long used in the treatment of respiratory illness in children and adults, has shown promise in the treatment of the apnea of premature infants. However, theophylline binds much less to plasma proteins and is metabolized much more slowly. Doses of theophylline that reach therapeutic concentrations in the blood of adults or mature children could easily be toxic for the premature infant. Clinical neonatal and pediatric pharmacology is quite recent as a discipline and is badly needed for sophisticated therapeutics.

Turning now to drugs in the prevention of mental retardation, the most dramatic examples of these are in the treatment of genetic disorders like PKU or galactosemia (Kaufman, 1975; Tedesco, 1975) or in the treatment of neonatal hypothyroidism. The first is negative pharmacotherapy. Nutrients that are normal for most individuals are toxic for those with the. illness. Withholding phenylalanine or galactose until the brain is mature permits normal development and apparently prevents mental retardation. Use of phenylalanine ammonia lyase from yeast for very rapid reduction of elevated blood levels of phenylalanine holds even greater therapeutic promise. The second example, treatment of congenital hypothyroidism using thyroid hormone, is pharmacotherapy in the broad sense. A hormone synthesized and therefore not needed by normal infants must be administered to infants suffering from congenital hypothyroidism in order to permit normal maturation of the central nervous system. In some cases the hormone must be given for life.

THE VITAMIN DEPENDENCY DISEASES

The vitamin dependency illnesses are another example of genetic illnesses that can be prevented from expressing themselves and, in this sense, can be prevented or cured. They are autosomal recessives that must be present in the homozygous state to express themselves, and consequently they are quite rare. Nonetheless, there are now about 25 of them and at least 15 are associated with neurological disturbances or mental retardation (Rosenberg, 1974). More are being found every year. They can be detected because they produce specific syndromes, and they can be identified by specific abnormalities in the blood and urine. Biochemically, they are caused by genetically transmitted mutant enzymes that are not totally nonfunctional but that require extraordinarily high concentrations of coenzymes in order to function properly. The water soluble vitamins are converted into coenzymes and then function in association with protein apoenzymes to make haloenzymes, i.e., complete enzymes necessary for specific metabolic reactions. The chemical affinity of an apoenzyme for its coenzyme depends upon the structure of the protein, and, in the case of these mutant proteins, the affinity is low. Consequently, the coenzyme concentration must be increased, and this, in turn, means that the dietary requirement of the vitamin is massively increased. In the treatment of these conditions, ten to several hundred times the usual daily requirement of specific vitamins is needed. When this is furnished the illness is prevented or cured.

These illnesses are of special interest with regard to the purposes of this chapter for several reasons. First, they require the use of vitamins in doses that would be considered pharmacological for the ordinary individual, but that for such patients are physiological (Rosenberg, 1974). This emphasizes the difficulties in defining precisely the meaning of drug treatment. Second, the rate at which new vitamin dependency illnesses are being discovered is logarithmic, and thus we undoubtedly shall find still more illnesses that can be prevented if methods for early detection and intervention are applied. Third, the evidence that these illnesses exist has been used, along with some other concepts, to establish the notion that many illnesses of unknown etiology, like schizophrenia and childhood autism, are really molecular illnesses that respond to megavitamin therapy (Pauling, 1973). This school of thought is led by a prominent figure, Linus Pauling, our only double Nobel Laureate. This subject has been discussed elsewhere in detail (Lipton et al., 1973) and space does not permit its full discussion here. Suffice it to say that there is no hard clinical evidence to support it. There is, however, a small amount of soft evidence that some children with autism may improve somewhat on large doses of pyridoxine (Rimland, 1973). I agree with Rosenberg (1974) that a short trial of vitamins in large amounts may offer a useful therapeutic trial in children with neurological or psychiatric problems of unknown nature. But this is a far cry from the advocacy of long-term, uncritical use of megavitamins, because they can do harm in addition to raising false hopes.

Hyperkinesis is commonly associated with learning disability (Werry and Sprague, 1972). It is a complex syndrome, most likely with multiple etiologies. It should be diagnosed by the presence of certain symptoms and the absence of others. It is probably often misdiagnosed, and large numbers of children may be inappropriately labeled and treated. For accurately diagnosed hyperkinesis the treatment of choice today is a central nervous system stimulant like dextro-amphetamine or methylphenidate. In substantially more than 50% of such children, there is a highly significant clinical improvement (Connors, 1972). Excessive motor activity, distractability, impetuosity, and aggressiveness diminish rapidly and significantly. Attention span improves and social and learning behavior improves both in the classroom and at home. However, the drugs have disadvantages. Perhaps the most common is that tolerance develops and the dose of drug must be continually raised over the years of management. Insomnia, failure to gain weight and to grow are undesirable side effects especially at higher doses (Safer and Allen, 1975). We know little of how the drugs, which are stimulating to normal children, exert their calming effects upon children who clinically appear to be overstimulated. Knowing as we do that these drugs, which are chemically related to the catecholamine neurotrans-mitters, alter various aspects of catecholamine metabolism (Sieden and Camp-bell, 1974), we hypothesize defects in neurotransmitter metabolism (Breese, Cooper, and Hollister, 1974) resulting perhaps in an imbalance of excitatory and inhibitory neurotransmitters (Moser, 1975). However, a specific biochemical lesion has not been established, so we are still in the position of knowing for certain only that they are empirically useful with some seriously detrimental side effects.

The need for better treatment is evident and some alternatives have been proposed. One hypothesis, which has been widely publicized, is that common food additives such as artificial colors and flavors are causative. It has been claimed that up to 50% of hyperactive children are cured on an additive-free diet, and that another 25% are significantly improved. These claims have been based upon what is commonly called clinical experience rather than upon carefully controlled clinical trials (Feingold, 1975). Some of these trials have been conducted in a few centers (Connors and Goyette, 1976), and their results show that the claims are quantitatively in error. Most of the children do not get well on the diet, but some of the data hint that a small subpopulation may show some degree of improvement (Connors, 1976). The results of all the controlled clinical trials thus far must be considered preliminary, but studies are continuing.

PHARMACOTHERAPY OF ILLNESSES
OF UNKNOWN ETIOLOGY OR IRREVERSIBLE DAMAGE

It is difficult to quantify the number of cases of learning disability or mental retardation in which we still lack understanding of etiology, but it is certainly at least 25% of our population of retardates. To these we must add those illnesses like Down's syndrome with its chromosomal defect and those genetic illnesses like the lipidoses or the glycogen storage diseases in which we sometimes know the defect but are unable to alter the symptoms or course. Finally, we also must add the many cases of antenatal or perinatal injury that might have been prevented but were not, and that have left the children with defects that we presently consider irreversible. Totaled, these types of illness probably add up to about 50% of the retarded population (Popjak, 1974).

What does clinical pharmacology have to offer such cases? The answer is certainly not cure. In some cases, the drugs we employ may tap into basic pathogenic processes. However, in most they do not alter the basic problem but, instead, treat associated symptoms which are themselves damaging. (The following chapters will address this topic in greater depth, but let me illustrate briefly.)

Almost every type of drug that has been found to be useful in the treatment of adult psychiatric illness has been tried with the mentally retarded. These include: the drugs used in the treatment of anxiety, like the benzodiazapines; the drugs used in the treatment of affective disorders, like lithium; the monoamine oxidase inhibitors and the tricyclic antidepressants; and the drugs used in the major psychoses, like the phenothiazines and butyrophenones. The vast literature has been reviewed by Werry and Sprague (1972) and Freeman (1970). They conclude that much of it is methodologically and statistically unsound and that very few generalizations can be drawn about the utility of these drugs.

The rationale for the use of these drugs is that mental retardation is commonly associated with other types of disturbed behavior. To some extent this is true, and certainly there is no reason why retarded patients should not be anxious, depressed, or psychotic. The existence of one illness does not confer immunity to others. When such illnesses are present the use of these drugs is justified, and a few reports indicate gratifying results. Naylor and co-workers (1974) reported positive results in the prophylactic use of lithium on 14 affectively disturbed retarded patients. In a two-year double blind study, they found that the number of weeks ill on the lithium was significantly less than the number while on placebo. Miav and Lynch (1974) treated ten severely disturbed retarded adults, who had failed on other drugs and on behavior modification with lithium and noted a very significant decrease in aggressive and self-mutilative behavior. The phenothiazines are discussed in greater detail in other chapters in this volume. Despite the paucity of good data in the literature, it seems clear that the phenothiazines have a beneficial effect upon retarded children and adults who are highly disturbed, especially if psychomotor overactivity is present. That they offer the best type of treatment is a less certain deduction. Usually they are prescribed for treatment of that behavior which brings the patient in conflict with society and particularly with those responsible for the patient's care. A survey by Lipmann (1970) showed that drug use in both public and private hospitals was very extensive and that the sedative neuroleptics like thioridazine or chlorpromazine led the list. The doses employed were often above the manufacturer's label recommendation for adult schizophrenics, and the average duration of usage was more than four years. This type of usage is open to severe criticism. At high doses, these drugs interfere with reactivity and learning. Prolonged use can lead to irreversible neuronal damage in the basal ganglia with clinical manifestations of tardive dyskinesia. This disabling and disfiguring illness is not uncommon in adults who have received high doses of phenothiazines for years and it is beginning to appear in children (Werry and Sprague, 1972).

It is unfortunate that in mental retardation, as in the psychoses, the use of drugs in disturbed patients is often a competitive substitute for other types of psychological and social treatment. I know of no carefully controlled research that has tested whether or not drugs, in relation to other treatments, are competitive or cooperative or that has tested whether or not their interaction is additive, subtractive, or interactive. Such research is badly needed.

It is interesting to note that the vast majority of research in neuro- and psychopharmacology for the past decade has been concerned with three chemical neurotransmitters: dopamine, noradrenaline, and serotonin. Our current notions about how psychotropic drugs work is based on their effects on the synthesis, release, inactivation, and turnover of these transmitters or upon the effect of drugs on the receptors for these transmitters. Yet only a very small fraction of the neurons of the brain contain or employ these transmitters. The other neurons, about which we know much less, employ transmitters like acetylcholine, amino acids like glycine, gammaaminobutyric acid, and, possibly, polypeptides. Perhaps more relevant to this discussion is the fact that with the possible exceptions of Down's syndrome, in which a defect in serotonin metabolism has been reported (Partington, Tu, and Wong, 1973), and of hyperkinesis, in which a disturbance of catecholamine metabolism has been suggested (Wender, 1975), there is no evidence that these transmitters are disturbed in mental retardation. Perhaps other putative transmitters should be examined.

One of the most exciting frontiers in neurobiology was opened several years ago when Guillemin   at the Salk Institute and Schally at Tulane University isolated tiny quantities of polypeptides with incredible potency from several hundreds of thousands of animal hypothalami. They were able to chemically identify them. These polypeptides are relatively simple compounds that can be readily synthesized by organic chemists and are thus available for study. Our laboratory, as well as many others throughout the world, has been engaged in such work.

Several interesting facts emerge from this research. Hypothalamic hormones are not found exclusively in the hypopthalamus but are widely distributed throughout the brain. Receptors for them also are distributed widely. Their classic and long-known actions in stimulating the pituitary to produce its hormones are not their only effects. They have behavioral effects upon animals without pituitaries. We have reviewed this topic extensively (Prange et al., 1977), and present only a few illustrative examples here. LHRH, which long has been known to stimulate the pituitary to release gonadotropins, will induce sexual behavior in hypophysectomized animals when administered subcutaneously at doses of one microgram (Moss and McCann, 1973). TRH, long known to stimulate the pituitary to release TSH, will enhance the stimulant action of some drugs and antagonize the sedative action of barbiturates in hypophysectomized rats (Prange et al., 1974). Neurotensin, on the other hand, induces hypothermia in several species (Nemeroff et al., 1977). Somatostatin reduces the spontaneous activity of intact rats when injected into the ventricles of the brain in nanogram quantities (Segal and Mandell, 1974). Many other examples could be given.

The pituitary hormones also seem to exert direct central nervous system activity. DeWied (1974), who has pioneered this work, has shown that small ACTH fragments that are devoid of corticotropic effects inhibit the extinction of learned condition-avoidance responses. Vasopressin, a posterior pituitary hormone, markedly enhances the memory of rats in a strain that is genetically deficient in this hormone. Very recently, Guillemin reported that he has isolated three different polypeptides from hypothalami, which he calls endorphins. One produces mild analgesia and tranquilization; another arouses rats to extremely violent behavior; the third produces a catatonic state (Lazarus, Ling, and Guillemin, 1976).

What has all of this to do with mental retardation? At the moment it would appear that the answer is "nothing." However, the field is so new that disturbances in these polypeptides have not yet been sought in different clinical conditions nor have they been extensively studied therapeutically. What has been done shows promise. Although when administered exogenously they have a very short half life and probably penetrate the blood-brain barrier very poorly, some interesting and controversial results have emerged when polypeptides are used. Melanocyte Stimulating Hormone-release Inhibiting Factor (MIF) for example, has been reported to be of some value in Parkinson's disease. Thyrotropin Releasing Hormone (TRH) has been reported to transiently improve the symptoms of depression and schizophrenia and to elevate the mood of normal women (Prange et al., 1976). One report claims that a child with cerebral gigantism, who showed strongly impulsive and regressive behavior, improved markedly, although transiently, after TRH. Another report claims that two hyperkinetic children, unresponsive to methylphenidate, improved transiently after TRH (Tiwary, 1975). These very preliminary findings coupled with the many animal findings about the direct action of these peptides on the brain, encourages optimism. Whether or not it will have anything to do with mental retardation remains to be seen.

SUMMARY

Pharmacology has made substantial contributions to the treatment of symptoms associated with some forms of mental retardation but thus far has not aided much in the prevention or cure of the most common forms of this heterogeneous group of illnesses. Some notable exceptions exist and these offer hope for future utilization of this approach. Examples can be found in the inborn errors of metabolism for which mental retardation can be prevented or cured by pharmacological doses of appropriate substances. Other examples, limitations, and potentialities of pharmacological strategy are discussed.

ACKNOWLEDGMENTS

We extend our appreciation to Nancy Harding and Pam Smith for help in the preparation of this manuscript.

REFERENCES

Aranda, J. V., Sitar, D. S., Parsons, W. D., Loughnan, P. M., and Neims, A. H. (1976) Pharmacokinetic aspects of theophylline in premature newborns. New Eng. J. Med., 295:413.

Breese, G. R., Cooper, B. R., and Hollister, A. S. (1974) Relationship of biogenic amines to behavior. J. Psychiat. Res. 11:125.

Connors, C. K. (1972) Pharmacotherapy. In Psychopathology Disorders of Childhood. New York: Wiley & Sons, p. 316.

Connors, C. K., and Goyette, C. (1976) Food additives and hyperkinesis. Pediatrics, 58, 154.

De Wied, D. (1974) Pituitary-adrenal system hormones and behavior. In The Neurosciences Third Study Program (Eds. Schmitt, F. O., and Worden, F. J.) Cambridge: MIT Press, p. 653.

Feingold, B. W. (1975) Why your Child is Hyperactive. New York: Random House.

Freeman, R. D. (1970) Psychopharmacology and the retarded child. In Psychiatric Approaches to Mental Retardation (Ed. Menolascino, F. J.) New York: Basic Books, p. 294.

Goodman, L. S., and Gilman, A. (1970) The Pharmacological Basis of Therapeutics, 4th Edition. London: MacMillan.

Hanninen, O. (1975) Age and exposure factors in drug metabolism. Acta Pharmac. Tox. 36: Suppl. 11, p. 3.

Kaufman, S. (1975) Hepatic phenylalanine hydroxylase and PKU. *In* Brain Mechanisms in Mental Retardation (Eds. Buchwald, C. N. A., and Brazier, M. A. B.) New York: Academic Press, p. 445.

Lazarus, L. H., Ling, N., and Guillemin, R. (1976) β-lipotropin as a prohormone for the morphinomimetic peptides endorphins and enkephalins. Proc. Nat. Acad Sci. 73:2156.

Lipman, R. S. (1970) The use of psychopharmacological agents in residential facilities for the retarded. *In* Biology of Brain Dysfunction I. (Ed. Gaull, G. E.) New York: Plenum Press, p. 387.

Lipton, M. A., Ban, T. A., Kane, F. J., Levine, J., Mosher, L. R., and Wittenborn, R. (1973) Megavitamin and orthomolecular therapy in Psychiatry. Task Force Report #7, American Psychiatric Association, Washington, D.C.

Miav, V., and Lynch, D. M. (1974) Effect of lithium on disturbed severely mentally retarded patients. Brit. J. Psychiat. 125:110.

Moser, H. W. (1975) Biochemical aspects of mental retardation. *In* The Nervous System. Vol. 2. The Clinical Neurosciences (Ed. Tower, D. B.) New York: Raven Press, p. 369.

Moss, R. L., and McCann, S. M. (1973) Induction of mating behavior in rats by luteinizing hormone-releasing factor. Science. 181:177.

Naylor, G. J., Arnold, J. M., LePoidevin, D., and Reid, A. H. (1974) A double-blind trial of long-term lithium therapy in mental defectives. Brit. J. Psychiat. 124:52.

Nemeroff, C. B., Bissette, G., Loosen, P. T., Prange, A. J., Barlow, T. S., and Lipton, M.A. (1977) Neurotensin: Central nervous system effects of a hypothalamic peptide. Brain Res. 128:485.

Partington, M. W., Tu, J. B., and Wong, C. Y. (1973) Blood serotonin levels in severe mental retardation. Develop. Med. Child Neurol. 15:616.

Pauling, L. (1973) Orthomolecular psychiatry. *In* Orthomolecular Psychiatry (Eds. Hawkins, D., and Pauling, L.) San Francisco: W. H. Freeman.

Popjak, G. S. (1974) Mental Retardation: Nature, Cause and Management. New York: Wiley & Sons.

Prange, A. J., Breese, G. R., Cott, J. M., Martin, B. R., Cooper, B. R., Wilson, I. C., and Plotnikoff, N. P. (1974) Thyrotropin-releasing hormone: antagonism of pentobarbital in rodents. Life Sci. 14:447.

Prange, A. J., Nemeroff, C. B., Lipton, M. A., Breese, G. R., and Wilson, I. C. (1977) Peptides and the central nervous system. *In* The Handbook of Psychopharmacology (Eds. Iversen, L. L., Iversen, S. D., and Snyder, S. H.) New York: Plenum Press (in press).

Rimland, B. (1973) High dosage levels of certain vitamins in the treatment of children with severe mental disorders. *In* Orthomolecular Psychiatry (Eds. Hawkins, D., and Pauling, L.) San Francisco: W. H. Freeman.

Rosenberg, L. E. (1974) Vitamin-responsive inherited diseases affecting the nervous system. *In* Brain Dysfunction in Metabolic Disorders (Ed. Plum, F.) New York: Raven Press.

Safer, K., and Allen, R. (1975) Side-effects from long term use of stimulants in children. Int. J. Ment. Hlth. 4:105.

Segal, D. S., and Mandell, A. J. (1974) Differential behavioral effects of hypothalamic polypeptides. *In* The Thyroid Axis, Drugs and Behavior (Ed. Prange, A. J.) New York: Raven Press, p. 129.

Seiden, L. S., and Campbell, A. B. (1974) Catecholamines, drugs, and behavior. Mutual Interactions. *In* Neuropsychopharmacology of Monoamines and Their Regulatory Enzymes (Ed. Usdin, E.) New York: Raven Press, p. 325.

Tedesco, T. A. (1975) Studies on the molecular defect in galactosemia. *In* Brain Mechanisms in Mental Retardation (Eds. Buchwald, N. A., and Brazier, M. A. B.) New York: Academic Press, p. 467.

Tiwary, C. M. (1975) Effects of thyrotropin-releasing hormone in minimal brain dysfunction. Pediatrics. 56:119.

Wender, P. (1975) Speculations concerning a possible biochemical basis minimal brain dysfunction. Int. J. Ment. Hlth. 4:11.

Werry, J. S., and Sprague, R. L. (1972) Psychopharmacology. *In* Mental Retardation. An Annual Review (Ed. Wortis, J.) New York: Grune & Stratton, p. 63.

RESEARCH TO PRACTICE IN MENTAL RETARDATION
Biomedical Aspects, Volume III
Edited by Peter Mittler
Copyright 1977 I.A.S.S.M.D.

THE DRUG TREATMENT OF MENTALLY HANDICAPPED PATIENTS IN HOSPITAL

W. A. Heaton-Ward
Stoke Park Hospital,
Bristol, BS16 1QU, England

The main uses of drugs in mental handicap hospital practice are: 1) to control disturbed behaviour and to facilitate care and training, 2) to improve performance, 3) to treat other conditions commonly associated with mental handicap, e.g., epilepsy, spasticity, and mental illness and 4) to treat general medical and surgical conditions arising in the mentally handicapped.

The world literature on drug trials in mentally retarded children was very comprehensively reviewed by Freeman (1970) and, in both children and adults, by Griffiths (1970) and Sprague and Werry (1971). At the same time, Colodny and Kurlander (1970) discussed the philosophical considerations underlying the often diametrically opposed attitudes of parents and different professionals to the use of drugs in the care of the mentally handicapped. Such opposing attitudes are as obvious today as they were then, and they are part of the current, wider, philosophical discussion of the nature and aetiology of mental handicap and the most appropriate forms of care. The populations of hospitals for the mentally handicapped in the United Kingdom have undergone striking changes during the past decade and a half as the result of the discharge into the community of the younger, mildly handicapped patients, and their subsequent replacement by patients with severe mental and often severe physical handicaps, or with grossly disturbed behavioural problems requiring highly skilled nursing and psychiatric care.

Reduction in the size of wards and increase in the ratio of staff to patients, and the introduction of behaviour modification techniques, have certainly led to some reduction in the prescription of drugs to control behaviour, but they certainly have not replaced the necessity for this; nor do I believe that they ever will for a certain proportion of cases. I personally regard drugs as vital, facilitating adjuncts to a wide range of other treatments that cannot be carried out if the patient is not there or is too hyperactive for any effective contact to be made with him—as Mrs. Beaton, I think, said, "first catch your hare."

In his 1970 survey, Freeman commented that pilot studies of drugs were almost uniformly favourable, yet many of the drugs were subsequently banned or disappeared from the market within a few years. He concluded, however, that the usefulness of chlorpromazine (Largactil) and thioridazine (Melleril) in reducing psychomotor excitement and disorganised psychotic behaviour seemed to be firmly based on numerous studies. Chlorprothixene (Taractan) seemed about as effective as chlorpromazine and related drugs but had no clear advantages. Haloperidol seemed to be an effective drug for use in the disturbed retarded child.

The seemingly paradoxical action of the central nervous system stimulants, the amphetamines, in quieting some hyperactive children, has usually been attributed to their stimulation of cortical inhibitory centres. In view, therefore, of the far greater stimulant action upon the central nervous system of dextro-amphetamine (Dexedrine) than that of laevo-amphetamine, Freeman saw no reason to suppose that amphetamine (the racemic mixture of laevo-amphetamine and dextro-amphetamine) would be superior therapy to dexedrine in such children. However, Freeman quoted a personal communication from Laufer (1968) that, purely on clinical grounds, he had found that some hyperactive children responded differentially to one or the other drug form. The latter is certainly in accord with my own somewhat limited experience in which amphetamine has appeared clearly more effective than dexedrine, in some cases, in reducing hyperactivity. Recent work by Montagu and Swarbreck (1975) has shown that the explanation may lie in the fact that the *sedative* central effect of *laevo*-amphetamine is greater than the *stimulant* central effect of *dextro*-amphetamine.

Griffiths, in his review, concluded that, despite the vast sums of money expended on tranquillisers, there was no clear answer to the question of the best drug to give in any particular circumstances. On the other hand, as the result of a trial by himself and Sylvester, he claimed that medical assessment provided undeniable evidence of the efficacy of diazepam (Valium) in reducing muscle spasm.

Since those two reviews, there has been relatively little literature on the use of drugs in mental handicap practice. During this period the widely sought magic drug that will control disordered behaviour in every case without affecting the level of consciousness or causing distressing side effects has not appeared. In fact, about a quarter of the references are to old friends like chlorpromazine, thioridazine, and haloperidol (Le Vann, 1971; Claghorn, 1972; Grabowski, 1973; Davis and White, 1975; Vaisenen et al., 1975).

Of these, the paper by Grabowski is of particular interest. As the result of the treatment of 148 mentally retarded children and adults with haloperidol, Grabowski concluded that this drug was the safest and most effective chemotherapeutic agent currently available for the treatment of emotionally disturbed and/or hyperkinetic mentally retarded patients. In addition, Grabowski found that haloperidol increased the attention span of patients and permitted their greater participation in educational programmes. Grabowski regarded the administration of 0.5 mg benztropine mesylate (Cogentin) 2–4 times per day as an important factor in the success of haloperidol because it prevented the development of extrapyramidal symptoms even when the daily dosage of that drug was as high as 120 mg. However, Davis and White (1975) have more recently reported briefly on the use of droperidol and claim that this drug is superior to haloperidol in its sedative effect on disturbed mentally subnormal patients, and that they had not observed any dystonic symptoms when used on more than 100 occasions.

Of the newer drugs, clozapine (Leponex) was said by Vyncke (1974) to be very effective in sedating mentally retarded patients with severe refractory behaviour disorders, being more effective in imbeciles than in idiots. It should be noted, however, that this drug has been reported to induce delirium in young patients who had no evidence of brain damage (Gross and Lagner, 1970), and that 18 cases of severe blood disorder, nine of them fatal, were reported in Finland in conjunction with clozapine treatment there (Idänpään et al., 1975).

There have been further reports during the past five years on the use of the stimulant drugs methylphenidate (Ritalin), dextro-amphetamine, and magnesium pemoline (Cylert) (Blacklidge and Ekblad, 1971; Conners, 1971). In a study of educable mentally retarded public school pupils, Blacklidge and Ekblad found no statistically significant difference in the pupils' behaviour on parents' ratings, or in their performance on the academic measurers, in response to treatment with methylphenidate. On the other hand, Conners found methylphenidate significantly more effective than dextro-amphetamine in improving the performance of children with minimal brain dysfunction on the WISC arithmetic and similarities subtests. Although both dextro-amphetamine and magnesium pemoline showed significant treatment effects, these appeared after two weeks with dextro-amphetamine but only after six weeks on magnesium pemoline. Most improved were conduct disturbances, impulsivity, immaturity and, antisocial behaviour, but there was no effect on hyperactivity. Conners concluded that there were a number of rather different responses to the drugs by children with minimal brain dysfunction, which were predictable by different patterns of baseline performance on psychological tests. Recent research has indicated that genetic temperamental mechanisms as well as brain damage may be operative in the aetiology of hyperactivity (Cantwell, 1975). One of the more serious side effects of the long-term use of amphetamines in children is premature closure of the epiphyses and depression of growth (Safer, Allen, and Barr, 1972).

Claims have been made for the effectiveness of lithium in controlling disturbed and aggressive behaviour in the mentally retarded. Dostal (1971) reported reduced aggression in a group of 14 aggressive mentally defective adolescent boys in an open trial of lithium. Micev and Lynch (1974) found a significant improvement in aggressive tendencies on lithium, with levels maintained between 0.6 and 1.4 mEq/litre, in five out of nine severely mentally retarded patients in whom previous treatment with tranquillisers and behaviour modification therapy had had little or no effect. In addition, six of eight patients with self-mutilating behaviour improved to a point where this tendency disappeared. Worrall and his co-workers (1975) found a reduction in aggression scores in the group as a whole of eight aggressive severely subnormal female patients in whom plasma lithium levels were maintained in the range 0.6 to 1.4 mEq/litre They concluded that their study added further weight to the evidence that lithium had an anti-aggressive effect at normal therapeutic dosage in nonmanic depressives, and they felt that this had implications for hypotheses about the mode of action of lithium. They reemphasized the caution required in the treatment by lithium in brain damaged patients in whom serious signs of neurotoxicity might occur with plasma lithium levels not inordinately high.

Spasticity is one of the most common accompaniments of mental retardation in hospitalized patients, and baclofen (Lioresal), a derivative of gamma-amino butyric acid, has joined diazepam as an effective reducer of both spasticity and flexor spasms, but it should be avoided in epileptic patients because it may increase the frequency of their fits (Calne, 1974). Hudgson and Weightman (1971) claimed that baclofen was less likely than diazepam in effective doses to induce unacceptable drowsiness.

Cyproterone acetate (Androcur), used initially in the treatment of sexual offenders of normal intelligence, more recently has been given to similar offenders of subnormal intelligence and has been used to reduce socially unacceptable sexual behaviour, such as masturbation in public, in the mentally subnormal. Davis (1975) reported a successful treatment of six intellectually subnormal male patients, convicted of repeated sexual assaults on women or children, on doses of cyproterone acetate ranging from 50 mg to 200 mg daily. The duration of drug treatment varied from six months to three years, and no sexual offences were committed during this period or for the period up to three years after the treatment was stopped in each case. A similar group of patients, about six, with a history of repeated indecent exposure showed a similar pattern of response. Davis also reported a marked improvement on cyproterone acetate in the nonsexual, physically aggressive behaviour toward other patients and staff of three severely subnormal adolescent male patients who had shown no response to conventional forms of treatment.

Recently in the United Kingdom, there has been an upsurge of interest in mental illness superimposed on mental handicap, and there have been several reports of the effectiveness of various neuroleptics in the treatment of psychosis in these patients. Reid (1972) reported that tricyclic anti-depressants and ECT appeared to be effective in most cases of depressive psychosis in his series of 18 imbecile, feeble-minded and borderline defectives at Strathmartine Hospital, Scotland. In a later paper, Reid was the co-author with Naylor and others of a paper which reported the result of a two-year double blind trial of the prophylactic effect of lithium therapy in a group of mentally defective hospital patients who were suffering from frequently recurring affective or behavioural changes.

My own experience in the Stoke Park Group of hospitals has been that the tricyclic anti-depressants are less predictable in their effect on the depressive episodes than chlorpromazine and haloperidol are in their ability to control manic episodes. Of particular interest was a patient with intermittent porphyria with manic depressive psychosis, under the care of my colleague Dr. Jozé Jancar, who has remained free from manic or depressive episodes for the past four years during which he has been taking lithium (Heaton-Ward, 1977).

Reid (1972) reported a satisfactory response to phenothiazines in 25% of mentally retarded patients with schizophrenic psychosis, and a reduction of agitation and irritability in those with paranoid psychosis. My own experience approximates to that of Reid.

We have become increasingly aware of the serious side effects and interactions of a number of drugs in daily use in our mental handicap practice. To counteract the disturbance of folic acid and vitamin B_{12} balance in epileptic patients on anti-convulsants we give each patient three yeast tablets daily as a routine and carry out periodic checks of red cell folate and serum vitamin B_{12} levels (Eastham and Jancar, 1971). Eastham and Jancar have reported macrocytosis in mentally subnormal hospital patients receiving phenobarbitone alone (Eastham and Jancar, 1970).

Reversible encephalopathy and choreoathetosis have been reported in patients treated with large doses of phenytoin (Glaser, 1973; McLellan and Swash, 1974). Chorea also was reported by Hosking et al. (1975) in a 16-year-old epileptic who developed osteomalacia. Thirteen years ago my colleague Dr. Jancar reported the development of rickets in a profoundly retarded epileptic girl, about four years old, on a normal diet, who had been receiving anti-convulsants as an in-patient at Stoke Park Hospital for the previous two years and ten months (Jancar, 1963). Other workers have reported osteomalacia and rickets as a result of long-term anti-convulsant therapy and have advocated the prophylactic use of vitamin D in epileptics (Lifshitz, 1973; Christiansen and Rødbro, 1974).

The suppression of immune responses by phenytoin has been suggested by a number of workers (Masi et al., 1976; Massimo et al., 1976; Seager et al., 1975). Penttilä and his co-workers (1974) have reported the failure of doxycycline in normal therapeutic doses to maintain the maximum inhibitory concentration necessary for proper bacteriostasis in patients taking diphenyl hydantoin or carbamazepine. Neuvonen and his colleagues had earlier shown that when ferrous sulphate and the recommended dose of various tetracyclines were given orally, the plasma levels of antibiotic reached only 10–50% of the expected level (Neuvonen, 1970).

It is thus becoming increasingly clear that the effective and safe drug treatment of the mentally handicapped is a highly skilled matter demanding a high degree of specialist knowledge in the psychiatric staff who care for them. The tragedy is that there is, at least in the United Kingdom, if not elsewhere, a powerful lobby who claim that the care of the mentally handicapped is not a psychiatric matter, or indeed a medical matter at all; as a result, the number of medical staff who possess such specialist knowledge is dropping to dangerously low levels. The institution of such admirable teaching training programmes as that described by Di Mascio in 1974 becomes a matter of urgent necessity if much of the present, often bizarre and idiosyncratic, prescribing is to be avoided.

There is a need for all drug regimes to be monitored regularly with regular blood counts and serum estimations whenever necessary. No drug should be continued longer or in higher dosage than the therapeutic response demands. My colleague, Dr. Jancar, has described the successful withdrawal of tranquillisers from patients who had previously received them for many years (Jancar, 1970). The price of freedom of the mentally handicapped from drug disasters is indeed eternal vigilance on the part of each of us who has a responsibility to care for them.

SUMMARY

This chapter lists the main uses of drugs in mental retardation practice. It briefly reviews the world literature on the subject, with comments based on the experience of the author and his colleagues with the 1,400 mentally handicapped patients in the Stoke Group of Hospitals, Bristol, England.

ACKNOWLEDGMENTS

I wish to express my very sincere thanks to the following people, without whose invaluable help the completion of this paper would have been impossible: Dr. H. McNulty, Regional Information Pharmacist, South Western Regional Health Authority, Bristol; Mr. R. A. Moorehouse, Staff Pharmacist (information), Southmead Hospital, Bristol; Mrs. Stella M. Waller, F.L.A., Medical Librarian, Postgraduate Centre, Frenchay Hospital, Bristol; and Mrs. Joyce White and Miss Anita England of the Patient Services Department, Stoke Park Hospital, Bristol, for typing the manuscript.

REFERENCES

Blacklidge, V., and Ekblad, R. L. (1971) The effectiveness of methylphenidate on learning and behaviour in public school, educable mentally retarded children. Pediatrics. 47:923.

Calne, D. B. (1974) Drugs for spasticity. Prescrib. J. 14:58.

Cantwell, D. P. (1975) Genetics of hyperactivity. J. Child Psychol. Psychiat. 16:261.

Christiansen, C., and Rødbro, O. S. (1974) Anticonvulsant action of Vitamin D in epileptic patients. Brit. Med. J. 2:258.

Claghorn, J. (1972) A double blind comparison of haloperidol and thioradiazine in out-patient children. Curr. Ther. Res. 14:785.

Colodny, D., and Kurlander, L. F. (1970) Psychopharmacology as a Treatment Adjunct for the Mentally Retarded, Problems and Issues. New York: Basic Books.

Conners, C. K. (1971) Psychchological effects of stimulant drugs in children with minimal brain dysfunction. Pediatrics. 49:702.

Davis, T. S. (1975) Collaborative clinical experience with cyproterone acetate. J. Int. Med. Res. 3: Suppl.(4):16.

Davis, T. S., and White, M. (1975) Droperidol in emotional states in subnormal patients. Brit. Med. J. 1:559.

Di Mascio, A. (1974) Changing patterns of psychotropic drugs in Massachusetts Mental Hospitals. Psychopharmacol. Bull. 10:24.

Dostal, T. (1971) Antiaggressive effect of lithium salts in mentally retarded adolescents. Proc. 4th U.E.P. Congr., Stockholm.

Eastham, R. D., and Jancar, J. (1970) Macrocytosis associated with anticonvulsant therapy. Epilepsia. 11:275.

Eastham, R. D., and Jancar, J. (1971) Epilepsy and folate deficiency. Brit. Med. J. 4:361.

Freeman, R. D. (1970) Psychopharmacology and the retarded child. In Psychiatric Approach to Mental Retardation (Ed. Menolascino, F.) New York: Basic Books.

Glaser, G. H. (1973) In Antiepileptic Drugs. New York: Raven Press.

Grabowski, S. W. (1973) Safety and effectiveness of haloperidol for mentally retarded behaviourally disordered and hyperkinetic patients. Curr. Ther. Res. 15:856.

Griffiths, A. W. (1970) Drug Trials. In Mental Subnormality: Modern Trends in Research. (Ed. Richards, B. W.) London: Pitman Medical.

Gross, H., and Lagner, E. (1970) Int. Pharmaco. Psychiat. 4:220.

Heaton-Ward, W. A. (1977) Psychosis in mental handicap. Brit. J. Psychiat. 130:525.

Hosking, D. J., Williams, A., Godwin-Austen, R. B., and Allison, S. P. (1975) Osteomalacia presenting as chorea. Brit. Med. J. 3:136.

Hudgson, P., and Weightman, D. (1971) Baclofen in the treatment of spasticity. Brit. Med. J. 4:15.

Idänpään-Heikkila, J., Alhave, E., Olkinuora, M., and Palva, I. (1975) Clozapine and agranulocytosis. Lancet. 2:611.

Jancar, J. (1970) Gradual withdrawal of tranquillisers with the help of ascorbic acid. Brit. J. Psychiat. 117:238.

Jancar, J. (1963) Rickets with secondary hyperparathyroidism in a severely subnormal child. Arch. Dis. Child. 38:412.

LeVann, L. J. (1971) Clinical comparison of haloperidol with chlorpromazine in mentally retarded children. Amer. J. Ment. Defic. 75:719.

Lifshitz, F. (1973) Vitamin D-dependent rickets in institutionalised, mentally retarded children receiving long term anticonvulsant therapy. J. Pediatr. 83:612.

Masi, M., Paolucci, P., Perocco, P., and Franceschi, C. (1976) Immunosuppression by phenytoin. Lancet. 1:860.

Massimo, L., Pasino, M., Rosanda-Vadala, C., and Tonini, G. P. (1976) Immunological side effects of anticonvulsants. Lancet. 1:860.

McLellan, D. L., and Swash, M. (1974) Choreoathetosis and encephalopathy induced by phenytoin. Brit. Med. J. 2:204.

Micev, V., and Lynch, D. M. (1974) Effect of lithium on disturbed severely mentally retarded patients. Brit. J. Psychiat. 125:110.

Montagu, J. D., and Swarbreck, L. (1975) Effects of amphetamines in hyperkinetic children—stimulant or sedative: A pilot study. Develop. Med. Child Neurol. 17:293.

Naylor, G. J., Donald, J. M., LePoivedin, D., and Reid, A. H. (1974) A double blind trial of long term lithium therapy in mental defectives. Brit. J. Psychiat. 124:52.

Neuvonen, P. J., Gothoni, G., Hackman, R., and Björksten, K. (1970) Interference of iron in the absorption of tetracyclines in man. Brit. Med. J. 4:532.

Neuvonen, P. J., and Penttilä, O. (1974) Interaction between doxycycline and barbiturates. Brit. Med. J. 1:535.

Penttilä, O., Neuvonen, P. J., Aho, K., and Lehtovaara, R. (1974) Interaction between doxycycline and barbiturates and some anti-epileptic drugs. Brit. Med. J. 2:470.

Reid, A. H. (1972) Psychosis in mental defectives. Brit. J. Psychiat. 120:205.

Safer, D., Allen, R., and Barr, E. (1972) Depression of growth in hyperactive children on stimulant drugs. New Engl. J. Med. 287:217.

Seager, J., Jameson, D. L., Wilson, J., Hayward, A. R., and Soothill, J. (1975) IgA deficiency, epilepsy and phenytoin treatment. Lancet. 2:632.

Sprague, R. L., and Werry, J. S. (1971) International Review of Research in Mental Retardation. Vol. 5. New York: Academic Press.

Vaisenen, K., Kainulainen, P., Paaviainen, M. T., and Viukari, M. (1975) Sulpiride versus chlorpromazine and placebo in the treatment of restless mentally subnormal patients. Curr. Ther. Res. 17:202.

Vyncke, J. (1974) The treatment of behaviour disorders in idiocy and imbecility with clozapine. Pharmakopsychiatr. 7:225.

Worrall, E. P., Moody, J. P., and Naylor, G. (1975) Lithium in non-manic depressives. Antiaggressive effect and red blood cell lithium. Brit. J. Psychiat. 126:463.

RESEARCH TO PRACTICE IN MENTAL RETARDATION
Biomedical Aspects, Volume III
Edited by Peter Mittler
Copyright 1977 I.A.S.S.M.D.

MEDICAL MANAGEMENT OF MONGOLISM OR DOWN SYNDROME

F. de la Cruz
Mental Retardation and Developmental Disabilities Branch,
National Institute of Child Health and Human Development,
National Institutes of Health,
Bethesda, Maryland, United States

In an effort to help mentally retarded individuals attain a higher level of psychomotor and intellectual development, various special diets and supplementary materials, including hormones, vitamins, minerals, and other pharmacological agents have been given to children with mongolism or Down syndrome, and have been reported to have beneficial effects. Table 1 is a list of some of the substances or methods that have been tried or are presently being used in the treatment of mongolism. Space does not permit a thorough discussion of all these methods; however, I have devoted most of the chapter to the "U" Series of drugs and dimethylsulfoxide (DMSO). I have not discussed anti-convulsants, anti-depressants, tranquilizers, and sedatives here, although these psycho-pharmacological agents are known to affect a child's ability to attend to stimuli or to cope better with his environment when administered for their indicated usage and when given in proper amounts.

SICCA-CELL THERAPY

In 1931, Dr. Paul Niehans from Switzerland introduced a form of treatment which he called Sicca-cell therapy. This method of treatment consists of the injection of lyophilized cells prepared from the organs of fetal or young animals, based on the belief that the action of embryonic cells will substitute for whichever biological function a retarded individual lacks. The injected cells are

---

This article was written by the author in his private capacity. No official support or endorsement by the National Institute of Child Health and Human Development, National Institutes of Health is intended or should be inferred.

Table 1. Treatment of mongolism or
Down syndrome

Sicca-Cell Therapy (P. Niehans)
Postnatal Maturation (H. Haubold)
5-Hydroxytryptophan
Vitamin B_6
"U" Series (H. Turkel)
Gerovital/Aslavital (Aslan)
DMSO

---

alleged to migrate to the organ analogous to their origin and to provide stimulus toward growth and development. Proof to the claim that the cells remain intact and continue to produce whichever hormone they are expected to produce is still forthcoming.

In 1966, a group of Canadian investigators (Black, Kato, and Walker, 1966) reported the results of a double blind study to evaluate the effects of Sicca-cell treatment on a group of 50 mentally retarded children, 36 of whom had mongolism. The subjects were 5 to 25 years old with IQs below 70. The treatment group received three injections of the prescribed Sicca-cell therapy at intervals of nine months, while the controls received placebos of lyophilized lung, liver, or muscle. None of the analyses provided any evidence that the treatment group did better than the control group.

POSTNATAL MATURATION (HAUBOLD TREATMENT)

The Haubold method consists of a powder or an emulsion that contains vitamins, trace elements, and hormones, including thyroid, pituitary, and thymus. This form of treatment is based on the premise that increased incidence of congenital anomalies during World War II was caused by a combination of vitamin A deficiency in the mother and "endocrine disturbances explainable by anomalies in the intermediary metabolism of vitamins D, E, B_1 and B_2, and with deficiencies in nicotinamide or pantothenic acid" (Haubold, 1958, 1959, 1960). Haubold did not include a control group of children in his series, and the physical and mental improvement attributed to the treatment was based on subjective impressions unsupported by objective facts.

5-HYDROXYTRYPTOPHAN

Because of evidence of low levels of blood 5-hydroxytryptamine (serotonin) in infants with trisomy 21, 5-hydroxytryptophan, a precursor of serotonin, was administered to children with mongolism. Initial observations of improvement in hypotonia, tongue protrusion, and activity levels were reported. However, a subsequent double blind study led Coleman (1975), and Weise et al. (1974) to conclude that 5-hydroxytryptophan is not effective in accelerating the rate of development of Down syndrome patients.

VITAMIN B$_6$

Mary Coleman (1976) is currently conducting a double blind study comparing children on large doses of vitamin B$_6$ to patients receiving placebo in the newborn period. The amount of vitamin B$_6$ given is based on blood levels of serotonin, but averages about 25 milligrams of pyridoxine per kilogram of body weight during the first year of life. This study is still in progress and the "code" will not be broken until next spring. Despite the lack of objective evidence to support its usefulness, a number of physicians are prescribing vitamin B$_6$ to children with mongolism, purportedly to improve their development.

"U" SERIES (H. TURKEL)

In 1959, Henry Turkel presented a paper at a meeting of the American Association for the Advancement of Science concerning the use of about 50 different kinds of drugs, including hormones, vitamins, minerals, and other substances, in the treatment of mongolism. Turkel called his method the "U" Series from the Greek prefix eu to indicate normalization of abnormal factors in the cells (Turkel, 1975). Suggested starting dosages, treatment schedules, and supplementary medications are carefully outlined. The treatment is designed to remove "... the harmful or defective expression of excessive genes in a trisomic syndrome and also (to remove) the unmetabolized substrate in a single-gene defect as well as supplementation of needed nutrients or normal physiological products" (Turkel, 1974).

Prompted by Turkel's reported success, Bumbalo from Buffalo did a double blind study of 24 children, 12 females and 12 males, ranging in age from three months to 11 years with typical clinical manifestations of mongolism, including karyotypes showing trisomy 21 on each patient. One half of the group received the "U" Series of drugs and the rest were placed on placebo. Turkel supplied the drugs and randomly assigned the experimental and control groups. All 24 children received the medication for 12 months. Comparison of data such as height, weight, psychometrics, x-ray, including bone age, hemograms, and urinalysis before and after treatment did not show any significant difference between the two groups. A significant degree of improvement in socialization, "attributed to the supervision of those children by an experienced staff," was observed in both groups (Bumbalo, Morelewicz, and Berens, 1964).

Turkel argued that the negative results reported by Bumbalo resulted primarily from the addition of "... supplemental oral vitamins containing vitamin D, contrary to instructions not to supply supplemental vitamins, as the unbound vitamin D produces premature calcification and calcium deposits within various structures and counteracts the beneficial activities of the "U" Series drugs, which contain No unbound vitamin D" (Turkel, 1974, p. 89). It should be noted that in a number of Turkel's pamphlets, published before and after Bumbalo's report, vitamin D supplement was not considered to be a contraindicated drug (1961, 1962, 1963, 1965).

Two Japanese investigators published a manuscript that was sent to me by Turkel in its original Japanese prose with an accompanying English translation, dealing with the use of a modified "U" Series on 52 children with Down syndrome ranging in age from less than one year to six years and 11 months. Preliminary results of this uncontrolled study showed that 50% of the children showed more than a ten-point increase in their development quotient, 21% showed a decrease, while the rest were described as "stable." None of the seven children who were not on the modified "U" Series showed any improvement. The drugs were considered to be less effective with children less than two years old. Three ingredients of the "U" Series (aminophylline magnesium glycinate, thyroglobulin, and pentylenetetrazole) were excluded from the series (Iida and Kurita, 1975).

In the United States, before a new drug can be marketed, the sponsor must submit a New Drug Application to the Food and Drug Administration with scientifically adequate evidence of its safety and effectiveness for the recommended uses. It is the opinion of the Food and Drug Administration that "Dr. Turkel has not been able to provide sufficient preclinical, clinical, and toxicological data to obtain approval of his "U" Series for the treatment of mongolism" (FDA, 1974).

GEROVITAL/ASLAVITAL (ASLAN)

Aslan (1975) from Romania claims that improvement has been observed in moderately and mildly mentally retarded children following administration of Aslavital. Aslavital contains procaine hydrochloride, an activating factor and an anti-atherogenous or lipotropic factor. The alleged improvement was attributed to the "role of the procaine in the stimulation of the nervous cell . . . and also (to) its activity in the inhibition of the monoamine oxidase." Whether or not this mode of treatment will stand the test of time needs to be determined with further scientific evaluation.

DIMETHYLSULFOXIDE (DMSO)

Dimethylsulfoxide (DMSO) is a chemical with remarkable solvent properties and a unique ability to penetrate and diffuse through plant and animal tissues. It comes from lignin, which is obtainable from wood pulp. It was first prepared by Alexander Saytzeff in 1866 by the oxidation of dimethylsulfide, but it remained a chemical curiosity until the 1940s when the plastic industry noted its unique solvent properties (Jacob, Rosenbaum, and Wood, 1971). In 1964, DMSO first became the subject of clinical investigation with the approval of the U.S. Food and Drug Administration. In 1965, after approximately 100,000 patients had received the drug, clinical testing of DMSO was discontinued because of a question of safety, especially with regard to changes in the lens of experimental animals. One year later, investigations involving the cutaneous application of DMSO were authorized for serious conditions for which no satisfactory therapy existed, such as scleroderma, persistent herpes zoster, and rheumatoid arthritis. Using the drug for other than research purposes is currently prohibited by the FDA. In 1972, the FDA asked the National Academy of Sciences–National Research Council to evaluate all of the safety and efficacy data available to the FDA. The National Academy of Sciences concluded that, in view of the reported toxicity and the lack of demonstrated effectiveness, DMSO should be restricted to investigational use until its therapeutic effect could be demonstrated to warrant the attendant side effects.

In April 1972, a fact-finding trip was made to Santiago, Chile by a representative from the FDA and by a representative from the National Institutes of Health to evaluate the claimed efficacy and safety of DMSO when prescribed for various medical indications. In Chile, DMSO is contained in five different commercially available drugs, one of which, Merinex, is used for the treatment of mongolism (Departmento Medico-Cientifico, 1973). After reviewing available information and meeting with various investigators, it was not possible to attribute the claimed improvement following DMSO administration because of a number of methodological deficiencies identified in several studies, including lack of suitable controls and the basing of beneficial effects on anecdotal and subjective information. DMSO was mixed with a combination of amino acids and lidocaine, and in no instance was it administered alone.

In February 1973, with the approval of the FDA, a pilot study was initiated in Eugene, Oregon to assess the effects of orally administered DMSO on the behavior and learning ability of retarded children (Gabourie, Becker, and Bateman, 1974, 1975).

The study lasted for 3½ months. The subjects were severely and moderately retarded children, ages four to 17 years, who attended the Pearl Buck Center, a private school for the mentally retarded located in Eugene, Oregon. The 67 subjects were paired by approximate age and level of functioning within the broad classifications of Down syndrome, brain damage evidenced by observed motor impairment, and other etiologies. One subject from each pair was randomly assigned to the high dose group and the other to the low dose group. An additional group of 23 children enrolled at the school did not receive any DMSO because their parents declined to have them participate in the study. While there were no significant differences between these nonstudy children and the study children on any tested demographic variables, they were not treated as a control group because they were not randomly assigned to the no-dosage condition.

Table 2. Total number of significant and not significant probabilities for all total raw test change scores, DMSO pilot study, 1973

	H > L	L > H	H > ND	ND > H	L > ND	ND > L
Significant ≤ 0.05	12	10	2	0	5	4
Not Significant	38	24	35	11	28	11

H = High Dose; L = Low Dose; ND = No Dose.

The low dose group received 0.01 g per kg of body weight once daily, five times a week throughout the study. The high dose group received 0.1 g per kg of body weight once daily, five times a week for seven weeks, which was subsequently raised to 0.5 g per kg for the remaining seven weeks. Medical grade DMSO mixed with fruit juice was given by mouth. The random assignment and coding was done by individuals other than the investigators. It was not possible to conduct a true double blind controlled study in which one group of children received DMSO and another group a placebo because of the unique odor of DMSO. The investigators hoped that the low dose of DMSO would produce just enough odor, without having any effect, to maintain the confidentiality of the two groups. However, no one has yet demonstrated that even a very small amount does not exert a significant pharmacological action.

Language and cognitive development changes were measured using standardized normative instruments, while motor behavior was assessed using psychomotor instruments. Social and emotional behavior changes were measured for each subject using structured parental interviews and anecdotal reports. Using the Mann-Whitney U probabilities of changes in the raw test scores for all tests and all groups, at a significance level of 0.05 or less, the following hypotheses were made: 1) the high dose group will show more gain than the low dose group; 2) the high dose group will show more gain than the nonstudy group; 3) the low dose group will show more gain than the nonstudy group.

The hypotheses were accepted on 19 and rejected on 14 variables based on the total number of total raw test change scores (Table 2). On the Illinois Test of Psycholinguistic Abilities (ITPA), the hypotheses were accepted on 16 variables and rejected on ten (Table 3). These data indicate that no conclusive evidence in favor or against the utilization of DMSO in the treatment of mental retardation has been obtained from this pilot study. Test results on a number of subjects

Table 3. Total number of significant and not significant probabilities for the ITPA subtest change scores, DMSO pilot study, 1973

	H > L	L > H	H > ND	ND > H	L > ND	ND > L
Significant ≤ .05	5	3	9	2	2	5
Not Significant	55	45	49	48	57	44

H = High Dose; L = Low Dose; ND = No Dose.

were inconsistent with group trends. Children who did not receive DMSO or those who were on the "low dose" schedule, showed significant improvement over the children who received the "high dose" on a number of tests.

Laboratory studies did not show any evidence of renal, hepatic, hematopoietic, or ophthalmologic complications that can be attributed to DMSO (Dunn and Jacob, 1975).

CONCLUSION

Fundamental research in cell biology, genetics, molecular biology, and other basic sciences must continue if we are to find the cause of a host of disabling conditions including Down syndrome. While basic research may not appeal to some individuals because of its apparent lack of relevance or a sense of remoteness to the immediate problem, we must remind ourselves that scientific discoveries frequently result from untargeted experiments that often astonish the investigator himself. Scientific creativity must be supported if our understanding of mongolism is to advance and flourish. While basic research is progressing, we must not lose sight of the medical, psychological, social, educational, and other pressing needs of children who are in our midst. Research on primary prevention and amelioration must continue to help mentally retarded and disabled children become happy and participating members of our society.

SUMMARY

This chapter reviews the current status of the medical management of Down syndrome using pharmacological agents. Special emphasis is made on the use of dimethylsulfoxide (DMSO), the "U" series of drugs proposed by Dr. Turkel, and vitamin B_6.

REFERENCES

Aslan, A. (1975) National Institute of Gerontology and Geriatrics, Bucharest, Romania. Personal communication.

Black, D. B., Kato, J. G., and Walker, G. W. (1966) A study of improvement in mentally retarded children accruing from Sicca-cell therapy. Amer. J. Ment. Defic. 70:499.

Bumbalo, T. S., Morelewicz, H. V., and Berens, D. L. (1964) Treatment of Down's syndrome with the "U" series of drugs. J. Amer. Med. Assoc. 187:125.

Coleman, M. (1975) The use of 5-hydroxytryptophan in patients with Down's syndrome. In Down's Syndrome (Mongolism)—Research, Prevention, Management (Eds. Koch, R. and de la Cruz, F.). New York: Brunner/Mazel.

Coleman, M. (1976) Personal communication.

Departamento Medico-Cientifico (1973) DAT (DMSO-Amino Acid Therapy): An Advance in the Treatment of Mental Deficiency. Santiago, Chile: Laboratorios Recalcine.

Dunn, M., and Jacob, S. (1975) Oral dimethylsulfoxide in mental retardation.

Part 2: Preliminary medical data. *In* Biological actions of dimethylsulfoxide (Eds. Jacob, S. W. and Herschler, R.). Ann. N.Y. Acad. Sci. 243:1.

Food and Drug Administration (1974) "U" series—Dr. Henry Turkel, FDA Consumer Memo, Current and useful information from the Food and Drug Administration, U.S. Department of Health, Education and Welfare, DHEW Publication Number (FDA) 74—3024, May.

Gabourie, J., Becker, J. W., and Bateman, B. (1974) Progress Report to FDA on Pearl Buck DMSO study.

Gabourie, J., Becker, J. W., and Bateman, B. (1975) Oral dimethylsulfoxide in mental retardation. Part 1: Preliminary behavioral and psychometric data. *In* Biological actions of dimethylsulfoxide. (Eds. Jacob, S. W. and Herschler, R.). Ann. N.Y. Acad. Sci. 243:1.

Haubold, H. (1959) Gedanken und Anregungen zur Mütterprophylaxe. Der Landarzt. 25:945.

Haubold, H., and Haubold, E. (1958) Mütterprophylaxe und Nachreifungsbehandlung entwicklungsgehemmter Kinder. Int. J. Prophyl. Med. Soc. Hyg., Wien, 3:89.

Haubold, H., Loew, H., and Haefele-Niemann, R. (1960) Möglichkeiten und Grenzen einer Nachreifungsbehandlung entwicklungsgehemmter, insbesondere mongoloider Kinder. Der. Landarzt. 11:378.

Iida, M., and Kurita, I. (1975) Investigational studies of nutritional and medical treatment of Down's syndrome children especially its influence on development of mental function. National Institute of Mental Health, and Department of Pediatrics, National Hospital in Monodae, Japan.

Jacob, S. W., Rosenbaum, E. E., and Wood, D. C. (1971) Dimethyl Sulfoxide. Vol. 1. Basic Concepts of DMSO. New York: Marcel Dekker, p. 479.

Turkel, H. (1959) Medical treatment of mongolism and other retardations. Presented as Lecture and Scientific Exhibit, Amer. Assoc. for the Advancement of Science, Chicago, Illinois.

Turkel, H. (1961) Medical treatment of mongolism. Proc. 2nd Int. Congr. Ment Retard., Vienna. 1:409.

Turkel, H. (1963) Medical breakthrough in mongolism. Presented as Lecture and Scientific Exhibit at the National Medical Association, Inc., Statler Hilton Hotel, Los Angeles, California, August 12—15.

Turkel, H. (1974) Medical amelioration of Cytogenetic Anomalies—A Handbook for the Practicing Physician. Detroit, Michigan: Graphic Service, p. 2, 89.

Turkel, H. (1975) Medical amelioration of Down's syndrome incorporating the ortho-molecular approach. J. Ortho-Molecular Psychiat. 4:102.

Turkel, H., and Turkel, J. (1962) Medical breakthrough in mongolism. Presented as Lecture and Scientific Exhibit at the Annual Meeting of the Society of Biological Psychiatry, Royal York Hotel, Toronto, Canada, May 4—6.

Turkel, H., and Turkel, J. (1962) Medical breakthrough in mongolism. Presented as Lecture and Scientific Exhibit at the 9th Annual Meeting of the Academy of Psychosomatic Medicine, Radisson Hotel, Minneapolis, Minnesota, Nov. 1—3.

Turkel, H., and Turkel, J. (1965) Medical amelioration of cytogenetic anomalies. Prepared for the 89th Annual Meeting of the American Association on Mental Deficiency, Americana Hotel, Miami Beach, Florida, June 8—12.

Weise, P., Koch, R., Shaw, K. N. F., and Rosenfeld, M. (1974) The use of 5-HTP in the treatment of Down's syndrome. Pediatrics. 54:165.

RESEARCH TO PRACTICE IN MENTAL RETARDATION
Biomedical Aspects, Volume III
Edited by Peter Mittler
Copyright 1977 I.A.S.S.M.D.

NEW APPROACHES TO TREATMENT OF PHENYLKETONURIA

H. K. Berry, R. E. Butcher, R. L. Brunner, N. W. Bray, M. M. Hunt, and C. H. Wharton
Institute for Developmental Research,
Children's Hospital Research Foundation,
Elland Avenue and Bethesda,
Cincinnati, Ohio, United States

In spite of efforts directed toward study of phenylketonuria (PKU) over four decades, the exact mechanism whereby the enzymatic defect in metabolism of phenylalanine leads to abnormal development of the central nervous system remains obscure. Once the mechanism is understood, therapeutic attempts could be directed toward correcting the basic defect. At present, restriction of phenylalanine content of the diet, thereby reducing concentration of phenylalanine and/or its metabolites in blood and tissues, including the brain, is the only empirical treatment used.

Treatment of children with phenylketonuria by use of phenylalanine restriction in the diet was used first in this country in 1955 (Armstrong and Tyler, 1955) and in Cincinnati beginning in 1956 (Berry, Sutherland, and Guest, 1958). There have been no significant improvements in this highly restrictive treatment since its inception.

Initially, it was assumed that treatment could be terminated when major phases of brain growth were completed. Studies in our clinic with liberalization or termination of the diet at ages varying from 5 to 10 years suggest that behavioral changes occurred that interfered with school learning when serum phenylalanine levels rose above 20 mg/100 ml (Berry and Sutherland). It therefore seems unwise to terminate the low phenylalanine diet during the school years. The recognition that phenylketonuric women bore children with congenital abnormalities and subsequent mental retardation argued for continuation of the diet into adult years for women with phenylketonuria (Trouche et al., 1974). A report of psychotic behavior associated with phenylketonuria in individuals with normal intelligence (Perry, 1973) makes us cautious about termination of the diet at any age.

This work was supported by NICHD-00324 and Project 427, Maternal and Child Health Services, Mental Health and Health Services Administration, USPHS.

However, continuation of the treatment diet becomes increasingly difficult as the patient grows older. Phenylalanine requirements steadily decrease while the desire for a more normal life, particularly regarding food habits, becomes urgent as the treatment is successful in producing normal physical and intellectual development.

In this chapter, we describe the exploration of alternate methods for treatment of phenylketonuria so that either control of blood phenylalanine levels can be continued into the adult years, or some form of treatment may be developed that might inhibit the deleterious effect of phenylalanine on the central nervous system.

METHODS

For several years we have carried on a program of investigation of an animal model of phenylketonuria that was developed in our laboratory. Experimental phenylketonuria was induced in animals by the combined feeding of a moderate excess (3%) of phenylalanine in the diet and an inhibitor of phenylalanine hydroxylase, p-chlorophenylalanine. Learning deficits were shown in animals exposed either in utero (Butcher, 1970) or postnatally to the PKU-inducing diet (Butcher et al., 1970; Vorhees et al., 1972) compared to control animals pair-fed with either excess phenylalanine, inhibitor, or normal diet. Pair feeding was used for control animals to compensate for reduced food intake by animals fed the PKU-inducing diet. Pregnant female rats were fed the PKU-inducing diet and control diets between days 10 and 20 of gestation (day of conception = 0). On day 20 of pregnancy, mothers were lightly anesthetized; fetuses were removed, decapitated, and blood was drained into heparinized tubes. Brains were quickly removed from fetal animals and weighed. Brains were then homogenized in water and aliquots were deproteinized with sulfosalicyclic acid before amino acid analyses were made. Brain weights of fetal animals from mothers fed the PKU-inducing diet from day 10 to 20 of gestation, shown in Table 1, were significantly lower than from mothers fed any of the control diets. Concentrations of the essential amino acids—isoleucine, leucine, valine, methionine, and

Table 1. Effect of maternal diet on fetal brain weight

Maternal diet	Fetal brain weight (mg)
PKU	
Purina Chow + 3% PHE, 0.12% pCLPHE	111 ± 11
Controls	
1. Purina Chow + 3% PHE (PHE)	147 ± 11
2. Purina Chow + 0.12% pCLPHE (pCLPHE)	143 ± 11
3. Purina Chow (PFN)	148 ± 11
4. Purina Chow (ADLIB)	168 ± 4

Diets 1, 2, and 3 fed in amounts consumed by matched animal receiving PKU diet.

Table 2. Concentrations of essential amino acids in brain and plasma of rats with experimentally induced PKU compared to pair-fed controls

| | μM/liter | | | |
| | Brain | | Plasma | |
Amino acid	PKU	Control	PKU	Control
Arginine	181	111	179	167
Isoleucine	66	112	91	140
Leucine	183	209	184	262
Lysine	1137	646	1260	1430
Methionine	48	44	52	118
Phenylalanine	2460	240	2452	297
Threonine	990	678	281	315
Tryptophan	24	63	40	98
Valine	172	298	229	364

tryptophan—shown in Table 2, were reduced in both blood plasma and brain of fetal PKU rats compared to control animals. Values shown are from three or more litters of at least ten animals in each experimental or control group.

Using as a measure the reduced brain weight of PKU fetal animals, experiments were undertaken to determine the extent to which the physical and psychological abnormalities associated with induced PKU might be moderated by counter-feeding with those essential amino acids shown to be decreased in plasma and brain of animals with experimental PKU.

Pregnant female rats were fed the PKU-inducing diet supplemented with essential amino acids as shown in Table 3. Design of the experiment was similar to that just described. On day 20 of pregnancy, mothers were anesthetized and fetuses were removed. Blood was collected and brains were removed and weighed. Amino acid analyses were carried out on blood plasma and fetal brains.

Brain weights of animals fed the PKU-inducing diet plus essential amino acids are shown in Table 4. Fetuses from PKU animals fed the supplement of valine, isoleucine, and leucine (VIL) had brain weights in the range of pair-fed

Table 3. Composition of experimental diets in counter-feeding study

PKU—Purina Chow + 3% PHE, 0.12% pCLPHE
Controls—PHE, pCLPHE, PFN (all pair-fed), ADLIB
PKU-VIL—Purina Chow + 3% PHE, 0.12% pCLPHE, 1% valine, 0.5% isoleucine, 1% leucine
PFN-VIL—Purina Chow + 1% valine, 0.5% isoleucine, 1% leucine (pair-fed to PKU-VIL)
PKU-T—Purina Chow + 3% PHE, 0.12% pCLPHE, 2% tryptophan
PFN-T—Purina Chow + 2% tryptophan (pair-fed)
PKU-M—Purina Chow + 3% PHE, 0.12% pCLPHE 2% methionine
PFN-M—Purina Chow + 2% methionine

Table 4. Effect of maternal diet on fetal brain weight

PKU-inducing	Fetal brain weight (mg)	Control	Fetal brain weight (mg)
		ADLIB	168
PKU	118	PFN	147
		PHE	153
		pCLPHE	159
PKU-VIL	145	PFN-VIL	165
PKU-T	128	PFN-T	155
PKU-M	117	PFN-M	147

control animals, while fetuses from PKU animals fed tryptophan or methionine had lower brain weights, comparable to fetuses from mothers fed the PKU-inducing diet alone.

Amino acid concentrations in brain and plasma of fetal animals fed the PKU-inducing diet supplemented with VIL are shown in Table 5.

The VIL supplement resulted in approximately 30% increase in the concentrations of valine, isoleucine, and leucine in brain and plasma in PKU-VIL animals compared to PKU animals. The most striking difference, however, was the lower content of phenylalanine in brain of PKU-VIL fetal animals compared to PKU fetal animals. Phenylalanine concentrations in blood were in the same range.

Subsequently, pregnant females were fed the PKU-inducing diet together with VIL supplement or the appropriate control diets. The diets were terminated on day 17 or 19 of pregnancy and the young were not exposed to experimental diets postnatally. Behavioral testing was carried out and results are shown in Table 6. Analysis of variance showed the PKU group to be significantly different from other groups. A paired t-test comparing the PKU and PKU-VIL groups showed them to be significantly different. The data suggested that supplementation of the PKU-inducing diet with branch chain amino acids reduced the behavioral deficit associated with the high concentration of phenylalanine in plasma.

Table 5. Effect of VIL supplement on concentrations of amino acids in brain and plasma of rats with experimentally induced PKU

Amino acid	μM /liter			
	Brain		Plasma	
	PKU	PKU-VIL	PKU	PKU-VIL
Isoleucine	66	94	91	117
Leucine	183	178	184	195
Valine	172	225	229	359
Phenylalanine	2,460	1,586	2,452	2,408

Table 6. Effect of VIL supplement on maze-learning in rats with experimentally induced PKU

Diet group	Number of subjects	Errors to criterion in T-maze	No. trials to criterion
PKU	16	39.3	145.6
PKU-VIL	16	29.8	125.9
PFN-VIL	16	21.9	87.1
PFN	16	26.2	108.9
AD LIB	12	25.4	108.1

The counter-feeding study was extended to test whether or not addition of the VIL supplement to the diet of adult animals might affect maze learning performance if animals were tested while blood phenylalanine concentrations were elevated, a situation comparable to the phenylketonuric child with elevated serum phenylalanine concentrations. Adult male rats at 40 days of age were assigned to five diet groups of 12 animals per group. The experimental diets for PKU, PFN, PKU-VIL, PFN-VIL, and ADLIB groups were shown in Table 3. Animals were assigned to groups randomly, but pair-fed controls were chosen so that initial body weights were within ±2.0 g of the index animals. Diets were fed for 14 days and behavioral testing took place while animals were on the experimental diets. After nine days on the diets, testing in a multiple-T (Biel) water maze was begun and continued for six days. The rats were run in blind order through the backward path of the maze which increased the difficulty. Animals were scored according to number of total errors per trial. PKU, PKU-VIL, and PFN-VIL animals lost weight during the period; PFN animals gained approximately 6 g, while animals fed ADLIB gained approximately 60 g. There were no significant differences in brain weights taken after completion of the testing. Results of daily testing in the multiple-T water maze on days 9 through 14 showed that PKU-VIL animals were not significantly different from control animals and were significantly different from PKU animals, although blood phenylalanine values were comparable. The learning deficit usually associated with high concentrations of phenylalanine was not apparent in animals fed the PKU-VIL diet.

These results were sufficiently encouraging that a trial of adding an amino acid supplement of valine-isoleucine-leucine to the diet of phenylketonuric children was undertaken.

The subjects were children under treatment for phenylketonuria in whom blood phenylalanine levels had been above control range for at least three months and in whom behavioral or neurological changes had been observed. The first patient was a 15-year-old boy in whom the diagnosis of phenylketonuria was first made at three years of age. He had been on a low phenylalanine diet since the age of 3½ as a means of improving his excessive irritability and hyperactivity. He functioned in the mildly retarded range with a measured IQ of

Table 7. Counterfeeding plan for phenylketonuric child taking 300 g/day of lofenalac

Amino acid	Former intake (g/day)	Added (g/day)	Current intake (g/day)
Valine	3.6	3.6	7.2
Isoleucine	2.2	2.2	4.4
Leucine	4.2	4.2	8.4
Phenylalanine	0.5	0	0.5

60–65. Dietary management became increasingly difficult as he grew older and serum phenylalanine concentrations were consistently over 15 mg/100 ml. Perceptual motor deficits beyond those expected for his mental age, short attention span, hyperactive behavior, limited impulse control, and psychotic ideation contributed to his being almost unmanageable at home. Placement in a residential treatment facility was suggested, but VIL supplement was tried as an alternative.

The second patient was a 15-year-old girl in whom the diagnosis of phenylketonuria was made at nine months of age. She had been treated with a low phenylalanine diet since that time. Dietary control became increasingly difficult as she grew older, and serum phenylalanine concentrations were usually over 15 mg/100 ml. She had low to normal intelligence (IQ 90), but perceptual and visual motor deficits, distractability, poor impulse control, and hyperactivity accounted for her placement in learning disability classes. VIL supplement was tried because the mother was concerned that some alternative therapy should be found for her daughter for long-term use. Neither patient was considered ideal for testing the supplement. Both patients imposed a severe test on the efficacy of the alternate treatment.

Dosage of the VIL supplement was chosen to approximately equal that contained in the daily prescription of the low phenylalanine protein substitute, thus doubling the intake of the branch chain amino acids, as shown in Table 7. The VIL supplement was added directly to the low phenylalanine formula, taken at meals and at bed time. Study periods of four to six weeks, during which the supplement was given, were alternated with four to six week periods of no supplement for a total of about six months of study. No other changes were

Table 8. Concentrations of amino acids in plasma of patient 1 during periods off and on VIL supplement (μM/liter)

Amino acid	Off	On	Normal
Isoleucine	58	64	67
Leucine	102	112	120
Valine	270	316	220
Phenylalanine	798	782	57

made in the routine treatment program. Plasma amino acids were measured during each interval of *off* and *on* the supplement. Only slight increases in plasma concentration of the branch-chain amino acids were seen in patient 1, shown in Table 8. Higher doses may be required to bring concentrations into the normal range. Phenylalanine concentrations were similar *on* or *off* the supplement.

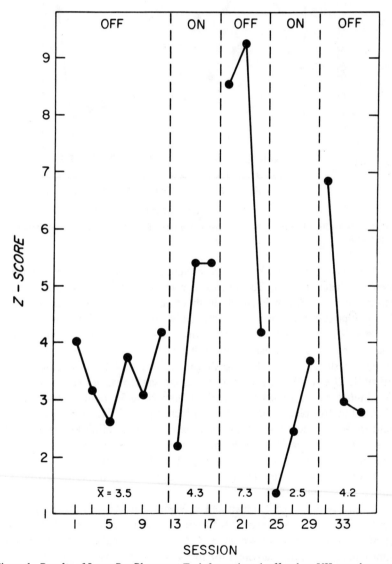

Figure 1. Results of Large Peg Placement Task for patient 1 *off* and *on* VIL supplement.

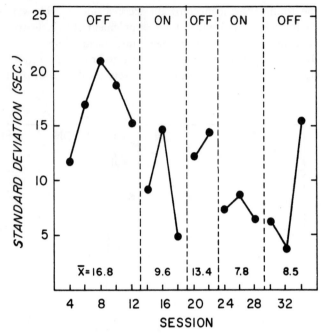

Figure 2. Results of Attention Diagnostic Method Task for patient 1 *off* and *on* VIL supplement.

A series of behavioral learning, attention, and motor tasks were administered weekly to each patient. The results in a motor coordination task, Large Peg Placement are shown in Figure 1. In this task, the child must transfer ten pegs that are placed horizontally to the child, into ten holes one-half inch in diameter. The score is the amount of time taken to place all ten pegs. A shorter time was required to transfer pegs during the second period *on* supplement. In Figure 2, results of the Attention Diagnostic Method (ADM) task are shown for patient 1. The ADM is a procedure for measuring temporary lapses of attention. The child is shown a display of numbers from 10 to 59, randomly arranged with a 5 X 10 matrix placed on an 18 X 36 inch piece of black mat board. The five numbers within each row are all the same color. The child's task is to name the color of the numbers, in order, beginning with ten. The cumulative time taken to name the color of each number is recorded. The results suggest reduced variability of attention during the periods *on* supplement. Again, the second period showed the greatest effect.

A third type of task is illustrated in Figure 3 for patient 2. The purpose of this test, Memory for Position, is to obtain a measure of nonverbal short-term retention. The child is shown an 8 X 8 inch white paper with one black dot (approximately 1/8 in diameter) for five seconds. The paper was covered for 30 seconds and the child was then asked to place a dot in the same position as the original. The measure is the distance between the original and the reproduced dot. Better memory for position is demonstrated during the first session of testing while patient 2 was *on* the supplement. Figure 4 illustrates serial learning by patient 2. The purpose is to measure the amount of study needed for one type of learning task. The child is shown a series of colored pictures of common objects (cup, book, flower), at the rate of one picture every three seconds. From seven to 12 pictures are shown, depending on age. The pictures are shown again in the same order with the child attempting to anticipate the next picture in the series before it is shown. The measure is the number of repetitions of the series necessary before all pictures are anticipated correctly. Figure 4 shows that fewer trials were required to learn the order of pictures in the series while *on* supplement.

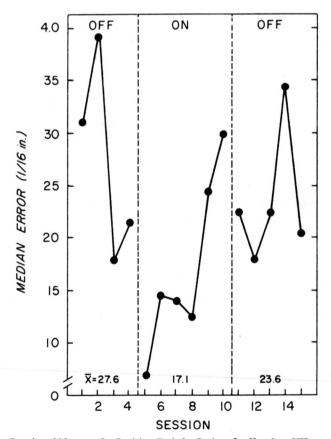

Figure 3. Results of Memory for Position Task for Patient 2 *off* and *on* VIL supplement.

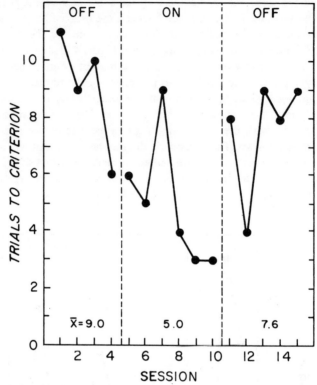

Figure 4. Results of Serial Learning Task for patient 2 *off* and *on* VIL supplement.

These results suggest improvement in motor and cognitive functioning by these two patients while taking the VIL supplement.

The addition of valine, leucine, and isoleucine to the present low phenylalanine diet for treatment of phenylketonuria would be simple. In animal studies, it prevented the maze learning deficits observed in animals with high concentrations of phenylalanine in blood. If it has the same effect in humans, as the data suggest, the diet may be liberalized. It prevented the reduction in brain weight seen in fetuses exposed in utero to high concentrations of phenylalanine in the mother. It prevented the subsequent behavioral deficits in offspring of mothers with high levels of phenylalanine in blood. If it has the same effect in humans, it might improve the prospects for phenylketonuric women with normal intelligence to bear normal children.

SUMMARY

An animal model of PKU was used to explore methods for prevention of the harmful effects of phenylalanine. Prenatal induction of PKU in rats resulted in small brains and later maze-learning deficits. Phenylalanine in brain of rats with PKU was raised while concentrations of other essential amino acids were decreased, suggesting interference by phenylalanine with amino acid transport. A supplement of valine, isoleucine, and leucine (VIL) given together with the PKU-inducing diet reduced the brain/blood ratio of phenylalanine, prevented the reduction of brain weights and prevented the behavioral deficits found postnatally in offspring of rats with maternal PKU. A supplement of VIL was then added to the low-phenylalanine diet of children under treatment for PKU. They showed improved performance in a series of tests of motor skill and coordination during periods of the VIL supplement that was not sustained off the supplement.

REFERENCES

Armstrong, M. D., and Tyler, F. H. (1955) Studies on phenylketonuria. 1. Restricted phenylalanine intake in phenylketonuria. J. Clin. Invest. 34:565.

Berry, H. K., Sutherland, B. S., and Guest, G. M. (1958) Chemical and clinical observations during treatment of children with phenylketonuria. Pediatrics 21:929.

Berry, H. K., and Sutherland, B. S. Effect of liberalization or termination of the diet for treatment of phenylketonuria. Unpublished observations.

Butcher, R. E. (1970) Learning impairment associated with maternal PKU in rats. Nature. 226:555.

Butcher, R., Vorhees, C., and Berry, H. (1970) A learning impairment associated with induced phenylketonuria. Life Sciences I. 9:1261.

Perry, T. L. (1973) Unrecognized adult phenylketonuria: Implications for obstetrics and psychiatry. N. Engl. J. Med. 289:395.

Trouche, A. M., Gigonnet, J. M., Darche, C., Nivelon-Chevallier, A., Nivelon, J. L., and Alison, M. (1974) Les enfants nés de mère phenylketonurique, a propos d'une nouvelle fratrie. Pediatrie. 29:33.

Vorhees, C., Butcher, R., and Berry, H. (1972) Reduced activity in rats with induced phenylketonuria. Devel. Psychobiol. 5:175.

RESEARCH TO PRACTICE IN MENTAL RETARDATION
Biomedical Aspects, Volume III
Edited by Peter Mittler
Copyright 1977 I.A.S.S.M.D.

REVERSAL OF APPARENT RETARDATION IN A PATIENT WITH EPILEPSY AND HYPERURICOSURIA

M. Coleman
2525 Belmont Road, N.W.,
Washington. D.C. 20008, United States

Although the overwhelming majority of older children who are classified as mentally retarded have irreversible syndromes that cannot be altered, occasionally a child is classified as mentally retarded when he actually has a depressed level of functioning caused by reversible factors. This very unusual situation arises when a patient has completely normal development of the brain for the first 18 months of life, with an onset of the disease process after that time, and it is most commonly found in patients on large doses of anticonvulsants.

In this chapter, we present one such unusual case. The child described was first seen at eight years of age and was classified in the range of severe mental retardation; today, at 14 years of age, he is functioning in a normal classroom and entering a normal seventh grade class.

CASE HISTORY

An eight-year-old boy presented with uncontrollable seizures. (A case report has already been published (Coleman, 1974)). An administrative decision had just been made by the Board of Education to move him from the special education classroom of the nearby public school into a school for the mentally retarded.

He was born at full term after an uneventful gestation and delivery, weighing 3.77 kg (8 lb, 6 oz). At first, the child progressed quite well in psychomotor milestones, walking at 10 months, and speaking little sentences, such as "I see you" and "Where is bird?" at 13 months of age.

At 22 months of age, the patient had his first seizure. He stopped in his tracks, stared, held his arms out, did not fall, then walked on. It lasted 20 seconds. The episodes rapidly progressed to both grand mal patterns and to a series of brief episodes consisting of loss of consciousness, assumption of the tonic neck position with face and eyes deviated to the left, and clonic jerking of the left side of the face. After the episodes, he was sleepy. Later, incontinence also occurred.

Initially, the seizure disorder was not controlled, although by both two and three years of age, electroencephalograms were read as normal. At four years of age, a successful anticonvulsant regimen was finally achieved with four drugs, and the child was seizure free for nine months. After that time, however, intermittent seizures of both the grand mal and atypical variant type persisted despite large doses of anticonvulsants. Combinations of phenobarbital, diphenyl-hydantoin sodium, primidone, mephobarbital, acetozolamide, carbamazepine, and diazepam were tried. In the following years, his EEGs became progressively more abnormal. In March, 1970, the child's condition was evaluated by an independent pediatric neurologist who told the parents that it was unrealistic to expect the child to have adequate seizure control. Dextroamphetamine sulfate also had been prescribed in an effort to control hyperactivity and irritability.

A school report in June, 1970 showed a depressed level of mental functioning. The child, almost eight years old, was reported to "recognize numerals 1 through 7 but no letters." He still could not dress himself or catch a large ball. He wore a football helmet at all times, including in school, to prevent head trauma from multiple seizures.

The parents were not consanguineous, but there was a family history of a mild seizure disorder on the maternal side; an uncle, described as a genius, had his first seizure at 41 years of age. There was no history of retardation, birth defects, or other neurological or psychiatric disease in the family. Four members of the family on the paternal side had gout, and the maternal grandfather had pernicious anemia.

Findings on general examination were unremarkable, except for a greenish-yellow tint to the skin. The following abnormalities were found on neurological examination: hyperactivity, severe dysarthria, and mild truncal ataxia. Slight dysmetria and terminal tremor were present on finger-to-nose examination, although there was no true sustention or intention tremor and no nystagmus or changes in muscular tonus. Cranial circumference was in the 25th percentile. Sensory examination could not be completed satisfactorily, so the noteworthy insensitivity to pain suggested by the history (no pain in a severely abscessed tooth) could not be confirmed.

A hospital evaluation disclosed normal values for the following tests: in the blood-complete white cell count, glucose and two-hour postprandial glucose,

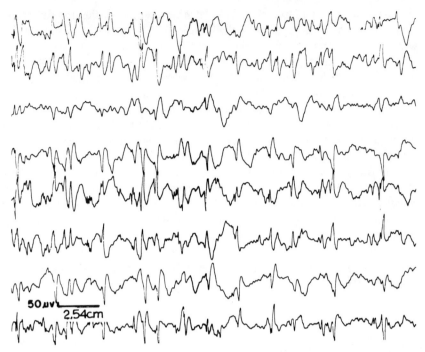

Figure 1. EEG taken in patient before allopurinol therapy. This tracing was described as "abnormal to a severe degree; background activity disorganized; almost constant high voltage spikes and 3 to 5/sec spike/wave discharges appear from both sides."

calcium, phosphorus, magnesium, blood urea nitrogen, total 5-hydroxyindoles, and creatinine determinations; in the urine-standard urinalysis, amino acid chromatogram, vanillylmandelic acid, homovanillic acid, dopamine, and 5-hydroxyindoleacetic acid determinations; and in creatinine clearance (102.6 ml/min/1.73 sq m). The only abnormal values were uric acid in the serum (7.3 mg/100 ml—borderline elevation) and the EEG (abnormal to a severe degree; background activity disorganized; almost constant high voltage spikes and 3 to 5/sec spike/wave discharges appearing from both sides—Figure 1).

Because the elevation of the uric acid content was the only abnormal finding in this deteriorating patient, a restricted purine diet was instituted. On this new diet, the serum uric acid level ranged from 5.4 to 6.6 mg/100 ml with one exception of 12.8 mg/100 ml. Levels in 24-hr urine specimens ranged from 25.1 to 30.6 mg/kg—all very abnormal values. The seizure pattern was unchanged on the diet.

On July 8, 1970, allopurinol, an established xanthine oxidase inhibitor, was added to the patient's therapeutic regimen after informed consent was obtained from the parents. The initial dose was 25 mg the first day, 50 mg the second day, and then a maintenance dose of 75 mg (2.4 mg/kg). Three days after starting to take allopurinol, the child became seizure-free for the first day in four years. On the third day, he had a slight fever (38.7° C, 101.6° F), in association with an upper respiratory infection, and still did not have any seizures.

One week later he remained seizure-free, seemed slightly less ataxic on examination, drooled less, appeared calmer with a longer attention span, and the tone quality of his voice had dropped. He still was hyperactive and still somewhat "dopey" during that examination. The parents reported that his usual sleeping pattern of six hours per night had stretched to 11 hours per night since being given allopurinol. When started on the drug, the child was taking four anticonvulsants; these were gradually tapered off during the course of the next six months. The patient gradually became more alert, developed a "tremendous" appetite for the restricted purine diet, became less constipated, and in six months, lost the yellow tint to the skin. Nine months after the initial dose of allopurinol, the EEG had become normal (Figure 2). The child's school performance improved remarkably and he began to learn rapidly. By September, 1973, three years after initiation of allopurinol therapy, he entered a normal fourth grade class, functioning at that grade level in every skill except reading (third grade level).

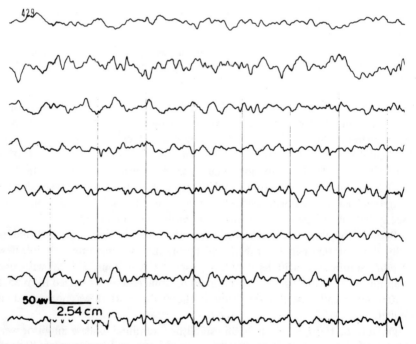

Figure 2. Fifth EEG taken in this patient after he received allopurinol for nine months. The tracing was described as "within normal limits."

By September, 1976, six years after the initiation of the therapy he had continued to progress and was entering a normal seventh grade classroom. During this period, his skills were commensurate with his age level. However, psychological testing, particularly the Bender-Gestalt still showed some residual of the previous disease process.

Between the ages of 12 and 14 the child broke through with seizures intermittently and the 24-hr urinary uric acid tended to jump up and down during this period. However, since the age of 14 he is again stabilized and been seizure-free.

DISCUSSION

The clinical reversal of this severe organic brain syndrome by use of a drug designed to normalize the patient's biochemistry has been an unexpected and gratifying result. Particularly surprising was the gradual reversal of the EEG abnormalities, including the focus of the EEG that had led previous examiners to assume there might have been a traumatic cause of this patient's disease process, although EEG foci have been described in other metabolic imbalances such as uremia. Although the EEG has remained normal for more than five years, the last time the patient broke through with a seizure he still had an asymmetrical pattern of left head-turning during the seizure.

Another surprising development was the rapid progress in school that began after allopurinol therapy was initiated. In retrospect, the presence of four anticonvulsants in a futile attempt to control seizures may have further compromised mental functioning already impaired by a progressive disease of the central nervous system (CNS). The patient now appears to be functioning mentally in the normal range, and he is progressing at the rate of one grade level per year. This type of recovery in a child classified as mentally retarded is, of course, only possible if the brain is essentially intact during the very early years of cerebral development with a later onset of the disease process. We now know that this child had a pseudo-retardation clinical picture when he was first seen by our research group.

The biochemical studies of this patient fall into two distinct categories. First is the identification of the increased rate of excretion of uric acid, with one serum level rising as high as 12.8 mg/100 ml and urinary levels up to 30.6 mg/kg per 24 hr, even on a restricted purine diet. It is important to note that the 24-hr urine levels were consistently abnormal, while the serum fluctuated, sometimes in the normal range. The enzyme error involved has not yet been identified. The child does not have the Lesch-Nyhan syndrome both because of clinical differences (e.g., no self-mutilation as well as seizures as the initial symptom rather than of late onset) and because the level of HPRT (hypoxanthinephosphoribosyl transferase) is normal in his leucocytes. Although all the CNA purine syndromes share many features, it is possible that this patient may have a separate, severe disorder of purine metabolism, which fortunately responds to an inhibitor of xanthine oxidase.

A study of several of the patient's urine samples both before allopurinol therapy by high-resolution liquid chromatography and while on the therapy has failed to reveal any abnormal metabolites known to be directly related to the purine biosynthetic pathway. Instead, elevated levels of tyrosine suggest that there is a functional depression of p-hydroxyphenylpyruvate oxidase in this child. There also was elevation of other compounds of the tyrosine pathway: 4-hydroxyhippuric acid, β(-hydroxyphenyl−) hydracrylic acid, and a newly identified compound named α-methyloxyhomovanillic acid. These abnormalities, however, are nonspecific. They also have been identified in autistic patients and patients with the Lesch-Nyhan syndrome as well as in patients without CNS symptoms who suffer from chronic leukemia, malignant carcinoid, synovial sarcoma, embryonic neoplasia, and multiple myeloma. Therefore, their relevance to the primary disease process in our patient is in doubt. Because p-hydroxyphenylpyruvate oxidase is an ascorbic acid-related enzyme, ascorbic acid was added to the patient's therapeutic regimen as part of the constant effort to replace a drug as toxic as allopurinol with a more benign medication. It seems to be of value and has allowed the dose of allopurinol to be reduced.

The patient is totally allopurinol-dependent. He has received it every four hours since his first dose in July, 1970, except for attempts to lengthen the time span between doses. Three times attempts were made to eliminate the 2:00 a.m. dose by increasing the previous evening doses, and each time the patient went out of seizure-control for a number of days following the unsuccessful trial. Since the turnover time of allopurinol is 3½ to 4 hours, one interpretation of these data is that continuous xanthine oxidase inhibition is essential.

However, allopurinol is a drug with many other biochemical actions that could effect the CNS: suppression of purine synthesis de novo, interference with pyrimidine metabolism, and inhibition of tryptophan pyrrolase activity. It also may inhibit the biotransformation of other drugs administered simultaneously and may deplete phosphoribosylpyrophosphate. It is interesting that the removal of the greenish-yellow tint from the skin of this patient by allopurinol (a color also seen in the skin or teeth of other hyperuricemic patients) suggests that the color may be caused by a purine metabolic product. At present, the mode of action of allopurinol responsible for the therapeutic effect is not established. None of the other purine syndromes associated with CNS disease has established treatments available, although the patient of Hooft, Nevel, and De Schaepdryver (1968) had an "undeniable improvement" on a low purine diet.

This patient's experience reinforces a number of clinical dicta of medicine. Uric acid abnormalities in children are determined more accurately in some patients by 24-hr urine specimens than by serum levels. An EEG focus is not always irreversible. Caution should be used in classifying the level of mental functioning in a child given large doses of four anticonvulsants. And the physician should never stop studying the history and examination results of a patient, looking for new leads, no matter how irreversible and hopeless the condition seems.

SUMMARY

A 22-month-old patient developed seizures that could not be controlled by anticonvulsants. By eight years of age, both the child's level of mental function and his electroencephalogram had markedly regressed out of the normal range. After identification of hyperuricosuria in the child, institution of a restricted purine diet and allopurinol was accompanied by control of the patient's seizures, a reversal of the abnormal electroencephalogram, and a striking improvement of mental functioning.

ACKNOWLEDGMENTS

The author is grateful to the editor of the *Archives of Neurology* for permission to reproduce Figures 1 and 2 originally published in 1974.

REFERENCES

Coleman, M., Landgrebe, M., and Landgrebe, A. (1974) Progressive seizures with hyperuricosuria reversed by allopurinol. Arch Neurol. 31:238.
Hooft, C., Nevel, C. V., and De Schaepdryver, A. F. (1968) Hyperuricosuric encephalopathy without hyperuricaemia. Arch. Dis. Child. 43:734.

ENVIRONMENTAL HAZARDS
Prenatal Infections

RESEARCH TO PRACTICE IN MENTAL RETARDATION
Biomedical Aspects, Volume III
Edited by Peter Mittler
Copyright 1977 I.A.S.S.M.D.

PRENATAL INFECTIONS AND PSYCHOSOCIAL DEVELOPMENT IN CHILDREN BORN INTO LOWER SOCIOECONOMIC SETTINGS

C. A. Alford
Department of Pediatrics,
University of Alabama in Birmingham,
Birmingham, Alabama 35294,
United States

Infections have long been recognized as prevalent problems of pregnancy, especially those acute forms that evidence dramatic onsets and run predictable or fulminant courses. The classical bacterial and acute communicable viral infections both fall in this category (Manson et al., 1960; Eichenwald, 1967; Mims, 1968; Monif, 1969; Klein et al., 1973). This group obviously contributes to the problems of pregnancy wastage through direct invasion of the conceptus by the pathogen or through expulsion of the embryo secondary to profound physiological disturbances in the mother that have not yet been precisely defined (Manson et al., 1960; Klein et al., 1973). However, the impacts of low grade, chronic, recurrent, and latent infections in pregnancy disturbances are much less well-understood; they are difficult to assess because of their subtle presentation in the mother. Indeed, in the conceptus they are also often too subtle to be recognized clinically, or they are completely asymptomatic. Yet, these "silent" forms of infections undoubtedly occur more commonly during the course of pregnancy than do the acute diseases. Clearly then, it becomes quite important from a public health standpoint to determine whether or not these less dramatic infections have an adverse effect on the outcome of pregnancy and the future performance of the offspring.

Perhaps the single most striking pathogenetic difference between the two arbitrary groups of infections described here is the self-limited nature of the acute forms and the tendency for chronicity or recurrence in the more subtle varieties (Alford et al., 1974a). In the self-limited groups, the infections run an acute course and are then cleared either by killing the host, with the more severe diseases, or by being eliminated by the host defense mechanisms followed by complete or partial immunity of the host to reinvasion by the pathogen. Thus, functional damage is thought to occur in a circumscribed period of time and thereafter can be assessed without the need to be concerned about persistent low-grade disease or recurrent episodes. Pregnancy infections, especially the bacterial types, have most often been viewed in this light in the past. Therefore, therapy has been designed to minimize the damage that occurs during the acute course of the disease, without regard for a continuing or a recurrent process. The resultant damage in both mother and baby has likewise been assessed mainly in the immediate postinfection period, and possible long-term effects are frequently overlooked. This approach is particularly inappropriate when the developing central nervous system or perceptual organs of the fetus or young infant has been involved. Clearly, insults to these organs, for which compensation might be made in older individuals, are likely to be more permanent and disabling when inflicted in the formative stages.

This chapter focuses attention on a group of infections characterized by chronicity and/or recurrence in the mother, baby, or both, and emphasizes their subtle effects on mental and perceptual morbidity in the child. The agents involved include cytomegalovirus (CMV), herpes simplex virus (HSV), rubella virus, *Toxoplasma gondii,* and *Treponema pallidum.* It is likely that Hepatitis A and B viruses and Epstein-Barr virus will be included in this group with time, but currently there is inadequate data about their role as perinatal pathogens to include them here. *Mycobacterium tuberculosis* (Corner et al., 1955), *Trypanosoma cruzi* (Howard et al., 1968), and the various agents that produce malaria (Covell, 1950) share the ability to produce chronic infection but will not be discussed because of the rarity of the former and the limited geographic distribution of the latter two.

INCIDENCE AND NATURE
OF CHRONIC PERINATAL INFECTION IN MOTHERS AND BABIES

The potential role of the chronic perinatal infections in the production of mental and perceptual disturbances is best reflected by their frequencies in pregnant females and their offspring. The incidence data are summarized in Table 1. At present in the United States, as determined by antibody prevalence, approximately 10%, 15%, 70%, and more than 99% of the female population in the child bearing age group are susceptible to rubella (Sever et al., 1969), CMV (Stagno et al., 1975a), toxoplasmosis (Feldman, 1968), and syphilis, respectively. The major variable influencing susceptibility is age; younger females are more susceptible than older ones. Other variables include socioeconomic status, geographic location, sexual promiscuity (HSV and syphilis), and consumption of undercooked meats or exposure to cats (toxoplasma). Clearly, the young and poor, especially those in developed countries, are more liable to acquisition of

Table 1. Incidence of maternal and chronic perinatal infection

Infection	Mother (per 1,000 pregnancies)	Fetus[a] (per 1,000 live births)	Natal—Newborn[b] (per 1,000 live births)
Cytomegalovirus	40–150	5–20	10–50
Rubella			
Epidemic	20–40	4–30	0.0
Interepidemic	1	0.5[c]	0.0
Toxoplasmosis	1.5–6.4	0.75–1.3	0.0
HSV	10–15	Rare	0.03–0.33
Syphilis	0.2[d]	0.1[d]	0.0
Cumulative total (excluding epidemic rubella)	53–173	6.3–27	10–50

[a]Designates intrauterine infection acquired before the immediate delivery period
[b]Designates infection acquired at or just before delivery
[c]Estimate
[d]Estimate derived from Center for Disease Control surveillance data
References: CMV: Feldman, 1969; Nankervis et al., 1972; Reynolds et al., 1973; Numazaki et al., 1970; Stern et al., 1973; Starr et al., 1970. Epidemic Rubella: Horstmann et al., 1965; Sever et al., 1969; Schiff et al., 1970. Interepidemic Rubella: Kimball et al., 1971. Toxoplasmosis: Kimball et al., 1971; Sever, 1966; Alford et al., 1974b. HVS: Nahmias et al., 1971; Ng et al., 1970; Florman et al., 1973.

the chronic perinatal infections, just as they are with most other types of infection. The figures shown in Table 1 refer mainly to developed nations. The situation is less clear in newly developing countries for lack of data, but the rates of infections with the two herpes virsus (CMV and HSV) probably are more exaggerated than those depicted because of the frequency of recurrent genital tract infections.

The overall incidence of active maternal infection during pregnancy (approximately 13%), is singularly impressive. By far the most common is CMV infection, which alone accounts for approximately 10% of the infections (range 4–15%) (Reynolds et al., 1973). The other maternal infections, listed in decreasing order of frequency, are: rubella (epidemic), 2–4% (Horstmann et al., 1965; Sever et al., 1969); HSV, 1–1.5% (Nahmias et al., 1971; Alford, personal observations); toxoplasmosis, 0.15–0.64% (Remington, 1969; Desmonts and Couvreur, 1974, 1975); rubella (endemic), 0.1% (Sever et al., 1969); and syphilis, variable but last recorded for the United States at about 0.02%. In terms of transmission to the fetus, rubella, toxoplasma, and syphilis are for the most part dangerous only during primary infections, i.e., when they are acquired for the first time by nonimmune females (Alford et al., 1974a). The organisms then gain access to the fetus via the blood stream, probably initially by infecting the placenta. Genital infection is incidental to the primary infections with these organisms, and recurrences in this site are unlikely. Thus, natal infections, those transmitted during delivery because exposure to the infectious agent in the lower genital area are thought not to occur with rubella, toxoplasma, and syphilis (Alford et al., 1974a). As far as transmission to the fetus or newborn is concerned, primary infection of the mother is less of a problem with CMV and HSV than are recurrent genital tract infections. These two viruses, most often acquired initially in childhood, are believed to cause latent infections and are prone to recurrent genital tract reactivations with or without pregnancy. Thus, both CMV and HSV may be transmitted during delivery causing, respectively, persistent and recurrent natal infection in the offspring (Nahmias et al., 1973; Alford et al., 1975). In addition, CMV is frequently transmitted (0.5–2.0% of the population) in utero in immune females by mechanisms currently unknown (Stagno et al., 1975b).

By comparing the overall maternal infection rates with the combined fetal and natal infection rates (Table 1), the former obviously exceed the latter by 3–8 fold. There is, then, inherent protection for the product of conception from invasion by the organisms harbored by the mother. This is fortunate given the inordinately high rates of maternal infection and the fact that each of these pathogens may damage the brain and perceptual organs of the offspring resulting in a constellation of abnormalities ranging from fetal death to asymptomatic but chronic infection (Alford et al., 1974a). Exactly what these protective mechanisms are is currently unknown, but solution is important from the standpoint of future therapy or prevention.

Even with this protection, as noted in Table 1, the incidence of intrauterine and natal infection is alarmingly high. Congenital acquisition occurs in 0.5–2.7%, and natal acquisition occurs in 1–5% of all deliveries. Anywhere from 1–7% of the infants in this country may then be infected by one of these organisms depending mainly on the age and socioeconomic status of the mother. CMV is currently believed to be the most important potential pathogen accounting for the great majority of perinatally acquired infections (Table 1). This is attributable to its high rate of maternal recurrences and its ability to invade both in utero and during delivery in the face of maternal immunity (Stagno et al., 1975b). The latter feature is shared by HSV, but the recurrent maternal infection rates are far less common than with CMV.

One could reasonably ask why such prevalent infections have been missed in the past. This is because they are more often asymptomatic in both mother and baby, in the latter case, whether congenitally or natally acquired. Not until large-scale laboratory screening studies were performed just recently, were their true frequencies uncovered. Although maternal rubella does cause German measles syndrome, it is just as often subclinical, and CMV and toxoplasma infections only rarely cause heterophil negative infectious mononucleosis. The genital lesions of syphilis, HSV, and CMV often go unnoticed because of their location and lack of symptoms, and, with the latter two infections, asymptomatic viral excretion most commonly occurs (Gluck, 1974). Among the infants with the congenitally acquired infections caused by CMV (Hanshaw, 1968), toxoplasma (Desmonts et al., 1974), rubella (Schiff et al., 1970), and syphilis

(Platou, 1949), over 90%, 70%, 65%, and 50% respectively, are born asymptomatically infected, as are virtually all those with natally acquired CMV. Perinatally acquired HSV infections are the exception to this rule; all neonates who acquire this infection are thought to be in jeopardy of an acute, severe, often lethal disease (Nahmias et al., 1970).

LONG-TERM OUTCOME OF THE
"SILENT" CONGENITALLY ACQUIRED INFECTIONS

In infants born with severe chronic intrauterine infections, those who are symptomatic at birth, a wide spectrum of central nervous system (CNS) involvement is notable (Alford et al., 1974a). Microcephaly, hydrocephalus, severe mental retardation, convulsive, and/or gross as well as fine motor disorders are often obvious at or soon after delivery (Alford et al., 1974a). Evident perceptual disorders in addition to CNS defects, may include: chorioretinitis, cataracts, glaucoma, keratoconjunctivitis, interstitial keratitis, and deafness (central and peripheral), among others. These grossly destructive presentations are fortunately rare among infants born with chronic intrauterine infections, as noted in the preceding data. However, they serve to emphasize the ability of these infectious agents to grow in and destroy a wide range of cells in the CNS axis. There is good reason to believe that the infections that are subclinical can be associated with less evident, low-grade pathology in the CNS axis that may not be detectable for months or years following delivery. In fact auditory, visual, intellectual, and behavioral functions cannot even be properly assessed for a few years following delivery. Only gross defects are demonstrable and minimal brain damage must await further maturation before testing. Clearly, then, even damage inflicted in utero may be missed in early life only to become more evident as time advances and the inappropriate integration of CNS and perceptual functions becomes overtly manifest. With the chronic intrauterine infections, especially CMV, which is the most persistent, pathology may be progressive or even recurrent because of exacerbations or reactivations from the latent state. Although not present at birth, continuing destruction in critical sites could lead, in time, to significant functional difficulties, including: hearing, visual, language, learning, and behavioral problems (Melish et al., 1973; Reynolds et al., 1974; Alford et al., 1975). Thus, in cases in which the mother is known to sustain one of these infections during pregnancy, the offspring's perceptual and CNS functions, including psychological testing, should be carefully and serially assessed. This is particularly true with "minimal" brain damage because many postnatal environmental factors (parent-child interactions, socioeconomic elements, stability of home, etc.) can profoundly influence the eventual performance of the child with regard to his/her ability to cope in his/her given social setting (Hanshaw et al., 1975).

The late onset CNS and perceptual sequelae is summarized for each of the silent chronic intrauterine infections in Table 2. Although the basic pathology

Table 2. Late CNS and perceptual sequelae of "silent" chronic intrauterine infections[a]

CMV:	Hearing loss, minimal brain dysfunction syndrome—learning, language, and behavioral problems.
Rubella:	Hearing and visual loss (cataracts, glaucoma, cloudy cornea), minimal brain dysfunction syndrome—learning, language, and behavioral problems. Potential problems—autism, and late onset degenerative brain disease.
Toxoplasmosis:[b]	Visual disturbances (missed or recurrent chorioretinitis), perhaps lowered IQ.
HSV:[b]	Visual difficulty (recurrent keratoconjunctivitis), perhaps recurrent acute encephalitis.
Syphilis:[b]	Visual difficulty (interstitial keratitis), degenerative brain syndromes.

[a]Alford et al. *Infections of the Fetus and the Newborn Infant.* New York: Alan R. Liss, Inc., 1975.
[b]Minimal brain dysfunction syndromes probably result from each of these infections, but the problem has not been adequately investigated to date.

differs with each agent, functional disturbances obviously overlap because their final expression may be similar depending on the combination of organs involved in an individual patient (Alford et al., 1974a). As a result of the frequency of congenital CMV, the occurrence of auditory defects and minimal brain dysfunction syndrome is a major concern (Reynolds et al., 1974; Hanshaw et al., 1975). Because infection in both the mother and baby is most often silent, well over 90% of the infected infants go undetected. Congenital CMV, therefore, conceivably contributes significantly to such common problems as learning and behavioral difficulties, the etiologies of which are currently unknown. Thus, determining exactly the proportion of infected infants with damage that is sufficient to produce functional problems is mandatory in order to appreciate the true public health significance of intrauterine CMV. Only large-scale laboratory screening of pregnant women and their offspring for diagnosis, followed by long-term follow-up studies to define outcome, can be used for this purpose because the infections are most often subclinical. Such kinds of studies are, of course, an incredible chore. However, a limited number have been partially completed to date (Starr et al., 1970; Reynolds et al., 1974; Hanshaw et al., 1975). The results of these indicate that silent congenital CMV may be a major contributor to deafness (Reynolds et al., 1974) and its attendant language and school difficulties, and that it probably causes lowered IQ, further complicating the capability of the infected child to achieve normal social goals (Reynolds et al., 1974; Hanshaw et al., 1975). The latter is particularly true in lower socioeconomic populations for whom postnatal social adjustments cannot adequately compensate for the original brain insult, as they appear to do in more affluent groups (Hanshaw et al., 1975). It is of major importance now to better define the relationship between low-grade organic damage produced by the silent perinatal infections and the psychosocial variables that may modify outcome in the large number of afflicted children, as discussed by Scheiner in the following chapter.

All too often school difficulties and social maladjustments are relegated to the realm of ill-defined "genetic propensity" and/or social deprivation per se. This is a somewhat depressing concept because prophylaxis of such disorders would be difficult, if not impossible, to achieve. In contrast, if the organic damage produced by finite but unseen environmental factors, such as the infections discussed here, were the initial stimulus for these all too common social maladjustments, then prophylactic and therapeutic measures could conceivably be designed in the near future. Just how many noxious environmental factors might mimic the chronic perinatal infections in diminishing the capacity of young infants to achieve their full genetic potential is unknown at present. It is hoped that studies directed at solving this matter will be forthcoming so that the immense body of medical knowledge can be directed toward the improvement of the quality of life for future generations.

SUMMARY

The type, incidence, and nature of maternal infections that cause persistent involvement of the offspring are summarized. The outcome of the infections in the child, especially as regards their effect on perceptual and mental development in lower socioeconomic settings, is reviewed.

REFERENCES

Alford, C. A. Personal observations.

Alford, C. A., et al. (1974a) Perinatal infections caused by viruses, toxoplasma and Treponema Pallidum. *In* Clinical Perinatology. St. Louis: C. V. Mosby.

Alford, C. A., et al. (1974b) Congenital toxoplasmosis: Clinical laboratory and therapeutic considerations with special reference to subclinical disease. Bull. N.Y. Acad. Med. 50:160.

Alford, C. A., et al. (1975a) Infections of the Fetus and the Newborn Infant. New York: Alan R. Liss, p. 133.

Alford, C. A., Jr., et al. (1975b) Modern Perinatal Medicine. Chicago: Year Book Medical Publishers, p. 285.

Corner, B. D., et al. (1955) Congenital tuberculosis: A report of a case with necropsy on mother and baby. Thorax. 10:99.

Covell, G. (1950) Congenital malaria. Trop. Dis. Bull. 47:1147.

Desmonts, G., and Couvreur, J. (1974) Toxoplasmosis in pregnancy and its transmission to the fetus. Bull. N.Y. Acad. Med. 50:146.

Desmonts, G., and Couvreur, J. (1975) Infections of the Fetus and the Newborn Infant. New York: Alan R. Liss, p. 115.

Eichenwald, H. F., et al. (1967) Virus infections of the newborn. Prog. Med. Virol. 9:35.

Feldman, H. A. (1968) Toxoplasmosis. New Engl. J. Med. 279:1370.

Feldman, R. A. (1969) Cytomegalovirus infection during pregnancy: A prospective study and report of six cases. Amer. J. Dis. Child. 117:517.

Florman, A. L., et al. (1973) Intrauterine infection with herpes simplex virus: Resultant congenital malformations. JAMA 225:129.

Gluck, L. (1974) Modern Perinatal Medicine. Chicago: Year Book Medical Publishers, Inc.

Hanshaw, J. B. (1968) Congenital cytomegalovirus infection—a fifteen year perspective. J. Infect. Dis. 123:555.

Hanshaw, J. B., et al. (1975) Infections of the Fetus and the Newborn Infant. New York: Alan R. Liss, p. 47.

Horstmann, D. M., et al. (1965) Maternal rubella and the rubella syndrome in infants. Amer. J. Dis. Child. 110:408.

Howard, J., et al. (1968) Congenital Chagas' disease I: Clinical and epidemiologic study of thirty cases. Bol. Chil. Parasitol. 23:107.

Kimball, A. C., et al. (1971) Congenital toxoplasmosis: A prospective study of 4,048 obstetric patients. Amer. J. Obstet. Gynec. 111:211.

Klein, J. O., et al. (1973) Infection in the newborn. In Obstetric and Perinatal Infections. Philadelphia: Lea & Febiger.

Manson, M. M., et al. (1960) Rubella and Other Virus Infections during Pregnancy. London: H.M.S.O.

Melish, M. E., et al. (1973) Congenital cytomegalovirus infection—developmental progress of infants detected by routine screening. Amer. J. Dis. Child. 126:190.

Mims, C. A. (1968) Pathogenesis of viral infections of the fetus. Prog. Med. Virol. 10:194.

Monif, G. R. G. (1969) Viral Infections of the Human Fetus. London: Macmillan.

Nahmias, A. J., et al. (1970) Infection of the newborn with herpesvirus hominis. Adv. Pediatr. 17:185.

Nahmias, A. J., et al. (1971) Perinatal risk associated with maternal genital herpes simplex virus infection. Amer. J. Obstet. Gynec. 110:825.

Nahmias, A. J., et al. (1972) Significance of herpes simplex virus infection during pregnancy. Clin. Obstet. Gynec. 15:929.

Nahmias, A. J., et al. (1973) Infection with herpes simplex viruses 1 and 2. New Engl. J. Med. 289:667.

Nankervis, G. A., et al. (1972) A prospective study of maternal cytomegalovirus and its effect on the fetus. Pediatr. Res. 6:385.

Ng, A. B. P., et al. (1970) Herpes genitalis: Clinical and cytopathologic experience with 256 patients. Obstet. Gynaec. 36:645.

Numazaki, Y., et al. (1970) Primary infection with human cytomegalovirus: Virus isolation from healthy infants and pregnant women. Amer. J. Epidemiol. 91:410.

Platou, R. V. (1949) Treatment of congenital syphilis with penicillin. Adv. Pediatr. 4:39.

Remington, J. S. (1969) The present status of IgM fluorescent antibody technique in the diagnosis of congenital toxoplasmosis. J. Pediatr. 75:1116.

Reynolds, D. W., et al. (1973) Maternal cytomegalovirus excretion and perinatal infection. New Engl. J. Med. 289:1.

Reynolds, D. W., et al. (1974) Congenital cytomegalovirus infection with elevated cord IgM levels—causal relationship with auditory and mental deficiency. New Engl. J. Med. 290:291.

Schiff, G. M., et al. (1970) Congenital rubella. *In* Perinatal Infections. Stuttgart: Georg Thieme Verlag.

Sever, J. L. (1966) Perinatal infections affecting the developing fetus and newborn, in the prevention of mental retardation through the control of infectious diseases. U.S. Public Health Service Publication No. 1962, Washington, D.C., Department of Health, Education and Welfare.

Sever, J. L., et al. (1969) Rubella in the collaborative perinatal research study. Amer. J. Dis. Child. 118:123.

Stagno, S., et al. (1975a) Comparative, serial virologic and serologic studies of symptomatic and subclinical congenital and natally acquired cytomegalovirus infections. J. Infect. Dis. 132:568.

Stagno, S., et al. (1975b) Congenital cytomegalovirus infection (C-CMV)—occurrence in an immune population. Program & Abstracts, 15th Interscience Conference on Antimicrobial Agents and Chemotherapy, Session 24, No. 232.

Starr, J. G., et al. (1970) Inapparent congenital cytomegalovirus infection: Clinical and epidemiologic characteristics in early infancy. New Engl. J. Med. 282:1075.

Stern, H., et al. (1973) Prospective study of cytomegalovirus infection in pregnancy. Brit. Med. J. 2:268.

RESEARCH TO PRACTICE IN MENTAL RETARDATION
Biomedical Aspects, Volume III
Edited by Peter Mittler
Copyright 1977 I.A.S.S.M.D.

THE STUDY OF CHILDREN WITH CONGENITAL CYTOMEGALOVIRUS INFECTION

A. P. Scheiner, J. B. Hanshaw, R. J. Simeonsson, and B. Scheiner
Monroe Developmental Services,
620 Westfall Road,
Rochester, New York 14620, United States

The study of perinatal factors that affect intellectual function must be approached cautiously. The pitfalls that could lead to spuriously positive results are many, and, even in the most meticulous studies, variables are difficult to control and measure.

We all are aware of the interaction of environmental factors and genetic endowment as determinants of intelligence. The problem has been studied extensively by such authors as Knoblock and Pasamanick (1976), Hunt (1961), Hardy (1965), Jensen (1968) and Heber et al. (1972). Although there is not a consensus among these authors as to the relative contributions of nature and nurture, they generally agree that the environment and the genetic makeup of the person interact to produce the observable behavior and intellect of the individual.

Anthony and Koupernik (1974) and Sameroff (1974) contributed to the complexity of the issue by including the transactional state, a dynamic, multi-variable environment that is in a constant state of change and adjustment over time. They describe a state that is the composite of the response of the environment to the individual, whose behavior is a sum of his previous experience and genetic makeup. The environment, at a minimum, consists of siblings, parents, relatives, and friends, who participate in the minute-to-minute caring for the child in settings with a variety of levels of sensory stimuli.

The selective, increased morbidity of the lower socioeconomic child to perinatal complications as compared to middle and upper class children can only be interpreted when one studies the physical, biological, and social environment, family genetics, and the transactional state which occurs within this environment. The continuum of reproductive casualty presented by Lilienfeld and Parkhurst (1951) and studied by Pasamanick and Knoblock (1966) implies a direct relationship between the degree of neonatal injury and the long-term neurological, affective, and cognitive outcome of the youngster. Although these authors have emphasized the contribution of the environment to intelligence, this cause and effect model traditionally does not include the parent/child interaction and the genetic vulnerability of the youngster. Current psychiatric risk and schizophrenia studies have increased our awareness of these important variables. Garmezy (1974) has stressed the interaction of genetic vulnerability of the child with life's events to produce mental illness. The synergism between the undesirable effects of infection and malnutrition described by Birch and Cravioto (1966) may test the ability of the child to withstand central nervous system injury that may result in decreased intelligence.

It is apparent that a profound neonatal insult may lead to severe intellectual and neurological dysfunction. However, the outcome of the more mildly affected infant or the infant with an inapparent perinatal injury may be determined by such variables as the infant's genetic threshold to withstand injury, his repair capabilities, his state of nutrition, and, subsequently, how the parent relates to the child, the stimuli in the home and the youngster's preschool experience. Bacola et al. (1966), in their study of 40 premature infants weighing 1,500 g or less, noted that their ability to survive the respiratory distress syndrome without neurological sequelae was closely related to the educational level of their parents. None of the parents of the borderline or retarded children had completed college, while 30 of the parents of the children, who subsequently tested in the normal range of intelligence, had either completed high school or college. The educational level of the parents is closely linked to their socioeconomic status, intellectual function, and childrearing practices. Deutsch, Katz, and Jensen (1968), Birch and Grissow (1970) and Wortis et al. (1963) identified the negative childrearing qualities of the lower socioeconomic (LSE) parent.

The study of children with inapparent cytomegalovirus (CMV) infection provides a model whereby these very complex variables can be researched. Alford (1969), Nankervis (1974), Hanshaw et al. (1976), and Stern (1968) have studied extensively children with congenital CMV infection. These authors have included socioeconomic status (SES) as one of the factors studied but have not included any of the other important variables. Hanshaw et al. (1976) tested 8,644 consecutive cord sera for CMV-IgM antibody, of which 53 were positive. Two infants had died during the neonatal period, and seven children could not be located or their parents were unwilling to participate in the study. The 44 remaining children, ages 3½ to 7 years, were matched according to their birthweight, SES, gestational age, sex, race, and the marital status of the mother at the time of the pregnancy. An equal number of random controls was chosen,

Table 1. Mean IQ levels in 3.5–7 year olds with positive and negative cord CMV-IgM titers

	No. tested	Mean IQ (unadjusted)	Standard deviation	Mean IQ (adjusted for covariate SES)
CMV-IgM positive	44	102.5	22.4	105.7
CMV-IgM negative (matched controls)	44	111.7	17.3	114.6
CMV-IgM negative (random controls)	44	119.2	16.7	113.1

and all children were evaluated on a double blind basis for intellectual, neurological, and sensory deficits. The Wechsler Preschool and Primary Scale of Intelligence (WPPSI), The Neurological Examination of the Child with Minor Nervous Dysfunction, by Touwen and Prechtl (1970), and puretone threshold audiometry were used to examine the youngsters.

There was a significant IQ difference between the infected infants and their matched and random controls (Table 1). None of the groups, regardless of SES, showed significant behavioral and neurological differences. The significance of SES of the youngster is emphasized if the infected, matched, and random groups are distributed according to their socioeconomic class (Table 2). When this is done, it is noted that none of the infected infants born to the upper and middle class mothers had IQs below 90, and none of the infants in the upper and middle class groups showed significant IQ differences between the infected, matched, and random controls. There were five youngsters with bilateral hearing loss in the infected group, and only one child in the noninfected group; similarly, these children were all in lower socioeconomic (LSE) families. The hearing of six youngsters could not be assessed accurately.

It was predicted that 16 of the 44 children would experience school failure. All of these youngsters were found in the LSE group. This prediction was based on an IQ of 91 or less with associated behavioral difficulties, except in the case of one youngster who had an IQ of 104 with a profound bilateral sensory hearing loss. Seven of the LSE infected children had associated hyperactivity; 75% of the LSE infected children who were predicted to experience school

Table 2. Relationship between social class, IQ and cord CMV-IgM antibody

Hollingshead Social class	CMV-IgM positive		Matched control		Random control	
	IQ	No.	IQ	No.	IQ	No.
I, II, III	122.3	(14)	129.3	(15)	124.1	(29)
IV, V	93.3	(30)	102.7	(29)	109.7	(15)

failure did not attend a preschool program. As one would anticipate, despite their high risk of experiencing school failure, the LSE children attended preschool programs only half as frequently as the upper and middle class children (Table 3). It should be noted that only 38% of all newborns tested were born to LSE mothers; however, LSE families accounted for 68% of the CMV-IgM positive children.

The finding of a 0.6% incidence of congenital CMV infection, associated with increased risk of hearing loss and intellectual impairment in children born to LSE, out-of-wedlock mothers are consistent with the epidemiological studies reported by Lang (1975). Our research effort differs from previous studies in the numbers of middle and upper class children evaluated, the length of follow-up, and the focus of preschool experience as it relates to predicted school failure and IQ in LSE children. The Hollingshead Classification of socioeconomic status is based on the educational and occupational level of the father; however, other striking differences between upper and lower socioeconomic class families do exist.

Melish and Hanshaw (1973), Alford (1974) and Hanshaw et al. (1976) have noted that congenital CMV is more prevalent in the young, out-of-wedlock mother, and although two of our mothers were 13 and 14 years of age, respectively, the average age of our mothers did not vary in the infected, matched, and random groups. All of the out-of-wedlock pregnancies in the infected group occurred in the LSE class and none occurred in the middle and upper classes. Efforts to ascertain emotional-state differences between LSE mothers and middle and upper class mothers were not successful using the IPAT Anxiety Level Examination (1963). Similarly, the out-of-wedlock status of the mother was not a reflection of her emotional state. It was anticipated that a significant number of children born to out-of-wedlock mothers would experience school failure. The converse was actually true. Five school failures were present in the unwed group, and eleven were present in the married group. Of interest but of no known significance, is that two of the mothers in the middle and upper class infected group had been previously diagnosed as schizophrenic. This is obviously a higher degree of prevalence than one would anticipate in a normal population.

Table 3. Predicted school failure and preschool experience in CMV-IgM positive children

Hollingshead social class	Preschool experience		Predicted school failure	
	Yes	No	Yes	No
I, II, III	9 (64%)	5 (36%)	0	14
IV, V	12 (40%)		4	8
		18 (60%)	12	6

As Bacola et al. (1966), Drillien (1964), Deutsch, Katz, and Jensen (1968), and Birch and Grissow (1970) indicated, untoward environmental conditions associated with the LSE of the infant compounds the perinatal factors that result in subsequent intellectual impairment. Efforts to identify the environmental qualities that lead to increased risk, have generally been limited to early intervention studies with infants who have not been subjected to perinatal insult. The exception to this has been psychiatric studies by Taft and Goldfarb (1964), and Knoblock and Pasamanick (1975) of psychotic children, which often revealed an associated perinatal injury. In the latter instance, it is speculated that genetic liability or vulnerability to emotional illness is compounded by a psychotoxic environment or a central nervous system injury to produce the affective disability.

The youngster with the inapparent congenital viral infection provides a similar model for speculation. Our study demonstrates that the LSE mother is more vulnerable to CMV infection during pregnancy than her upper and middle class peer. Although the prevalence of CMV in the LSE pregnant mother is greater at the onset of pregnancy as compared to the upper and middle class mother (80% vs 50%), the 20% of the uninfected LSE mothers made up 68% of our subsequently infected population. The reasons for this are unclear. Melish and Hanshaw (1973) attributed this to increased promiscuity. Once again, the study of the mother's emotional and nutritional status had been neglected. The possibility of a form of biological Freudianism that was described by Dubos, Savage, and Scaedler (1966) and subclinical states of inadequate nutrition as causes of increased vulnerability to CMV infection have not been ruled out in Melish's study.

The well-nourished infant with possibly greater intellectual potential, who is born into the stimulating upper and middle class environment, appears to be less vulnerable to an inapparent, congenital virological insult. This invulnerability may be enhanced by a positive transaction between a stable mother and an at-risk infant. The transaction between the child and parent is a complex variable. Measures by Thomas, Chess, and Burch (1968) assess the personality of the child. Brazelton (1973) has recently provided us with a measure of infant affect. Chamberlain (1976) and Kearsly et al. (1962) have developed measures of childrearing practices, but the assessment of the transaction between the parent and child continues to be complex and cumbersome. The Baldwins (1974) have described a computerized analysis of the verbal exchanges between the parent and the youngster. Brown and Rutter (1966) and Pless and Satterwhite (1975) have developed measures of effectiveness of family function. Brown's long history requires that the investigator have several weeks of training, and Pless' questionnaire seems to have a middle class bias in that a single parent family is perceived as being less adequate than its dual parent counterpart. Empirical evidence suggests that our children of out-of-wedlock, CMV infected mothers did not perform poorly. A reliable, easily administered method for assessing child/parent interaction and family strengths and weaknesses, that correlates well with intellectual outcome following a perinatal insult, does not appear to be available at this time.

The youngster born into the LSE environment with an inapparent congenital CMV infection appears to have a markedly diminished ability to escape injury as measured by IQ. The variabilities in the LSE environment, which increase this vulnerability, are unclear. Whether or not such factors as genetic makeup of the child, maternal undernutrition and ill health, or poor childrearing practices, or their combination are major secondary factors is unclear. A preschool experience seemed to mitigate against decreased intellectual function and school failure in the LSE congenital CMV infected children.

There seems to be little question that inapparent, congenital CMV infection is a significant variable in the decreased intellectual function of the infants studied. The morbidity associated with congenital CMV infection is sufficient to have stimulated the consideration of the development of a vaccine by Stern and Elek (1974). Hanshaw (1975) expressed concern related to the development of such a vaccine, and unless the reported 1 to 1,000 or 1 to 600 incidence of severe injury attributable to congenital CMV infection is sufficient to proceed with vaccine development, current studies suggest that our data in regard to the morbidity related to the inapparent infections is inconclusive.

One cannot overlook the increased liability of being born into an LSE home with all its associated untoward effects. How the variables interact to decrease intelligence is unclear. It would seem that it is necessary to integrate the genetic, psychological, and virological factors in the study of children who sustain a perinatal injury if the researcher is to identify the significant contributing variables. The results of such studies may identify a psychosocial vaccine as a primary method of prevention instead of the current suggested vaccine which has potential oncogenic side effects.

SUMMARY

The cord sera of 8,644 infants were tested for CMV-IgM antibody. Forty-four children and their matched and random controls were evaluated neurologically, intellectually, and behaviorally. The congenitally infected group had significant hearing losses and decreased intelligence (16/44). Further study of preschool experience and parent/child interaction is appropriate.

REFERENCES

Alford, G. A. (1969) Clinical central nervous system disease in neonates; A prospective study of infants born with increased levels of IgM. J. Pediatr. 75:1167.

Alford, G. A. (1974) Cytomegalovirus Workshop. Food and Drug Administration, Bureau of Biologies. Bethesda, Maryland: HEW.

Anthony, J. E., and Koupernik, X. (Eds.) (1974) The Child in His Family: Children of Psychiatric Risk. New York: Wiley & Sons, p. 990.

Bacola, E., Behrle, F. L., De Schweinitz, L., Muller, H. C., and Mira, M. (1966) Perinatal and environmental factors in late neurological sequelae. Amer. J. Dis. Child. 112:359.

Baldwin, A. L., and Baldwin, C. P. (1974) Personality and social development of handicapped children. Psychology and the Handicapped Child. U.S. Dept. of HEW, Office of Education, DHEW Pub. Co. (OE) 73−05000, p. 169.

Birch, H. G., and Cravioto, J. (1966) Infection, nutrition, environment in mental development. The Prevention of Mental Retardation through Control of Infectious Diseases. Cherry Hill, New Jersey: U.S. Dept. HEW, National Institute of Child Health and Human Development, p. 227.

Birch, J. G., and Grissow, J. D. (1970) Disadvantages of Children Health and School Failure. New York: Grune & Stratton.

Brazelton, B. T. (1973) Neonatal Behavioral Assessment Scale. London: Spastics International Medical Publications in association with William Heinemann Medical Books; Philadelphia: J. B. Lippincott.

Brown, G. W., and Rutter, M. (1966) The measurement of family activities and relationships. Hum. Relat. 19:3.

Chamberlain, R. W. (1976) Parental Use of "Positive Contact" in Child Rearing: Its Relationship to Child Behavior Patterns and Other Variables. (In press).

Deutsch, M., Katz, I., and Jensen, A. R. (Eds.) (1968) Social Class, Race and Psychological Development. New York: Holt, Rinehart & Winston.

Drillien, C. M. (1964) The Growth and Development of the Prematurely Born Infant. Baltimore, Maryland: Williams & Wilkins.

Dubos, R., Savage, D., and Scaedler, R. (1966) Biological Freudism. J. Pediatr. 38:789.

Garmezy, N. (1974) Children at risk; the search for the antecedents of schizophrenia—part II ongoing research programs, issues and interventions. Schizophr. Bull. 9:55.

Hanshaw, J. B. (1975) A cytomegalovirus vaccine. Amer. J. Dis. Child. 128:141.

Hanshaw, J. B., Scheiner, A. P., Moxley, A. W., Gaev, L., Abel, V., and Scheiner, B. (1976) New Engl. J. Med. (to be published).

Hardy, J. B. (1965) Perinatal factors and intelligence. In The Biosocial Basis of Mental Retardation. (Eds. Osler, S. F., and Cooke, R. E.) Baltimore, Maryland: The John Hopkins Press, p. 35.

Heber, R., Howard, G., Harrington, S., Hoffman, C., and Fallender, C. (1972) Rehabilitating Families at Risk for Mental Retardation. Progress Report Rehabilitation Research and Training Center in Mental Retardation, University of Wisconsin, Madison.

Hunt, McV. J. (1961) Intelligence and Experience. New York: Ronald Press Co.

Jensen, A. R. (1968) Part II, basic processes and intelligence development. Social Class, Race and Psychological Development. (Eds. Deutsch, M., Katz, I., Jensen, A. R.) New York: Holt, Rinehart & Winston.

Kearsley, R. J., Snider, M., Ridne, R., Crawford, J. D., and Talbot, N. B. (1962) Study of relations between psychologic environment and child behavior. Amer. J. Dis. Child. 104:46.

Knoblock, H., and Pasamanick, B. (1975) Some etiologic and prognostic factors in early infantile autism and psychosis. J. Pediatr. 55:181.

Knoblock, H., and Pasamanick, B. (Eds.) (1976) Gesell and Amatruda's Developmental Diagnosis, 3rd edition. Haverstown, Maryland: Harper & Row.

Lang, D. J. (1975) The epidemiology of CMV infections: interpretations of recent observations. *In* Infections of the Fetus and the Newborn Infant. (Eds. Krugman, S., and Gershon, A. A.) New York: Alan R. Liss, p. 35.

Lilienfeld, A. M., and Parkhurst, E. (1951) A study of the association of factors of pregnancy and parturition with the development of cerebral palsy: A preliminary report. J. Hyg. 53:262.

Melish, M. E., and Hanshaw, J. B. (1973) Congenital cytomegalovirus infection. Amer. J. Dis. Child. 126:190.

Nankervis, C. (1974) Cytomegalovirus Workshop. Food and Drug Administration, Bureau of Biologies. Bethesda, Maryland: HEW.

Pasamanick, B., and Knoblock, H. (1966) Prospective studies on the epidemiology of reproductive casualty: Methods, findings and some implications. Merrill-Palmer Q. 12:27.

Pless, I. B., and Satterwhite, B. (1975) Family functioning and family problems. *In* Child Health and the Community (Eds. Haggerty, R. J., Roghmann, K. J., and Pless, I. B.) New York: Wiley & Sons.

Sameroff, A. J. (1974) Infant Risk Factors in Developmental Deviancy. International Association for Child Psychiatry and Allied Professionals, Philadelphia.

Stern, H. (1968) Isolation of cytomegalovirus and clinical manifestations of infection at different ages. Brit. Med. J. 1:665.

Stern, H., and Elek, S. D. (1974) Development of a vaccine against mental retardation caused by CMV infection in utero. Lancet 1:1.

Taft, L., and Goldfarb, W. (1964) Prenatal and perinatal factors in childhood schizophrenia. Develop. Med. Child Neurol. 6:32.

Thomas, A., Chess, S., and Burch, H. G. (1968) Temperament and Behavior Disorders in Children. New York: University Press.

Touwen, B. C. L., and Prechtl, H. F. R. (1970) The neurological evaluation of the child with minor nervous dysfunction. Clinics in Developmental Med. 38. London: Spastics International Publications, Wm. Heinemann Medical Books.

Wortis, H., Bardack, J. L., Cutler, R., Rue, R., and Freedman, A. (1963) Childrearing practice in a low socioeconomic group. J. Pediatr. 32:298.

Toxic Origins

RESEARCH TO PRACTICE IN MENTAL RETARDATION
Biomedical Aspects, Volume III
Edited by Peter Mittler
Copyright 1977 I.A.S.S.M.D.

MENTAL RETARDATION AND MERCURY

R. A. P. Kark, N. K. Menon, and M. Kishikawa
Mental Retardation and Reed Neurological Research Centers,
Neuropsychiatric Institute and School of Medicine,
University of California,
Los Angeles, California 90024,
United States

The ingestion of methylmercury by pregnant women can result in mental retardation and other neurological abnormalities in their offspring. The signs may not appear until middle to late infancy (Matsumoto, Koya, and Takeuchi, 1965; Snyder, 1971; Bakir et al., 1973; Kojima and Fujita, 1973). The mothers themselves often have no signs of toxicity (Snyder, 1971; Kojima and Fujita, 1973; but see Amin-Zaki et al., 1974) despite an excess body burden of mercury. Blood, urine, and hair levels of mercury in the infants may be higher than in the mother (Snyder, 1971; Bakir et al., 1973; Amin-Zaki et al., 1974). The syndrome can include severe mental and motor retardation, irritability progressing to myoclonic seizures, loss of sight, loss of hearing, abnormal tone, abnormal postures, and choreoathetosis (Snyder, 1971, 1972; Amin-Zaki et al., 1974).

The reported cases are all from studies of environmental disasters with alkylmercury. There is concern that similar cases could occur in areas with low, constant levels of the toxin such as on the shores of the Great Lakes and of certain rivers in the United States and central Canada. Body levels of mercury do not necessarily correlate with toxicity and there are as yet no markers of toxicity nor certainty of the biochemical basis of alkylmercury poisoning. There is no satisfactory treatment.

Pathological changes in the brains of children with congenital methylmercury poisoning are similar to those reported in adults. Granule cells are lost from the cerebral cortex and from the cerebellum, and there are also changes ascribable to maldevelopment, such as sparse myelination and heterotopias (Matsumoto et al., 1965).

This work was supported in part by USPHS Grant ES–00625, and National Institute of Child Health and Development Grant HD–06576, HD–05615, and HD–04612. Dr. Kishikawa was a Rotary International Scholar of the University of Nagasaki, Japan.

The toxicological basis is not known. A number of enzymes are inhibited by mercury in vitro and a number of co-factors and metabolic intermediates can react with the metal (Vallee and Ulmer, 1972). Yoshino, Mozai, and Nakao (1966) and Cavanagh and Chen (1971b) have demonstrated that alkylmercurials inhibit protein synthesis in the brains of adult laboratory animals, but this can be transient (Cavanagh and Chen, 1971b), and Menon and Kark (1976) have suggested that carbohydrate oxidation is inhibited more than protein synthesis, at least in the rabbit. Neither inhibition of protein synthesis nor of oxidation immediately accounts for the decreased myelination of poisoned human infants. We therefore examined a number of metabolic conversions in the brains of rat pups continuously exposed to methylmercury in utero and after birth.

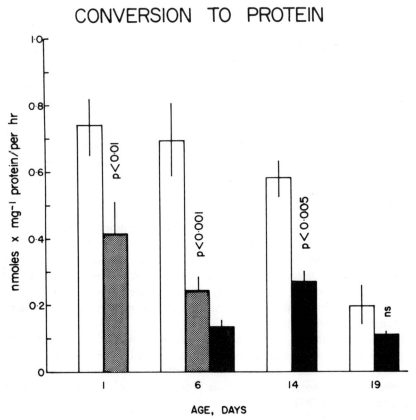

Figure 1. Conversion of [U-^{14}C] glucose to proteins. □ Control; ▨ Mother injected on 14th day of pregnancy; ■ Mother injected on 4th day of pregnancy. Slices from rat pups were incubated 60 min. Values are means ± S.E.M. for 3 determinations on the pups of a single litter for each bar.

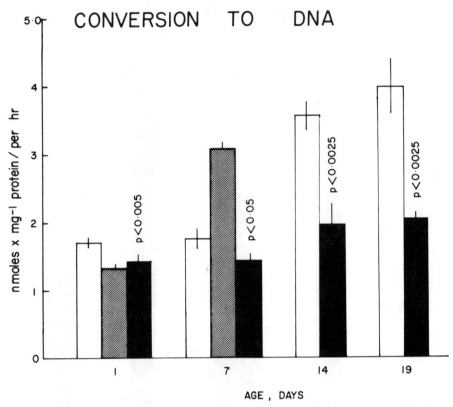

Figure 2. Conversion of $[U\text{-}^{14}C]$ glucose to DNA. □ Control; ▨ Mother injected on 14th day of pregnancy; ■ Mother injected on 4th day of pregnancy. Slices from rat pups were incubated 60 min. Values are means ± S.E.M. for 3 determinations on the pups of a single litter for each bar.

EXPERIMENTAL

Female Sprague-Dawley rats (250–300 g) were injected intravenously with a single dose of 10 mg/kg body wt. of CH_3HgCl on the 4th or 14th day after impregnation, and then bore and nursed their pups. Slices of whole brains from the pups were chopped into prisms with a McIlwain chopper at various days after birth (see Figures 1–3 and Table 1). An aliquot of the resulting mince equivalent to 10 mg protein was suspended in oxygenated Krebs-Ringer phosphate buffer, pH 7.4 (Itoh and Quastel, 1970), and added to incubation medium of the same buffer containing either 5 mM glucose (with 1 μCi $[U\text{-}^{14}C]$ glucose) or 1 mM β-hydroxybutyrate in the presence of 5 mM glucose (with 1 μCi β-$[3\text{-}^{14}C]$ hydroxybutyrate) (Gibson et al., 1976). The flasks were sealed with serum caps holding wells with 2 N NaOH in filter paper and incubated at 37°C for

CONVERSION   TO   RNA

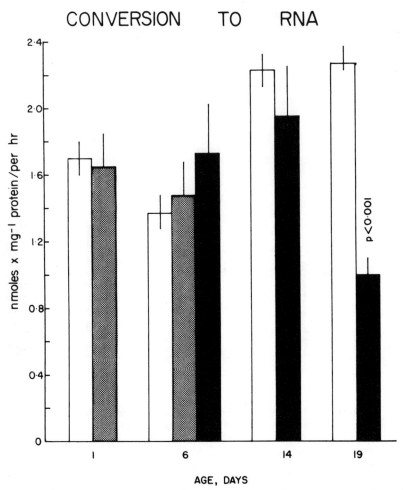

Figure 3. Conversion of [*U*-¹⁴C] glucose to RNA. □ Control; ▨ Mother injected on 14th day of pregnancy; ■ Mother injected on 4th day of pregnancy; Slices from rat pups were incubated 60 min.; Values are means ± S.E.M. for 3 determinations on the pups of a single litter for each bar.

60 min. After termination of the assay and fractionation by the method of Glazer and Weber (1971), the radioactivity in CO_2, lipids, RNA, DNA, and proteins was determined by liquid scintillation counting. Protein was determined by the method of Lowry et al. (1951).

One pup from each litter was perfused with buffered glutaraldehyde. The cerebral hemispheres, cerebellum, and dorsal root ganglia were imbedded in Epon, and 1 micron and ultrathin sections were taken for light microscopy and electronmicroscopy, respectively.

Table 1. Conversion of ^{14}C from β-[3-14C]hydroxybutyrate into lipids

Age (days)	nM/mg/hr		Significance
	Control	CH$_3$Hg	
1	1.29 ± 0.36	1.53 ± 0.10	n.s.
7	1.61 ± 0.64	1.59 ± 0.25	n.s.
14	3.81 ± 0.02	1.60 ± 0.25	$p < 0.001$
19	1.78 ± 0.37	0.14 ± 0.02	$p < 0.01$
21	3.26 ± 0.67	1.83 ± 0.07	$p < 0.05$

Slices of brain from rat pups were incubated 60 min.
Values are means ± S.E.M. for 3 determinations at each age.

RESULTS

Doses of 40 mg/kg of CH$_3$HgCl on the 14th day of pregnancy lead to stillbirth of all pups. No clinical abnormalities were seen in pups or dams with 10 mg/kg given early or late in pregnancy, and the total weights and protein concentration of brains did not differ significantly between mercury-treated and control pups one to 19 days of age, nor did wet weights of brains differ in pups 14 days of age or older.

Biochemical and ultrastructural results did not differ, in so far as they were examined, whether methylmercury was injected on the 4th or 14th day of pregnancy (Figures 1–3).

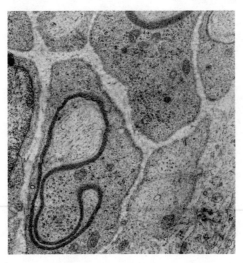

Figure 4. Myelin of peripheral nerve in the dorsal root ganglion of control newborn rat. Compare with Figure 5. Epon embedded, stained with uranyl and lead acetate. × 7,000.

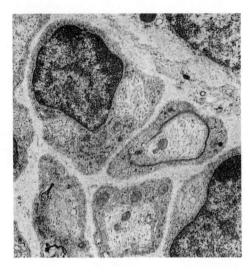

Figure 5. Myelin from newborn rat treated with methylmercury. The layers are immature and thin, although the pup is the same age as that of Figure 4. Epon embedded, stained with uranyl and lead acetate. × 7,000.

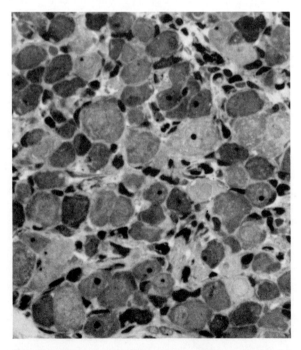

Figure 6. Dorsal root ganglion of control newborn rat. The two types of neuron are easily distinguished. Toluidine blue stain, Epon embedded, 1 μ section. × 125.

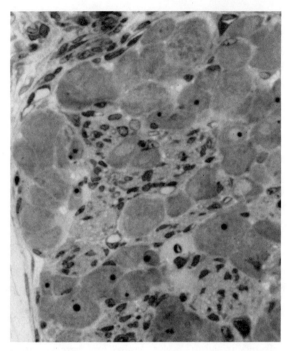

Figure 7. Dorsal root ganglion of newborn rat treated with methylmercury. Compare with Figure 6. In addition to the poor distinction of neuronal types, nuclei are eccentric. Toluidine blue stain, Epon embedded, 1 μ section. X 125.

There was a significant decrease of the conversion of labeled carbon from glucose into protein from one through 14 days and into DNA at all ages, from one to 19 days, in the mercury-treated pups (Figures 1 and 2). Conversion into RNA was only decreased at 19 days (Figure 3). There was no significant effect on the conversions to CO_2 or to lipids.

On the other hand, methylmercury produced a significant decrease in the conversion of labeled β-hydroxbutyrate into lipids from 14 days of age on (Table 1). There was no inhibition of $^{14}CO_2$ production. The conversion into proteins and nucleic acids appeared to be inhibited, but too little radioactivity was incorporated into these fractions in the treated or the control animals to be sure the effect was not caused by a radiochemical contaminant.

Microscopic examination of the dorsal root ganglia from mercury-treated pups showed eccentric nuclei with dispersal of rough endoplasmic reticulum in the neurones (as seen in chromatolysis), increased numbers of neurofibrils, and smooth, rather than interdigitated, contact between the neuronal and glial plasmalemmae. Myelin was immature, with one to two layers rather than six to seven layers of wrappings, and the Schwann-cell cytoplasm contained much debris (Figures 4 and 5). In addition, the normal distinction between two types of ganglion neurones could not be made (Figures 6 and 7). The changes in the complexity of neuronal-to-glial contacts, the number of neurofibrils, and the degree of myelination all improved with time, suggesting that the dose of methylmercury given had delayed rather than prevented maturation. No changes were evident in the cerebrum or cerebellum by light microscopy.

DISCUSSION

Methylmercury is lost from the body only very slowly. The experimental design reported above resembles the situation in human perinatal mercury poisoning in that the animals were constantly exposed to methylmercury in utero from the time of the injection and continued to be exposed to it, via the mother's milk, until weaned at 21 days. The treated pups did not have significant differences in weight, brain weight, or brain protein content from the controls, and the biochemical and ultrastructural changes that were present were discrete. These changes probably reflect, fairly directly, toxic effects of methylmercury.

Methylmercury clearly reduced the conversion of labeled glucose into protein. While actions of mercury on pools of intermediates within the brain cannot be excluded, the decreased conversion suggests a decrease in protein synthesis in the brains of the pups even though the effect of methylmercury was not so great as to change protein concentration. The effect is contrary to what Menon and Kark (1976) found in adult rabbit brain, but agrees with the findings of Cavanagh and Chen (1971b) and Brubaker et al. (1973) in adult rats. Brubaker et al. (1973) demonstrated increased nucleic acid synthesis from pyrimidine precursors and suggested the effect was at the level of translation. The decreased conversion of label to DNA and RNA from glucose in the pups, shown above, suggests an effect of ribose synthesis via the pentose shunt, or, alternatively, an effect on replication or transcription. An effect on purine or pyrimidine synthesis cannot be excluded.

Edmond (1974) has shown that ketone bodies are a major source of carbon for brain lipids in developing rats. Our observation, that more label entered the lipid fraction from β-hydroxybutyrate than from glucose, is in accordance with this view, especially as saturating concentrations of glucose were present in the medium. The peak of lipid synthesis in the control pups would appear to have been at 14 days, and this corresponds with the known rapid phase of brain myelination. Methylmercury prevented the rise of the conversion of β-hydroxybutyrate into lipids at days 14 through 19. The biochemical change might represent a delay in myelination such as is seen by microscopy in the dorsal root ganglia. It could also reflect a direct inhibition of lipid synthesis, some indirect consequence of decreased protein synthesis, or a combination of effects.

Striking structural changes were seen in the dorsal root ganglia of treated newborn pups. Many of these changes reverted to normal by the third week of life. At the dose used, methylmercury's toxicity was sufficient to delay maturation in the dorsal root ganglia, but not to prevent it.

The structural changes in dorsal root ganglia and the lack of changes at the level of light microscopy in the brain emphasize the point of Cavanagh and Chen (1971a, b) that methylmercury may be toxic to one group of cells but not to a related group. The biochemical changes in the brain do not entirely negate the idea of selective toxicity. Menon and Kark (1976) found quite different biochemical changes in the adult rabbit with chronic methylmercury poisoning, and Brubaker et al. (1973) found an *increase* of protein and nucleic acid synthesis in the brains of adult rats with acute loads of methylmercury. The selected actions of this environmental toxin raise the possibility that its mode of toxicity may differ from one kind of cell or circumstance to another. Future studies on the pathogenesis of mental retardation caused by alkylmercury may require that close correlations be sought between biochemical, functional, and morphological changes in defined, discrete groups of cells. However, even the more crude studies of entire tissues could lead to the discovery of biochemical markers for mercurial toxicity and could provide a basis for investigations of potential treatments.

SUMMARY

Mental retardation can be produced by mercury, especially methylmercury, if there is prenatal exposure. To study potential mechanisms, pregnant rats were injected with methylmercury. Various aspects of brain biochemistry and ultrastructure and the mercury concentrations in pups and mothers were examined at various times after birth. The resulting abnormalities and their implications are discussed.

ACKNOWLEDGMENTS

We thank Dr. W. Jann Brown and Dr. George J. Popjak for their help, advice, and encouragement.

REFERENCES

Amin-Zaki, L., Elhassani, S., Majeed, M. A., Clarkson, T. W., Doherty, R. A., and Greenwood, M. (1974) Intra-uterine methylmercury poisoning in Iraq. Pediatrics, 54:587.
Bakir, F., Damluji, S. F., Amin-Zaki, L., Murtadha, M., Khalidi, A., Al-Rawi, N. Y., Tikriti, S., Dhahir, H. I., Clarkson, T. W., Smith, J. C., and Doherty, R. A. (1973) Methylmercury poisoning in Iraq, an interuniversity report. Science. 181:230.
Brubaker, P. E., Klein, R. Herman, S. P., Lucier, G. W., Alexander, L. T., and Long, M. D. (1973) DNA, RNA and protein synthesis in brain, liver and kidneys of asymptomatic methylmercury treated rats. Exp. Mol. Biol. 18:263.
Cavanagh, J. B., and Chen, F. C. K. (1971a) The effects of methylmercury dicyandiamide on the peripheral nerves and spinal cord of rats. Acta Neuropathol., (Berl.). 19:208.

Cavanagh, J. B., and Chen, F. C. K. (1971b) Amino acid incorporation in protein during the "silent phase" before organo-mercury and *p*-bromophenylacetyl-urea neuropathy in the rat. Acta Neuropathol. (Berl.). 19:216.

Edmond, J. (1974) Ketone bodies as precursors of sterols and fatty acids in the developing rat. J. Biol. Chem. 249:72.

Gibson, G. E., Gruel, L., Barlass, L., and Blass, J. P. (1976) Acetylcholine synthesis in relation to glucose and ketone body utilisation (*in preparation*).

Glazer, R. I., and Weber, G. (1971) Incorporation of [6-^{3}H] glucose into lipid, protein, RNA and DNA of slices of differentiating rat cerebral cortex. J. Neurochem. 18:1569.

Itoh, T., and Quastel, J. H. (1970) Acetoacetate metabolism in infant and adult rat brain in vitro. Biochem. J. 116:641.

Kojima, K., and Fujita, M. (1973) Summary of recent studies in Japan on methylmercury poisoning. Toxicology. 1:43.

Lowry, O. H., Rosebrough, N. J., Farr, A. L., and Randall, R. J. (1951) Protein measurement with the folin phenolreagent. J. Biol. Chem. 193:265.

Matsumoto, H., Koya, G., and Takeuchi, T. (1965) Fetal Minamata disease. J. Neuropath. Exp. Neurol. 24:563.

Menon, N. K., and Kark, R. A. P. (1976) Inhibition of oxidation in chronic alkylmercury poisoning. Trans. Amer. Soc. Neurochem. 7:151.

Snyder, R. D. (1971) Congenital mercury poisoning. New Engl. J. Med. 284:1014.

Snyder, R. D. (1972) The involuntary movements of chronic mercury poisoning. Arch. Neurol. 26:379.

Vallee, B. L., and Ulmer, D. D. (1972) Biochemical effects of mercury, cadmium and lead. Ann. Rev. Biochem. 41:91.

Yoshino, Y., Mozai, T., and Nakao, K. (1966) Biochemical changes in the brain in rats poisoned with alkylmercury compound, with special reference to the inhibition of protein synthesis in brain cortex slices. J. Neurochem. 13:1223.

RESEARCH TO PRACTICE IN MENTAL RETARDATION
Biomedical Aspects, Volume III
Edited by Peter Mittler
Copyright 1977 I.A.S.S.M.D.

LOW LEVEL LEAD EXPOSURE AND NEUROPSYCHOLOGICAL FUNCTION
Current Status and Future Directions

H. L. Needleman
Children's Hospital Medical Center,
300 Longwood Avenue,
Boston, Massachusetts 02115,
United States

Lead is a useful metal and an enduring danger. Knowledge of its toxic potential reaches back into antiquity. Nikander in the second century B.C. described the hazards of white lead; Benjamin Franklin graphically described the symptoms afflicting tinkers, printers, and painters; and Sir George Baker in a classic study attributed the cause of the Devonshire colic to lead.

Awareness of childhood lead poisoning is relatively new. Blackfan and Aub described the disease in children in the early part of the twentieth century. The conventional cause was assumed to be the ingestion of paint by inner-city children. Undoubtedly, most cases of frank poisoning come from the ingestion of paint, but the role of airborne lead in general exposure, deriving primarily from automobile emissions, deserves careful scrutiny. Children who sustain lead encephalopathy are known to have frequent and often profound sequelae. Byers and Lord (1943) followed children known to have recovered from lead poisoning, half of whom had no clinical signs of encephalopathy. They found that 19 out of 20 children were having learning problems or behavioral disorders. More than 30 years ago, Byers asked whether some of the school problems being encountered were not because of undiagnosed lead exposure.

When broad based community screening studies were undertaken in the 1950s and 1960s, it was found that between 5% and 40% of children sampled

---

The research reported here was supported by Grant No. HD08945, awarded by NICHD, DHEW.

had lead levels greater than 40 μg/dl. At 80 μg/dl, a child is considered at considerable risk of encephalopathy. Approximately 600,000 American children under the age of six are believed to have elevated blood-lead levels > 40 μg/dl.

Does a threshold for lead toxicity exist? On both theoretical and empirical grounds, there is reason to believe that if there is a threshold, many children, assumed to be asymptomatic, have exceeded it. First, there is no known metabolic function for lead. Second, because global environmental levels of lead have increased only since the industrial revolution, most markedly since the invention of the automobile, the human organism has had only a brief opportunity in the evolutionary scale of time to adapt to contemporary environmental levels. Third, no toxicologist would accept a margin of safety of 50%, yet thousands of children carry blood-lead levels of 40 μg/dl. Fourth, the symptoms of lead toxicity are vague and easily missed. Headache, lethargy, colic, or clumsiness do not identify themselves as lead poisoning. Undoubtedly, many children with these symptoms are misdiagnosed by parent or physician.

Hernberg (1972) has shown that aminolevulinic acid dehydratase, an enzyme in the heme synthesis pathway, is inactivated at all levels of blood-lead. It is arguable whether or not this is an in vitro effect of health significance. More recently, Nathanson and Bloom (1975) have shown that cerebellar adenyl cyclase is inhibited at levels of lead as low as 0.1 μM. This study locates an effect on a critical brain enzyme at levels of lead found in "normal" human populations.

Animal studies have demonstrated that younger, developing nervous systems are more sensitive to lead toxicity. Schroeder (1971) produced runting, decreased litter size, and shortened life span in immature rodents at doses insufficient to produce effects in older animals. Silbergeld (1974) has produced hyperactivity in immature nursing mice by inserting lead in the maternal diet, which then is transported through breast milk. She reports that the response of these animals to methylphenidate and barbiturates parallels that of the hyperactive child. Carson (1974) exposed pregnant ewes to low amounts of lead sufficient to raise their blood-lead levels to 34 μg/dl. While the offspring lambs appeared normal at birth, at 15 months they were much slower at learning a visual discrimination task. Interaction between protein deprivation and lead exposure was reported by Der et al., 1974, measuring the sexual development of infant rats.

Studies of humans are, of course, more difficult to do as rigorously and, as a result, conclusions derived from such studies tend to conflict. Among the difficulties encountered in the undertaking of population studies are lack of suitable indices of exposure, insensitive outcome measures, and failure to control for other variables known to affect development that may confound the results. It is clear to me that a number of studies, no one of which is perfect, taken in sum, indicate that children with moderately elevated body burdens of lead, considered asymptomatic, are at significant risk for impaired neuropsychological function.

Brigitte Burde (1975) has shown that children with pica and elevated blood-lead levels have an increased incidence of perceptual dysfunction, behavior disorder, and speech problems when compared to controls matched on socio-economic status (SES) and race. David, Clark, and Voeller, (1972) have reported that hyperactive children with no discernible prior cause tended to have higher blood-lead levels and excrete more lead in their urine after a dose of penicil-lamine. Landrigan (1975) studied children with blood-lead levels greater than 40 μg/dl living near a smelter in El Paso and found significant deficit on the performance scale of the WISC when compared to other children from the same area with blood lead levels below 40 μg/dl. Perino and Ernhart (1974) reported that black preschoolers with blood-lead levels above 50 μg/dl had significant impairment on the McCarthy Scales of Mental Development, when compared to children matched for race and controlled for other variables with blood-lead levels below 30 μg/dl.

Of considerable interest to this audience is the report of Beattie and co-workers (1975). They identified 77 children with idiopathic mental retarda-tion, matched them with normal children on age, SES, and geographic residence. the place of residence of the mother was identified and a sample of the drinking water was analyzed for lead. No normal children came from homes with excess lead, while 11 mothers of retarded children lived in homes with high water-lead during the time they carried the child. The authors conclude that the risk of retardation is increased by 1:7 by living in a home with high lead in the water during pregnancy.

We are at present studying the effects on development of undiagnosed exposure to lead in first and second grade children. Since blood-lead levels decline after exposure ends, this measurement is inadequate to determine burden. Deciduous teeth store lead, and offer to the investigator a spontaneous, universal, and painless biopsy of bony tissue. We have found that lead-poisoned children have extremely high levels of dentine lead, and that "asymptomatic" children from the lead belt have five times the concentration of lead of children from areas where lead poisoning is rare. ($\overline{X}$ lead belt = 51.1±109 ppm; $\overline{X}$ suburbs = 11.0±14.8 ppm)

A study of 761 teeth from Philadelphia school children confirmed this finding, and also showed that children from good housing, who attended school adjacent to a major lead processor, had levels of lead as high as any found in our study (Needleman and Shapiro, 1974).

Circumpulpal Lead Dentine Concentrations

Lead Belt	$\overline{X}$ = 198 ppm
Near Processor	$\overline{X}$ = 136 ppm
Nonlead Belt	$\overline{X}$ = 40 ppm

Currently we are collecting teeth from a sample base of 3,000 Boston area children and analyzing them for lead. The mean dentine lead level of the teeth we have analyzed to date is 15.8 ppm. Eight percent of these children have dentine lead levels in the range of those found with children who are lead poisoned, above 32.0 ppm. We are selecting those children at the upper end of the distribution for dentine lead and at the lower end, identifying those variates that might confound, and giving each child a five-hour battery of neuropsychological tests that measure cognition, attention, perceptual performance, and motor performance. Should the children with elevated lead demonstrate deficit when compared to their nonleaded peers, the developmental costs of low level lead exposure will be more precisely fixed.

SUMMARY

This chapter reviews the relevant studies, both animal and clinical, that bear upon these questions: Does lead in quantities insufficient to cause frank clinical signs and symptoms cause neuropsychological deficit? What are the sources of lead for humans? Why has this problem continued to exist since antiquity in the presence of adequate knowledge?

REFERENCES

Beattie, A. D., Moore, M. R., and Goldberg, A. (1975) Role of chronic low-level lead exposure in the aetiology of mental retardation. Lancet. 1:589.

Burde, B. de la, and Choate, M. (1975) Early asymptomatic lead exposure and development at school age. J. Pediatr. 87:638.

Byers, R. K., and Lord, E. F. (1943) Late effects of lead poisoning on mental development. Amer. J. Dis. Child. 66:471.

Carson, T. L., and Van Gelder, G. (1974) Slowed learning in lambs prenatally exposed to lead. Arch. environ. Hlth. 29:154.

David, O., Clark, J., and Voeller, K. (1972) Lead and hyperactivity. Lancet. 2:900.

Der, R., Fahim, Z., Hilderbrand, D., and Fahim, M. (1974) Combined effect of lead and low protein diet on growth, sexual development and metabolism in female rats. Res. Commun. Chem., Pathol., Pharmacol. 9:723.

Hernberg, S. (1972) Biological effects of low lead doses. Presented at the International Symposium on Environmental Health Aspects of Lead, Amsterdam, October.

Landrigan, P. J. et al. (1975) Epidemic lead absorption near an ore smelter. The role of particulate lead. New Engl. J. Med. 292:123.

Nathanson, J. and Bloom, F. (1975) Lead-induced inhibition of brain adenyl cyclase. Nature. 255:419.

Needleman, H. L., and Shapiro, I. M. (1974) Dentine lead levels in asymptomatic Philadelphia school children: Subclinical exposure in high and low risk groups. Environ. Hlth. Perspectives. May, p. 27.

Perino, J., and Ernhart, C. B. (1974) The relation of subclinical lead level to cognitive and sensorimotor impairment in black preschoolers. J. Learn. Disabil. 7:26.

Schroeder, H. A., and Mitchener, M. (1971) Toxic effects of trace elements on the reproduction of mice and rats. Arch. Environ. Hlth. 23:102.

Silbergeld, E., and Goldberg, A. (1974) Lead-induced behavioral dysfunction: An animal model of hyperactivity. Exp. Neurol. 42:146.

RESEARCH TO PRACTICE IN MENTAL RETARDATION
Biomedical Aspects, Volume III
Edited by Peter Mittler
Copyright 1977 I.A.S.S.M.D.

LEAD TOXICITY AND EFFECTS ON BLOOD-BRAIN AND CNS TRANSPORT

L. A. O'Tuama
Departments of Neurology,
Pediatrics and Pharmacology,
The University of North Carolina School of Medicine,
Chapel Hill, N.C. 27514
United States

The neurological importance of acute inorganic lead poisoning has long been recognized because of its ability to cause permanent mental and motor handicap (Thomas and Blackfan, 1914). More recently, the issue of lead poisoning has attracted new interest in view of the association between childhood exposure to levels of the metal that were formally considered "safe" (blood levels $\geqslant$ 40μg/ml) and the occurrence of educationally disabling disorders such as hyperactivity (de la Burde and Choatte, 1972; Pueschel, Kopito, and Schwachman, 1972). The importance of solving this problem can be gauged by statistics provided by the Center for Disease Control (Morbidity and Mortality Weekly Report 1974) showing that between July 1, 1972 and April 1, 1974, of 80,000 children suspected of being at risk of lead poisoning, 12.2% were found to have a blood-lead level of this magnitude. These clinical studies have established an association between lower levels of blood-lead elevation and serious academic and/or behavior disorders of childhood, but have failed to prove that it is the elevation of blood lead rather than some other factor in the lead-exposed population (such as nutritional or sociocultural deprivation) which has caused the problem. Furthermore, the studies indicate that not all children exhibiting similar levels of blood lead have an equal chance of neurological deficit, so that individual vulnerability must play a role in determining the risk. It is of considerable importance to resolve this issue because, if a causal association can be established between these lower levels of lead exposure and neurotoxicity, there is need for a major public health effort to prevent the exposure of children

Supported by a grant from National Institutes for Environmental Health Sciences and the Environmental Protection Agency, ES01151-01A1.

to such levels. A related need is for a predictive test that would identify in the exposed population the individual at risk of brain damage and therefore requiring chelation. It seems unlikely that clinical study alone can establish whether or not low level lead exposure is a direct cause of encephalopathy. A more fruitful research strategy probably lies in an attempt to establish whether or not these "low levels" of lead cause impairment of neurological function that can be detected by biochemical or pharmacological methods.

The occurrence of these neurological deficits is presumably ultimately related to abnormal levels of inorganic lead in the nervous system. A study of the factors influencing lead penetration into, and distribution within, the brain would therefore seem to be a high research priority. However, until quite recently, little direct research has been performed on this topic.

Early studies that can be interpreted to give inferences about lead distribution in the brain include those of Kehoe, whose work is reviewed by Goyer and Rhyne (1973). The latter authors pointed out that, in the studies of Kehoe and others, in fatal cases of lead poisoning only trace amounts of inorganic lead (0.01 to 0.09mg/100g) have been reported for the brain with higher levels reported for the liver and the kidney. Such findings raised the possibility that lead entry into the nervous system may be subject to a degree of regulation not found for other soft tissue organs, and they indicate that this regulation may persist to some extent even in acute lead poisoning.

Earlier studies depicting neuropathological changes in lead poisoning may be reviewed as relevant to the matter of lead distribution because they give clues to brain sites showing predilection for pathological effects. Such sites might be presumed to be selectively involved in the distribution of lead. Both the studies of Blackman (1937) and Pentschew and Garro (1966) in childhood lead poisoning showed pathological changes that were maximal in the blood vessels of the cerebrum and the meninges and included capillary dilatation with endothelial cell swell and astrocytic proliferation. These findings were extended to an ultrastructural level by Thomas, Dallenbach, and Thomas (1971) who showed capillary and glial footplace swelling as the earliest change in lead-treated animals. These changes were interpreted as suggesting an increased permeability of the blood-brain barrier in lead encephalopathy. In fact, Pentschew and Garro (1966) had previously tested this hypothesis directly and showed an increased uptake of intravenously injected trypan blue in their encephalopathic animals.

More recently, autoradiography and tracer studies have been used to study neural distribution of lead. Thomas, Dallenbach, and Thomas (1973) found a selective accumulation of ^{210}Pb in the cerebellum using the suckling rat model, and it is of interest that this selective concentration correlated with a predominantly cerebellar deficit in this particular model. This would suggest that the process of lead uptake by the nervous system influences the behavioral expression of lead poisoning. O'Tuama, Kim, and Gatzy (1976) were interested in the findings of Goyer and Rhyne suggesting the operation of some factor or factors regulating lead access to the nervous system from the systemic circulation, and they also were interested, in results of the pathological studies emphasizing the vulnerability of the structures of the blood-brain and blood-CSF barriers. These considerations suggested a detailed study of the central neural distribution of ^{210}Pb given systematically to adult guinea pigs. The Weller model was used to induce encephalopathy by administering lead carbonate 165 mg p.o. daily for six days.

Lead was not detected in the choroid plexus. (Average concentration in control animals was < 1.2µg/g; < 1.5µg/g in poisoned animals.) Brain lead concentrations averaged 0.095 ± 0.016 µg/g wet weight in control animals and 0.427 ± 0.067 µg/g in poisoned animals (Table 1). The choroid plexus concentrated pulsed radiolead more than 70 times as avidly as the brain, and in the meninges and the ependyma the concentration of ^{210}Pb also markedly exceeded the concentration occurring in the brain. (Figures 1–3). It was suggested that the high initial uptake of radiolead by the choroid plexus and the other barrier tissues indicated that these structures might serve as a sink tending to reduce lead entry into the CSF and the brain. The pathological changes seen in the nervous system and the barrier tissues in the guinea pig model of lead encephalopathy were described by Bouldin et al. (1975). In sharp contrast to the suckling rat model, *no* morphological changes were seen either by light or electronmicroscopy in the cerebral capillaries or perivascular glial sheaths. Also, the blood-brain barrier to macromolecules was intact as measured by Evans blue-albumin complex and horseradish peroxidase.

A pattern of ^{210}Pb neural distribution similar to that noted in the guinea pig was found by O'Tuama, Kim, and Gatzy in a model of lead encephalopathy in the adult cat (O'Tuama, Kim, and Gatzy 1976). As in the guinea pig, there was a net concentration of lead by the brain where the lead levels were three to four

Table 1. Specific radioactivity and concentrations of neural tissue lead[a]

		Brain[b]		Choroid plexus[bc]
	Blood lead concentration (µg/g) Mean ± SE	Lead concentration (µg/g) Mean ± SD	Specific radioactivity (cpm ^{210}Pb/µg lead)	Lead concentration (µg/g) Mean ± SD
Control	10.54 ± 1.77 (5)	0.095 ± 0.016 (3)	505	< 1.2 µg/g (3)
Lead-poisoned	132.74 ± 40.8 (7)	0.42 ± 0.067 (3)	37	< 1.5 µg/g (3)

[a]O'Tuama et al., Toxicol. Appl. Pharmacol. 1976.
[b]Number of animals per group in parenthesis.
[c]Weights of choroid plexus samples ranged from 2.55 to 3.08 mg for control animals and from 3.88 to 4.78 mg for poisoned animals.

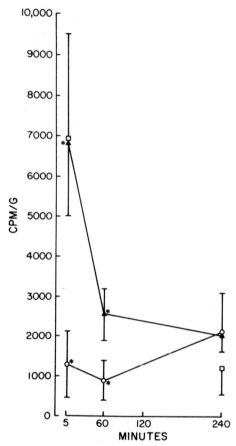

Figure 1. Time course of choroid plexus uptake of ^{210}Pb. Values labeled (▲) indicate control animals; (○), values for control animals treated with ouabain $(1.6–1.8 \times 10^{-9}$ M iv) 15 min before label injection; (□), values for animals pretreated with lead carbonate (165 mg p.o. for 6 days before label injection). Mean ± SE are given. Asterisks indicate differences of statistical significance $(p < 0.05)$ between values for control animals and control animals treated with ouabain.

times that found in plasma. Once again, a selective short term concentration of the pulsed lead was noted in the barrier tissues, but the tissue permeability to ^{210}Pb was not significantly different in control vs. lead-poisoned animals. The role of the high concentration of lead by neural barriers in the overall distribution of lead within the nervous system was further defined in this study by comparing the tissue distribution of lead in animals receiving ^{210}Pb i.v. with the group receiving a comparable dose via the CSF, delivered by ventriculocisternal perfusion. A striking contrast was noted between these two groups. In the CSF-injected group, the mean tissue concentration of ^{210}Pb was considerably higher than in the systemically injected animals, and the striking concentration differences between different organs seen in the latter group was much less evident. These results support the concept that the selective accumulation of systemically injected lead by the neural barriers influences the CNS distribution of the metal at least for tracer doses. Thus, when we circumvent the barrier by introducing lead directly into the CSF, the profile of tissue distribution is markedly different.

Further evidence pertinent to this point has been obtained from studies in which we have examined the accumulation of ^{210}Pb by excised choroid plexus, meninges, and brain slices from guinea pigs and bull frogs (Smith, Gatzy, and O'Tuama 1974). These tissues accumulated ^{210}Pb from a bathing solution with a lead concentration of 3×10^{-8} to 3×10^{-6} M (approximately an order of magnitude lower than to 10 times the estimated plasma levels in marginal lead

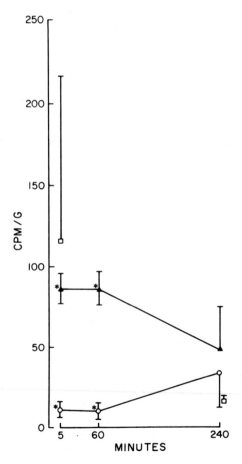

Figure 2. Time course of brain uptake of ^{210}Pb. Same details as for Figure 1.

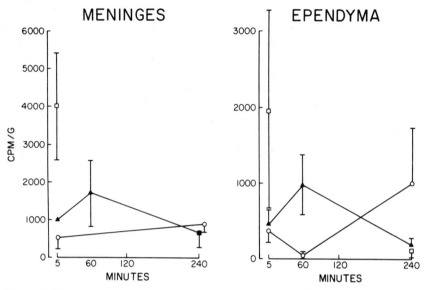

Figure 3. Time course of meninges and ependyma uptake of ^{210}Pb. Same details as for Figure 1.

intoxication). Tissue-to-medium ratios ranged from around 20 after 30 minutes of incubation to over 100 after four hours. These studies further support the conclusion that the selective concentration of radiolead by the barrier tissues in vivo influences the concentration contained in the brain, because the brain and the meninges take up lead rapidly when the neural barriers are removed by excision.

Some major differences are apparent between the conclusions reached by our group as to the mechanisms of lead uptake in the nervous system based on the experiments reported above and the conclusions of Goldstein, Asbury, and Diamond (1974). These workers claim that lead accumulation by the brain is passive and diffusional, whereas our conclusions are that a concentrative and presumably facilitated uptake occurs. Two comments seem appropriate concerning these different conclusions. First, it is not clear that the data of Goldstein and his colleagues support the conclusions they reach. From calculations based on their lowest dose for total lead injected, and taking into account the estimated initial volume of distribution of this injectate in their experimental animal (the young rat), we estimate that the lowest level of blood lead attained in their animals was 48μg/100ml, a value 5 times greater than that obtained by our group for untreated rats of comparable age (Krigman and Mushak, personal communication). Therefore, processes other than passive uptake might approach saturation at levels below this initial blood-lead level, and the results of Goldstein's group may not be pertinent to the situation in which small increments of lead enter the brain at slightly elevated blood levels. Second, there may be fundamental differences in the model of lead encephalopathy used by Goldstein and that used by us. His group employed a modification of the suckling rat preparation. Major differences exist at a pathological level between this preparation and the model employed in our studies. These differences are discussed in detail below.

It seems appropriate to examine the results of all the studies cited dealing with lead distribution of the nervous system to see whether or not they have advanced our knowledge about two fundamental questions: 1) What factors regulate neural distribution of lead; 2) What is the relationship of this distribution to the pathogenesis of lead encephalopathy?

On reviewing these studies, some major generalizations appear to be justified. It seems clear that a characteristic pattern of tissue destruction in the brain follows exposure to lead in young animals subjected to acute or subacute poisoning. This reaction is characterized by grossly apparent proliferative and/or hemorrhagic changes which are maximal in the capillaries of the cerebrum, meninges, and ependyma. A vasculitis of this general character is found consistently in cases of lead poisoning in children, as well as in the suckling rat, as detailed above. However, the several studies cited from our own laboratories show clearly that the full clinical behavioral and chemical picture of acute lead encephalopathy can be produced without any vasculitic changes and, indeed, without any discernable morphological changes in the nervous system. A possible explanation for these differences would be that the guinea pig/cat and child/suckling rat models of lead encephalopathy represent the differing responses of the immature and mature nervous system to a given dose of lead. This possibility is consistent with the finding that most species show increased absorbtion of lead in the developmental period, and CNS vulnerability to the metal is higher at that time. (Lin-Fu, 1972). This argument would predict that the differences between the neural effects of small and large doses of lead would be quantitative rather than qualitative. This is in fact the situation observed in our studies in both guinea pigs and cats, where pulses of lead are concentrated by the meninges and ependyma, i.e., tissues where marked vasculitic changes were found in the suckling rat and child.

The selective distribution of tracer doses of ^{210}Pb in the barrier tissues of "control" animals also raises the possibility that these minute amounts of lead may cause dysfunction of these tissues. Such dysfunction probably would be significantly damaging to neural function overall in view of the known physiological functions of the barrier tissues. These functions include a role in the transport of many solutes of importance for neural function, including amino acids (Lorenzo and Cutler, 1969), and calcium (Graziani, Escriva, and Katzman 1967). The demonstration of alternation in those critical barrier functions at relatively low amounts of lead would be of far-reaching importance because it would show clearly that such levels as are found in children with "marginal" lead

Table 2. Effects of inorganic lead on tyrosine accumulation by isolated choroid plexus (CP), hypothalamus (H) and caudate nucleus (CN)

Control		$V_{max} \pm$ S.E.M. (μM/ml/min)	$K_m \pm$ S.E.M. (mM)
	CP	0.205 ± 0.013	0.016 ± 0.003
	H	0.047 ± 0.009	0.018 ± 0.001
	CN	0.059 ± 0.007	0.020 ± 0.003
Lead nitrate (5×10^{-6}M)	CP	0.101 ± 0.009 ($p < 0.01$)	0.005 ± 0.001 ($p < 0.01$)
	H	0.036 ± 0.008 ($p > 0.05$)	0.026 ± 0.008 ($p > 0.05$)
	CN	0.046 ± 0.011 ($p > 0.05$)	0.025 ± 0.005 ($p > 0.05$)

toxicity are indeed potentially injurious to the nervous system. As discussed earlier, unaided clinical studies seem unlikely to resolve this problem fully.

We have commenced studies of the effects of lead poisoning on barrier-associated functions and one relevant result is reported here. The effects of lead on tyrosine accumulation by isolated neural tissues were evaluated (Kim and O'Tuama, 1976). Freshly excised cat tissues were preincubated for 15 minutes in artificial CSF only or in CSF with added lead nitrate (5×10^{-6}M) and then incubated for five minutes with varying concentrations of L-tyrosine. The results are shown in Table 2. It can be seen that under in vitro conditions, lead may adversely and selectively affect a choroidal function. Studies are in progress to define more fully the effects of lead on tyrosine transport by the choroid plexus and to determine whether or not similar effects occur with in vivo lead poisoning. Because tyrosine is a neurotransmitter precursor, these studies may be relevant to the diverse interactions of lead with central aminergic systems (Silbergeld and Goldberg, 1975).

Further studies of the effects of lead poisoning on barrier-associated functions are a continuing and major interest of our group.

SUMMARY

This presentation reviews studies of the distribution of inorganic lead in the nervous system, both in control animals and in experimental lead encephalopathy. Emphasis is placed on results from our laboratories which document a selective concentration of lead by the neural "barrier" tissues and assess lead effects on choroid and neural transport.

REFERENCES

Blackman, S. S. (1937) The lesions of lead encephalitis in children. Bull. Johns Hopkins Hosp. 61:1.

Bouldin, T. W. Mushak, P., O'Tuama, L. A., and Krigman, M. R. (1975) Blood-brain barrier dysfunction in acute lead encephalopathy: A reappraisal. Environ. Health Perspect. 12:81.

de la Burde, B., Choatte, M. S. (1972) Does asymptomatic lead exposure in children have latent sequelae? J. Pediat. 81:1088.

Goldstein, G. W., Asbury, A. K., and Diamond, I. (1974) Pathogenesis of lead encephalopathy. Arch Neurol. 31:382.

Goyer, R. A., and Rhyne, B. C. (1973) Pathological effects of lead. Internat. Rev. Exp. Path. 12:1.

Grazianai, L., Escriva, A., and Katzman, R. (1967) Exchange of calcium between blood, brain and cerebrospinal fluid. Arch. J. Physiol. 208:1058.

Kim, C. S., O'Tuama, L. A. (1976) Inorganic lead affects tyrosine accumulation by isolated choroid plexus, but not in other brain regions. Environmental Health Perspectives. (in press).

Lin-Fu, J. S. (1972) Undue absorbtion of lead among children—a new look at an old problem. New Engl. J. Med. 286:702.

Lorenzo, A. V., Cutler, R. W. P. (1969) Amino acid transport by choroid plexus in vitro. J. Neurochem. 16:577.

O'Tuama, L. A., Kim, C. S., and Gatzy, J. T. (1976) Inorganic lead penetration into cat brain, neural barrier tissues and CSF. Proc. Amer. Soc. Neurochem. 7:154.

O'Tauma, L. A., Kim, C. S., Gatzy, J. T., Krigman, M. R., and Mushak, P. (1976) The distribution of inorganic lead in guinea pig brain and neural barrier tissues in control and lead-poisoned animals. Tox. Appl. Pharma. 36:1.

Pentschew, A., and Garro, F. (1966) Lead encephalomyelopathy of the suckling rat and its implication on the porphyrinopathic nervous diseases. With special reference to the nervous system's capillaries. Acta Neuropathol. 6:266.

Pueschel, S. M., Kopito, S., and Schwachman, H. (1972) Children with an increased lead burden. A screening and follow-up study. JAMA. 222:462.

Silbergeld, E., and Goldberg, A. (1975) Pharmacological and neurochemical investigations of lead-induced hyperactivity. Neuropharmacology. 14:431.

Smith, P., Gatzy, J. T., O'Tuama, L. A. (1974) Uptake and release of ^{210}Pb by bullfrog neural tissues in vitro. The Pharmacologist 16:207.

Thomas, H. M., Blackfan, K. D. (1914) Recurrent meningitis due to lead in a child of five years. Amer. J. Dis. Child. 8:377.

Thomas, J. A., Dallenbach, F. D., and Thomas, M. (1971) Considerations on the development of experimental lead encephalopathy. Virchows. Arch. Path. Anat. Physiol. 352:61.

Thomas, J. A., Dallenbach, F. D., and Thomas, M. (1973) The distribution of radioactive lead (^{210}Pb) in the cerebellum of developing rats. J. Pathol. 109:45.

Malnutrition

RESEARCH TO PRACTICE IN MENTAL RETARDATION
Biomedical Aspects, Volume III
Edited by Peter Mittler
Copyright 1977 I.A.S.S.M.D.

MALNUTRITION AND MENTAL DEVELOPMENT
An Ecological Perspective

S. A. Richardson
Departments of Pediatrics and Community Health,
Albert Einstein College of Medicine,
Yeshiva University
1300 Morris Park Avenue, Bronx, N.Y. 10461, United States

The central hypothesis underlying the early studies of the consequences of severe malnutrition was that malnutrition causes brain damage which in turn causes intellectual impairment. Results of early studies showed that children and animals who had been malnourished in early life had lower intelligence than "controls" who were not malnourished. With varying degrees of caution, investigators interpreted their results as supporting the hypothesis. This support was based on the assumption that the social and biological histories of the experimental and control groups were similar in all respects except for the presence or absence of malnutrition. Further research made this assumption highly questionable. It was found that malnourished children have experienced a more disadvantageous set of social and biological circumstances for intellectual development and that these circumstances could be sufficient to account for the lower intelligence found in the malnourished subjects (Richardson, 1974). Where animals have been studied, experimenters have used methods to cause malnutrition that seriously disturbed the mother-infant relationship. Later differences found in the experimental and control animals could have been attributable to malnutrition, disturbance in the maternal-infant relationship, or some combination of these.

Given this knowledge, we now need to consider malnutrition as one of a wide array of factors that may influence intellectual development during growth and development. Further, we need to consider the relative contribution that each factor makes to the outcome of intellectual functioning. We must then deal with multiple independent variables and identify and assess each of the significant variables.

A further complication in research design is that malnutrition does not seem to be an additive variable that has the same effect under various social and biological conditions. Rather, malnutrition seems to be an interactive variable with differential effects depending on the overall ecological context, e.g., malnutrition may have no long-term effect within a generally advantageous set of conditions for intellectual development, but may have a significant effect within a generally disadvantageous set of conditions (Richardson, 1976). If further research supports the evidence that malnutrition is an interactive variable, then this would severely limit research designs using the experimental model.

A second hypothesis that has influenced research design is that there are critical periods when malnutrition is most likely to cause brain damage that will lead to mental impairment. This critical period of rapid brain growth for humans was first thought to begin with the last trimester of pregnancy and extend through the first six months of life. Studies that have tested this hypothesis have not found supporting evidence. More recent research has led to the suggestion that the brain growth spurt extends at least through the first two years of life. Testing the revised hypothesis will be difficult because severe malnutrition is found most often before the age of two, except where general conditions of famine exist. In such conditions, there are numerous related social and biological disturbances that make doing research and sorting out the relative role of contributing factors a very difficult task.

The term malnutrition has been defined in many different ways. Perhaps the only direct definition is a primary diagnosis of marasmus or kwashiorkor with a listing of symptoms given in each case. Most other definitions are inferences about malnutrition, e.g., height, residence in a poverty area where it is believed malnutrition is common, living in a time and place where a famine has occurred. Maternal malnutrition has been inferred from low weight gain during pregnancy and low birth weight of the child. It is essential to examine and consider separately whatever definition is used and not to consider the various definitions of malnutrition as equivalent.

Unfortunately, few studies provide any information about the overall life history of nutrition when a case is followed up. An episode of malnutrition may have different effects depending on the prior and subsequent nutrition. Studies have also generally failed to report the forms of treatment during the acute and convalescent phases of kwashiorkor or marasmus, and variation in treatment may have differing long-term consequences.

Unless the considerations outlined here are taken into account in malnutrition research, there is danger that the role of nutrition in intellectual development may be misunderstood.

REFERENCES

Richardson, S. A. (1974) The background histories of school children severely malnourished in infancy. *In* Advances in Pediatrics, 21. (Ed. I. Schulman) Chicago: Yearbook Medical Publications, Inc.

Richardson, S. A. (1976) The relation of severe malnutrition in infancy to the intelligence of school children having differing life histories. Pediatr. Res. 10:57.

RESEARCH TO PRACTICE IN MENTAL RETARDATION
Biomedical Aspects, Volume III
Edited by Peter Mittler
Copyright 1977 I.A.S.S.M.D.

MALNUTRITION, CHILD HEALTH, AND BEHAVIORAL DEVELOPMENT
Data from an Intervention Study

R. E. Klein, M. Irwin, P. L. Engle, J. Townsend, A. Lechtig,
R. Martorell, and H. Delgado
Division of Human Development,
Institute of Nutrition of Central America and Panama (INCAP),
Guatemala City, Guatemala

A child growing up in a developing country lives in a precarious situation. Poverty, disease, and a variety of other environmental factors expose the child to a high death-risk, malnutrition, and numerous other environmental insults that combine to limit his physical and mental development. For example, in developing countries, nearly two out of every ten children die during the first year of life, while the corresponding statistic for children in developed countries is roughly one out of fifty (United Nations, 1971). For the past eight years, our research group in Guatemala has been focusing broadly on problems of child development in developing countries and specifically on the effect of mild to moderate malnutrition and other environmental factors on mental development during preschool years (Klein et al., 1977).

This chapter reports preliminary results of an ongoing longitudinal intervention study in which two nutritional supplements were made available to all members of the chronically malnourished population of four isolated rural villages in Guatemala. Our special interest is on the impact of the supplementation to pregnant and lactating women, and to children in the first few years of life. In addition to the food supplement program, outpatient curative medical care is provided free of cost to all residents of the four villages. The principal foci of the study are physical growth and mental development.

This research was supported by Contract N01-HD-5-0640 from the National Institute of Child Health and Human Development, National Institutes of Health, Bethesda, Maryland, United States

MATERIAL AND METHODS

Experimental Design

The data presented here are drawn from a longitudinal study of the effects of chronic malnutrition on physical growth and mental development. Two types of food supplements are provided to residents of the study communities: atole, a high protein, high calorie beverage similar to a popular local corn gruel, and fresco, a beverage similar to kool-aid which contains one third of the calories contained in atole and no protein. In addition, both preparations contain similar concentrations of the vitamins and minerals that possibly are limited in the diets of this population. Two villages receive atole while the other two receive fresco. Coming to the supplementation center is voluntary, and consequently a wide range of supplement intake is observed.

Study Population   The study population is a rural population in which mild to moderate malnutrition and infectious diseases are endemic. The villages and their inhabitants are very poor, the median family income being approximately $400 per year. The typical house is built of adobe and has no sanitary facilities. Drinking water is contaminated with enteric bacteria. Corn and beans are the principal staples of the home diet; dietary intakes are mainly calorie-deficient.

Variables and Sample Size   Supplement intake was expressed in terms of calories, because the home diet seems to be more limited in calories than in proteins. We stress that while calories seem to be more limited in this study population, other populations may present very different nutritional situations. Nutritional supplementation has proved to be our most accurate indicator of overall nutritional status; supplement ingestion was found not to replace home dietary consumption, and to correlate consistently with physical growth. The measure of nutritional status employed in the analyses described in this chapter was membership in low, medium, or high supplement ingestion categories. Category membership was determined on the basis of total calories of supplement ingested by the mother during gestation and lactation (the first six months of postpartum life) and by the child from birth to the time of psychological testing, by reference to the following table:

Category	Amount
1	$< 5,000$ calories per three-month period
2	$5,000{-}10,000$ cals. per three-month period
3	$> 10,000$ calories per three-month period

The total number of supplement calories ingested was divided by the number of three-month intervals from conception to time of testing (i.e., for 36-month testing, the total number of calories was divided by 15, since $9 + 36 = 45$ months $\div 3 = 15$), and the resulting figure referred to the table above.

The principal outcome variables discussed here are the prevalence of physical growth retardation at birth and 36 months of age, and psychological test performance at 36, 48, and 60 months of age.

The total sample of 1,083 children was made up of 671 infants born in the four villages from January, 1969, through February, 1973, and 412 children alive and under the age of three years at the beginning of data collection in January, 1969.

RESULTS

Determinants of Physical Growth Retardation

Supplement Ingestion and Birthweight Figure 1 shows the percentage of low birthweight babies ($\leqslant$ 2.5 kg) by two categories of maternal supplement ingestion. The low group is comprised of women whose total supplement ingestion during pregnancy was less than 20,000 calories, while the high group consists of mothers whose supplement ingestion was greater than 20,000 calories. The percentage of low birthweight babies is consistently lower in the better supplemented group in both the fresco and the atole groups. In fact, the risk of delivering low birthweight babies among highly supplemented mothers is roughly half that of the low group. Because home caloric intake was similar in both groups, the supplemental calories represent additional calories to the maternal diet. In the high calorie supplementation group, this addition amounted to approximately 35,000 calories during the course of pregnancy, or about an extra 125 calories per day.

This association between caloric supplementation and birthweight is not explained by other important maternal variables such as size, home diet, morbidity, obstetric characteristics, or socioeconomic status. Most important, this association was not produced by undetected confounding factors related to the mother (such as a tendency for some women to have bigger babies) because it was also observed across two consecutive births for the same mother. That is, if a woman consumes more supplemental calories during one pregnancy than during another, there is a tendency for the baby of that pregnancy to be heavier at birth. Thus, based on the pattern of findings, we have concluded that caloric supplementation during pregnancy is causally associated with the decrease in small babies in this population.

The issue of calories requires a comment. The fact that the effect observed on birthweight was similar for calories with or without proteins indicates a caloric rather than a protein effect. This finding is consistent with analyses of home dietary intake data showing deficiencies in calories but not in protein. Thus, we believe it feasible to improve the total diet of mothers by adding more calories. In other populations with different patterns of dietary intake, the situation could be quite different. The best supplement for one population need not be the best and indeed may even be harmful for another.

Supplement Ingestion and Growth at 36 Months of Age For these analyses, we define retardation in growth, whether in weight, height, or head circumfer-

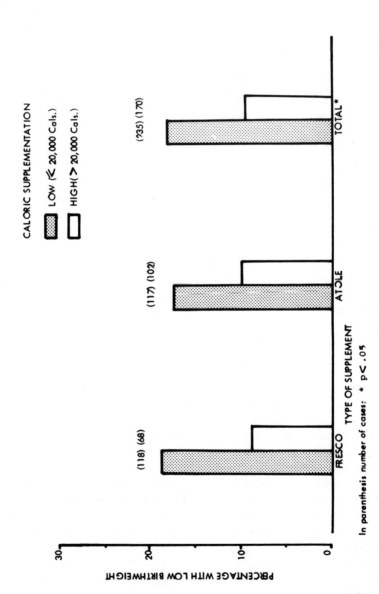

Figure 1. Relationship between supplemented calories during pregnancy and proportion of low birth weight (≤ 2.5 kg)

ence, as being below the 30th percentile of the study population distribution. These limits are below the tenth percentile of the distribution of a well-nourished reference sample from Denver, Colorado (Hansman, 1970). Since we do not believe these populations differ in genetic potential (Habicht, et al., 1974; Martorell, et al., 1975), we regard these deficits as true retardation.

Figure 2 shows the proportion of children with retardation in weight, height, and head circumference at 36 months of age for the low, middle, and high supplemented groups. The groups with low and high supplementation were composed of those children who ingested, either directly or through their mothers, less than 5,000 or more than 10,000 supplemented calories per quarter, during at least 14 quarters. The group with middle supplementation was composed of children who fell in neither the low nor the high group. There is a strong relationship between level of supplementation and physical growth retardation. In fact, we estimate that the final result of food supplementation up to seven years of age will be approximately a 50% reduction of the deficit in height between the low supplemented children and the Denver standards (DDH/INCAP, 1975).

Determinants of Psychological Test Performance

The central question in the longitudinal study is whether or not the condition of mild to moderate malnutrition, a condition affecting the majority of children growing up today in developing countries, affects the mental development of these children. *Our data argue strongly that the answer is yes.* Tables 1, 2, and 3 present mean psychological test scores at ages three, four, and five years for children falling into three supplementation categories, plus analysis of variance test *F* values. It will be noted that both a composite score constructed by standardizing and then summing test scores, as well as several individual tests, show significant effects of nutritional status at each age. Tests that illustrate effects of nutritional status cover a wide range of skills, including verbal reasoning, learning and memory, and visual analysis.

We have also attempted to determine if crucial periods exist in which nutritional status has particularly strong impact upon subsequent mental test performance. To examine this question, we have employed regression analyses in which supplementation during various developmental epochs was regressed on mental test performances at three and at four years. (Such analyses were not interpretable at five years because of insufficient numbers of children yet studied who have been well supplemented very early in life.) These analyses pinpoint the periods of gestation and of birth to 24 months as the most important in determining later mental development.

Alternative Explanations for Our Findings,
and the Role of Social and Economic Factors

We have considered the possibility that the associations we have found between nutritional status and mental development actually have some nonnutritional

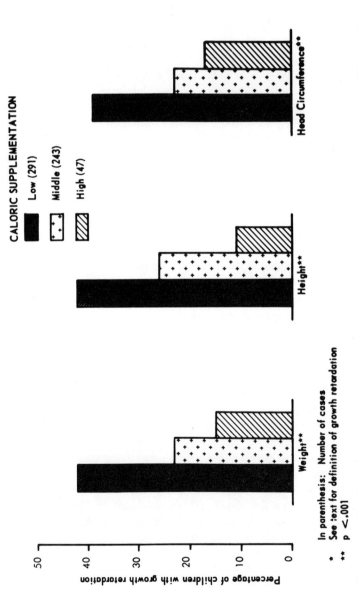

Figure 2. Relationship between categories of caloric supplementation since conception and percentage of children with growth retardation in weight, height, and head circumference at 36 months of age ($N = 581$, Fresco and Atole combined).

Table 1. Means, pooled standard deviations and analysis of variance F values of psychological test scores at 36 months for children falling into various cumulative supplementation categories

	1	2	3	Standard deviation	F
Composite score	−0.41 (452)	0.60 (119)	0.78 (147)	3.64	8.09**
Embedded figures	9.78 (440)	9.94 (119)	10.12 (144)	3.32	0.60
Digit memory	10.19 (367)	12.42 (107)	11.96 (129)	8.23	4.28**
Sentence memory	12.67 (385)	15.05 (108)	15.87 (134)	12.85	3.78**
Vocabulary naming	6.66 (426)	8.28 (114)	8.04 (143)	4.18	10.52**
Vocabulary recognition	19.90 (426)	20.98 (114)	20.66 (143)	5.72	2.11
Verbal inferences	1.38 (191)	1.87 (53)	2.06 (50)	1.27	7.63**
Memory for objects	1.94 (199)	1.95 (83)	2.19 (114)	1.39	1.32
Reversal Disc. learning	23.79 (393)	25.70 (115)	24.18 (137)	20.61	0.38
Knox cubes	0.62 (88)	0.41 (46)	0.69 (62)	1.30	0.65

* $p = 0.05$ ** $p = 0.01$

basis. For example, it is possible in a quasi-experimental study like ours in which treatment (supplement ingestion) was entirely voluntary, that bright, cooperative families would drink more supplement and do well on psychological tests without ingestion and good performance being causally related; or that the stimulating effect of attending the supplementation centers per se, rather than drinking supplement, made children more intelligent; or that poorly supplemented children were also more sick and being more ill made them perform less well. However, each of these possible alternative explanations, as well as a number of others have been statistically tested and rejected (Progress Report, 1975).

Probably the best candidate for an alternative explanation of our finding of an association between nutritional status and mental development is family socioeconomic status (SES). It is generally known that family characteristics are

Table 2. Means, pooled standard deviations, and analysis of variance F values of psychological test scores at 48 months for children falling into various cumulative supplementation categories

	1	2	3	Standard deviation	F
Composite score	−0.41 (473)	0.59 (132)	0.98 (120)	3.87	8.21**
Embedded figures	2.71 (451)	2.74 (129)	3.24 (119)	1.80	4.31**
Digit memory	21.56 (448)	22.18 (128)	21.65 (115)	11.90	0.14
Sentence memory	31.94 (442)	33.91 (128)	37.33 (113)	20.04	3.37**
Vocabulary naming	12.11 (461)	13.95 (130)	14.49 (118)	5.13	14.36**
Vocabulary recognition	25.70 (461)	27.79 (130)	27.3º !8)	5.34	10.65**
Verbal inferences	2.92 (364)	3.19 (110)	3.22 (91)	1.49	2.41
Memory for objects	3.63 (221)	3.80 (91)	3.68 (105)	1.68	0.32
Reversal disc. learning	35.52 (458)	39.00 (131)	40.80 (118)	19.62	4.24**
Knox cubes	1.36 (163)	1.75 (83)	1.22 (82)	2.02	1.57

* $p = 0.05$ ** $p = 0.01$

Table 3. Means, pooled standard deviations, and analysis of variance F values of psychological test scores at 60 months for children falling into various cumulative supplementation categories

	1	2	3	Standard deviation	F
Composite score	−0.70 (452)	0.87 (135)	1.90 (104)	7.64	6.05**
Embedded figures	4.12 (450)	4.40 (135)	4.84 (103)	2.21	4.72**
Digit memory	35.82 (441)	35.20 (135)	34.09 (103)	13.10	0.75
Sentence memory	51.27 (442)	51.56 (134)	52.17 (104)	21.16	0.08
Vocabulary naming	17.08 (449)	18.78 (135)	18.40 (104)	5.06	7.53**
Vocabulary recognition	30.08 (449)	31.13 (135)	31.35 (104)	4.39	5.40**
Verbal inferences	4.07 (422)	4.44 (128)	4.23 (99)	1.89	1.98
Memory for objects	5.51 (197)	5.89 (88)	5.81 (88)	1.85	1.60
Reversal Disc. learning	23.73 (438)	25.56 (133)	29.68 (103)	21.20	3.37*
Knox cubes	3.44 (202)	4.74 (88)	4.91 (89)	3.53	7.57**
Conservation of material	0.29 (197)	0.34 (86)	0.26 (86)	0.60	0.40
Conservation of area	0.35 (193)	0.40 (85)	0.38 (87)	0.67	0.16
Conservation of content quantity	0.20 (202)	0.21 (86)	0.17 (87)	0.43	0.17
Incomplete figures	5.59 (203)	5.73 (86)	5.15 (84)	2.64	1.15
Elimination	5.10 (199)	5.24 (83)	5.33 (87)	2.16	0.40
Block design	39.58 (202)	42.84 (88)	47.75 (88)	20.46	5.04**
Incidental learning	1.34 (448)	1.77 (135)	1.79 (103)	1.27	9.36**
Intentional learning	2.18 (448)	2.44 (135)	2.87 (103)	1.40	10.96**
Haptic-Visual match	3.86 (351)	4.22 (126)	4.45 (103)	2.87	2.01
Face-hands	2.44 (200)	2.37 (87)	2.42 (87)	1.39	0.09
Matching family figures	2.75 (443)	2.85 (134)	2.86 (103)	1.35	0.51
Memory for designs	11.66 (444)	13.04 (131)	14.76 (102)	11.37	3.37*
Animal house	118.64 (196)	113.76 (88)	120.16 (87)	54.08	0.35

* $p = 0.05$ ** $p = 0.01$

consistently associated with mental test performance, and this was true in these villages. Family SES level also generally covaries with children's nutritional status in untreated populations. For these reasons, family SES must be carefully measured in studies of malnutrition and mental development.

In the present study, family SES level is unrelated to supplement ingestion. Furthermore, we know the associations between nutritional status and mental test performance are not merely caused by SES differences between good and poor test performers; regression analyses in which successive offspring of the same mother are compared have been performed. These analyses, by making within family comparisons, hold constant all family level variables, including SES level. They indicate mental test performance differences as a function of differences in nutritional status within families are as large as the between family effects seen in Tables 1, 2, and 3.

Family SES level does appear to interact with nutritional status in affecting mental development; although effects of supplement ingestion exist within both the upper and lower halves of the family SES distribution, these effects are somewhat different for children of low and high SES families. This is illustrated in Table 4, which presents contingency tables showing the numbers of children in the lowest 0–24 month supplementation category falling, or not falling, into the lowest percentile of composite scale performance at 36, 48, and 60 months, by SES level. Relative risk of lowest percentile performance as a function of SES level (high or low) has been computed (MacMahon and Pugh, 1970). Low SES children who received very little supplementation are seen to be at significantly greater risk of poor mental test performance than higher SES children who received little supplementation. As we have noted previously, supplement ingestion is our best estimate of overall nutritional status in the study population.

Table 4. Number of children in lowest supplementation category falling into the lowest percentile of composite score performance or not, by SES level

36 months	Lowest percentile	Not lowest percentile	
Low SES	61	166	
			Relative risk = 1.41*
High SES	47	200	
48 months	Lowest percentile	Not lowest percentile	
Low SES	82	169	
			Relative risk = 2.10**
High SES	43	233	
60 months	Lowest percentile	Not lowest percentile	
Low SES	69	183	
			Relative risk = 1.68**
High SES	47	241	

* $p = 0.05$ ** $p = 0.01$

Table 5. Correlations between various family variables related to intellectual stimulation and of family wealth indicators, and composite score on the preschool battery at ages 3, 4, and 5

Age (years)	Mother composite[a]		Sibling schooling		Books & objects		House quality[b]		Parents' clothing	
	boys	girls	boys	girls	boys	girls	boys	girls	boys	girls
3	.13*	.02	.14*	.01	.02	−.02	.05	.03	.16**	.02
4	.17*	.06	.26**	.00	.04	−.05	.05	.07	.16**	.10
5	.20**	.12	.31**	.22**	.20**	.23**	.13*	.20**	.12*	.15*

[a]Cell n's 300 for Mother Composite, Sibling Schooling, Books and Objects.
[b]Cell n's 600 for Home Quality and Parents' Clothing.

Thus, these data argue that poor nutrition early in life is more damaging to subsequent intellectual development of children from poorer families than to those from less poor families.

As we have noted, family SES variations not only interacted with nutritional status to affect mental development, but also seem to have exerted an effect directly upon mental development. Table 5 presents correlations between mental test performance and family economic indicators of House Quality and Quality of Parents' Clothing, as well as with a number of family measures constructed to index aspects of intellectual stimulation available in the home. These are: 1) Mother Composite, which combines the mother's vocabulary test score, literacy test score, years of school passed, and modernity into a single index of intellectual characteristics; 2) Sibling Schooling, which indexes average years passed by all older siblings living at home; and 3) Books and Objects, which is an index of the number of books, magazines, and visually stimulating objects such as drawings, photographs, pictorial calendars, diplomas, and decorated furniture found in the home.

As Table 5 indicates, the Mother Composite and Sibling Schooling intellectual characteristics both correlated consistently with test performances for boys, although for girls Mother Composite was unrelated to test performance and Sibling Schooling only related significantly to performance at five years of age. Our measure of material stimulation, Books and Objects, also correlated with test performance, but only at age five. The economic indicators of House Quality and Parents' Clothing related significantly to test performances of both boys and girls at five years of age, and Parents' Clothing also related to boys' test performances at three and four years.

To date, the INCAP longitudinal study data suggest effects on mental development of early nutritional status and of social and economic variables characterizing families, as well as an interaction between nutrition and socio-economic status. At present, work is proceeding on the development of more measures descriptive of study children's home environments from data collected under the auspices of another investigation. Multivariate analyses of the complicated and important interrelationships among nutritional status and of these environmental influences on mental development are also planned.

SUMMARY

This investigation focuses on the mental and physical development of malnourished children living under impoverished conditions in rural Guatemala. Maternal malnutrition during pregnancy and malnutrition of the child during the first two years of life were found to be detrimental to optimal physical and mental development. Other micro-environmental factors also were found to be importantly related to measures of mental development.

REFERENCES

DDH/INCAP. (1975) Nutrición, crecimiento y desarrollo. Boletín de la Oficina Sanitaria Panamericana 78:38.
DDH/INCAP. (1975) Progress Report.
Habicht, J.-P., Martorell, R., Yarbrough, C., Malina, R. M., and Klein, R. E. (1974) Height and weight for preschool children: Are there really ethnic differences in growth potential? Lancet 1:611.
Hansman, C. (1970) Anthropometry and related data. In Human Growth and Development (Ed. McCammon, R. W.) Springfield, Ill.: Charles C Thomas, p. 101.
Klein, R. E., Irwin, M. H., Engle, P. L., and Yarbrough, C. (1977) Malnutrition and mental development in rural Guatemala: An applied cross-cultural research study. In Advances in Cross-Cultural Psychology (Ed. Warren, N.) New York: Academic Press, pp. 91-119.
MacMahon, B., and Pugh, T. F. (1970) Epidemiology: Principles and Methods. Boston: Little, Brown.
Martorell, R., Yarbrough, C., Lechtig, A., Delgado, H., and Klein, R. E. (1975) Nutrition and physical growth: Results from a feeding experiment in Guatemala. In: Abstracts of Papers, Symposia and Free Communications of the Xth International Congress of Nutrition, Kyoto, Japan, August, Abstract No. 2507, p. 154.
United Nations (1971) Demographic Yearbook, 23rd. Edition. Geneva: United Nations.

RESEARCH TO PRACTICE IN MENTAL RETARDATION
Biomedical Aspects, Volume III
Edited by Peter Mittler
Copyright 1977 I.A.S.S.M.D.

PRENATAL NUTRITION AND SUBSEQUENT DEVELOPMENT

M. Susser, Z. A. Stein, and D. Rush
Division of Epidemiology,
School of Public Health, Faculty of Medicine,
Columbia University, and N. Y. Psychiatric Institute,
600 West 168th Street,
New York, N.Y. 10032, United States

In this chapter, we will discuss two studies carried out by our group at Columbia University: 1) the Dutch Famine Study (with Drs. Zena Stein, Gerhart Saenger, and the late Frank Marolla), and 2) the Prenatal Project (with Drs. David Rush and Zena Stein). These studies aimed to clarify the effects of prenatal nutrition on fetal growth, on fetal viability and infant mortality, and on subsequent physical and mental development.

THE DUTCH FAMINE STUDY

When the idea of this study occurred to us, it was 20 years after Clement Smith's 1947 paper on the effects of the Dutch famine on pregnancy. We realized with excitement that the survivors among those exposed to the famine in utero would be in their 20s.

The Dutch famine was a tragic cadenza to World War II. The relevant aspects are fully described in our book (Stein et al., 1975), and we omit description here. The famine was unique in a number of important respects. It was sharply demarcated in time and in place, and thus permitted the identification of those exposed and those unexposed according to the time and place of birth. Furthermore, the famine lasted a relatively short time—six months in all, or less than a term pregnancy. From this there followed several advantages. The extreme conditions extending over a short period of time provided the natural equivalent of a deliberate intervention. Consequently, the common difficulty of separating prenatal from postnatal malnutrition was not an obstacle, and exposure to the famine could be specified in terms of each phase of pregnancy, thus permitting a test of the critical period hypothesis (Dobbing, 1964; Winick and Noble, 1966). Finally, the country was not so disorganized that it could not maintain its

Figure 1. The Netherlands. (Taken from Stein, Z., Susser, M., Saenger, G., and Marolla, F. (1975. *Famine and Human Development: The Dutch Hunger Winter of 1944–1945.* Oxford University Press, New York, p. 58.)

excellent system of vital statistics, and extensive documentation on the famine, including nutritional intake of the population in terms of food rations, was readily available.

The design of the study rested on two prongs. Exposed and unexposed birth cohorts were assigned by time and place of birth to create two comparison groups, a place control and a time control. To achieve control by place, the exposed and unexposed cohorts were derived from total births occurring at the same time in all cities of over 40,000 population in famine and nonfamine areas. The accompanying map (Figure 1) indicates their distribution.

The time control was based on monthly births throughout the period, January, 1944, through December, 1946. The design is illustrated in Figure 2. This diagram also indicates the level of official rations, which declined to less than 500 calories at the worst period. Each horizontal bar represents one month of births from conception to delivery. The bars are grouped according to their stages of gestation at famine exposure in order to test the critical period hypothesis. The crucial exposure in terms of maximum prenatal brain growth is during the third trimester. In the diagram, the B-2 cohort suffered the maximum exposure at this time. (It should be noted, from the recent work of Dobbing and Sands, 1973, that the period of maximum brain growth now appears to extend through the first two years of life, an amendment that must be taken into account in assessing the ultimate effects of malnutrition on brain growth.)

In this study, we were able to examine effects of prenatal famine exposure on the following outcomes: 1) fertility, 2) fetal growth, 3) mortality through 19 years of age, and 4) adult mental, physical, and health states.

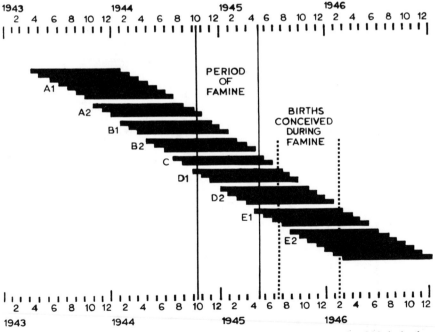

Figure 2. Design of study. Cohorts by month of conception and month of birth, in the Netherlands, 1943 through 1946, related to famine exposure. Solid vertical lines bracket the period of famine, and broken vertical lines bracket the period of births conceived during famine. (Taken from Stein, Z., Susser, M., Saenger, G., and Marolla, F. 1975. *Famine and Human Development: The Dutch Hunger Winter of 1944–1945.* Oxford University Press, New York, p. 57.)

Fertility

Effects on fertility were profound. Here we note only that the effects differed across social class, thus altering the social class composition of the birth cohorts affected, and requiring control of confounding factors in analysis.

Prenatal Famine Effects on Fetal Growth

About 6,000 births in maternity hospitals were studied, which allowed us to reach the following conclusions. Growth retardation occurred in all the fetal dimensions measured. The effects were attributable solely to third trimester exposure to the famine; thus the maximal effects were seen in the B-2 cohort. Most important, they occurred only below a threshold value of caloric intake in the population. Below that threshold level, there was a dose-response relationship between deprivation and fetal growth retardation. The results of birthweight are illustrated in Figure 3.

Mortality Through 19 Years

The study of mortality was based on all deaths up to 20 years of age in the study cohorts. Age-specific death rates were developed for the 120,000 births involved.

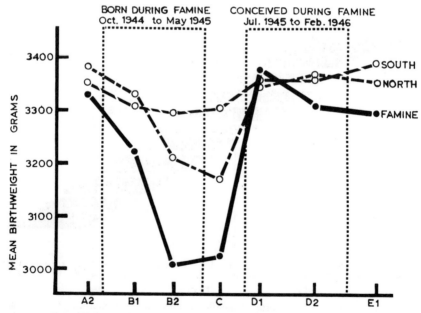

Figure 3. Birthweight by time and place (mean birthweight in grams for births in maternity hospitals for seven birth cohorts: famine, Northern control, and Southern control areas compared for the period August, 1944, to March, 1946, inclusive). (Taken from Stein, Z., Susser, M., Saenger, G., and Marolla, F., 1975. *Famine and Human Development: The Dutch Hunger Winter of 1944–1945.* Oxford University Press, New York, p. 93.)

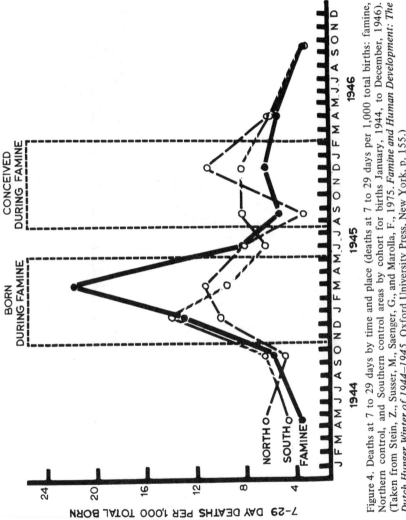

Figure 4. Deaths at 7 to 29 days by time and place (deaths at 7 to 29 days per 1,000 total births: famine, Northern control, and Southern control areas by cohort for births January, 1944, to December, 1946). (Taken from Stein, Z., Susser, M., Saenger, G., and Marolla, F., 1975. *Famine and Human Development: The Dutch Hunger Winter of 1944–1945*. Oxford University Press, New York, p. 155.)

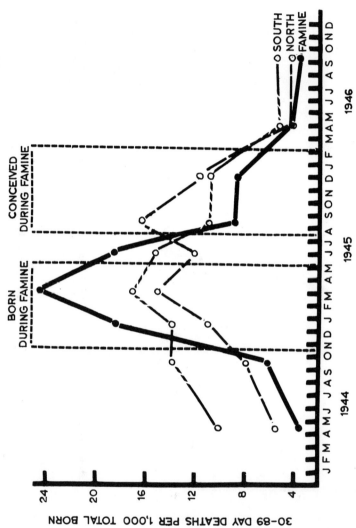

Figure 5. Deaths at 30 to 89 days by time and place (deaths at 30 to 89 days per 1,000 total births: famine, Northern control, and Southern control areas by cohort for births, January 1944 to December 1946). (Taken from Stein, Z., Susser, M., Saenger, G., and Marolla, F., 1975. *Famine and Human Development: The Dutch Hunger Winter of 1944–1945*. Oxford University Press, New York, p. 158.)

In summary, third trimester famine exposure caused a sharp increase of mortality up to three months of age. These effects, while apparent in the first week of life, became marked after that stage through the first three months of life. The peak mortality in the B-2 cohort, for deaths at 7–29 days and at 30–89 days, are illustrated in Figures 4 and 5.

Prenatal Famine Effects on Adult Health State

In this part of the study the data were taken from military induction records of examinations of 19-year old men. These data comprised virtually a total population of 120,000 men. The losses in data between birth and survival at 19 years that could not be accounted for by migration or mortality were an estimated 3%.

Five psychometric tests were available, of which the most sensitive was Raven's Progressive Matrices test. Figure 6 shows that there were no detectable effects of famine exposure on test performance in either the manual or the nonmanual classes.

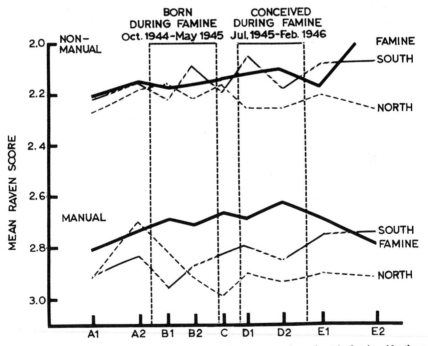

Figure 6. Raven scores by area and class (mean Raven scores by cohort in famine, Northern control, and Southern control areas, comparing manual and non-manual occupational classes). (Taken from Stein, Z., Susser, M., Saenger, G., and Marolla, F., 1975. *Famine and Human Development: The Dutch Hunger Winter of 1944–1945.* Oxford University Press, New York, p. 203.)

Similarly, analysis of classified diseases yielded no detectable famine effects related to third trimester exposure and fetal growth retardation. The conditions tested included mild mental retardation, severe mental retardation, and a number of psychiatric conditions among many others.

Finally, anthropometric measures such as height, weight, and Quetelet's index yielded no detectable effects of prenatal famine exposure with one exception. Exposure in the latter part of pregnancy and early postnatal life led to a decreased number of obese individuals; exposure in the first half of pregnancy led to an increased number of obese individuals. These results have considerable import for hypotheses relating to obesity.

We may conclude that prenatal exposure to famine had unequivocal somatic effects on fetal growth and on infant vitality through 90 days of age. Effects persisting in adults were undetectable, with the exception of the frequency of obesity.

THE PRENATAL PROJECT

The ultimate aim of the studies upon which we embarked was the prevention and treatment of adverse nutritional effects. It is a logical fallacy to translate directly from ill effects of nutritional deprivation—for instance on fetal growth and mortality as seen in the famine study—to a presumption of benefits from nutritional supplementation. Such a presumption requires empirical tests. Hence, we designed a second study based on nutritional intervention with the object of trying to eliminate, in a population at risk of low birthweight, retardation of fetal growth attributable to poor nutrition, and its subsequent effects (Rush et al., 1974).

About 1,000 black women were selected from a clinic population known to be at high risk of low birthweight (about 18% vs. 5–6% in the most favored health areas of New York City). With their permission, they were assigned at random to a double blind control trial, at different levels of nutritional supplementation. Before assignment to treatment, the women were stratified by individual attributes that placed them at particularly high risk of low birthweight (± 25%), attributes that we believed might differentiate among conditions of varying sensitivity to nutritional intervention.

There were three treatment groups in all, 1) the high protein supplement (40 grams protein, 470 calories, vitamins, and minerals) group, 2) the balanced protein caloric supplement (6 grams protein, 320 calories, vitamins, and minerals) group, and 3) a sleeping control group assigned to regular clinic care (routine supplements of vitamin and mineral tablets).

Results of Supplementation

Figure 7 shows an unequivocal failure to negate the null hypothesis at the time of birth. There was no difference detected in birthweight, nor in other fetal

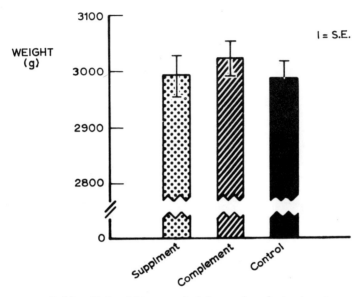

Figure 7. Mean birthweight among singleton survivors by treatment groups.

dimensions, between the three treatment groups, each comprised of about 300 women.

Naturally, all available explanations of the absence of effect have been tested, including distributions of confounding factors that might have been biased despite the randomization of the design, the degree to which supplementation took place, and the degree to which supplementation might have been substituted for the regular diet. Unfortunately, with further analysis, things got worse rather than better.

An important control variable was length of gestation, a factor intimately related to birthweight. The most proper means of controlling for length of gestation is by life table analysis. Figure 8 shows the cumulative delivery rate by stage of gestation throughout the study period. Excess of premature deliveries among the women in the high protein supplement group before 35 weeks gestation is evident. This excess rate of prematurity led directly to an excess of neonatal deaths. Figure 9 shows a life table analysis of neonatal mortality by treatment group that illustrates this outcome. Furthermore, over and above the excess of premature deliveries, the high protein supplement led to fetal growth retardation before 35 weeks gestation (Figure 10).

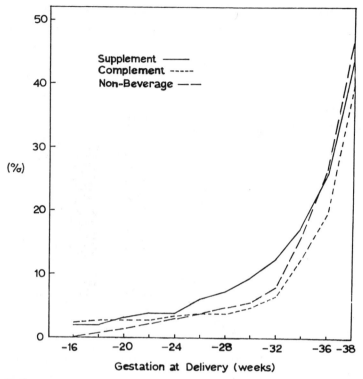

Figure 8. Cumulative delivery rates (percent) by length of gestation for each treatment group, including deaths.

Fortunately, the result of high protein supplementation was not adverse throughout gestation. Term pregnancies were defined as those carried beyond 37 weeks gestation. Figure 10 shows that, at term, there was some indication of an increased birthweight in the supplement or high protein treatment group. This result was not in itself statistically significant. A stratification of the data in accord with our initial hypotheses, however, showed that a coherent result was present. It will be recalled that, at the outset, a number of factors were specified because they carried a special or conditional risk of a low birthweight outcome. Without violating the conventions of hypothesis testing, therefore, we could test for nutritional effects in relation to these conditions, although at the cost of reduced power.

Analysis by these high risk conditions showed that the high protein supplement produced a significant birthweight increment at term under two conditions, namely, smoking and low prepregnant weight. Figure 11 illustrates this result. It also shows that these two risk conditions accounted for the total effect of high protein supplement at term. Nutritional supplementation produced no effect among nonsmokers and women of prepregnant weight above 110 pounds. A number of other outcomes measured at birth, such as maturity and neonatal behavior, and also biochemical indices of placental state at birth, showed no relationship to nutritional supplementation.

At follow-up at one year of age, an array of measures of physical growth, six psychometric tests, and clinical data were available. (D. Nathan Brody is our co-investigator in this aspect of the study.) Virtually all the expected relations of measures of infant development with birthweight were present. However, none of the expected relations of development with treatment was present, with two exceptions.

On a test of visual habituation in response to a repeated stimulus, we found that the supplement treatment group lost their attention sooner, and when the stimulus changed, paid attention again as soon as expected. In the *Hunt-Uzgiris* procedure for observing the infants at play, the duration of attention, as indicated by the time a child spent with each toy, turned out to be longer. The combination of these two results suggests that there may be a general effect of the high protein supplement on some faculty of attention. This improved

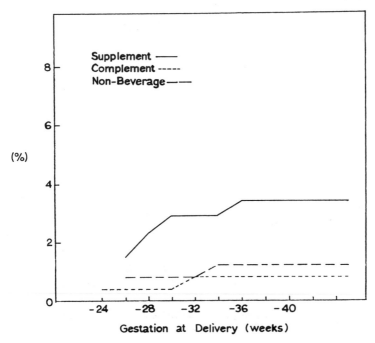

Figure 9. Cumulative neonatal mortality rates (percent) by length of gestation for each treatment group.

performance was unrelated to birthweight, and therefore, not mediated by an accelerated rate of fetal growth or the correction of growth retardation.

In summary, the outcome of this study was ambiguous. High protein supplement led to unpredicted, adverse effects on fetal growth, time of delivery, and viability. The presence of three such indicators makes attribution to chance unlikely. These effects are not coherent with any known properties of the supplement. The high protein used was casein, and the beverage contained nothing that is not used in regular foods at a level within the recommended daily allowances. Hence, whether we consider undertaking new studies or whether we consider practical applications, this result cannot be ignored.

At the same time, high protein supplement had a protective effect on fetal growth consistent with the initial hypotheses of the study which, like the famine effects, was *conditional.* A favorable effect on a specific psychological function, i.e., attention at one year of age, was independent of fetal growth and unconditional.

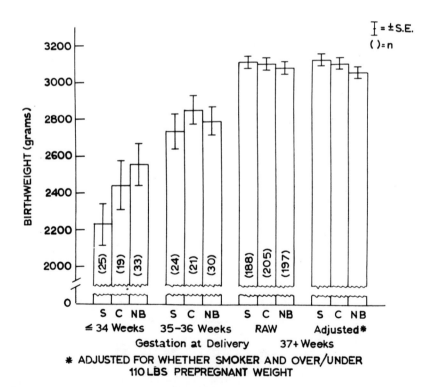

Figure 10. Mean singleton birthweight among survivors by duration of gestation for each treatment group.

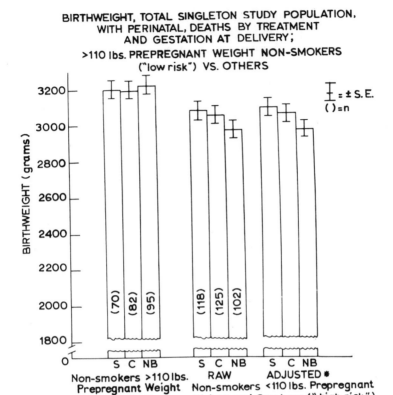

Figure 11. Mean singleton birthweight at term, stratified by smoking and prepregnant weight, for each treatment group.

DISCUSSION

These two studies—the Dutch Famine Study and the Prenatal Project—together with the Guatemala study (Lechtig et al., 1976; Lasky et al., 1975) represent the first published results of a new generation of studies that move us somewhat closer to securing causal inferences about the effects of prenatal nutrition in humans.

Technical advances in research design, however, do not advance our capacity to reconcile conflicting and disconcerting results. How shall we conclude? In the

Dutch famine, a population, well-nourished in previous times, when exposed to prenatal deprivation of nutrients below a threshold value during the third trimester of pregnancy, showed unequivocal but conditional effects of depressed fertility, retarded fetal growth, and increased mortality up to three months of age. However, among adults no effects could be detected except on the frequency of obesity.

In the Prenatal Project, the study population was at high risk of low birthweight, but only segments of it could be described as poorly nourished. In this population, too, a high protein supplement benefited growth conditionally; in that respect, the result was congruent with the threshold found in the Dutch famine study. In addition, the high protein supplement benefited specific psychological test performance. This benefit, while unconditional, was not mediated by fetal growth, and it has unknown significance for later ages.

The published data of the Guatemalan study afford some reassurance with regard to supplementation. In this instance, the total population suffers from chronic malnutrition, and hence the favorable effects observed on fetal growth and later test performance are subject to that condition. Data supplied by Dr. Klein indicate, however, that even within this population the results are conditional, and that increments in fetal growth are most notable among women most likely to be malnourished.

Taking together the three studies available to us, three conclusions present themselves. First, we can be sure that prenatal nutrition affects fetal growth, viability, and vitality, but only under certain conditions. We need to know more about these conditions and the specifics of the nutrients involved. We need also to explore the meaning of the adverse effect of the high protein supplement observed among premature deliveries. Second, we can be almost as sure that prenatal nutrition is unlikely to affect adult mental performance given reasonable nutritional conditions in the postnatal environment. Third, it is possible, but it is not finally established, that prenatal nutrition affects aspects of early mental development, especially when there is chronic postnatal malnutrition. Here we need to know more about the interaction and interrelations of prenatal nutrition with family and social dynamics as well as with postnatal nutrition.

Critical pieces of the puzzle of chronic malnutrition are still missing. For example, in such populations, do effects on early cognitive function, *solely* attributable to nutrition, actually occur? Do effects on early cognitive function occur in response to the interaction of nutrition with the social environment? Or are the observed relationships of early cognitive function with prenatal nutrition solely attributable to social environment? Existing studies still allow the possibility that malnutrition is a result of the social environment, separate from but confounded by cognitive performance; in other words, that a harsh social environment is the common cause of malnutrition and retarded cognitive performance.

In this respect, one may advance a unifying hypothesis to encompass the work of Chavez (1975) and Cravioto (1974) in Mexico, and of Richardson (1976), and Hertzig et al. (1972) in Jamaica, as well as the animal experiments of Frankova (1974). This work suggests that the main effect of both prenatal and postnatal nutritional supplementation on the infant may well be to promote somatic growth, while the main influence on psychological test performance is to be found in the social environment. The data taken together also suggest that supplementation improves the affective state and activity of a malnourished mother. This in turn is a likely intermediate variable in a path leading from maternal nutrition through maternal affective change to improvement in the psychological performance of their offspring. In other words, the report by Klein et al. in Guatemala (see p. 299 of this volume) of a prenatal nutritional effect on early psychological test performance (subsequently increasing with age) may in reality be caused by improvements in the mother's health and affective state that influence her care of the child after birth.

These three separate effects may set up a dynamic interactive process.

This hypothetical process can be illustrated in a path diagram:

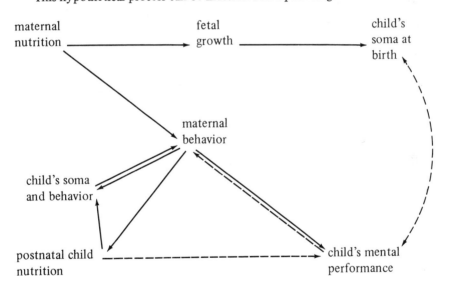

Still another generation of studies will be required to address these questions.

ACKNOWLEDGMENTS

Our colleague Dr. Frank Marolla died suddenly on July 27, 1976. This chapter is dedicated to him.

REFERENCES

Chavez, A. (1975) Consequences of insufficient nutrition on child character and behavior. Cornell Conference on Malnutrition and Behavior, November, Ithaca, N.Y.

Cravioto, J., and Delicardie, E. R. (1974) The relation of size at birth and preschool clinical severe malnutrition. Acta Paediat. Scand. p. 63:577.

Dobbing, J. (1964) The influence of early nutrition on the development and myelination of the brain. Proc. Roy Soc. (Biol.) 159:503.

Dobbing, J., and Sands, J. (1973) Quantitative growth and development of human brain. Arch. Dis. Child. 48:757.

Frankova, S. (1974) Interaction between early malnutrition and stimulation in animals. In Symposia of the Swedish Nutrition Foundation XII. Early Malnutrition and Mental Development. (Eds. Cravioto, J., Hambraeus, L., and Vahlquist, B.) Uppsala: Almqvist and Wiksells, p. 226.

Hertzig, M. F., Birch, G. G., Richardson, S. O., and Tizard, J. (1972) Intellectual levels of school children severely malnourished during the first two years of life. Pediatrics. 49:814.

Lasky, R. E., Lechtig, A., Delgado, H., et al. (1975) Birthweight and psychomotor performance in rural Guatemala. Amer. J. Dis. Child. 129:566.

Lechtig, A., Delgado, H., Yarbrough, C., Habicht, J., Martorell, R., and Klein, R. (1976) A simple assessment of the risk of low birthweight to select women for nutritional intervention. Amer. J. Obstet. Gynec. 125:25.

Richardson, S. A. (1976) The relation of severe malnutrition in infancy to the intelligence of school children having differing life histories. Pediatr. Res. 10:57.

Rush, D., Stein, Z., Christakis, G., and Susser, M. (1974) The Prenatal Project: The first 20 months of operation. In Malnutrition and Human Development (Ed. Winick, M.) New York: Wiley & Sons.

Stein, Z., Susser, M., Saenger, G., and Marolla, F. (1975) Famine and Human Development: The Dutch Hunger Winter of 1944/45. New York: Oxford University Press.

Winick, M., and Noble, A. (1966) Cellular response in rats during malnutrition at various ages. J. Nutr. 89:300.

RESEARCH TO PRACTICE IN MENTAL RETARDATION
Biomedical Aspects, Volume III
Edited by Peter Mittler
Copyright 1977 I.A.S.S.M.D.

ASPECTS OF PHYSICAL GROWTH AND NUTRITION IN SEVERELY MENTALLY RETARDED CHILDREN

C. J. de Groot and A. Stutterheim
*"Maartenswouden," Home for Residential
Care of Mentally Retarded Children,
Drachten, The Netherlands*

Irrespective of etiology, the severely mentally retarded child tends to be short for his/her age and to have delayed bone development. In addition, microcephaly is observed very often. He is also likely to be underweight (Dooren, 1967; van Gelderen, 1962; Moser, Grossman, and Dingman, 1965; Roberts and Clayton, 1969; Rundle, 1970).

Elucidating a cause of the observed dwarfism in mentally retarded children was the main object in several studies in previous years. Although the influence of socioeconomic (Rundle, 1970), hormonal (Frasier, Hilburn, and Smith, 1970; Rundle, 1970) and nutritional (Roberts and Clayton, 1969) factors were studied, none of them could be shown to be a major factor. A recent study by Castells et al., (1974) suggests there may be in some cases a disturbed regulation of the growth hormone secretion rate as a result of defects in the hypothalamic centers. However, definite conclusions about the cause of the degree, as well as the frequency, of stunted growth have not yet been made (Frasier, 1974).

The idea that linear growth in man is partly caused by the dynamics of brain function is supported by studies concerning growth in intellectually normal children who were emotionally deprived (Croughs, 1971; Powell et al., 1967). Looking at growth this way, an eventual increase or decrease of growth rate in a deeply mentally deficient child, could give an indication of the relative emotional stability. Particularly with these children where psychological methods are

Table 1. The code used for construction of Figure 2

Length in relation to age	Weight in relation to length
0 = more than 3rd percentile	0 = more than 10th percentile
1 = 3rd percentile	1 = 10th percentile
2 = less than 3rd percentile	2 = less than 10th percentile
3 - far less than 3rd percentile	3 = far less than 10th percentile
Gain in length in relation to age	Gain in weight in relation to length
0 = more than 3rd percentile	0 = more than 10th percentile
1 = parallel to 3rd percentile	1 = parallel to 10th percentile
2 = less than 3rd percentile	2 = less than 10th percentile
3 = far less than 3rd percentile	3 = far less than 10th percentile or a weight loss

difficult to apply, this could possibly be of help for establishing optimal care. This was the reason we made another attempt to measure length and other aspects of growth in severely retarded children.

Our study investigated the linear growth of a group of severely retarded children over a three-year period. The relationship of weight, bone age, skinfold thickness, nutritional state, intercurrent illnesses, and anti-epileptic drugs was also studied. In a separate part of this study the relationship of linear growth and nail and hair growth was investigated.

The first study concerned a group of 72 institutionalized children. We did not make an etiological selection. The sole criterion was severe mental retardation. A division was made between a group in a prepubertal stage (A) and a group of children who were approaching puberty or had reached puberty (B). (Groups A and B combined included 25 children with Down's syndrome.) Length, weight, and skinfold thickness were measured every six months. We measured nail growth by making a scratch at the nail root. Then, after a month, we read the distance the scratch had made from the nail root. After each reading a new mark was made for the subsequent reading. Hair growth was measured monthly, by cutting a small patch of hair at skin level, each month at the same place, mid-frontal. As the actual length, the mean of ten cutoff hairs was used.

To obtain further information about the nutritional state, a yearly blood sample was taken for electrolytes, calcium, phosphorus, alkaline phosphatase, hemoglobin, total protein, γ globulins, urea, kreatine, and cholesterol. During the three-year period the frequency of intercurrent infections and major changes in care and nursing were noted. For nail and hair growth comparisons were made with normal school children. During a one-year period, monthly readings of nail and hair growth were taken. The nail and hair growth of the normal children were compared with those of a group of severely retarded children and a group of less retarded children with Down's syndrome. All the readings were made by the same person. Length was measured on the same Harpenden Infant Measuring Table. Weight was measured on a standardized weighing chair (Berkel). Skinfold thickness was measured by a Harpenden Skinfold Caliper. The nomographs used for length and weight were those for Dutch children (van Wieringen et al., 1968). A code was used for the graphic presentation of the measurements of length and weight (Table 1).

RESULTS

The Length and Gain in Length During the Three-Year Follow-Up

About half of the children in the prepubertal age group and half of the children in the older age group were below −2 SD of the normal length for age (Figure 1). During the follow-up, eight children of Group A (27%) showed a higher than expected gain in growth, and two children (6%) showed a lower than expected gain. In Group B, these figures were respectively 33% and 10%; here, however, some children could be expected to be in their adolescent spurt or to be just out of it (Figure 2).

The Relationship of Length with Weight and Weight Gain

In Group A, 50% of the children were of low weight even for their length (less than the 10th percentile for length). For Group B, this figure was 25%. This higher weight to length ratio in Group B probably reflects the extra weight gain which is normally seen in puberty. In most children, a satisfactory gain in length (following the individual percentile or catching up) was accompanied by a good gain in weight for length.

Satisfactory gain in length with a low or absent gain in weight was observed in 18% of the children in Group A and 2% of the children in Group B. On the other hand, good weight gain with low gain in length was seen in 21% of the children in Group A and 13% of those in Group B. This shows that factors responsible for linear growth are not strictly related to weight gain or loss.

The Relationship of Weight Gain and Skinfold Thickness

A gain in weight along or above the 10th percentile was accompanied by a gain in skinfold thickness in only 27% of Group A and in 39% of Group B. This shows that good weight gain can be obtained without gain in skinfold thickness.

The Relationship of Length and Bone Age

As was shown by previous reports (Dooren, 1967; Rundle, 1970) abnormal linear growth was in many cases accompanied by delay in bone age maturation. In our study, 16% of the children in Group A who were showing linear growth below the third percentile had a bone age according to chronological age. The relative independence of linear growth and bone age determining factors was further shown by a few children with length above the third percentile, but with a marked delay in bone age maturation (Group A: 6%, Group B: 5%).

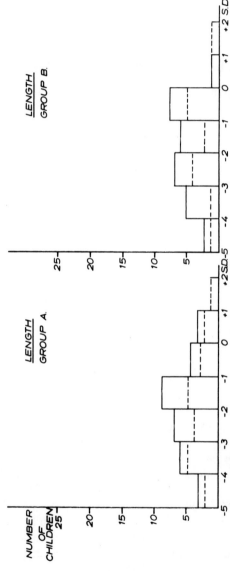

Figure 1. The standard deviation of the mean length for age.   The dotted line divides the bars in two parts. The upper part indicates the number of boys, the lower part the number of girls. This figure excludes the children with Down's syndrome. Of the children with Down's syndrome, 74% had a length lower than −2 SD.

GA

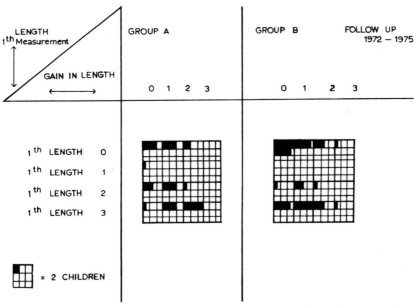

Figure 2. The children were classified according to the criteria of Table 1. Growth along a particular percentile is indicated on this diagram by a correspondence between class of length and class of gain in length. If all children had a growth along their percentile, the diagram would have shown a diagonal from upper left to bottom right.

In accordance with the results of the study of Dooren (1967), it was shown that in children with Down's syndrome skeletal age was more advanced than the age for length.

The Relationship of Length with Nail and Hair Growth

Nail and hair growth were not related in normal children to length, weight or age. Hair and nail growth of mentally retarded children was significantly lower than in normal children (Figure 3), but within this group no relation with length or weight was found.

In children with Down's syndrome, however, hair growth was significantly increased, while nail growth was significantly decreased (Figure 4). These data suggest that the regulation of hair and nail growth are not related to each other, and not related to the linear growth regulating factors. Taking into account the absence of a relationship with length and weight, the association of slower hair and nail growth with mental deficiency is even more surprising. This could be an indication that the central nervous system has pathways for the regulation of nail and hair growth that are different from those for linear growth.

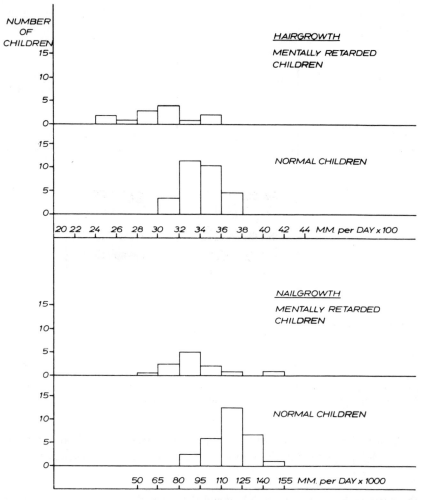

Figure 3. The distribution of hair and nail growth in a group of mentally retarded children and normal children. The mean values were significantly different between both groups ($p <$ 0.001).

The Relationship of Length with the Nutritional State and Interview Data

Biochemically, we could not find in either group of children any sign of protein or caloric deficiency. The only indication of a relevant biochemical abnormality in the groups was a significantly higher chloride and sodium level in the blood (Figure 5). This probably reflects slight dehydration. The special problem of feeding severely retarded children is concerned with the intake of sufficient fluid. Swallowing is easier when the food is of a more solid consistency. Fluid food is more often refused and seems to be more difficult to handle for the child. Excessive drooling could also play a role. Intercurrent infections were in fact rare.

Relationship with Anti-Epileptic Treatment

We could not find a relationship between the different observed items with anti-epileptic treatment. Calcium, phosphorus, and alkaline phosphatase were

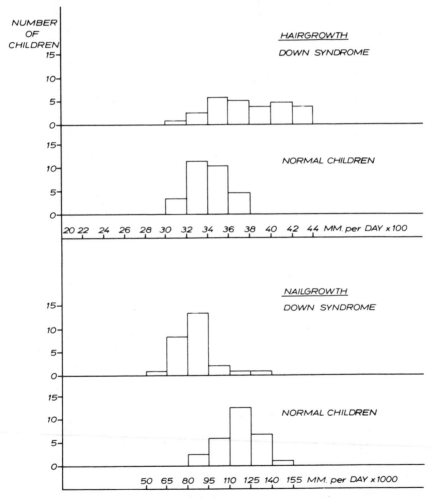

Figure 4. The distribution of hair and nail growth in a group of children with Down's syndrome and normal children. The mean value was significantly different between the groups ($p < 0.001$).

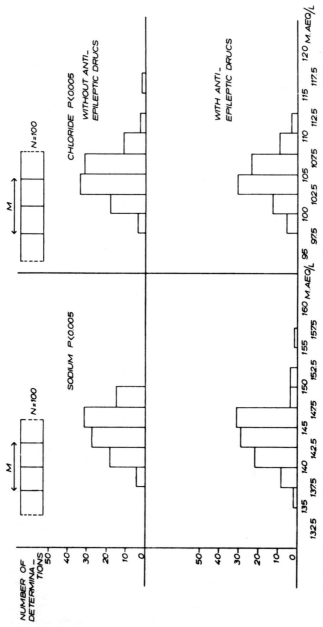

Figure 5. Distribution of sodium and chloride concentrations in mentally retarded children compared with a sample of routine laboratory measurements of mentally normal patients ($p < 0.005$). Treatment with anti-epileptic drugs is not related to the observed shift to the right.

not significantly different in children with or without anti-epileptic drugs. Probably the routine prescription of 200 I.U. vitamin D daily to all children was sufficient to prevent the symptoms of vitamin D deficiency in children on anti-epileptic drugs.

DISCUSSION

Dwarfism as a sign of abnormality in a severely mentally retarded child is not, as it is in mentally normal children, much of a handicap. One can even argue that the seriously mentally retarded child has an advantage when he is dwarfed. Those caring for the child will notice he is more infantlike or childlike than a normal length would suggest, and so his/her whole physical appearance is more in accordance with the intellectual performance. In addition, when a motor handicap is present as well, which is often the case, the children are easier to look after and to carry when they are small. The same argument holds for minor underweight and microcephaly.

Taking anthropometric measurements, however, could be of help either for making a diagnosis or for getting an indication of the time when potentially normal development has been interrupted. In many syndromes of mental retardation, dwarfism and delay in bone age are secondary but essential features. In his thesis, Dooren (1967) made the observation that perinatal damage causing mental retardation was usually not accompanied by small stature and bone age retardation. He also differentiated between dwarfism caused by early prenatal disturbances, as in cases with chromosomal disorders, and dwarfism of late onset in pregnancy. The first or "primordial" dwarfism was usually without marked bone age retardation; in the late onset type, the skeletal maturation was usually much more retarded. We did not investigate this aspect in depth. In many children, no firm diagnosis could be made.

Two aspects of this study are of particular significance. The first is the observed large variability in growth rate (Figures 1 and 2) and the second is the absence of a consistent relationship between length or gain in length and any of the studied items. Rundle's figures in his extensive ten-year survey of growth and sexual maturation in mental defectives (Rundle, 1970) also show large variability of length gain.

A remarkable aspect of Dooren's study (1967) is that there is a large variation of gain in length shown in all his differently defined etiological groups, except in a group of mildly retarded children. The small number of children and the high standard error in measuring length in a mental defective child do not permit definite conclusions. We think, however, that these data do suggest that, superimposed on an acquired or genetic growth disturbance as a consequence of the particular structural impact of the brain damaging factors, state of mind and emotional stability also influence linear growth.

SUMMARY

Unrelated to the cause of mental retardation, dwarfism, microcephaly and a retarded skeletal development tend to be the phenotype of the severely mentally retarded child. This study was undertaken in order to try to recognize some of the underlying mechanisms leading to this single phenotype. Some data about nail and hair growth are included.

ACKNOWLEDGMENTS

The authors wish to thank the staff of "Huize Maartenswouden" for their full cooperation. Also, the financial support of the "Stichting Maartenswouden," which made this study possible, is gratefully acknowledged.

Dr. J. E. Vos (Department of Developmental Neurology) performed the statistical analysis of the nail and hair data.

REFERENCES

Castells, S., Voeller, K. K., Vinas, C., and Lu, C. (1974) Cerebral dwarfism: Association of brain dysfunction with growth retardation. J. Pediatr. 85:36.

Croughs, W. (1971) The influence of emotional deprivation on growth and behavior. In Normal and Abnormal Development of Brain and Behavior(Boerhaave series). Leiden University Press.

Dooren, L. J. (1967) Growth and sexual maturation in cerebral defects. Thesis, Lieden, The Netherlands.

Frasier, S. D. (1974) Growth hormone deficiency and dwarfism in mental retardation. J. Pediatr. 86:155.

Frasier, S. D., Hilburn, J. M., and Smith, F. G. (1970) Dwarfism and mental retardation: The serum growth hormone response to hypoglycemia. J. Pediatr. 77:136.

Gelderen, H. H. van (1962) Studies in oligophrenia. 1. Growth in mentally deficient children. Acta Paediat. 5:643.

Moser, H. D., Grossman, H. J., and Dingman, H. F. (1965) Physical growth in mental defectives. A study in an institutionalized population. Pediatrics 36:465.

Powell, G. F., Brasel, J. A., Raiti, S., and Blizzard, R. D. (1967) Emotional deprivation and growth retardation simulating idiopathic hypopituitarism. Endocrinological evaluation of the syndrome. New Engl. J. Med. 276:1276.

Roberts, G. E., and Clayton, B. E. (1969) Some findings arising out of a survey of mentally retarded children. Develop. Med. Child Neurol. 11:584.

Rundle, A. T. (1970) A ten year survey of growth and sexual maturation. In Mental Subnormality: Modern Trends in Research (Ed. Richards, B. W.) London: Pitman Medical and Scientific Publications.

Wieringen, J. C. van, Wafelbakker, F., Verbrugge, H. P., and De Haas, J. H. (1968) Groeidiagrammen Nederland 1965. Groningen: Wolters-Noordhof N.V.

RESEARCH TO PRACTICE IN MENTAL RETARDATION
Biomedical Aspects, Volume III
Edited by Peter Mittler
Copyright 1977 I.A.S.S.M.D.

UNDERNUTRITION AND HUMAN BRAIN DEVELOPMENT

H. P. Chase and L. S. Crnic
University of Colorado Medical Center,
Department of Colorado Medical Center,
Department of Pediatrics,
B. F. Stolinsky Laboratories,
4200 East Ninth Avenue,
Denver, Colorado 80262, United States

Undernutrition is the most common cause of substandard health in children in the world. The World Health Organization estimated one of every two children born in the 1960s suffered some degree of undernutrition. Although severe forms of undernutrition are relatively rare in the United States, they do occur. Three cases of kwashiorkor were treated at Colorado General Hospital within one month in early 1976. More subtle forms of undernutrition, such as the vitamin A deficiency described in one-third of Mexican-American preschool children in the United States (Chase et al., 1971; Ten State Nutrition Survey, 1972; Chase et al., 1973), are unfortunately more common. At present, we know that severe forms of environutritional deprivation impair later functioning in intellectual and sensorimotor testing, possibly attributable to motivational and attentional factors in addition to intellectual impairment; however, the consequences of the less severe forms of undernutrition are less clearly established.

Many scientists have attempted to attribute the brain alterations following undernutrition solely to lack of food, or to assign a portion of the insult to food and a portion to environment. However, the interactions between environment and nutrition are so complex in humans that they are inseparable, and the term "environutritional deprivation" should now be used. The effects of nutritional deprivation in the environmental context in which it usually occurs may be described on several levels (Figure 1). First, the primary effect of undernutrition upon the brain consists of decreased availability of nutrients for growth. Secondary effects of undernutrition upon the physiological status of the child include lowered blood sugar levels, fluid and electrolyte alterations, low thyroid hormone levels, and increased susceptibility to infections. All of these secondary

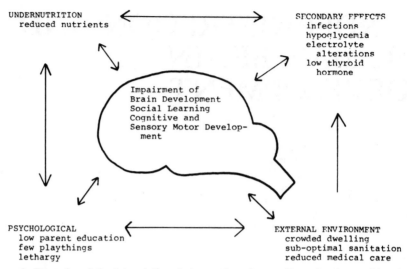

Figure 1. Examples of the interrelations between the primary effect of under-nutrition, its secondary effects, the influences of the external environment, and psychologic factors on brain and child development.

factors have been associated with impaired brain development. These internal alterations interact with the external environment. For example, while the physiological status of the undernourished child makes him/her more susceptible to infections, the crowded dwellings and suboptimal sanitation that often accompany undernutrition increase the risk of exposure to infectious agents. In addition, the lack of funds for medical care along with the low availability of medical services and less advanced medical technology found in some Third World Countries make it likely that the child will receive too little care too late to prevent infections from seriously threatening his/her future development.

On the psychological level, optimal interactions with the environment are necessary for normal intellectual development. Here, environutritional deprivation works on two levels. First, ". . . the environment in which children at risk of undernutrition live is highly effective in reducing mental competence" (Cravioto and DeLicardie, 1973) through such factors as low educational levels of parents, lack of playthings, and reduced contact with the outside world. On a second level, the lethargy produced by undernutrition leads to a lower level of interaction with the environment and thus to a reduction in important early cognitive, sensorimotor, and social learning.

NORMAL HUMAN BRAIN DEVELOPMENT

In order to understand the effects of any insult on the brain, it is helpful to have some knowledge of normal human brain development (Figure 2). Approximately

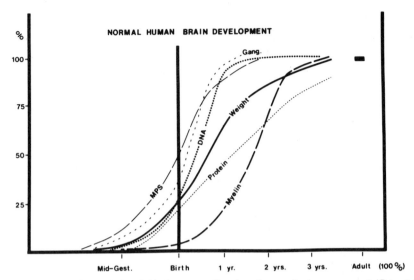

Figure 2. The initial periods of development of various human brain components. Prenatal period expanded for clarity. Abbreviations: MPS = mucopolysaccharide; Gang. = ganglioside.

one-fourth of adult brain weight (1,200 g) is present at birth (300 g) and three-fourths at age one year (900 g). About one-fourth of the brain cells, as estimated by DNA, are present at birth, with 66% present by six months, and 90–95% by one year. Myelin is slower to develop, with over half of myelin lipid forming between 12 and 24 months of age. Brain protein formation is linear between the sixth intrauterine month and second postnatal year with the rate of formation then diminishing. Both mucopolysaccharides and axon-dendritic connections, as estimated by gangliosides, begin to accumulate earlier in utero, with higher percentages of adult levels present at birth than for the above factors (Figure 2). The human brain is quite mature biochemically by the age of four years.

EFFECT OF ENVIRONUTRITIONAL DEPRIVATION ON BRAIN BIOCHEMICAL DEVELOPMENT

Intrauterine Environutritional Deprivation

Relatively few investigations have evaluated brain biochemical alterations in small for gestational age (SGA) infants who have presumably suffered some intrauterine nutritional restriction (Chase et al., 1972; Sarma and Rao, 1974; Vasan and Chase, 1976). Brain biochemical analyses have been done by necessity only on infants who died, and they were probably the more severely affected infants.

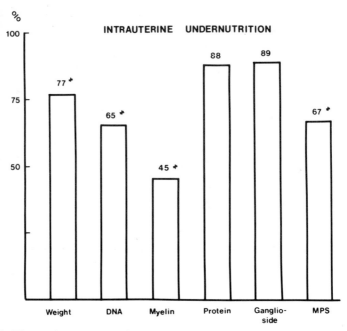

Figure 3. The numbers represent the percentage of various constituents in brains from SGA infants compared to AGA infants which were set at 100% (Chase et al., 1972). The asterisks indicate the values that were significantly lower in the SGA brains. Values represent total brain quantities except for mucopolysaccharide (MPS), which represent concentration (Vasan and Chase, 1976).

In brain specimens analyzed in our laboratory (Figure 3), SGA infants' brains weighed 77% of those of infants who were appropriate in body weight for their gestational age (AGA). The reduction in cerebellar weight was greater (37%) than the reduction in the remainder of the brain (21%). The same pattern was revealed in brain cell number, as estimated by DNA. Total myelin content and myelin concentration were reduced in the brains of the SGA infants, but, because a very small percentage of myelin is present at birth, complete postnatal recovery should be possible with adequate postnatal nutrition. Brain protein was not significantly reduced in the SGA infants, but the enzymatic protein important in the formation of the myelin lipid sulfatide, galactolipid sulfotransferase, was greatly reduced in the brains of the SGA infants. Ganglioside NANA, which may represent nerve terminal endings (Svennerholm, 1974) was not significantly altered in SGA infants. Brain mucopolysaccharides, whose alteration has been associated with mental retardation, were reduced 33% in SGA infants (Vasan and Chase, 1976).

In summary, intrauterine undernutrition can affect human brain development. However, as most of the components have their major period of growth following birth, the deficiencies should be correctable in the postnatal period.

An exception might be neuronal cell multiplication, with most neurones currently believed to be formed in utero.

Postnatal Environutritional Deprivation

Reports of brain biochemical alterations following postnatal environutritional deprivation have come primarily from two groups (Winick and Rosso, 1969; Winick, Rosso, and Waterlow, 1970; Chase et al., 1974). Brown (1965) initially described reduced brain weights in autopsies of children who had died of undernutrition. The specimens analyzed in our laboratory (Figure 4) revealed that the brains of poorly nourished children weighed 78% of those of well-nourished children. Cerebellar weight was reduced to 76% of normal. Results of studies of cell number alterations have varied with the timing of the period of undernutrition. Nine infants who died of malnutrition between age 0.5 to 6 months in Chile (Winick and Rosso, 1969) had reductions in brain DNA of over 50%. In contrast (Figure 4), we found no significant reduction in DNA in children who had died of malnutrition between 12 and 24 months of age. These differences can be explained on the basis of timing of the undernutrition in

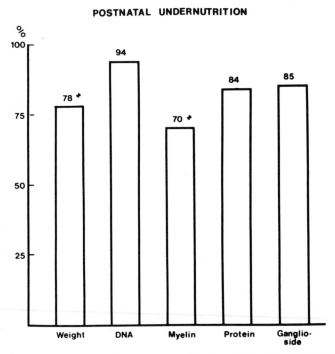

POSTNATAL UNDERNUTRITION

Figure 4. The numbers represent the percentage of various total brain constituents in brains from infants dying of postnatal undernutrition (Chase et al., 1974) compared to controls (values set at 100%). Asterisks represent values that were significantly lower in brains from undernourished compared to control children.

conjunction with an understanding of the normal periods of brain cellular formation. All of the infants in our study were initially breast fed and the malnutrition presumably began after the period of rapid brain cell division.

Brain cholesterol and lipid-phosphorous, which are found in all brain membranes including myelin, were measured in brains from Chilean infants who had died of undernutrition (Rosso, Hormanzabal, and Winick, 1970). Quantities of both lipids in undernourished compared to control infants were similar in three undernourished infants who had died before age one year, but were markedly reduced in three undernourished infants who had died after age one year. In a second study (Chase et al., 1974), the total quantities and concentrations of the myelin lipids cerebroside and sulfatide were reduced in brains from six Guatemalan infants (ages 12 to 24 months) who had died of undernutrition compared to control infants (Figure 4). It thus seems that early environutritional deprivation does not result in reduced myelin lipid formation, whereas later deprivation, after age one year, does cause a reduction.

Total brain protein levels in children who had died of undernutrition have varied considerably even within the same laboratory (Winick and Rosso, 1969; Winick, Rosso, and Waterlow, 1970) but have generally been reduced in children who died in their first year of life. In our laboratory, total brain protein values from the 12- to 24-month-old undernourished and control infants were similar in the cerebrum, but were significantly lower for the cerebellum from the children who had died of undernutrition. Thus the reduction seems less when the deprivation occurs after age one year.

The total quantities of brain gangliosides, used as an estimate of axon-dendritic terminals, have been reported to date only in infants with onset of undernutrition after termination of breast feeding (Chase et al., 1974). Statistically significant differences were not found in either concentration or total quantities of brain gangliosides between the control infants and the undernourished infants. This suggests that the axon-dendritic terminals have normal development at least when environutritional deprivation occurs after age one year. Brain mucopolysaccharide levels have been measured in only two children who died of undernutrition and were found to be reduced in both children compared to controls (Chandrasekaran et al., 1971).

In summary, biochemical analyses of brains from human infants suffering from intrauterine or postnatal undernutrition have demonstrated alterations in quantities of brain cells, myelin lipid, brain protein, and brain mucopolysaccharides. The degree of reduction of any of these components is related to the timing, severity, and the type of environutritional deprivation.

FROM RESEARCH TO PRACTICE

As the world population continues to increase at the rate of 100,000 people daily, or 37 million per year, environutritional deprivation in childhood will not only continue but will increase as a problem in the future. What practices can be drawn from the above review to aid in enabling every child in the world to reach his/her optimal potential?

The data presented above reveals that intrauterine underdevelopment can result in brain alterations. Research in Guatemala (Read et al., 1975) has shown that nutritional supplements given to pregnant women will result in improved birthweight. Thus, the first recommended practice would be for governments of countries with high rates of suboptimal nutrition routinely to provide nutritional supplements to pregnant women. These should specifically include minerals such as iron, vitamins such as folic acid, calories, and protein, as the needs for all of these increase during pregnancy.

A second recommendation in this same area would be that optimal postnatal care and nutrition be provided to any infant low in birthweight. Nutritional supplements are probably even more important for the mother during nursing than during pregnancy. Most intrauterine insults to the brain may be correctable postnatally with good nutrition. However, because the effects of combined intrauterine and postnatal undernutrition are probably additive, every effort must be made to prevent postnatal undernutrition when intrauterine undernutrition is already present. Methods will have to be found to record birthweights and to alert local health workers to pay extra attention to the infant who is low in birthweight. Body weight, length, and head circumference growth should be followed routinely by a community health worker, and when inadequate growth is detected, the family should be referred to an infant-family center where proper environutritional help can be offered.

A third recommendation in moving from research to practice concerns the great importance of breast feeding. Undernutrition after age one year seems to have little effect on numbers of brain cells, in contrast to undernutrition in the first six months of life, when numbers of brain cells are decreased greatly. In the critical first six months of life, breast feeding provides adequate nutrients to ensure normal brain growth. Thus, countries should train health workers and allocate funds to encourage mothers to breast feed.

A fourth recommendation for change is in the area of fortification of vegetable protein. Vegetable proteins currently provide 80% of the protein eaten in the Third World Countries, in contrast to the United States, where 80% of the proteins consumed are from animal sources. The need to obtain protein from vegetable sources will increase as the world population rises. For every kilogram of beef produced, a steer must eat 20–25 kg of grain. Likewise, in water input, one kg of beef is 2,500% more expensive than one kg of bread. Animal protein intake will have to decrease, but, at the same time, vegetable protein can be improved through combinations of vegetable proteins such as soy, which is deficient in methionine, and wheat, which is deficient in lysine. It is also possible that amino acid fortification of vegetable proteins such as wheat could provide an adequate protein source, which, when given to pregnant and lactating

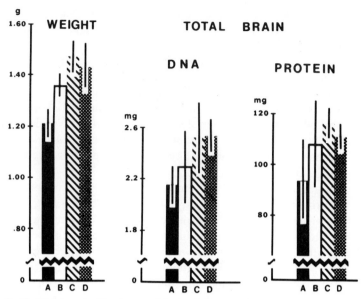

Figure 5. Changes in rat offspring total brain weight, DNA, and protein while maternal bread diet (A) was supplemented with lysine (B) or lysine plus threonine (C). Results are compared with offspring from a mother receiving Purina Stock diet (D) (Chase and Jansen, 1976). Values for groups A, B, and C were significantly different ($p < 0.001$) from each other for all three parameters.

mothers, would allow optimal offspring brain development. To look briefly back at the laboratory, Figure 5 shows the correction of deficiencies in offspring brain development when wheat fed to pregnant and lactating rats was fortified first with lysine or with lysine and threonine (Chase and Jansen, 1976). Routine fortification of vegetable proteins for pregnant and lactating mothers, and perhaps for children during the preschool years of rapid growth, might prevent the protein deficiency states that are now so common.

The final recommendation as we move from research to practice would be in the area of environmental stimulation. We have purposely used the term enviro-nutritional deprivation to refer to the situation of a malnourished child. Providing food without providing an optimal environment and adequate medical care will not totally alleviate the impaired brain development of undernourished children. Elimination of the environmental miseries that accompany poverty and undernutrition is a monumental task. However, there is evidence that simple types of stimulating interactions with children by their caregivers can be useful in rehabilitating children who have experienced malnutrition (McKay, McKay, and Sinisterra, 1973, 1974; Yaktin and McLaren, 1970). Such interactions may also reduce the harmful effects of an environment of poverty on children who are not severely malnourished.

SUMMARY

Undernutrition is the most common disease in the world to affect the health of children and is often accompanied by altered environmental stimulation. "Environutritional deprivation" has been shown to result in altered human brain growth, particularly of the myelin lipids, and in altered behavior. Adequate nutrition and infant stimulation should be a goal for all of the world's children.

REFERENCES

Brown, R. E. (1965) Decreased brain weight in malnutrition and its implications. East Afr. med. J. 42:584.

Chandrasekaran, E. V., Mukherjee, K. L., and Bachhawat, B. K. (1971) Isolation and characterization of glycosaminoglycans from brains of children with protein-calorie malnutrition. J. Neurochem. 18:1913.

Chase, H. P. (1973) The effects of intrauterine and postnatal undernutrition on normal brain development. Ann. N.Y. Acad. Sci. 205:231.

Chase, H. P., Canosa, C. A., Dabiere, C. S., Welch, N. N., and O'Brien, D. (1974) Postnatal undernutrition and human brain development. J. Ment. Defic. Res. 18:355.

Chase, H. P., and Jansen, G. R. (1976) Effect of feeding lysine and threonine fortified bread during gestation and lactation on growth of the brain in rats. J. Nutr. 106:41.

Chase, H. P., Kumar, V., Dodds, J. M., Sauberlich, H. E., Hunter, R. M., Burton, R. S., and Spalding, V. (1971) Nutritional status of preschool Mexican-American migrant farm children. Amer. J. Dis. Child. 122:316.

Chase, H. P., Larson, L. B., Massoth, D. M., Martin, D. L., and Niernberg, M. M. (1973) Effectiveness of nutrition aides in a migrant population. Amer. J. Clin. Nutr. 26:849.

Chase, H. P., Welch, N. N., Dabiere, C. S., Vasan, N. S., and Butterfield, L. J. (1972) Alterations in human brain biochemistry following intrauterine growth retardation. Pediatrics. 50:403.

Cravioto, J., and DeLicardie, E. R. (1973) Nutrition and behavior and learning. World Rev. Nutr. Diet. 16:80.

McKay, H. E., McKay, A., and Sinisterra, L. (1973) Behavioral Intervention Studies With Malnourished Children: A Review of Experiences. Washington, D.C.: U.S. Government Printing Office, p. 121.

McKay, H. E., McKay, A., and Sinisterra, L. (1974) Intellectual Development of Malnourished Preschool Children in Programs of Stimulation and Nutritional Supplementation. Uppsala, Sweden: Almqvist & Wiksell, p. 226.

Read, M. S., Habicht, J-P, Lechtig, A., and Klein, R. E. (1975) Maternal malnutrition, birthweight, and child development. Mod. Probl. Paediatr. 14: 203.

Rosso, P., Hormanzabal, J., and Winick, M. (1970) Changes in brain weight, cholesterol, phospholipid and DNA content in marasmic children. Amer. J. Clin. Nutr. 23:1275.

Sarma, M. K. J., and Rao, K. S. (1974) Biochemical composition of different regions in brains of small for date infants. J. Neurochem. 22:671.

Singh, J., and Bachhawat, B. K. (1968) Isolation and characterization of glycos-aminoglycans in human brain of different age groups. J. Neurochem. 15:249.

Svennerholm, L. (1974) Lipid biochemical changes of brain during development. *In* Early Malnutrition and Mental Development (Eds. Cravioto, J., Hambraeus, L. and Vahlquist, B.) Uppsala, Sweden: Almqvist & Wiksell, p. 67.

Ten-State Nutrition Survey 1968–1970 (1972) Highlights. Washington, D.C.: Department of Health, Education and Welfare, Publication Number (HMS) 72–1834.

Vasan, N. S., and Chase, H. P. (1976) Brain glycosaminoglycans (mucopolysac-charides) following intrauterine growth retardation. Biol. Neonate. 28:196.

Winick M., and Rosso, P. (1969) The effect of severe early malnutrition on cellular growth of human brain. Pediatr. Res. 3:181.

Winick, J., Rosso, P., and Waterlow, J. (1970) Cellular growth of cerebrum, cerebellum, and brain stem in normal and marasmic children. Exp. Neurol. 26:393.

Yatkin, U. S., and McLaren, D. S. (1970) The behavioural development of infants recovering from severe malnutrition. J. Ment. Defic. Res. 14:25.

RESEARCH TO PRACTICE IN MENTAL RETARDATION
Biomedical Aspects, Volume III
Edited by Peter Mittler
Copyright 1977 I.A.S.S.M.D.

EARLY PRENATAL MALNUTRITION AND BRAIN DEVELOPMENT IN RATS

S. Zamenhof
Mental Retardation Research Center,
and Brain Research Institute,
School of Medicine,
University of California,
Los Angeles, California 90024, United States

Although prenatal malnutrition has been, by now, the subject of many studies, the period of malnutrition *early in pregnancy* has not attracted the attention it deserves. In most studies, malnutrition was applied throughout pregnancy; many investigators also felt that prenatal malnutrition could have an effect only if it occurred in the second part of pregnancy. Some investigators felt that because cerebral neuron proliferation ceases in humans before the 20th week of pregnancy, i.e., when the nutritional requirements of the fetus are still low, the neuron number in the human fetal brain is "highly protected" against malnutrition (Dobbing and Sands, 1973).

We have reported (Zamenhof, van Marthens, and Grauel, 1971a) the study of the effects of *timing* of maternal dietary restriction in rats on fetal development. Because of the short periods of malnutrition, a diet completely protein-free was used to get demonstrable results. This diet was fed to pregnant rats during five periods of pregnancy; the normal diet was fed during the remaining time. The most striking effect, also reported by others (Nelson and Evans, 1953), was that protein deprivation on days 0 to 10 reduced the number of actual deliveries to 40% of positively mated females. Another finding was that at day 16 the placental weights of the experimental animals were 25% lower than in the controls. Thus, evidence was obtained that fetal development *can* be harmed even if maternal malnutrition occurs as early as the first half of pregnancy.

These studies were supported by Grants HD-04612, HD-05615, HD-05394, and HD-08927 from the National Institute of Child Health and Human Development

The purpose of the present work was to obtain more information on the effects of *early* maternal dietary protein deprivation on fetal brain development. We find that, indeed, in malnourished rat pregnancy two different main periods can be recognized. 1) The early period (the first half of the pregnancy), when the actual nutrient needs of the embryo are still negligible, yet fetal growth can be restricted, or even destroyed, by the action of a regulatory mechanism presumably involving hormones. 2) The late period (the second part of pregnancy), when growth restriction of the fetal brain is caused by the actual deficiency of substances needed for the protein and DNA synthesis in the proliferating neurons. The two periods differ in many respects as will be discussed later.

METHODS

The rats were Sprague-Dawley derived and were randomly bred in our laboratory as a closed colony for 38 generations. Three-month-old virgin females were mated; the presence of a vaginal plug was considered day 0 of pregnancy.

The control animals were fed a pelleted diet containing 20.5% protein, while the experimental animals received a powdered, protein-free diet on specified days of pregnancy, and a normal pelleted diet at other times. All animals were removed by cesarean section on day 16, 18, or 20. The fetuses were weighed and then decapitated; their cerebral hemispheres, with cerebellum and olfactory lobes, were immediately removed and weighed; they were then frozen and subsequently used for colorimetric DNA analysis (Zamenhof et al., 1972) and protein analysis (Lowry et al., 1951), as in our previous work.

RESULTS AND DISCUSSION

Table 1 represents the effects of short-term total protein deprivation upon decidual response in mated rats. The experimental animals did form implanta-

Table 1. The effects of protein-free diet on decidual response in mated rats

| Period of protein deprivation (days after mating) | Days when tested | Number of pregnant animals | | Decidual response, % mated |
		mated	Decidual response detected	
None (controls)				
	6	11	8	72.7%
	7	4	4	100%
Experimentals				
0–5 and 0–6	6	44	33	75%
0–7	7	9	5	55.5%

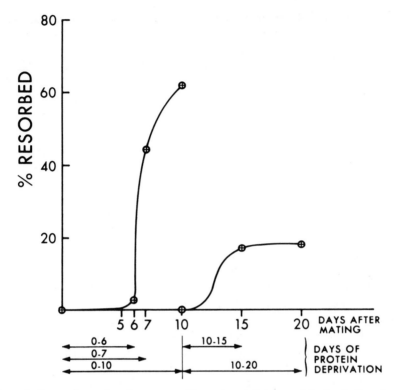

Figure 1. Resorptions of rat fetuses caused by maternal dietary protein deprivations for the indicated periods during the first and the second half of pregnancy.

tion sites. There was no significant difference in the percentage of these animals forming the decidual response on days 5–6, as compared to the controls. However, as can be seen, protein deprivation did reduce this percentage to 55% on day 7, while all the control animals *maintained* decidual response.

Figure 1 illustrates the two different main periods of pregnancy: in the first period, maternal protein deprivation produces a steep increase in resorptions. The critical period seems to be between days 6 and 7, that is, right after implantation, which in the rat is on day 5½: the percentage of resorptions increases in one day from 3 to 45%. In contrast, protein deprivation for the same length of time in the second half of pregnancy produces a low and constant number of resorptions.

The average size of the implantation sites for 7th day animals was 4.6 mm for the controls, as compared to 4.2 mm for the experimental animals; this difference was not statistically significant.

The average number of corpora lutea in the pregnant experimental animals (days 5 and 6) was the same as the average in nonpregnant experimentals, and

Table 2. The effects of maternal protein-free diet on fetal parameters at day 16 of pregnancy

Time of protein deprivation	Body weight (mg)	Cerebrum			Placenta		
		weight (mg)	DNA (μg)	protein (mg)	weight (mg)	DNA (μg)	protein (mg)
0–10th day	407[a]	23.5	158	0.95	275	754	21
(N = 45)	±119	±11	±81	±0.48	±69	±134	±6
0–6th day	570	33	225	1.38	361	769	26.5
(N = 31)	±225	±12	±79	±0.51	±70	±124	±5.4
Difference in % of 0–6	−39	−39	−30	−31	−24	−2	−21
p	<.001	<.001	<.001	<.001	<.001	n.s.	<.001

[a]Mean weights ± standard deviation. p = significance (Students' t-test).

both these averages were within the range of the pregnant and nonpregnant control value. Since protein deficiency did not affect the number of corpora lutea, this deficiency is unlikely to influence directly the maintenance of decidual response by means of altering the number of these hormone-producing bodies.

The next study was concerned with the effects of short-term maternal protein deprivations on subsequent fetal development. All animals were visually inspected on day 6 of pregnancy for decidual formation.

The experimental animals that showed decidual formation on day 5 and day 6 maintained pregnancy until the 16th, 18th, and 20th day. Therefore, on day 6, the implantation sites were still alive.

The results are represented in Table 2. The results of a 0–10 day protein-free diet are compared with those of a 0–6 day diet. Highly significant decreases were found in all measured parameters in the 16-day-old fetus. These differences could be partially attributable to the fact that the total time of protein deprivation was substantially different (ten days compared with six days) and so was subsequent rehabilitation (control diet). However, in addition, there may be an effect of deficient placenta which is smaller in 0–10 than in 0–6 days. The number of placental nuclei (represented by placental DNA) is essentially unchanged, but the ratio of placental protein to placental DNA is 19% smaller. Such underdevelopment of the placenta is likely to result in a deficient transfer of nutrients to the fetus.

The effects of protein deprivation for comparative lengths of time on fetal development on day 16 are represented in Table 3. It can be seen that protein deprivation for five or six days produced different effects, depending on when it occurred in pregnancy. Protein deprivation in the first, preimplantation period, i.e., from mating until implantation (0–6 days), does not affect placental weight and fetal brain parameters at day 16; however, it does produce considerable variability among the fetuses, as estimated from standard deviations of their parameters. This period is comparatively long in the rat (5½ days which is one quarter of total pregnancy); in humans, however, the length of this period, 7 days, is comparatively negligible (2.5% of total pregnancy).

Protein deprivation in the next period, around implantation (5–10 days) in rats, already has a considerable effect on fetal development at day 16. As can be seen in the table, the values of placental, brain, and body parameters are well below the controls. On the other hand, the fetuses are much more uniform as evidenced by their lower variability.

The effects of protein deprivation in the next period, 10–15 days, show the same trend: there is a considerable decrease in placental weight and fetal brain and body parameters at day 16 of pregnancy; the variability between fetuses is also lower than in the 0–6 day period. This decrease in fetal parameters occurs despite the fact that the total protein needed to build the fetuses and their supporting tissues until day 15 is only 620 mg or 1.3% of the maternal protein intake during the same period.

In conclusion, we can say that the total maternal dietary protein deprivation on days 0–6, 0–7, or 0–10 of pregnancy has no effect on the number of corpora lutea, on the time of implantation, or on the size of implantation sites. In contrast, there seems to be a critical period for the early fetal resorption or underdevelopment: maternal protein deprivation on days 0–6 gives normal maintenance of pregnancy and fetal development on day 16, whereas deprivation of *one* day longer duration, that is, until day 7, reduces maintenance of pregnancy to 55% and results in a significant fetal underdevelopment on day 16 and placental underdevelopment until term.

The actual amount of protein needed by the embryos and the supporting tissues until day 10 is minuscule—less than 0.1% of total maternal protein intake. Thus, the effect obtained was *not* caused by actual deficiency of building

Table 3. The effect of maternal protein deprivation during various periods of pregnancy on 16 day fetus

		Protein deprivation (days)		
		0–6	5–10	10–15
Differences to control, in % of control	body weight		−12	−9
	brain { weight	−2	−16	−14
	brain { DNA	−1	−21	−6
	brain { protein	−13	−21	−18
	placental weight	+1	−12	−29
Standard deviation in % of control standard deviation	body weight	140	45	40
	brain { weight	220	78	90
	brain { DNA	210	118	110
	brain { protein	260	152	130

materials for the embryo, but rather by a regulatory mechanism triggered by maternal protein deprivation. This mechanism was studied by others; it is believed to be hormonal and quite complex. Presumably, the organ sensitive to malnutrition is the hypothalamus; reduced food intake results in lower hypo-thalamic content of releasing factors (LH-RF and FSH-RF), (Meites, 1970) which in turn depresses the output of pituitary gonadotropins (Hays and Kendall, 1961; Callard and Leathem, 1963; Kinzey and Srebnik, 1963). This lack of pituitary gonadotropins produces a deficiency of estrogen and progesterone, which in turn results in faulty implantation and placentation, in most cases followed by resorption of the fetus. (Nelson and Evans, 1954; Hays and Kendall, 1961; Kinzey and Srebnik, 1963; Fisher and Leathem, 1965; Hazelwood and Nelson, 1965; Kinzey, Sands and Bonds, 1970). This controlling mechanism was developed during evolution to protect the female during famine, by destroying the fetuses.

Around day 10 and thereafter until day 16 or so, the mother normally shows a net weight gain: she deposits fat for future energy emergencies, of which the first is to provide enough nutrients for fetal growth toward the end of preg-nancy. The situation in humans (in the comparative period of pregnancy) seems to be quite similar (Hytten and Thomson, 1965). The malnourished female is unable to do this, and she will be handicapped in the future; in fact, she is already mobilizing her nutrient reserves to be able to maintain herself and to maintain the fetuses at all, however underdeveloped.

The fetus from 0–10 days protein-deprived mothers, which is so underdevel-oped at day 16, appears to "recover" at the end of pregnancy, if the mother is put back on a normal diet. This "recovery," however, may be deceptive. For one thing, placenta never recovers. One must also bear in mind that by day 16 the neuroblast proliferation in the cerebrum is already slowing down, and in the cortical layer VI it is already finished (Berry, 1974); there is no indication that the gross deficiency at that time can be repaired later. Thus, such early prenatal malnutrition might distort the neuron distribution in the cortex, just as the postnatal malnutrition has been shown to distort distribution of cortical glial cells (Dobbing, Hopewell, and Lynch, 1971).

SUMMARY

The effects of *early* maternal dietary protein deprivation on rat fetal develop-ment, in general, and fetal *brain* development, in particular, have been studied. Several different periods of pregnancy can be recognized.

Maternal protein deprivation in the period between mating and implantation had no demonstrable effect on percentage of successful pregnancies and on brain and body development of the fetuses. In contrast, maternal protein deprivation around implantation time may produce resorption of the majority of fetuses, and a deficient brain and body development (as well as deficient placentas) in those surviving until day 16. Since at that time the actual fetal nutrient requirements are still minuscule, the mechanisms involved must be regulatory: they seem to be hormonal and involve hypothalamus, pituitary, and ovary. In addition, the malnourished mother fails to deposit fat normally needed for emergencies toward the end of pregnancy. Protein deprivation in the second half of pregnancy does not produce many resorptions, but it does reduce fetal brain and body parameters as well as placental development; the mechanisms involved may include deficiency in placental size and function and, toward the end of pregnancy, actual deficiency of building materials for the fetus.

ACKNOWLEDGMENTS

The author wishes to thank Dr. Edith van Marthens and Miss Suzan Y. Shimomaye with regard to the experimental part of this work.

REFERENCES

Berry, M. (1974) Development of the cerebral neocortex of the rat. *In* Aspects of Neurogenesis vol. 2 (Gottlieb, G.) New York: Academic Press, p. 21.

Callard, I. P., and Leathem, J. H. (1963) Pregnancy maintenance in protein-deficient rat. Amer. Zool. 3:491.

Dobbing, J., Hopewell, J. W., and Lynch, A. (1971) Vulnerability of developing brain: VII. Permanent deficit of neurons in cerebral and cerebellar cortex following early mild undernutrition. Exp. Neurol. 32:439.

Dobbing, J., and Sands, J. (1973) Quantitative growth and development of human brain. Arch. Dis. Child. 48:757.

Fisher, C. J., and Leathem, J. H. (1965) Effect of protein-free diet on protein metabolism in the pregnant rat. Endocrinology. 76:454.

Hays, R. L., and Kendall, K. A. (1961) Maintenance of pregnancy with prolactin or progesterone in rats on a sucrose diet. Endocrinology. 68:177.

Hazelwood, R. L., and Nelson, M. M. (1965) Steroid maintenance of pregnancy in rats in the absence of dietary protein. Endocrinology. 77:999.

Hytten, F. E., and Thomson, A. M. (1965) Pregnancy, childbirth and lactation. *In* The Physiology of Human Survival. (Eds. Edholm, O. G., and Bachrach, A. L.) New York: Academic Press, p. 327.

Kinzey, W. G., Sands, L., and Bonds, P. (1970) Maintenance of pregnancy in absence of dietary protein with progesterone. Proc. Soc. Exp. Biol. Med. 134:72.

Kinzey, W. G., and Srebnik, H. H. (1963) Maintenance of pregnancy with pituitary hormones in protein-deficient rats. Anat. Rec. 145:249.

Lowry, O. H., Rosebrough, N. J., Farr, A. L., and Randall, R. J. (1951) Protein measurement with the Folin phenol reagent. J. Biol. Chem. 193:265.

Meites, J. (1970) Modification of synthesis and release of hypothalamic factors induced by exogenous stimuli. *In* Neurochemical Aspects of Hypothalamic Function (Eds. Martini, L., and Meites, J.). New York: Academic Press, p. 6.

Nelson, M. M., and Evans, H. M. (1953) Relation of dietary protein levels to reproduction in the rat. J. Nutr. 51:71.

Nelson, M. M., and Evans, H. M. (1954) Maintenance of pregnancy in the absence of dietary protein with estrone and progesterone. Endocrinology. 55:543.

Zamenhof, S., Grauel, L., van Marthens, E., and Stillinger, R. A. (1972) Quantitative determination of DNA in preserved brains and brain sections. J. Neurochem. 19:61.

Zamenhof, S., van Marthens, E., and Grauel, L. (1971a) DNA (cell number) and protein in neonatal rat brain: Alteration by timing of maternal dietary protein restriction. J. Nutr. 101:1265.

Zamenhof, S., van Marthens, E., and Grauel, L. (1971b) Prenatal cerebral development: Effect of restricted diet, reversal by growth hormone. Science. 174:954.

Zamenhof, S., van Marthens, E., and Shimomaye, S. Y. (1976) The effects of early maternal protein deprivation on fetal development. Fed. Proc. 35:422.

RESEARCH TO PRACTICE IN MENTAL RETARDATION
Biomedical Aspects, Volume III
Edited by Peter Mittler
Copyright 1977 I.A.S.S.M.D.

TRACE ELEMENT NUTRITION AND BRAIN DEVELOPMENT

P. A. Walravens
Department of Pediatrics and Preventive Medicine,
B. F. Stolinsky Laboratories,
University of Colorado Medical Center,
Denver, Colorado 80220, United States

Trace elements occur in low concentration in tissues of plants, animals, and microorganisms. Each contributes less than 0.01% of the total body weight. Presently, ten of the trace elements have known functions and can be considered dietary essentials for higher animals. These ten elements are iron, iodine, copper, zinc, chromium, manganese, molybdenum, selenium, cobalt, and tin.

While the importance of an adequate nutritional intake of trace elements for normal brain development is a new concept, changes in central nervous system morphology, biochemical composition, and behavioral modifications have been demonstrated in association with deficiencies of copper, zinc, manganese, and iodine. In this review, the latter two elements will be considered briefly, while the roles of copper and zinc in mammalian metabolism and central nervous system functions will be discussed more extensively.

IODINE

The main physiological function of iodine derives from its presence in thyroid hormone. Untreated congenital hypothyroidism leads to mental retardation and sometimes to ataxia and seizures. However, a discussion of the multiple effects of thyroid hormone on brain morphology and biochemical composition goes beyond the scope of this chapter.

The original work reported in this paper was supported by Grant R01-AM-12432 from the National Institutes of Arthritis and Metabolic and Digestive Diseases, and by Grant RR-69 from the General Clinical Research Centers Program of the Division of Research Resources, National Institutes of Health.

MANGANESE

The offspring of manganese-deficient chicks, rats, guinea pigs, and mice show ataxia with loss of equilibrium, incoordination, and head retraction (Lassiter and Hambidge, 1973). They also display multiple skeletal abnormalities, which result from impaired activity of the epiphyseal cartilage plates. Maternal manganese supplementation before the 14th day of gestation prevents the appearance of neonatal ataxia, which, however, cannot be corrected by manganese supplementation after birth.

Histological studies have shown that the ataxia results from a faulty embryonic development of the inner ear. The otoliths of the utricular and saccular maculae are absent or deformed in mice, rats, and chicks, and histochemical studies point to a local defect in mucopolysaccharide synthesis. A similar defect is responsible for skeletal abnormalities. From animal experiments, manganese also seems to be necessary for carbohydrate metabolism, reproduction, lipid metabolism, and growth. The striking neurological findings shown by the offspring of manganese-deficient animals can, however, be ascribed to a defective vestibular system, and not to a more generalized central nervous system malfunction. Whether or not similar defects occur in humans following a deficiency of manganese during pregnancy, is at present unknown.

COPPER

A role for copper in the maturation of the central nervous system was first established in 1937, when it was discovered that a disease called enzootic neonatal ataxia, or swayback, was associated in Australia with subnormal levels of copper in the pastures (Underwood, 1971). Low levels of copper were also found in the blood of both the ewes and the affected lambs.

In affected lambs, the swayback either appears at birth or a few weeks later. Characteristically, uncoordinated movements of the hind limbs, a stiff and staggering gait, and swaying of the hind quarters become evident as the disease develops. Different degrees of severity can be present, ranging from paralysis and ataxia at birth, followed by rapid death, to minimal ataxia revealed only when the lambs are startled. Copper supplementation of the ewes' diet during pregnancy prevents the appearance of the disease.

The histopathology and biochemistry of the brain in enzootic neonatal ataxia have been studied extensively. Cavitation or gelatinous lesions of the white matter and a characteristic picture of chromatolysis, neurone necrosis, and demyelination in the brain stem and spinal cord are the main features. Biochemically, the primary lesion is low content of copper in the brain, leading to a deficiency of neuronal cytochrome oxidase. Copper also seems necessary for phospholipid synthesis, and phospholipids are important components of myelin.

Hence, the changes noted in myelin formation could derive both from decreased phospholipid synthesis and from demyelination produced by decreased cytochrome oxidase activity. While swayback was originally thought to be present only in lambs, later studies showed that copper deficiency in utero could lead to a similar picture in the progeny of copper-deficient goats, guinea pigs, pigs, and rats.

Copper is an ubiquitous element, and copper deficiency in humans was long considered impossible because of the presence of this element in most forms of animal and plant products. Copper forms part of the molecular structure of many proteins (Evans, 1973), the most important of which is cytochrome oxidase, the terminal oxidase in the electron transport chain and the only enzyme that can reduce molecular oxygen to water. In the electron transport chain, energy is conserved by the synthesis of high-energy phosphate bonds, thus, cytochrome oxidase controls the energy producing metabolic reactions of aerobic cells. Other copper enzymes include ferroxidases, among them ceruloplasmin, necessary for iron metabolism, amine oxidases required for the cross-linking of elastin and collagen, tyrosinase, necessary for the formation of melanin, and hyperoxide dismutases, that remove hyperoxide free radical anions and ascorbic acid oxidase. Two other cuproproteins deserve mention; metallothionein is a copper binding protein whose function is controversial, but appears to play a central role in copper metabolism in hepatic cells. Neonatal hepatic mitochondrocuprin is a copper protein complex that contains 2–4% copper and that accumulates in fetal liver during gestation, where presumably it serves as a storage form. A role for copper has been demonstrated, at present, in the processes of growth, reproduction, hematopoiesis, bone synthesis, myelination, connective tissue formation, and keratinization.

In 1964, Cordano and co-workers published the first report of a copper deficiency syndrome occurring in four children recuperating from severe protein-calorie malnutrition. These children were fed with an iron-fortified milk formula supplemented with cane sugar and cotton seed oil. They developed a syndrome of anemia, neutropenia, leukopenia, bone lesions, and failure to thrive. The anemia did not respond to the administration of iron and vitamins, but copper supplementation was followed by rapid reticulocytosis, correction of the neutropenia after two weeks, and disappearance of the bone lesions over a period of two to three months.

Later reports of infants with copper deficiency added the findings of skin rashes of the seborrheic dermatitis type, pallor, decreased pigmentation of skin, and enlarged veins. More interesting were the neurological findings associated with copper deficiency, namely apneic spells in a premature infant (Al-Rashid and Spangler, 1971) and hypotonia, developmental delay, and a question of blindness in a six-month-old infant (Ashkenazi, et al., 1973).

In 1972, Danks and co-workers showed that the genetic defect in the kinky hair syndrome was associated with abnormal metabolism of copper, characterized by low levels of copper in plasma, low ceruloplasmin levels, and decreased hepatic copper content. This syndrome was first described by Menkes and co-workers in 1962 as a progressive neurodegenerative disorder transmitted in an X-linked fashion and leading to death during early infancy. Premature birth is a frequent finding but birthweights are within normal limits for gestational age. Hypothermia, feeding difficulties, and prolonged jaundice are sometimes noted in the neonatal period, and associated anomalies include club feet, high arched palate, micrognathia, inguinal hernias, and undescended testicles.

The disease is usually recognized when seizure activity starts at two to three months of age. By this time, the hair that seemed normal at birth, has been progressively replaced by a short, stubby, twisted growth of a lighter pigmentation that feels like steel wool. Seborrheic dermatitis often is present. The patients present a striking facial resemblance, with frontal bossing, pudgy cheeks, a lack of expression, and horizontal twisted eyebrows. Pallor and drowsiness often are present but may go unnoticed. Development usually proceeds to the stage of smiling and minimal head control. As the disease progresses, seizure activity increases and becomes harder to control. Changes in body tone toward hyper or hypotonicity develop. Progressive mental deterioration is accompanied by increasing infections, feeding difficulties, and failure to thrive. Neurogenic bladders and diverticulum formation have been reported in two patients (Wheeler and Roberts, 1976), and also have occurred in one of our patients (Hambidge and Walravens, 1975). Progressive venous dilatation with aneurysm formation also can occur.

The radiological changes in bones are striking, although evanescent (Wesenberg, Gwinn, and Barnes, 1969). Excessive wormian bone formation is the earliest change, followed by flaring of the anterior ribs, the appearance of metaphyseal spurs in long bones, and periosteal reaction. Spontaneous fractures can occur. These osseous changes can disappear spontaneously and be replaced by diffuse osteoporosis. The lesions are similar to those seen in nutritional copper deficiency and sometimes are interpreted as lesions of scurvy or as a result of child abuse. Pneumoencephalographic studies have shown cerebral hypoplasia, hygromas, and subdural hematomas.

Pathologically, three types of hair anomalies are described. Most frequently reported is pili torti, ot twisting of the hair shaft around its axis, but trichorrhexis nodosa—fractured hair at a point of swelling, and monilethrix—bead-like enlargements of the hair shaft have also been noted. In the central nervous system, widespread neuronal loss is present in the cerebrum, accompanied by a reduction of white matter, and moderate dilatation of the ventricular system, reactive astrocytosis, and microcyst formation occur. The cerebellum is atrophic, shows neuronal loss, and the Purkinje cells show dendritic thickening and branching. From the body of the Purkinje cells arise stubby processes, thus giving them a prickly appearance (Menkes et al., 1962).

Microscopic changes in the systemic arteries consist mainly of fragmentation, splitting, and beading of the elastic lamina interna, which is covered in places by a hyperplastic intima. It is the similarity between the changes in hair and blood vessels of patients with the steely hair syndrome and those changes seen in nutritional copper deficiency in sheep that led the Australian workers to explore copper metabolism in these patients. The arterial changes can be demonstrated by angiography where elongation, tortuosity, and multiple supernumerary vessels are seen mainly in the cerebral and mesenteric arteries (Wesenberg, Gwinn, and Barnes, 1969; Danks et al., 1972; Hambidge and Walravens, 1975). Narrowing of the arteries and sometimes occlusion of branches can be seen and may help in the establishment of a diagnosis.

The pathogenesis of many of the findings in steely hair syndrome can be explained through our knowledge of the metabolic functions of copper. Defective keratinization and decreased skin pigmentation result from the role of copper in the synthesis of keratin and from deficient tyrosinase function. The arterial, venous, and bone lesions derive from impaired amine oxidase activity, and the cerebral lesions have been postulated to result from decreased cytochrome oxidase function. Biochemically, a decrease in long-chain polyunsaturated fatty acids has been reported (French et al., 1972; O'Brien and Sampson, 1966) that might result from decreased hyperoxide dismutase activity. The discovery of low serum and hepatic copper levels in Menkes' steely hair syndrome led to multiple attempts at providing copper and to many studies of the basic biochemical defects. Oral administration of copper sulfate was not followed by any rise in plasma copper levels (Danks et al., 1972). Parenteral administration of copper salts by either intravenous, subcutaneous, or intramuscular routes is accompanied by rises in the copper levels of blood and liver, but also by excessive urinary copper excretion (Bucknall, Haslam, and Holtzman, 1973; Walker-Smith, et al., 1973; Garnica and Fletcher, 1975). Most cases of parenteral administration of copper did not succeed in reversing the progressive neurological deterioration of the patients, but therapy may have been instituted too late. In one patient of Grover and Scrutton (1975), copper supplementation was started at four weeks of age. The infant is presently 30 months old, seizure-free and functions at an adaptative level of 18 months and at a gross motor level of 6 months (Grover, personal communication, 1976). Other early attempts at therapy, however, have not been so successful.

Biochemically, excessive copper concentration was first demonstrated in the intestinal mucosa cells, implying an intracellular block in copper transport (Danks et al., 1973). Later studies showed excessive levels of copper in brain, muscle, pancreas, and kidney of a fetus presumed to have Menkes' syndrome (Heydorn et al., 1975). Red blood cell copper levels have generally been normal. Recent studies on fibroblasts have shown excessive copper levels (Goka et al., 1976) and increased ^{64}Cu uptake. Similar findings pertain to cultured amniotic cells and also to the levels of copper in the amniotic fluid (Horn, 1976). Surprisingly, the hepatic levels of copper both in the fetus and neonates have been low. The steely hair syndrome thus apparently results from a genetic defect in intracellular copper metabolism, the exact nature of which remains to be determined. Genetic counseling and therapeutic abortion of the affected male fetuses now seem to be possible.

ZINC

Zinc plays an important role in mammalian physiology. Carbonic anhydrase, carboxypeptidases A and B, alkaline phosphatase and alcohol, and lactic and glutamic dehydrogenases are some of the more than 20 presently known zinc metalloenzymes. In zinc-deficient animals, thymidine kinase and DNA-dependent RNA polymerase activities are reduced concurrently with decreased utilization of amino acids for protein synthesis.

In animal studies, nutritional zinc deficiency causes profound anorexia and decreased growth. Alopecia, defective keratinization, lethargy, and increased susceptibility to infections are also present.

Human zinc deficiency was first described in Iran by Prasad and co-workers in 1961, who postulated that the syndrome of nutritional dwarfism was related to zinc deficiency. This syndrome occurs in adolescents who are dwarfed, have absent sexual development, roughened skin, lethargy, poor appetite, and sometimes hepatosplenomegaly. The bone age is grossly retarded and the epiphyses may remain open in subjects more than 20 years of age. While the nutritional dwarfism syndrome may be associated with concurring deficiencies of protein and iron, the importance of zinc for growth and sexual maturation was demonstrated by Halsted and co-workers in 1972. Other zinc-responsive syndromes were later described, including disturbances of taste and smell, delayed wound healing, some forms of failure to thrive with peculiar eating habits, and most, recently, acrodermatitis enteropathica. The latter disease has its onset in early infancy often after weaning from breast feeding, with the appearance of an erythematous vesicular skin rash affecting mainly the body orifices and the extremities. Diarrhea, alopecia, lethargy, and failure to thrive are prominent. Death often occurred during the first year of life, before the chance observation was made that diiodoquin administration was of help in controlling the symptoms. This disease is inherited in an autosomal recessive manner, and present evidence points to a severe degree of zinc deficiency in this syndrome (Neldner and Hambidge, 1975; Walravens and Hambidge, 1976), presumably through impaired intestinal absorption of zinc (Lombeck et al., 1975). The symptoms can be alleviated by the daily administration of 1–2 mg of zinc per kilogram of body weight.

The importance of zinc for normal brain development and function is substantiated by animal studies and by some recent epidemiological and clinical observations. In pregnant rats, a nutritional deficiency of zinc from the 6th through the 14th day of gestation, the period of organogenesis, is accompanied by a high incidence of fetal resorptions in utero, of stillborn births, and of congenital malformations. The studies of Hurley et al. (1967, 1972, 1973) and those of Warkany and Petering (1973) have defined the malformations induced by short-term zinc deficiency during pregnancy, which include hydrocephaly, anencephaly, exencephaly, microphthalmia, and anophthalmia. Cleft lip and palate, bone anomalies such as clubbed feet, syndactyly, and tail deformities, and malformations of the heart and lungs also occur. Mean weight at birth and survival capacity are reduced. Tritiated thymidine incorporation was markedly decreased in the fetuses of zinc-deficient rats implying deficient DNA synthesis (Swenerton, Shrader, and Hurley, 1969).

Other interesting findings derive from the studies of Sandstead and collaborators (1975) on the effects of zinc deficiency during the latter third of gestation in rats and throughout the suckling period. Zinc deprivation during the final week of pregnancy resulted in decreased total fetal weight and decreased brain weight. The latter could not be explained on the basis of starvation alone, since pair-fed controls, i.e., animals fed the same amount of food as that consumed by the zinc-deficient females on the previous day, showed a reduction in total fetal weight but a preservation of brain weight. Impaired synthesis of brain lipids was postulated for both the zinc-deficient and the pair-fed starvation group.

Postnatal zinc deficiency was accompanied by decreased forebrain growth and decreased DNA content, but similar effects resulted from starvation. However, the brains of the zinc-deficient pups contained less protein per mg DNA than did the brains of the pups nursed by pair-fed control dams. While the biochemical effects of starvation are sometimes hard to separate from those of zinc deficiency, behavioral studies in rehabilitated male rats suggested that persistent adverse effects had resulted from the dietary manipulations. Shock avoidance conditioning was markedly impaired after intrauterine zinc deficiency, more so than by intrauterine starvation as a consequence of pair feeding. Similar findings pertained for both pair-fed and zinc-deficient groups to the acquisition of a Tolman-Honzig maze.

The experimental work on zinc deficiency during pregnancy and the suckling period in rats has raised the question of whether or not similar findings apply to humans (Sever and Emanuel, 1973). Clinically recognizable human zinc deficiency is frequent in Egypt and Iran, and it is interesting to note that in Alexandria the rate of CNS malformation is 7.88 per 1,000 births. In Shiraz, Iran, the reported incidence for anencephaly is 1.6 per 1,000 births, and this rate is exceeded only by those of Belfast, Alexandria, and Bombay.

Other epidemiological data on the importance of zinc for normal brain development in utero derived from studies on the outcome of pregnancies in female patients with acrodermatitis enteropathica (Hambidge, Neldner, and Walravens, 1975). One of our patients became pregnant twice before commencement of zinc therapy. Her first pregnancy terminated through an abortion at three months; the second yielded an anencephalic stillbirth. The pregnancy outcomes of two other females with acrodermatitis enteropathica are reported in the literature. One patient, with a mild form of the disease, was maintained in complete remission with diiodoquin and had a normal offspring. The third patient's disease exacerbated during her first pregnancy, and she delivered a newborn with multiple skeletal abnormalities resembling those of an achondroplastic dwarf. The infant died shortly after delivery. Later, her disease was controlled with diiodoquin and she had three normal pregnancies. Of seven pregnancies, two were associated with severe congenital malformations of the type seen in zinc-deficient rats. This suggests that maternal zinc deficiency in humans may be teratogenic as it is in rats.

Limited observations also indicate a role for zinc in normal psychological development and function. In acrodermatitis enteropathica, lethargy and emotional lability are prominent. One three-year-old girl we have followed was a quiet child while on diiodoquin therapy and seldom laughed. With zinc therapy, her personality changed to that of a happy, smiling, active child. Formal psychological testing was undertaken in another of our patients, a three-year-old boy. Before zinc therapy, his IQ was 90, and 13 months after starting zinc, his IQ was 110.

Other interesting psychological changes have been noted in patients receiving parenteral hyperalimentation with solutions devoid of zinc. In some subjects, skin lesions similar to those seen in acrodermatitis enteropathica have occurred, accompanied by marked depression. Both skin and mood changes were reversed by supplemental zinc administration (Kay and Tasman-Jones, 1975).

More detailed observations on the role of zinc in behavior have been reported recently by Prasad (1976), who fed two volunteers an artificial diet of low zinc content and followed longitudinally the changes in laboratory parameters of zinc nutrition. These volunteers displayed slowing of memory, difficulties in concentration, and decreases in initiative and ambition, and complained of loss of sound sleep and increased irritability.

While the studies to date on the effect of adequate zinc nutrition on behavior are too limited to be conclusive, they open a wide field of research. Some of our recent studies performed in Denver have shown that inadequate zinc nutrition is a quite frequent finding among low-income children (Hambidge et al., 1976). Whether or not this inadequate intake of zinc is accompanied by learning problems in school remains to be determined. It should however be cautioned that the administration of zinc to children with behavioral disorders does not at the present time have any scientific foundation.

SUMMARY

Nutritional copper deficiency in pregnant animals results in neurodegenerative disease in offspring. Similarly, zinc deficiency causes frequent congenital CNS malformations in rat pups. In humans, nutritional copper deficiency causes psychodevelopmental delay in infants, and impaired metabolism of copper has been demonstrated in the neurodegenerative process of Menkes' steely hair syndrome.

REFERENCES

Al-Rashid, R. A., and Spangler, J. (1971) Neonatal copper deficiency. New Engl. J. Med. 285:841.

Ashkenazi, A., Levin, S., Djaldetti, M., Fishel, E., and Benevisti, D. (1973) The syndrome of neonatal copper deficiency. Pediatrics. 52:525.

Bucknall, W. E., Haslam, R. H. A., and Holtzman, N. A. (1973). Kinky hair syndrome: Response to copper therapy. Pediatrics. 52:653.

Cordano, A., Baertl, J. M., and Graham, G. G. (1964) Copper deficiency in infancy. Pediatrics. 34:324.

Danks, D. M., Campbell, P. E., Stevens, B. J., Mayne, V., and Cartwright, E. (1972) Menkes' Kinky hair syndrome. Pediatrics. 50:188.

Danks, D. M., Cartwright, E., Stevens, B. J., and Townley, R. R. W. (1973) Menkes' Kinky hair disease: Further definition of the defect in copper transport. Science. 179:1140.

Evans, G. W. (1973) Copper homeostasis in the mammalian system. Physiol. Rev. 53:535.

French, J. H., Sherard, E. S., Lubell, H., Brotz, M., and Moore, C. L. (1972) Trichopoliodystrophy I. Report of a case and biochemical studies. Arch. Neurol. 26:229.

Garnica, A. D., and Fletcher, S. R. (1975). Parenteral copper in Menkes' Kinky hair syndrome. Lancet. 2:659.

Goka, T. J., Stevenson, R. E., Hefferan, P. M., and Howell, R. R. (1976) Menkes disease: A biochemical abnormality in cultured human fibroblasts. Proc. Nat. Acad. Sci. 73:604.

Grover, W. D., and Scrutton, M. C. (1975) Copper infusion therapy in trichopoliodystrophy. J. Pediatr. 86:216.

Halsted, J. A., Ronaghy, H. A., Abadi, P., Haghshenass, M., Amirhakemi, G. H., Barakat, R. M., and Reinhold, J. G. (1972) Zinc deficiency in man: The Shiraz experiment. Amer. J. Med. 53:277.

Hambidge, K. M., and Walravens, P. A. (1975) Trace elements in nutrition. In Practice of Pediatrics. Vol. I. Hagerstown, Maryland: Harper & Row, p. 24.

Hambidge, K. M., Neldner, K. H., and Walravens, P. A. (1975) Zinc, acrodermatitis enteropathica and congenital malformations. Lancet. 1:577.

Hambidge, K. M., Walravens, P. A., Brown, R. M., Webster, J., White, S., Anthony, M., and Roth, M. L. (1976) Zinc nutrition of preschool children in the Denver Head Start program. Amer. J. Clin. Nutr. 29:734.

Heydorn, K., Damsgaard, E., Horn, N., Mikkelsen, M., Tygstrup, I., Vestermark, S., and Weber, J. (1975) Extra-hepatic storage of copper. Humangenetik. 29:171.

Horn, N. (1976) Copper incorporation studies on cultured cells for prenatal diagnosis of Menkes' disease. Lancet. 1:1156.

Hurley, L. S. (1967) Studies on nutritional factors in mammalian development. J. Nutr. 91: Suppl. 1, 27.

Hurley, L. S., and Tao, S. (1972) Alleviation of teratogenic effects of zinc deficiency by simultaneous lack of calcium. Amer. J. Physiol. 222:322.

Hurley, L. S., and Mutch, P. B. (1973) Prenatal and postnatal development after transitory gestational zinc deficiency in rats. J. Nutr. 103:649.

Kay, R. G., and Tasman-Jones, C. (1975) Zinc deficiency and intravenous feeding. Lancet. 2:605.

Lassiter, J. W., and Hambidge, K. M. (1973) Manganese. Washington, D.C.: National Academy of Sciences, p. 87.

Lombeck, I., Schnippering, H. G., Kasperek, K., Ritzl, F., Kastner, H., Feinendegen, L. E., and Bremer, H. J. (1975) Akrodermatitis enteropathica, eine Zinkstoffwechselstorung mit Zinkmalabsorption. Z. Kinderheilk. 120:181.

Menkes, J. H., Alter, M., Steigleder, G. K., Weakley, D. R., and Sung, J. H. (1962) A sex-linked recessive disorder with retardation of growth, peculiar hair and focal cerebral and cerebellar degeneration. Pediatrics. 29:764.

Neldner, K. H., and Hambidge, K. M. (1975) Zinc therapy of acrodermatitis enteropathica. New Engl. J. Med. 292:879.

O'Brien, J. S., and Sampson, E. L. (1966) Kinky hair disease. II. Biochemical studies. J. Neuropath. Exp. Neurol. 25:523.

Prasad, A. S., Halsted, J. A., and Nadimi, M. (1961) Syndrome of iron deficiency anemia, hepatosplenomegaly, hypogonadism, dwarfism, and geophagia. Amer. J. Med. 31:532.

Prasad, A. S. (1976) American College of Nutrition Award Lecture. Zinc deficiency in man: Consideration in sickle-cell anemia and other medical disorders. (in press).

Sandstead, H. H., Fosmire, G. J., McKenzie, J. M., and Halas, E. S. (1975) Zinc deficiency and brain development in the rat. Fed. Proc. 34:86.

Sever, L. E., and Emanuel, I. (1973) Is there a connection between maternal zinc deficiency and congenital malformations of the central nervous system in man. Teratology. 7:117.

Swenerton, H., Shrader, R., and Hurley, L. S. (1969) Zinc-deficient embryos: Reduced thymidine incorporation. Science. 166:1014.

Underwood, E. J. (1971) Trace Elements in Human and Animal Nutrition. (3rd edition) New York: Academic Press. p. 83.

Walker-Smith, J. A., Turner, B., Blomfield, J., and Wise, G. (1973) Therapeutic implications of copper deficiency in Menkes's steely-hair syndrome. Arch. Dis. Child. 48:958.

Walravens, P. A., and Hambidge, K. M. (1976) Unpublished observations.

Warkany, J., and Petering, H. G. (1973) Congenital malformations of the brain produced by short zinc deficiencies in rats. Amer. J. Ment. Defic. 77:645.

Wesenberg, R. L., Gwinn, J. L., and Barnes, G. R. (1969) Radiological findings in the kinky hair syndrome. Radiology. 92:500.

Wheeler, E. M., and Roberts, P. F. (1976) Menkes's steely hair syndrome. Arch. Dis. Child. 51:269.

RESEARCH TO PRACTICE IN MENTAL RETARDATION
Biomedical Aspects, Volume III
Edited by Peter Mittler
Copyright 1977 I.A.S.S.M.D.

EFFECT OF MALNUTRITION AND EARLY ENVIRONMENT ON BEHAVIORAL DEVELOPMENT AND LONG-TERM MENTAL DISTURBANCES IN RATS

S. Fraňková
Institute for Clinical and Experimental Medicine,
Prague, Czechoslovakia

Extensive studies of long-term consequences of early malnutrition in children have demonstrated that severe nutritional deprivation, experienced during infancy, may result in mental retardation and in behavioral abnormalities.

Laboratory experimentation with animals completes the human research by modeling situations that, for various reasons cannot be induced in human subjects. It makes possible comparisons of responses to malnutrition on different phylogenetic and ontogenetic levels; it shows which fundamental biological properties and functions of the brain can be affected by malnutrition.

Interest in the study of behavioral responses to early malnutrition has rapidly increased during recent years. It is gratifying that clinicians and child psychologists realize the value of animal research and that they stress the necessity for an interdisciplinary approach to the study of interaction between nutrition and mental development.

This chapter deals with the effect of early protein and/or calorie malnutrition (PCM) on behavior, with environmental factors that codetermine the development of the PCM infant and, finally, with attempts to influence therapeutically mental conditions following early PCM.

When comparing findings of various laboratories, and when taking into account the diversity of nutritional plans, the large scale behavioral tests, and the different kinds of experimental animals, the similarity in behavioral symptoms observed by individual authors is surprising.

Severe PCM, which affects the young from the first days of postnatal life, or which already acts in the course of fetal development, results in the retardation of physical and mental development. When a low-protein diet was provided to rat mothers from the first day of lactation, significant suppression of growth was recorded in pups from the 10th day of life (Barnes et al., 1968).

In the malnourished pups, delayed development of reflexes and of motor coordination was observed (Simonson et al., 1969; Smart and Dobbing, 1971). They display poor exploratory activity in a new environment (Fraňkova and Barnes, 1968a). While normal pups quickly become independent and move freely in the breeding cage, exploring and playing with their littermates, the PCM pups rest passively under or beside their mother, exhausted by acute malnutrition (Fraňkova, 1973a; Massaro, Levitsky, and Barnes, 1974).

LONG-TERM BEHAVIORAL SYMPTOMS OF EARLY PCM

Malnutrition that lasts longer than the preweaning period (e.g., during both the prenatal and suckling period, or from birth until sexual maturation), results in long-term, if not permanent, behavioral disturbances that are resistant to later nutritional therapy. Adult animals, previously deprived of protein or of calories, differ from normal subjects in the response to a changed environment, to sensory stimuli, and to new objects. They show a low level of spontaneous exploratory activity in a novel situation (Fraňkova and Barnes, 1968a; Simonson et al., 1971) and slower habituation of response to acoustic stimuli (Fraňkova, 1973b). Zimmerman, Strobel, and Maguire (1970) observed fear of new objects that were induced into the familiar environment, in malnourished monkeys. On the other hand, total spontaneous locomotor activity of undisturbed rats was not affected by the early PCM (Guthrie, 1968).

Marked behavioral abnormalities appear in the PCM animals in more complex conditions or in stress situations. They respond with an elevated "emotionality," with increased excitement that manifests itself in panic reactions, freezing, defecation, and aggressivity. Their responses often seem to be inappropriate to the intensity of stimulation. The fixation of the aversive experience is extremely strong (Levitsky and Barnes, 1970). According to Smart, Whatson, and Dobbing (1975), they have a lowered pain threshold.

There are certain controversies concerning the learning performance of the PCM animals. Some authors reported worse learning (Simonson and Chow, 1970), others did not observe any difference between the PCM and the control animals. In certain tasks, the early malnourished rats performed even better than the controls when latencies or speed of learning were recorded (Fraňkova and Barnes, 1968b).

Despite the contradictory results, it is possible to find common features in the learning performance of the PCM animal. Apparently, these animals have no serious problems in solving a simple task, but they fail in situations in which it is necessary to discriminate, to evaluate time intervals, to inhibit a certain response or to modify it, or to reverse the learned reaction. They extinguish once-learned responses with difficulty, as observed in rats (Fraňková and Barnes, 1968b) or in pigs (Barnes et al., 1970). In the course of avoidance learning, the PCM animals may develop inadequate responses, perseverative activities, stereotypes, panic reactions, and other symptoms of seriously impaired behavior.

Whether these behavioral manifestations reflect lower functional capacity of the brain, or disturbances of general processes underlying the ability to adapt to novel demands, remains an open question. Nevertheless, it seems that, principally, motivation and emotional stability is grossly affected in malnourished individuals and that malnutrition accounts for at least some of the observed learning problems.

COMPLEXITY OF EARLY PCM,
ROLE OF THE EXTERNAL ENVIRONMENT

When modeling conditions of the early PCM, it is necessary to realize that malnutrition does not affect selectively only an individual, but that it interacts with the psychological and social situation within, or even outside the family.

The PCM infant is apathetic, does not initiate active contacts with litter-mates, and is less demanding on the mother. Because all pups are malnourished in the litter, the total sum of mutual contacts and stimulation is very low. The development of social behavior is at a decreased level from the very beginning (Fraňková, 1973a).

Not only the behavior of pups, but also maternal behavior, is adversely affected by the acute severe malnutrition. The PCM lactating dams display a low level of maternal activity as tested in various experimental situations (Fraňková, 1971; 1974a).

In rats, the suckling period is important for later development. Early experience, gained by the pup in interaction with the external environment makes a base for cognitive development. The level of stimulation of the close environment and of activity of the infant through which he seeks new stimuli is the precondition of the quantity and quality of the experience. As is evident, both external and internal sources of experience are limited in the malnourished infant.

When analyzing the conditions that accompany human malnutrition, sensory deprivation of the child is often stressed. The child is sensorially deprived in the unstable family with a low cultural level, low parental care, by long-term hospitalization, etc. Experimentally, it was demonstrated that early sensory deprivation markedly intensified the behavioral symptoms of malnutrition (Fraňková, 1972; Elias and Samonds, 1974). As observed, the adult rats, deprived of protein and of sensory stimuli during the suckling period, almost lost their curiosity in a new environment and showed an enhanced response to a low dose of psychotropic drug (Fraňková, 1972).

EXPERIMENTAL THERAPY OF THE PCM

Before suggesting any possibilities for therapeutic treatment of malnutrition, it is necessary to find out on which ontogenetical level PCM interferes with neural and behavioral development and which components, or processes, it influences. Based on experimental findings, we suggest that several ways of active intervention exist.

Interference with the early psychological environment might be the first way. As mentioned, malnutrition is accompanied by decreased stimulation from the close environment. On the other hand, ample literature gives evidence of the beneficial effect of increased stimulation on development and later behavior (Fraňková, 1974b). Our earlier study demonstrated that increased sensory stimulation by means of regular manipulation, handling, and exposure to a new environment during the suckling period resulted in long-term elevation of the exploratory activity in rats that were calorically deprived in the preweaning period. The early-stimulated undernourished rats did not differ in this behavioral characteristic from the well-nourished rats which were not provided with any extra stimulation during the first three months of life (Fraňková, 1968).

There is another, more natural way to increase stimulation within the malnourished "family." A normal, healthy, virgin female ("the aunt") was induced into the breeding cage with the malnourished mother and pups. As observed, this aunt undertook part of the maternal role; she provided pups with the missing maternal stimulation. When comparing the PCM aunt-reared pups with well-fed young reared by the mother only, it was found that they did not differ in behavioral development nor in some behavioral characteristics in adult age (Fraňková, 1974c).

Most probably, there are various other possibilities of interfering experimentally with the psychological milieu in the course of behavioral development. It seems that psychological stimuli are extraordinarily strong factors in behavioral development of the PCM infant even if they are not able to compensate for all the deficits, especially for physical handicap.

There is another, quite different approach to the therapy of behavioral symptoms following early PCM: pharmacological treatment. We were looking for a drug with a relation to brain metabolism without undesirable side effects. In pediatric practice, satisfactory therapeutic experience was reported with pyrithioxine, the derivate of pyridoxine (Encephabol, Merck), in behavioral disturbances after perinatal cerebral injuries, encephalitis, mechanical and hypoxic brain damage, and mental retardation of various etiologies (Quadbeck et al., 1962; Hoffecker, 1964; Adam and Hammelmann, 1964). It was found that pyrithioxine increased mental efficiency, reduced motor agitation, and harmonized affective states (Heinze and Stöckmann, 1964).

Pyrithioxine was applied to protein-deficient rats either during the period of sexual maturation or in adult animals after nutritional rehabilitation. It was found that pyrithioxine, applied for 10 consecutive days from weaning onward tended to normalize behavior of the PCM rats. The beneficial effect of pyrithioxine was long-term; it also promoted the growth rate of the PCM animals. On the other hand, therapy with pyrithioxine in adult life, from the 100th day of life, failed to improve behavioral abnormalities of the PCM rats (Fraňková and Benešová, 1973).

All experimental designs evidenced the inefficacy of nutritional or pharmacological therapy, if started in adulthood. Nevertheless, we tried to examine one way. As demonstrated (Fraňková and Barnes, 1968b), the early malnourished rats responded to the learning situation in adulthood with increased excitement, fear, and marked behavioral abnormalities. We were interested in whether or not it would be possible to normalize behavior in the course of learning. Based on our finding that the adaptation to the novel situation goes slowly in PCM rats, the rats were allowed to become familiar with the environment and gradually to adapt to the experimental situation. It appeared that this adaptation prior to learning helped to normalize later behavior and it reduced fear-motivated responses, i.e., special care helped the PCM rats to solve the situation, otherwise stressful for them (Fraňková, 1973b).

Experimental studies on laboratory animals show that early malnutrition interferes with behavioral development. Behavioral abnormalities persist into adulthood. Unfavorable psychological conditions, such as sensory deprivation, or poor maternal care, make the behavioral symptoms of PCM even more profound.

Contrary to the pessimistic view of the persistence of disturbances, we suppose possibilities exist of moderating mental conditions in the malnourished individual, even later in his life. For the laboratory worker, it means studying mechanisms underlying behavioral abnormalities and looking for all ways that can help to compensate for the deficits.

SUMMARY

The study stresses the importance of the complex approach to the investigation of interaction between malnutrition and mental retardation. The animal model gives evidence that both early malnutrition and external environment contribute to later behavioral abnormalities of the malnourished animal.

REFERENCES

Adam, D., and Hamelmann, H. (1964) Pyrithioxin- Behandlung und Schädeltraumen. Med. Wschr. 106:1045.

Barnes, R. H., Moore, U. A., and Pond, W. G. (1970) Behavioral abnormalities in young adult pigs caused by malnutrition in early life. J. Nutr. 100:149.

Barnes, R. H., Neely, C. S., Kwong, E., Labadan, B. A., and Fraňková, S. (1968) Postnatal nutritional deprivations as determinants of adult behavior toward⁻ food, its consumption and utilization. J. Nutr. 96:467.

Elias, M. F., and Samonds, K. W. (1974) Exploratory behavior and activity of infant monkeys during nutritional and rearing restriction. Amer. J. Clin. Nutr. 27:458.

Fraňková, S. (1968) Nutritional and psychological factors in the development of spontaneous behavior in the rat. In Malnutrition, Learning and Behavior. (Eds. Scrimshaw, N. S., and Gordon, J. E.) Cambridge, Mass. MIT Press. p. 312.

Fraňková, S. (1971) Relationship between nutrition during lactation and maternal behaviour of rats. Activ. Nerv. Super. (Prague). 13:1.

Fraňková, S. (1972) Effects of early dietary and sensoric reduction on behaviour of adult rats. Activ. Nerv. Super. 14:1.

Fraňková, S. (1973a) Effect of protein-calorie malnutrition on the development of social behavior in rat. Devel. Psychobiol. 6:33.

Fraňková, S. (1973b) Interaction among the familiarity with the environment, avoidance learning and behaviour or early malnourished rats. Activ. Nerv. Super. (Prague). 15:207.

Fraňková, S. (1974a) Effects of protein deficiency in early life and during lactation on maternal behaviour. Baroda J. Nutr. (India). 1:21.

Fraňková, S. (1974b) Interaction between early malnutrition and stimulation in animals. In Early Malnutrition and Mental Development. (Eds. Cravioto, J., Hambraeus, L., and Vahlquist, B.) Symp. Swedish Nutr. Found. XII, 202.

Fraňková, S. (1974c) Influence of early social environment on behaviour of the protein-calorie malnourished rats. Activ. Nerv. Super. (Prague). 15:199.

Fraňková, S., and Barnes, R. H. (1968a) Influence of malnutrition in early life on exploratory behavior of rats. J. Nutr. 96:477.

Fraňková, S., and Barnes, R. H. (1968b) Effect of malnutrition in early life on avoidance conditioning and behavior of adult rat. J. Nutr. 96:485.

Fraňková, S., and Benešová, O. (1973) Effect of pyrithioxine (Encephabol) on growth and exploratory behaviour of rats malnourished in early life. Psycho-pharmacol. (Berlin), 28:63.

Guthrie, H. A. (1968) Severe undernutrition in early infancy and behavior in rehabilitated albino rats. Physiol. Behav. 3:619.

Heinze, H., and Stöckmann, F. (1964) Jugendpsychiatrische Erfahrungen über die Wirkung von Pyrithioxin. Med. Klin., 59:1913.

Hoffecker, F. (1964) Erfahrungen mit Encephabol in der kinderärztlichen Praxis. Ther. Ggw. 103:913.

Levitsky, D. A., and Barnes, R. H. (1970) Effect of early malnutrition on the reaction of adult rats to aversive stimuli. Nature. 225:468.

Massaro, T. F., Levitsky, D. A., and Barnes, R. H. (1974) Protein malnutrition in the rat: its effects on maternal behavior and pup development. Devel. Psychobiol. 7:551.

Quadbeck, G., Landmann, K. R., Sachsse, W., and Schmidt, I. (1962) Der Einfluss von Pyrithioxin auf die Blut- Hirn-schranke. Med. Exp. (Basel). 7:114.

Simonson, M., and Chow, B. F. (1970) Maze studies on progeny of underfed mother rats. J. Nutr. 100:685.

Simonson, M., Sherwin, R. W., Anilane, J. K., Yu, W. Y., and Chow, B. F. (1969) Neuromotor development in progeny of underfed mother rats. J. Nutr. 98:18.

Simonson, M., Stephan, J., Hanson, H., and Chow, B. F. (1971) Open field studies in offspring of underfed mother rats. J. Nutr. 101:331.

Smart, J. L., and Dobbing, J. (1971) Vulnerability of developing brain. II. Effects of early nutritional deprivation on reflex ontogeny and development of behaviour in the rat. Brain. Res. 28:85.

Smart, J. L., Whatson, T. S., and Dobbing, J. (1975) Thresholds of response to electric shock in previously undernourished rats. Brit. J. Nutr. 34:511.

Zimmermann, R. R., Strobel, D. A., and Maguire, D. (1970) Neophobic reactions in protein malnourished infant monkeys. Proc. 78th Ann. Convent. APA, p. 197.

NEUROSCIENCE

RESEARCH TO PRACTICE IN MENTAL RETARDATION
Biomedical Aspects, Volume III
Edited by Peter Mittler
Copyright 1977 I.A.S.S.M.D.

SOME RULES GOVERNING SPECIFICITY OF SYNAPTIC CONNECTIONS IN THE DEVELOPING MAMMALIAN BRAIN

R. L. Sidman
Department of Neuroscience,
Children's Hospital Medical Center,
300 Longwood Avenue,
Boston, Massachusetts 02115,
United States

Experienced clinicians and pathologists estimate that the pathological basis for mental retardation is known in only a minority of cases. Even when a given case can be assigned to a disease category, the targets of the disease process (regions of the nervous system, cell types) and the pathological mechanisms at play are rarely identifiable. Sometimes the basic biochemical genetic error may be known, but the consequent epigenetic events in the developing nervous system remain undeciphered, with a few notable exceptions.

One obvious reason for this gross lacuna in our knowledge of mental retardation is that we rarely have the opportunity to examine the nervous system systematically at the developmental stages when the disease process is active, and we are forced instead to seek clues at uninformative or misleading terminal stages. Another reason is methodological. Our ultimate objective is to establish the clinico-pathological correlation in terms of qualitative and quantitative abnormalities of synaptic organization, and a methodology appropriate to this task is just beginning to evolve.

The approach that my colleagues and I have taken has been to concentrate on development of the brain in the mouse, a relatively simple and accessible mammalian species for which an expanding list of inherited developmental diseases of the nervous system is known (Sidman, Green, and Appel, 1965; Sidman, 1974). Most of these inherited disorders are thought to result from spontaneous point mutations. Many have been assigned to specific chromosomes and are carried in breeding stocks in which affected and control animals are genetically identical except at the mutated locus (defined as coisogenic strains) or differ only over a limited chromosome segment that includes the locus of interest (congenic strains). Marker genes have sometimes been incorporated into the stocks to allow recognition of affected mice before overt expression of the neurological disease and as an aid in selecting heterozygotes for breeding purposes. In this chapter, I have concentrated on a few mutants with major effects on cell number, shape, and synaptic connections in the cerebellum, and have attempted to extract a few principles of synaptogenesis that may alert us to possible disease mechanisms in the developing human nervous system.

THE PROBLEM OF CLINICO-PATHOLOGICAL CORRELATION

In the 1970s, three independent mutations in mice have been recognized that cause a relatively selective postnatal loss of Purkinje neurons in the cerebellum. Their names are Nervous, gene symbol *nr* (Sidman and Green, 1970), Purkinje cell degeneration, *pcd* (Mullen et al., 1976), and Lurcher, *Lc* (Wilson, 1975, 1976; Caddy and Biscoe, 1975, 1976). If the patients were human, they probably would be considered to have the same disease, but in the mouse it is clear on the basis of genetic and histopathologic criteria that we are dealing with three separate diseases producing similar end results.

Figure 1 shows the position of Purkinje cell bodies in the cerebellum of a normal 24-day-old mouse. The axons of these cells are unstained, but traverse the granule cell layer and pass inward to synapse mainly on deep cerebellar neurons. The granule cells send their axons outward into the lightly stained molecular layer, where they branch, run parallel to each other, and make synaptic contacts with the outward-directed dendrites of Purkinje cells. The middle panel of the figure shows the corresponding cerebellar region of a 24-day-old *pcd* littermate in which Purkinje cell loss already is far advanced. The lowest panel illustrates a four-month *pcd* cerebellum, with hardly a single residual Purkinje cell. Other cell types are essentially intact in the cerebellar cortex.

Figure 2 compares the rate and extent of Purkinje cell loss in the *nr* and *pcd* mutants, and allows correlation of clinical and pathological signs. In both mutants, loss of Purkinje cells is rapid in the 4th and 5th weeks after birth, a bit earlier and more extreme in *pcd*. Interestingly, the onset and progression of clinical ataxia parallels the cell loss in *pcd* but antedates it in *nr*. By 15 days of age in *nr*, when the mutant is distinguishable behaviorally from its normal littermates, every Purkinje cell soma shows abnormal mitochondrial morphology

Figure 1. Culmen of cerebellar cortex of 24-day-old control (top panel) and *pcd* (middle panel) mice, and 113-day-old *pcd* mouse (bottom panel). Aldehyde fixed, celloidin embedded, 20 μm sections stained with cresyl violet. Arrows point to degenerating cells. × 270.

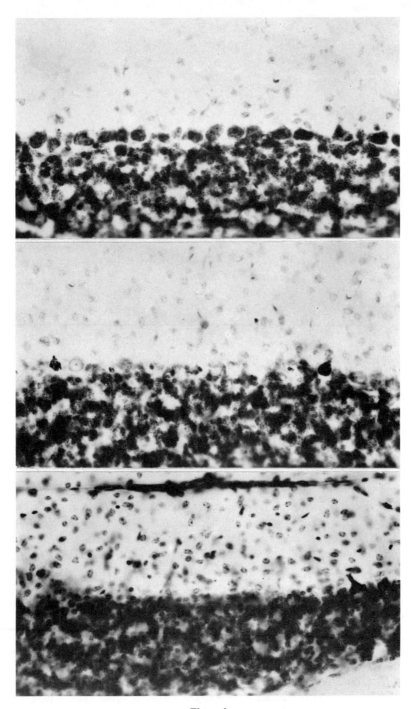

Figure 1.

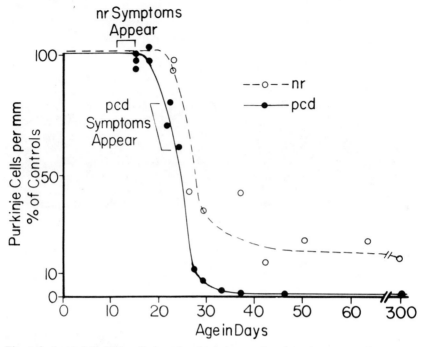

Figure 2. Loss of Purkinje cells in *pcd* and *nr* mice as a function of age (R. Mullen, personal communication).

(Landis, 1973). Subsequently most Purkinje cells die, while in the survivors mitochondrial shape reverts permanently to normal. A few other populations of neurons also show this transient mitochondrial change but do not degenerate; their involvement in the pathological process would pass unrecognized if only the end stage of the disease were available for examination.

The selective loss of a major neuronal population poses the question, what are the consequences for synaptic organization? Examination of deep cerebellar neurons, the normal targets of Purkinje cell axons in the 60-day-old mouse (Figure 3), shows that the surfaces of neurons in the lateral nucleus of the cerebellum (essentially corresponding to the human dentate nucleus) are studded with Purkinje axon terminals, forming characteristic axosomatic inhibitory synapses. In a *pcd* littermate, also 60 days old (Figure 4), most Purkinje terminals have degenerated; the cell soma is now almost denuded of synaptic inputs, and is invested instead with an astrocytic coating. A modest number of large synaptic terminals of an undefined class, not normally present on these somas, has come in during the month or so since degeneration of the Purkinje cells. (S. O'Gorman and R. L. Sidman, unpublished observations).

Purkinje axon terminals are known to use gamma aminobutyric acid (GABA) as their neurotransmitter (Ito and Yoshida, 1966; McLaughlin et al., 1975).

Roffler-Tarlov, Beart, and Sidman (1976) have been attempting to assess deep cerebellar synaptic organization in *pcd* by biochemical criteria. To our surprise, there is only a 20–50% drop in net GABA content in the cerebellar cortex and deep nuclei (measured separately) and persistence of normal values in both regions for activity of the GABA-synthesizing enzyme, glutamic acid decarboxylase, as well as for synthesis of [^{3}H]GABA from [^{3}H]glutamate by cerebellar slices. These data pose a worrisome caveat as one considers assessing

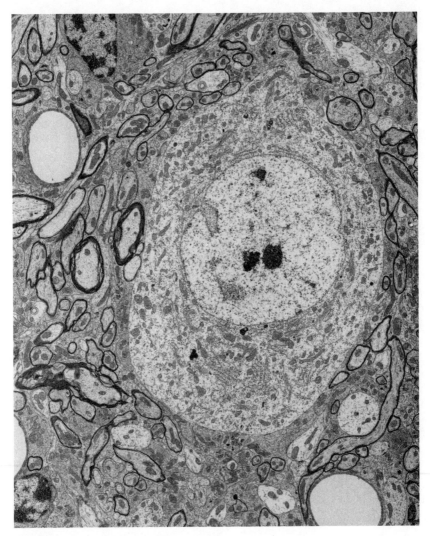

Figure 3. Neuron of lateral nucleus of cerebellum in 60-day-old normal mouse. Most of the cell surface is contacted synaptically by Purkinje axon terminals. × 5,350.

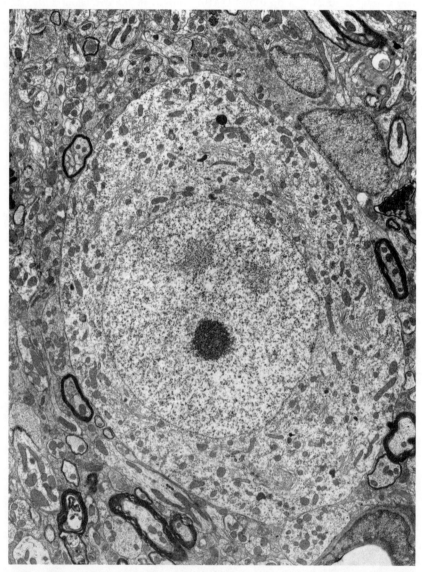

Figure 4. Neuron of lateral nucleus of cerebellum in 60-day-old *pcd* mouse, littermate to that illustrated in Figure 3. See text. × 5,550.

synaptic organization in human mental deficiency by means of cytopathology or neurotransmitter chemistry: Do either the cytological or chemical data, as currently obtained, accurately reflect the functional status of the synaptic circuitry? Further, the locomotor derangement in *pcd* is curiously mild in light of the almost total loss of Purkinje cells, the central neuronal elements of the cerebellar cortex. Have we exaggerated the importance of the cerebellar cortex, or has there been a fairly effective compensatory synaptic reorganization at some site we have not explored, say on the dendritic surfaces of deep cerebellar neurons or even outside the cerebellum entirely?

Thus, the Purkinje neuron-deficient mutants suggest several reasons why answers may be generally elusive in human developmental neuropathology: the classification of diseases in terms of clinical behavior or end-stage pathology is inadequate; the denominating pathological events may be transient; the available cytological and chemical methods for assessing synaptic organization are limited, even if suitable specimens were available; and it is usually not clear what region of the nervous system actually merits detailed analysis in a given case.

CELL INTERACTIONS IN SYNAPTOGENESIS

A broad range of studies, too extensive to review here (see Sidman, 1974; Cotman and Lynch, 1976), are consistent with the generalization that synaptogenesis is nonrandom, and that the extent of its selectivity and stability are dependent on a series of interactions between pre- and postsynaptic elements, perhaps involving glial cells as well. Some of the most interesting data on this theme come from analysis of another cerebellar mutant mouse named Staggerer, *sg* (Sidman, Lane, and Dickie, 1962).

While the normal mouse cerebellum grows extensively in the first few weeks after birth, the staggerer cerebellum remains permanently close to its neonatal size and configuration. The small size is mainly the result of a decreased rate of proliferation of granule cell precursors (Yoon, 1976) and a degeneration, predominantly in the third week after birth, of most of the granule cells that do form (Sidman, 1968). It is intriguing that although the granule cell neuron bears the obvious brunt of the pathology, the actual target of the *sg* genetic locus is very probably the Purkinje cell (Sidman, 1968; Sotelo and Changeux, 1974). The volumes of the Purkinje cell soma and dendrites are smaller in *sg* mice compared to littermate controls at all postnatal ages and, unique among all mutants studied to date, exhibit very few spines on tertiary dendritic branches (Sidman, 1972; Sotelo, 1975). The surface membranes of such spines normally develop specialized features that mark them as postsynaptic target sites for granule cell axons, and in the absence of such spines in Staggerer, that particular synapse is essentially missing.

Figure 5 shows Ramon y Cajal's (1960) classic drawing of Purkinje cell dendrite differentiation, from an immature cell with a single stubby dendritic

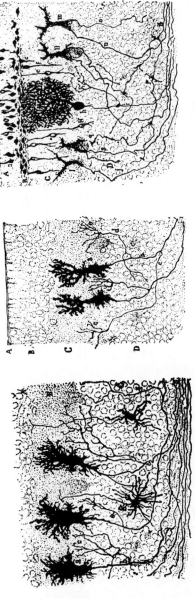

Figure 5. Drawings of Golgi preparations to illustrate early postnatal differentiation of mammalian Purkinje cells. From Ramon y Cajal (1960).

Figure 6. Drawings of Golgi preparations of Purkinje cells from a 16-day-old *sg* mouse. Dendrites are smaller in volume than normal, are not confined to the sagittal plane and lack tertiary dendritic branches and branchlet spines. Calibration bar equals 50 nm. From Landis and Sidman (1977).

arbor and a soma with abundant filopodia, gradually to a mature cell with an elaborate dendritic tree and a smooth-surfaced soma. Figure 6 illustrates staggerer Purkinje cells (Landis and Sidman, 1977) with absence of the type of spines normally contacted by granule cell axons. The remarkable selectivity of the genetic lesion is diagrammed in Figure 7, which shows the presence in Staggerer of every other class of synaptic contact made by granule cell axons, and every type of input onto Purkinje cell dendrites except the granule cell input (Sidman, 1972).

These data are consistent with the generalization expressed by Mugnaini (1970) and others that the postsynaptic element controls the specificity of synaptic relationships. However, as emphasized elsewhere (Sidman, 1974; Vaughn et al., 1976), synaptic recognition probably involves a series of interactions between pre-and postsynaptic elements rather than an all-or-none control

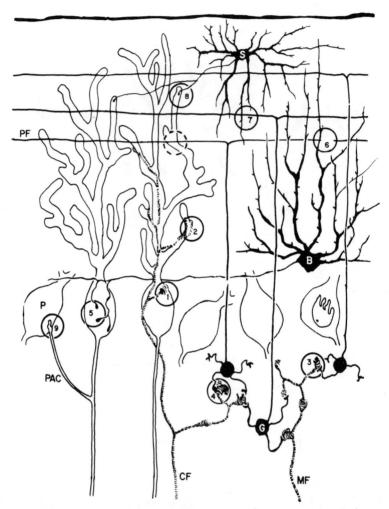

Figure 7. Schematic drawing of the cerebellar circuitry in the staggerer mouse with each major class of synapses encircled and numbered: 1, climbing fiber-Purkinje cell soma; 2, climbing fiber-Purkinje cell dendrite; 3, mossy fiber-granule cell dendrite; 4, climbing fiber-granule cell dendrite; 5, basket cell axon-Purkinje cell soma; 6, parallel fiber (granule cell axon)-basket cell dendrite; 7, parallel fiber-stellate cell dendrite; 8, stellate cell axon-Purkinje cell dendrite; 9, Purkinje cell axon collateral-Purkinje cell soma. Synapses between parallel fibers and Purkinje cell dendrites (broken circles below synapse #8) were not encountered. Abbreviations: B, basket cell; CF, climbing fiber; G, granule cell; MF, mossy fiber; P, Purkinje cell; PAC, Purkinje axon collateral; PF, parallel fiber; S, stellate cell. From Sidman, 1972.

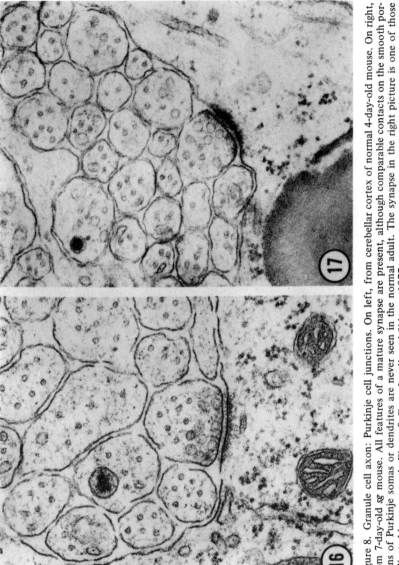

Figure 8. Granule cell axon: Purkinje cell junctions. On left, from cerebellar cortex of normal 4-day-old mouse. On right, from 7-day-old *sg* mouse. All features of a mature synapse are present, although comparable contacts on the smooth portions of Purkinje somas or dendrites are never seen in the normal adult. The synapse in the right picture is one of those indicated by an arrow in Figure 9. From Landis and Sidman, 1977.

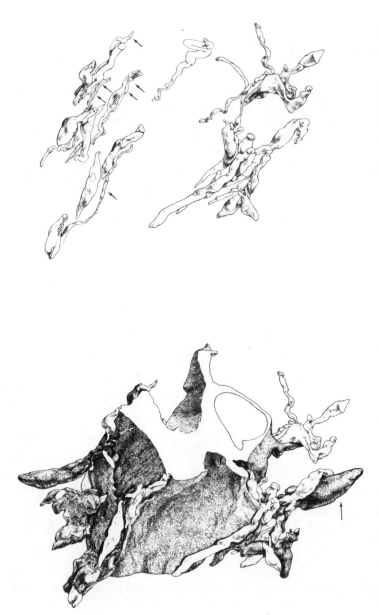

Figure 9. Serial section reconstruction of a Purkinje cell (left) and of its afferents alone (right) from a 7-day-old sg mouse. The Purkinje cell axon is at the bottom of the left picture (arrow) and the apical cytoplasmic cone at the top. Afferent climbing fibers and granule cell axons are lightly stippled. See text for further details. From Landis and Sidman, 1977.

by either element, and a closer look is worthwhile at the early, transient contacts between granule cell axon and Purkinje cell soma and dendrites in Staggerer. During the first two weeks after birth, well-developed synaptic junctions are present between granule cell axons and the smooth apical part of the Purkinje cell soma, as in the example (Figure 8) from a four-day-old normal mouse. On the right is a similar synapse with enlarged presynaptic bouton, a collection of synaptic vesicles, and asymmetrically disposed electron-dense fuzz from a seven-day-old *sg* mouse. The identification of this terminal, and its distinction from climbing fiber synapses, was made by reconstructing a three-dimensional image from 90 consecutive serial sections encompassing a total thickness of about 7 nm, as shown in Figure 9 (Landis and Sidman, 1976). On the left is the reconstructed immature Purkinje cell surface with persistent basal somatic cytoplasmic processes intertwined with climbing fibers, characterized by irregular synaptic swellings and branchings. Dendritic processes emerge from the apex of the cell body and are contacted by both climbing fibers and granule cell axons, the latter characterized by their orientation in the long axis of the cerebellar folium, the lack of branches, and the presence of only one synaptic swelling per axon within the reconstructed territory. The drawing on the right shows the same axons with the Purkinje cell "subtracted." Postsynaptic membrane thickenings are indicated by cross-hatching, or, when obscured by a fiber, by dashed circles. Most of the granule cell axons in contact with the Purkinje cell lack specialized junctions at any given moment in time.

It would appear, then, that the granule cell axon and Purkinje cell soma or dendrite can recognize each other and interact to a limited extent in early postnatal *sg* mice, but the contact in general is not sustained, and it fails to differentiate into a mature spine synapse. A limited number of the contacts with smooth somatic or dendritic sites on the Purkinje cell surface may persist for at least three weeks (Sotelo, 1975) and may function to drive Purkinje cells (Crepel and Mariani, 1975). The *sg* genetic locus, then, may affect not the Purkinje cell's ability to form an initial recognition site for granule cell axons, but its ability (directly or indirectly) to elaborate that site into a spine. The *sg* locus does not control Purkinje cell synaptic sites in general; it is especially noteworthy that dendritic thorns contacted by climbing fibers are abundant in Staggerer.

CONCLUDING COMMENTS

Various other mutants serve as unique experiments for analysis of additional factors possibly affecting synaptogenesis. For example, in Weaver, most granule cells die but some survive and remain in ectopic positions external to Purkinje cell bodies. Their major axonal input, the mossy fibers, can find them in the abnormal site and discriminate among several potential synaptic partners to form normal-appearing synapses with them selectively (Rakic and Sidman, 1973). Synaptogenesis in this case would appear to proceed quite accurately, despite abnormal geometric coordinates and abnormal timing. This conclusion is reached even more dramatically in the case of the reeler mutant, in which the majority of cerebellar and cerebral cortical neurons are in abnormal positions (Sidman, 1974) and yet axons may seek out their usual target cells and reach them by very unusual trajectories (Caviness, 1976), form morphologically normal classes of synaptic connections (Rakic, 1976), and attain a reasonably accurate functional state (Bliss and Chung, 1974; Drager, 1975). These phenomena pose an intense challenge to account for at the molecular level.

This survey has been necessarily superficial and sharply limited to topics within the author's personal experience. Rudimentary as our facts and ideas may be, one can glimpse the general shape of a forthcoming set of concepts that may give us some control over developmental mechanisms that go wrong and lead to mental retardation.

SUMMARY

A description is given of 1) the temporal sequences of synapse formation in cerebellar and cerebral cortices in primates and rodents and 2) effects of specific cerebellar neuron-deleting mutations and of abnormal neuron positions on synaptogenesis in mice. Data are interpreted in terms of a developmental hierarchy, rather than an absolute set, of synaptic specificities.

REFERENCES

Bliss, T. V. P. and Chung, S.-H. (1974) An electrophysiological study of the hippocampus of the "reeler" mutant mouse. Nature 252:153.

Caddy, K. W. T., and Biscoe, T. J. (1975) Preliminary observations on the cerebellum in the mutant mouse Lurcher. Brain Res. 91:276.

Caddy, K. W. T., and Biscoe, T. J. (1976) The number of Purkinje cells and olive neurones in the normal and Lurcher mutant mouse. Brain Res. 111:396.

Caviness, V. S., Jr. (1976) Patterns of cell and fiber distribution in the neocortex of the reeler mutant mouse. J. Comp. Neurol.

Cotman, C. W., and Lynch, G. S. (1976). Reactive synaptogenesis in the adult nervous system: the effects of partial deafferentation on new synapse formation. In Neuronal Recognition (Ed. Barondes, S. H.) New York: Plenum Press.

Crepel, F., and Mariani, J. (1975) Anatomical, physiological, and biochemical studies of the cerebellum from mutant mice. I. Electrophysiological analysis of cerebellar cortical neurons in the staggerer mouse. Brain Res. 98:135.

Drager, U. C. (1975) Physiological properties of cells in the primary visual cortex of the reeler mutant mouse. Neurosci. Abstr. 1:102.

Ito, M., and Yoshida, M. (1966) The origin of cerebellar-induced inhibition of Deiter's neurons. I. Monosynaptic initiation of the inhibitory postsynaptic potentials. Exp. Brain Res. 2:330.

Landis, D. M. D., and Sidman, R. L. (1977) Electron microscopic analysis of postnatal histogenesis in the cerebellar cortex of Staggerer mutant mouse. J. Comp. Neurol. (in press).

Landis, S. (1973) Ultrastructural changes in the mitochondria of cerebellar Purkinje cells of nervous mutant mice. J. Cell. Biol. 57:782.

McLaughlin, B. J., Wood, J. G., Saito, K., Roberts, E., and Wu, J. Y. (1975) The fine structural localization of glutamic decarboxylase in developing axonal processes and presynaptic terminals of rodent cerebellum. Brain Res. 85:355.

Mugnaini, E. (1970) Neurones as synaptic targets. In Excitatory Synaptic Mechanisms (Eds. P. Anderson, and J. K. S. Jansen, Jr.). Oslo: Universitets Forlaget, p. 149.

Mullen, R. J., Eicher, E. M., and Sidman, R. L. (1976) Purkinje cell degeneration, a new neurological mutant in the mouse. Proc. Nat. Acad. Sci. USA. 73:208.

Rakic, P. (1976) Synaptic specificity in the cerebellar cortex: a study of anomalous circuits induced by single gene mutations in mice. Cold Spring Harbor Symposia on Quantitative Biology. 40:333.

Rakic, P., and Sidman, R. L. (1973) Organization of cerebellar cortex secondary to deficit of granule cells in weaver mutant mice. J. Comp. Neurol. 152:133.

Ramon y Cajal, S. (1960) Studies on Vertebrate Neurogenesis (L. Guth, transl.). Springfield, Ill.: Charles C Thomas.

Roffler-Tarlov, S., Beart, P. M., and Sidman, R. L. (1976) Studies of GABA synthesis in Purkinje cell deficient mice. ICN-UCLA Winter Conference on Mol. and Cellular Biol., Neurobiology. Abstract.

Sidman, R. L. (1968) Development of interneuronal connections in brains of mutant mice. In Physiological and Biochemical Aspects of Nervous Integration (Ed. F. D. Carlson). Englewood Cliffs, New Jersey: Prentice-Hall, p. 163.

Sidman, R. L. (1972) Cell interactions in developing mammalian central nervous system. In Cell Interactions: Proceedings of the Third Lepetit Colloquium (Ed. L. G. Silvestri) Amsterdam: North-Holland.

Sidman, R. L. (1974) Contact interaction among developing mammalian brain cells. In The Cell Surface in Development (Ed. A. A. Moscona). New York: Wiley & Sons, Inc. p. 221.

Sidman, R. L., Lane, P., and Dickie, M. (1962) Staggerer, a new mutation in the mouse affecting the cerebellum. Science. 137:610.

Sidman, R. L., and Green, M. C. (1970) "Nervous," a new mutant mouse with cerebellar disease (Symposium of the Centre National de la Recherche Scientifique, Orleans-la-Source, France). In Les Mutants Pathologiques chez l'Animal Leur Intérêt dans la Recherche Biomédicale (Ed. M. Sabourdy). Paris: CNRS, p. 69.

Sidman, R. L., Green, M. C., and Appel, S. H. (1965) Catalog of the Neurological Mutants of the Mouse. Cambridge: Harvard University Press.

Sotelo, C. (1975) Dendritic abnormalities of Purkinje cells in the cerebellum of neurologic mutant mice (Weaver and Staggerer). In Advances in Neurology, Vol. 12 (Ed. G. W. Kreutzberg). New York: Raven Press.

Sotelo, C., and Changeux, J.-P. (1974) Transsynaptic degeneration "en cascade" in the cerebellar cortex of staggerer mutant mice. Brain Res. 67:519.

Vaughn, J. E., Henrikson, C. K., and Wood, J. G. (1976) Surface specializations of neurites in embryonic mouse spinal cord. Brain Res. 110:431.

Wilson, D. B. (1975) Brain abnormalities in the lurcher (Lc) mutant mouse. Experientia. 31:220.

Wilson, D. B. (1976) Histological defects in the cerebellum of adult lurcher (Lc) mice. J. Neuropath. Exp. Neurol. 35:40.

Yoon, C. H. (1976) Pleiotropic effect of the staggerer gene. Brain Res. 109:206.

RESEARCH TO PRACTICE IN MENTAL RETARDATION
Biomedical Aspects, Volume III
Edited by Peter Mittler
Copyright 1977 I.A.S.S.M.D.

DOWN'S SYNDROME AND AGING OF THE BRAIN

A. J. Dalton and D. R. Crapper
Surrey Place Center,
Toronto Canada, M5S 2C2
Department of Physiology,
University of Toronto, Canada

It has long been known that the brain pathology which is characteristic of Alzheimer's disease is also present in the brain tissues of aging persons with Down's syndrome. Malamud, in a recent neuropathological survey (1972), has reported the presence of Alzheimer's disease in all cases of Down's syndrome over the age of 40 years. This type of brain pathology in persons with Down's syndrome who were younger than 30 years of age was very rare, and it occurred in only two out of 302 brains examined (Malamud, 1972).

While the histopathology of Alzheimer's disease has been well documented (e.g., Wolstenholme and O'Connor, 1970), considerably less is known about the clinical features of this disease in persons with Down's syndrome. Owens, Dawson, and Losin (1971) reported few neuropsychiatric signs in a group of persons with Down's syndrome between the ages of 35 and 50 years. Short-term memory deficits have been described (Dalton, Crapper, and Schlotterer, 1974) in the presence of remarkably few signs of disturbed electroencephalographic (EEG) activity (Crapper et al., 1975).

The present study was undertaken to assess the incidence and nature of deterioration in clinical state compatible with a diagnosis of Alzheimer's disease in aging adults with Down's syndrome. Data were collected over a three-year period and the findings were related to measures of brain pathology as determined by the method of computerized transaxial tomography (CTT) and to measures of physiological disturbances as reflected in EEG activity. For comparative purposes, similar observations were made with a group of young, adult persons with Down's syndrome and a group of mentally retarded adults without Down's syndrome.

This work was supported in part by Grant MA-5364 from the Medical Research Council of Canada and by Grant HD 08893 from the National Institute of Child Health and Human Development of the United States.

METHODS AND PROCEDURES

The subjects were 18 individuals with Down's syndrome ranging in age from 19 to 58 years at the start of the study, and ten mentally retarded persons without Down's syndrome who participated as "Retarded Control" subjects. All the subjects were residents of the same institution. They had been hospitalized for periods ranging from three to 44 years with an average stay of 25.4 years. There were no statistically reliable differences between the groups of subjects on the basis of IQ scores from the Leiter International Performance Scale. Selection of subjects was based on the following criteria: a normal birth record, no history of seizures, no gross sensory or motor impairment, minimal or no evidence of focal neurological signs at the start of the study, and successful mastery of a circle-square visual discrimination task employing matching-to-sample procedures.

Learning and Memory Test Procedures

Tests were conducted with an automated intelligence console measuring 50 cm by 50 cm by 80 cm that contained three rear-projection plastic keys, each 10 cm by 10 cm, located 5 cm apart in a row on the front panel. Three carousel projectors mounted in the interior of the console were used to project images of a circle and a square of the same brightness, size, and colour, on each of the keys. Figure 1 shows the essential elements of the learning and memory test procedures.

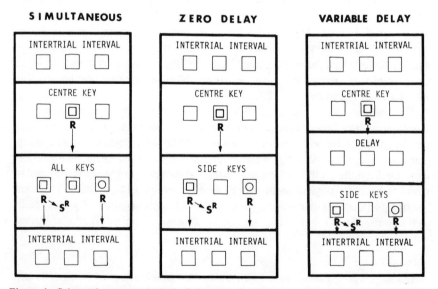

Figure 1. Schematic representation of the essential elements of the learning and memory test procedures. R = press; S^R = reward stimulus.

The Learning Test consisted of trials as depicted in the "simultaneous" condition. A press (R) on the centre key following stimulus onset produced the simultaneous appearance of two choice stimuli on the side keys. A press on the correct side key produced automatic delivery of a poker chip reward (S^R) that was later exchanged for chocolate bars, etc., as part of an incentive system to motivate performance on the task. A press on the incorrect side key produced no reward. A press on either side key terminated the stimuli and initiated an intertrial interval of four to six seconds. The Learning Test required correct matching of the two stimuli during ten consecutive trials. Failure to meet this acquisition criterion led to termination of the experiment after 108 practice trials had been completed.

The Memory Test employed the same apparatus and procedures with two modifications: during "zero delay" and "variable delay" conditions (Figure 1), a press on the centre key produced termination of the stimulus on the centre key and the two choice stimuli appeared on the side keys only after predetermined time intervals had elapsed, which ranged from 0–60 sec (0–30 sec on the 3.0 year retest). Ninety-six memory trials (48 trials on the 3.0 year retest) were administered in a fixed-random order of stimulus and delay interval presentations. The same test procedures were repeated with each subject 1.5 years and 3.0 years after the original test with the differences noted above.

Measures of Brain Pathology

Five of the subjects (Nos. 1, 5, 7, 10, and 11 of Table 1) were admitted as in-patients for CTT brain scans four to nine months after the 3.0 year retest was completed. Two other persons with advanced Alzheimer's disease associated with Down's syndrome also were examined. Photographs of slices through the brain were obtained for each subject using an EMI brain scanner according to procedures described by Wortzman (1975). Each slice was 13 mm thick and each was produced from the computer analysis of 43,200 density readings obtained on a 160 by 160 matrix. Cortical atrophy, ventricular enlargements, tumours, and many other types of brain pathology can be readily detected by this x-ray procedure. Data from the remaining subjects were not available at the time of writing.

Measures of Electrophysiological Disturbances

Electroencephalographic records were obtained from 13 of the 18 subjects with Down's syndrome on two separate occasions separated by three years. EEG recordings were not obtained from the "Retarded Control" subjects. Recording sessions were held under the usual clinical conditions with electrodes placed according to the international 10–20 system. A Grass model 78 ink-writing polygraph was used for all tests. At least two 20-minute records were obtained during each recording session. EEG frequency analyses were performed as described elsewhere (Crapper et al., 1975). Samples of 50 consecutive seconds of artifact-free tracings from occipital and temporal regions were analyzed. The percentages of each run, which was occupied by frequencies of 1–2.9 Hz, 3–7.9 Hz, 8–12.9 Hz, and greater than 13 Hz were measured by an observer who was kept uninformed about the experimental and recording conditions. The aim was to determine the possible presence of EEG abnormalities over the three-year period of the study that might be correlated with observed alterations in performance measures and brain scan measures of pathology in the same subjects.

RESULTS AND DISCUSSION

Results of the first test, the second test held 1.5 years later, and the third test held 3.0 years later, are shown for each subject in Table 1. Separate columns show the individual characteristics of each subject, the number of trials that were required to achieve the criterion of acquisition on the Learning Test, and the overall percentage of correct trials on the Memory Test.

The performances of four subjects (Nos. 1, 2, 3, and 7) in the "Old Down's" group declined to the extent that they were no longer able to relearn the visual discrimination task after their initial success, and thus further testing was terminated. Contrary to expectation, five of the remaining seven subjects in the "Old Down's" group showed improvements in Memory Test scores over the three-year course of the study. These improvements and the final levels of performance attained were indistinguishable from the results obtained with the "Young Down's" group and the "Retarded Control" group. The superior performances of the "Young Down's" and "Retarded Control" groups were expected because it is known that there is a low incidence of the pathological alterations of Alzheimer's disease in deceased persons with Down's syndrome who are younger than 30 years of age (at the time of autopsy) and in mentally retarded persons of any age without Down's syndrome (Malamud, 1972).

The results shown in Table 1, therefore, indicate that four out of eleven "aged" persons with Down's syndrome sampled in the present study performed in such a way as to provide a clinical picture compatible with a diagnosis of Alzheimer's disease. The CTT brain scans provided evidence consistent with the presence of diffuse parenchymal degeneration in Subjects No. 1 and No. 7 and in the two cases of advanced Alzheimer's disease associated with Down's syndrome. No signs were observed of cortical atrophy or ventricular enlargements in Subjects No. 10 and No. 11. Signs of cerebral infarction secondary to atherosclerosis, tumours, or other lesions were absent in all of the subjects studied to date. Calcification associated with the choroid plexus and a right-temporal cavitation, which was apparently left following a cerebrovascular accident sustained one year before the 3.0 year retest, were evident in the CTT brain scans of one subject (No. 5).

Table 1. Learning and memory performance

	S No.	Sex	Age	Leiter IQ	Test	1.5 yr	3.0 yr	Test	1.5 yr	3.0 yr
		Description of subjects			Learning test number of trials			Memory test percent correct		
	1	M	58	20	31	108[a]	108[a]	58		
	2	F	55	33	13	24	108[a]	46	64	
	3	F	51	?	11	108[a]	108[a]	59		
	4	M	49	?	20	10	20	57	74	58
"Old Down's"	5	M	48	27	20	10	31	74	82	83
	6	F	44	23	29	57	15	56	67	88
	7	M	43	20	17	108[a]	108[a]	57		
	8	F	43	21	26	10	12	88	83	60
	9	M	42	23	10	22	10	75	68	79
	10	M	41	?	14	13	10	70	73	77
	11	M	39	40	18	10	10	64	67	75
	12	F	23	33	18	12	17	69	67	69
	13	F	23	21	13	10	10	61	85	73
"Young Down's"	14	M	22	21	20	16	11	73	68	77
	15	F	21	29	10	12	12	60	66	85
	16	F	21	25	22	10	14	77	85	90
	17	M	19	20	26	13	12	56	72	90
	18	M	19	35	20	10	10	68	70	88
	19	M	61	44	14	10	10	69	98	100
	20	M	58	46	10	10	10	100	96	98
	21	M	53	54	12	10	12	76	88	90
	22	M	50	33	10	13	10	86	93	96
"Retarded Controls"	23	M	50	?	10	10	19	96	91	85
	24	M	50	38	12	10	10	73	80	100
	25	M	50	27	10	10	10	99	92	88
	26	M	46	42	10	10	10	83	95	100
	27	F	45	31	17	15	20	56	71	63
	28	M	42	42	11	10	13	93	89	100

[a] These subjects failed to attain the acquisition criterion within 108 practice trials, and, consequently, all further testing was terminated as a result of confounding factors entering into the performance scores.

Figures 2 and 3 illustrate some of the relationships that were noted between the presence or absence of brain pathology as indicated by CTT brain scans and progressive changes in measures of learning (Learning Trials and data represented by the vertical bars) and of memory (Memory Percent Correct and data represented by dots). The cerebral atrophy and ventricular enlargement which appeared in the CTT scans of Subject No. 1 were also found in Subject No. 7 and, in both cases, were correlated with profound deterioration in performance measures during the 1.5 year and the 3.0 year follow-up retests. There was an

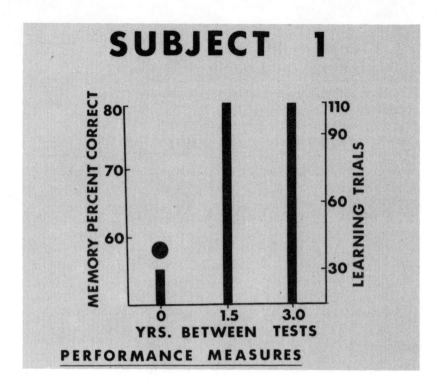

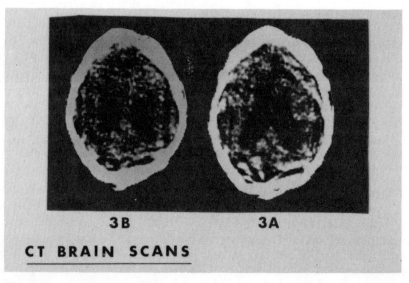

Figure 2. Relationships between two measures of performance and CTT brain scans for a man with Down's syndrome who was 58 years old at the start of the study.

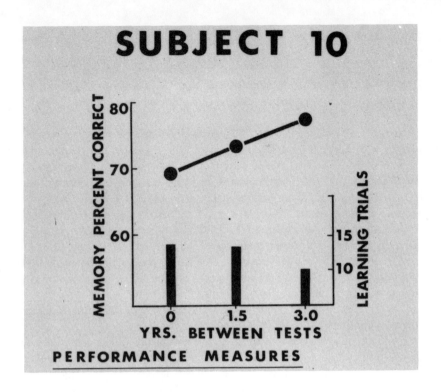

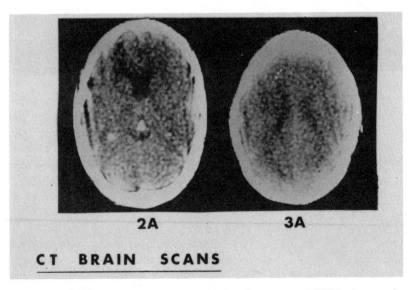

Figure 3. Relationships between two measures of performance and CTT brain scans for a man with Down's syndrome who was 41 years old at the start of the study.

absence of cortical atrophy and ventricular enlargement in the CTT scans of Subject No. 10 (Figure 3) and Subject No. 11 (not shown). In both cases, improvements in performance measures were observed over the three-year course of the study.

Analyses of variance failed to distinguish statistically the EEG activity of the subjects with Down's syndrome when they were separated into two groups on the basis of age. The two groups were neither distinguishable at the time of the first EEG test nor at the time of the second EEG test held three years later, nor were there any significant within-subject changes in the percentages of the various frequency bands. It would seem, therefore, that signs of electrophysiological disturbances, as evidenced by EEG activity, occurred with insufficient frequency or severity to discriminate aging persons with Down's syndrome who may be suffering from Alzheimer's disease from younger persons with Down's syndrome who were expected to remain unaffected. This observation was consistent with a previous finding (Crapper et al., 1975), and it suggests that EEG alterations may be relatively late manifestations of Alzheimer's disease in Down's syndrome.

Evidence of some abnormalities were noted in the EEG tracings of two of the thirteen subjects with Down's syndrome. Figure 4 shows a number of three-second samples of EEG tracings drawn at random from the first five minutes of occipital recordings over the left hemisphere of the four subjects whose data were discussed in some detail above (i.e., Nos. 1, 7, 10, and 11). Slow-wave abnormalities were present in the first EEG and the EEG obtained three years later from Subject No. 1, and in the EEG obtained three years later from Subject No. 7; both of these subjects showed learning and memory performance deficits and cerebral atrophy and ventricular enlargements. On the other hand, there were no discernible differences or abnormalities noted on inspection of the EEG tracings obtained from the other two subjects shown in Figure 4 (Nos. 10 and 11), nor from any of the remaining subjects.

In general, the results indicated that progressive declines in learning abilities were among the early clinical manifestations of Alzheimer's disease in certain aging persons with Down's syndrome. This observation was consistent with an earlier report of short-term memory deficits in persons with Down's syndrome over 44 years of age (Dalton, Crapper, and Schlotterer, 1974). Deterioration in performance levels also was associated with evidence of cerebral atrophy and ventricular enlargements, while improved performance levels seemed to be associated with an absence of pathology as measured by CTT brain scans.

The results further showed that no simple age-related decline in the clinical state of older persons with Down's syndrome occurred. Contrary to expectations based on study of the neuropathological research literature, many of the subjects (five out of eleven) in the "Old Down's" group of the present study showed progressive improvements, rather than declines, in performances over a three-year period. These observations suggest two alternative hypotheses: 1) The extent and distribution or activity of the pathology of Alzheimer's disease may be

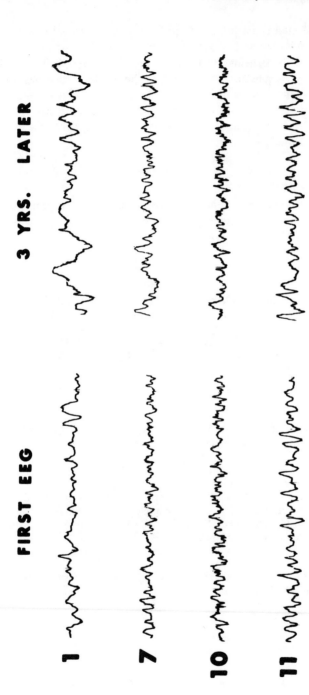

Figure 4. Three-second samples of occipital tracings observed in four adults with Down's syndrome. Tracings were obtained three years apart.

insufficient to be reflected clinically, or, 2) no brain pathology may be present in those individuals who showed progressive improvements in performances. Possibly, the incidence of Alzheimer's disease among older, living persons with Down's syndrome may be substantially lower than the incidence that has been reported among those who come to autopsy. The autopsy-based findings of 100% incidence of Alzheimer's disease in aging Down's syndrome may reflect the possibility that Alzheimer's disease may be a contributing factor to the death of older persons with Down's syndrome.

SUMMARY

Relationships between behavioural, electrophysiological, and histopathological findings are presented in the context of changes observed over a three-year period in aging persons with Down's syndrome.

ACKNOWLEDGMENTS

The assistance and cooperation of the staff and the generous participation of residents and their families from the Huronia Regional Centre, Orillia, Canada are gratefully acknowledged. The authors are also indebted to Mr. G. R. Schlotterer and Mrs. M. Berssenbrugge for their assistance in collecting the performance data. Special thanks are extended to Dr. V. Hachinski, Dr. J. W. Scott, and Dr. G. Wortzman.

REFERENCES

Crapper, D. R., Dalton, A. J., Scott, J. W., Skopitz, M., and Hachinski, V. (1975) Alzheimer degeneration in Down's syndrome: Electrophysiological alterations and histopathology. Arch. Neurol. 32:618.
Dalton, A. J., Crapper D. R., and Schlotterer, G. R. (1974) Alzheimer's disease in Down's syndrome: Visual retention deficits. Cortex. 10:366.
Malamud, N. (1972) Neuropathology of organic brain syndromes associated with aging. In Aging and the Brain (Ed. Gaitz, C. M.). New York: Plenum, p. 63.
Owens, D., Dawson, J. C., and Losin, S. (1971) Alzheimer's disease in Down's syndrome. Amer. J. Ment. Defic. 75:606.
Wolstenholme, G. E. W., and O'Connor, M. (Eds.) (1970) Alzheimer's Disease and Related Conditions. London: Churchill.
Wortzman, G. (1975) Computerized tomography of intracranial lesions. Modern Medicine of Canada. 30:1068.

RESEARCH TO PRACTICE IN MENTAL RETARDATION
Biomedical Aspects, Volume III
Edited by Peter Mittler
Copyright 1977 I.A.S.S.M.D.

A STUDY OF ANTI-BRAIN AUTOIMMUNE ANTIBODIES IN MENTAL RETARDATION OF PARASYPHILITIC ORIGIN

L. V. Sazonova and V. M. Yavkin
Central Institute for Research in Skin and Venereal Diseases,
USSR Ministry of Health; and
Institute of Defectology,
USSR Academy of Pedagogical Sciences,
Moscow, USSR

It is now generally recognized that the mechanisms of autoimmunity are involved in a vast majority of morbid processes. In the last few years, the pathogenesis of a number of diseases (nephritis, rheumatic fever, disseminated lupus erythematosus, etc.) has been reconsidered because autoimmunity can be understood only in the light of recent developments in the field of so-called noninfectious immunology.

That autoimmune mechanisms are involved in the development of various nervous diseases was pointed out by Khoroshko as far back as 1912. However, because of the insufficient development of immunology at that time, interest in the manifestations of autoimmunity disappeared and did not revive until the 1950s and 1960s. Autosensitization to brain antigens has been shown to play a major part in the pathogenesis of multiple sclerosis (Leontovich, 1967), postvaccine neurological complications, traumatic and vascular brain lesions (Gannushkina, 1974), congenital encephalopathies and schizophrenia (Semenov, Nazarov, and Chuprikov, 1973), and epilepsy (Chuprikov, 1973). Antibodies to brain tissue have been detected in 47% of patients with schizophrenia and in 56% of persons with senile dementia (Gurevich, 1969). In recent years, autoanti-

---

As a courtesy to Soviet colleagues, the Editor includes this paper here and regrets that unforseen circumstances prevented it from being read by the authors.

bodies have also been demonstrated to appear in morbid processes associated with the breakdown or defects of tissues (Koliaskina and Kushner, 1969), Semenov and Semenova (1966) have concluded from their clinical immunological studies that autosensitization has a substantial role to play in the pathogenesis of vascular diseases of the brain. Markov (1967) has shown experimentally that allergic sensitization may promote the development of hypertensive disease in the presence of neurotic states. A number of investigators have demonstrated that sensitization with brain antigens promotes the development of convulsive seizures in animals (Gusarov, 1969, 1970). Antibodies to brain tissue have also been found in neurosyphilis (Georgi and Fichery, cited in Skvirsky, Neelova, and Aronovich, 1930). In all such cases, autoimmune reactions either complicate, or are a consequence of, the morbid process.

The mechanism of autoaggression is at present interpreted as follows (Semenov and Popova, 1969). Since the antigen composition of normal antibodies and of those pathologically changed by tissue is similar, the antibodies elaborated in the organism will act not only against those antigens that have caused their formation (i.e., not only against damaged tissues) but also against normal cells. Autoantibodies bring about a secondary damage to the primarily normal cells, and this results in the appearance of autoantigens which in turn stimulate the immunogenic systems of the body. A "vicious circle" is thus formed. This pathogenic mechanism has been used as the basis for singling out a group of autoimmune diseases.

Semenov (1973) has emphasized that the morbid process primarily activates the less specific heterologous brain antigens resulting in earlier and more frequent appearances of antibodies to a heterologous brain.

Studies of autoimmune processes occurring in the maternal body during pregnancy have shown them to affect the neuropsychic development of the child. Semenov, Chuprikov, and Kokhanov (1968) have shown that anti-brain antibodies are detectable in the maternal blood serum if the expectant mother had encephalopathy of infectious-allergic, vascular, or endocrine origin, or was affected with mental diseases (schizophrenia, epilepsy). Anti-brain antibodies are also detectable in the blood of some newborn babies. For that reason, diseases of the central nervous system in postnatal life may sometimes be associated with the autoimmune processes of cerebral origin that occurred in the maternal body. Such women are usually characterized by increased fatigability, irritability, emotional instability, decreased memory, rapid exhaustion of mental functions, and hypochondria. These symptoms often appear in the form of a clinically well-defined asthenic syndrome.

On the basis of his own and other studies, Semenov (1973) considers it a proven fact that anti-brain antibodies produce a neurotropic effect.

Golubovskaya (1970, cited in Semenov, Nazarov, and Chuprikov, 1973) has studied 200 mother-baby pairs. All the mothers had a difficult pregnancy. Of these 200 pairs, anti-brain antibodies were detected in 99 pairs. In the control group of 29 mother-baby pairs, pregnancy and labor were uneventful, and anti-brain antibodies were found in only one pair. In the seropositive group of pregnant women and newborns, the effects of various hazards on the expectant mother were noted twice as often as in the seronegative group, and premature babies were born twice as often in the former group. Follow-up studies of the children over a period of three years showed that symptoms of impairment or delay in the development of brain structures were much more frequent in the seropositive group than in the seronegative one—in 80.4% and 26.0% of the cases, respectively.

Semenov et al. (1972) have carried out immunological studies of young pupils attending general and special auxiliary schools as well as of a group of children with retarded mental development. Comparison of the results of these studies revealed a much larger proportion (40%) of immunepositive cases among mentally retarded children compared to those having uncomplicated oligophrenia or to their normal peers. Reidiboim has shown (1974) that, among oligophrenic children, pathological immune reactions chiefly occur in those with complicated forms of oligophrenia.

METHODS

In view of the fact that the mechanism of origin of parasyphilitic diseases has not yet been fully elucidated and taking into consideration the results of immunological studies discussed above, we have studied anti-brain antibodies in patients suffering from various parasyphilitic diseases as well as in those with different forms of neurosyphilis. The control groups included patients with schizophrenia, oligophrenia of nonsyphilitic origin, chronic alcoholics, and normal subjects.

Blood was taken in the conventional way from the bend of the elbow, inactivated at $36°C$ for 30 min, and absorbed with washed ovine erythrocytes to remove heterophilic antibodies.

Antigen was prepared using a modified procedure of Kuznetsova and Semenov (1961). Antigen I was prepared from cerebellar tissue and antigen II from the gray and white substance of a patient who died of progressive paralysis.

The procedure for preparing the antigen was as follows: brain tissue was homogenized for 10 min and a mixture consisting of one part of ethyl alcohol ($90°C$) and two parts of physiological saline (10 ml of the mixture per g of brain substance) was poured over it. Extraction was continued for 10 days at $2-4°C$, with daily shaking. After the extraction, the material was centrifuged for 1 hr at 2,000 rpm. The supernatant material represented the antigen.

The antigens were tested for protein in a precipitation test with sulfosalicylic acid. The antigens were diluted to half their strength (beginning with 1:50 dilution), and a 20% solution of sulfosalicylic acid was placed under the solution. After 20 min, the highest dilution of the antigens at which the precipitation ring was clearly seen, was determined. The 1:10 dilution with a protein titre of 1:200 was taken to be the initial antigen dilution.

In this test, the method of long-term complement fixation in the cold was used. Before the test, the complement was titrated in the presence of the antigen. The working dose of the complement was equal to its titre plus 70%.

The inactivated test serum was diluted with physiological saline (1:5) and dispensed into three test tubes—0.25 ml in each; 0.25 ml of antigen I, antigen II, and physiological saline were poured into each test tube, respectively. The complement, diluted to the working dose, was added in the amount of 0.25 ml to each test tube. The test tubes were shaken and placed in a refrigerator for 18 hours at 2–4°C and then transferred to a thermostat for 10 min at 37°C; 0.5 ml of the hemolytic system was then added to each of the test tubes. After shaking, the test tubes were placed in a thermostat for secondary incubation until complete hemolysis occurred in the control test tubes.

To obtain positive results, the 4+ serum was diluted with physiological saline to 1:20, 1:40, 1:80, 1:160, and 1:320, and these dilutions were then studied in complement-fixation tests as described above. The result was considered positive if repeat tests gave a serum titre of 1:40 or higher, relative to the antigen at the reaction intensities of 1+ to 4+. If the serum reacted with the brain antigen to 1:20 dilution, the result was considered doubtful, and if it reacted below that dilution, the result was regarded as negative.

RESULTS AND DISCUSSION

A total of 134 blood sera were studied in complement-fixation tests, including 39 from patients with neurosyphilis, 19 from those with chronic alcoholism, 6 from those with schizophrenia, 20 from children with oligophrenia of non-syphilitic origin, 43 from normal subjects, and 47 from patients with para-syphilitic diseases. Concurrently, all subjects were studied in tests of complement fixation with toxoplasma antigen as well as in standard serologic tests for syphilis and in treponemal immobilization tests. The results are shown in Table 1.

In all the control groups, the tests of complement fixation with brain antigen were negative except in five doubtful cases.

The positive reaction of complement fixation by brain antigen and, consequently, the presence of autoimmune antibodies in patients with parasyphilitic diseases could not be considered as accidental because the percentage of positive cases was more than twice as great as the mean percent error (Genes, 1967).

As is known, the clinical course of neurosyphilis is partly determined by the neuroallergic processes that complicate the toxic-infectious effects of an etiological factor, i.e., of *Treponema pallidum*, on the nervous tissue and on the body as a whole. As a result of destructive processes occurring in nervous tissues of patients with neurosyphilis in conditions of increased permeability of the blood-brain barrier, and also partly because of the constitutional predisposition of such patients to antibody formation, a situation probably may develop in which the

Table 1. Results of a study of blood sera in complement-fixation tests with brain antigens and toxoplasma antigen and in serologic tests for syphilis

Diagnosis	No.	Complement-fixation test with brain antigens						Complement-fixation test with toxoplasma antigen			Treponemal test		Standard serologic tests		
		Antigen I			Antigen II										
		Pos.	Doubtl.	Neg.	Pos.	Doubtl.	Neg.	Pos.	Doubtl.	Neg.	Pos.	Neg.	Pos.	Doubtl.	Neg.
Parasyphilitic diseases	47	14 (30 ± 7%)		33 (71 ± 7%)	15 (32 ± 7%)		32 (68 ± 7%)	2 (4 ± 3%)		45 (96 ± 3%)		47 (100%)			47 (100%)
Neurosyphilis	39	23 (59 ± 8%)	7 (18 ± 6%)	9 (23 ± 7%)	22 (56 ± 8%)	9 (23 ± 7%)	8 (20 ± 6%)			39 (100%)	23 (59 ± 8%)	16 (41 ± 8%)	14 (36 ± 8%)	6 (15 ± 6%)	19 (49 ± 8%)
Oligophrenia of non-syphilitic origin	20		4 (20 ± 9%)	16 (80 ± 9%)	1	4 (20 ± 9%)	16 (80 ± 9%)			20 (100%)		20 (100%)			20 (100%)
Schizophrenia	6		1 (17 ± 17%)	5 (83 ± 17%)	2 (33 ± 21%)		4 (67 ± 21%)			6 (100%)		6 (100%)			6 (100%)
Chronic alcoholism	19			19 (100%)			19 (100%)		3 (16 ± 9%)	16 (84 ± 9%)		19 (100%)			19 (100%)
Normal subjects	43			43 (100%)			43 (100%)			43 (100%)		43 (100%)			43 (100%)

organism is sensitized with brain antigens and in which antibodies to brain tissue are formed. This appears to be an important factor in the development of diseases of the brain with a more or less pronounced progradient course such as brain syphilis, tabes dorsalis, progressive paralysis, etc. Many authors believe that the occurrence of autoimmune chain reactions is a sign of a severe disease of destructive type. A similar situation apparently develops in other late forms of syphilis (late congenital syphilis, latent syphilis, secondary relapsing syphilis, etc.), although the clinical picture is less clear. However, in these forms there are also signs of cerebral asthenia.

If the pregnant woman has a late form of syphilis, *Treponema pallidum* may be expected not to penetrate the placenta so that a picture of true congenital syphilis may not develop. However, as has been indicated by many authors, dystrophic processes in fetal tissues do occur (the so-called dystrophic forms of syphilis) under the effect of breakdown products of *Treponema pallidum* and of toxic agents arising when metabolic processes are impaired in the maternal body. Such conditions have been referred to as embryo- and fetopathies (Raits, 1948; Pashkov, 1955; Sukhareva, 1955; Studnitsyn and Stoyanov, 1970; Ilyin, 1975; Pavlov et al., 1975; and others).

CONCLUSIONS

Our results suggest that in addition to the above-mentioned mechanisms, of considerable importance in the diseases under discussion are processes of auto-immunization occurring in the maternal body affected with syphilis. It appears that such processes may be initiated as a result of cerebrospinal fluid pathology and brain tissue injuries that cause the appearance of anti-brain antibodies as well as of brain antigens capable of penetrating the placenta and damaging the tissues of the developing fetal brain. As pointed out by Semenov, Nazarov, and Chuprikov (1973), clearcut clinical symptoms may not appear in the expectant mother and consequently the pathological process sometimes may not be recognized when she is admitted to the maternity home. It is worthy of note that among our subjects, tests of complement fixation by brain antigens were positive almost exclusively in only those children whose mothers had late syphilis (13 cases); in only one case was the test positive in a child whose father had brain syphilis.

The present studies of anti-brain antibodies in the blood of patients with parasyphilitic diseases thus represent an attempt to elucidate one of the pathogenic mechanisms of the origin of these diseases.

SUMMARY

In blood serum of patients with neurosyphilis and patients with mental retardation of parasyphilitic etiology autoantibodies toward cerebral tissue were found that show a significant role of autoimmunization processes in pathogenesis of these diseases.

REFERENCES

Gannushkina, I. V. (1974) Immunologicheskiye aspekty travmy i sosudistykh porazhenii golovnogo mozga (Immunological Aspects of Injuries and Vascular Lesions of the Brain). Moscow: "Meditsina" Publishing House.

Genes, V. S. (1967) Nekotoriye prostiye medoty kiberneticheskoi obrabotki diagnosticheskikh i fiziologicheskikh issledovanii (Some Simple Methods of Cybernetic Processing of the Results of Diagnostic and Physiological Studies). Moscow: "Nauka" Publishing House.

Gurevich, Z. P. (1969) Incomplete anti-tissue autoantibodies in schizophrenia. Zhurnal Nevropathologii i Psikhiatrii im. S. S. Korsakova. 69:11:1683.

Gusarov, V. G. (1969) Experimental confirmation of the role of autoimmunity in the genesis of epilepsy. In Trudy Vsesoyuznoi Konferentsii po Immunopatologii. Leningrad.

Gusarov, V. G. (1970) Sravnitelnoye kliniko-immunologicheskoye issledovaniye bolnykh epilepsiyei (Comparative clinical-immunological study of patients with epilepsy). Author's synopsis of his Candidate's Dissertation. Moscow.

Khoroshko, V. K. (1912) Reaktsii zhivotnogo organizma na vvedeniye nervnoi tkani (nevrotoksiny, anafilaksiya, endotoksiny) (Reactions of the animal organism to administration of nerve tissue (neurotoxins, anaphylaxia, endotoxins). Moscow.

Koliaskina, G. I., and Kushner, S. G. (1969) On some regularities in the appearance of anti-brain antibodies in the blood serum of patients with schizophrenia. Zh. Nevropatol. Psikhiatr. 69: 11:1679.

Kuznetsova, N. I., and Semenov, S. F. (1961) Detection of antibodies to the brain in the serum of patients with nervous and mental diseases. Zh. Nevropatol. i Psikhiatr. 61:6:869.

Leontovich, A. L. (1967) Complement-fixing anti-brain antibodies to an encephalomyelitic brain in patients with disseminated sclerosis. In Voprosy Immunopatologii Nervno-Psikhicheskikh Zabolevanii. Moscow.

Markov, Kh.M. (1967) Allergic sensitization and neurogenic hypertension. Sofia: "Medistina i Fizkultura" Publishing House. (In Bulgarian)

Pashkov, B. M. (1955) Pozdnii vrozhdennii sifilis (Late congenital syphilis). Moscow: "Medgiz" Publishing House.

Pavlov, S. T., Shaposhnikov, O. K., Sampov, V. I., and Ilyin, I. I. (1975) Kozhniye i venericheskiye bolezni (Skin and venereal diseases.) Moscow: "Meditsina" Publishing House.

Raits, M. M. (1948) Sifilis u detei (Syphilis in children). Moscow: "Medgiz" Publishing House.

Reidiboim, M. G. (1974) Nekotoriye immunopatologicheskiye pokazateli deteioligofrenov (Some immunopathological indices in oligophrenic children) (Manuscript). Moscow.

Semenov, S. F., and Semenova, K. A. (1966) Vascular diseases of the brain and phenomena of neuroallergy. In Voprosy pathologii nervnoi sistemy, No. 5. Kishinev.

Semenov, S. F., Chuprikov, A. P., and Kokhanov, V. P. (1968). Anti-brain antibodies in women with brain abnormalities and in their newborn babies. Zh. Nevropathol. i Psikhiatr. 68:12:1819.

Semenov, S. F., and Popova, N.N. (1969) Nervno-psikhicheskiye zabolevaniya v svete immunopatologii mozga (Nervous and mental diseases with special reference to immunopathology of the brain). Moscow: "Meditsina" Publishing House.

Semenov, S. F., Pevzner, M. S., Reidiboim, M. G., and Kogan, R. D. (1972) Comparative study of anti-brain antibodies and brain antigens in the blood serum of children with some developmental abnormalities. Pediatriya. 5:49.

Semenov, S. F., Nazarov, K. N., and Chuprikov, A. P. (1973) Autoimmunniye protsessy pri vrozhdennykh entsefalopatiyakh, epilepsii i shizofrenii (Autoimmune processes in congenital encephalopathy, epilepsy and schizophrenia). Moscow: "Meditsina" Publishing House.

Skvirsky, P., Neelova, N., and Aronovich, G. (1930) Brain antigens and antibodies. Mikrobiol. Zh. 11:2:138.

Studnitsyn, A. A., and Stoyanov, B. G. (1970) Uchebnik kozhnykh i venericheskikh boleznei (Textbook of skin and venereal diseases), Vol. I. Moscow: "Medgiz" Publishing House.

Sukhareva, G. E. (1955)' Klinicheskiye lektsii po psikhiatrii detskogo vozrasta (Clinical Lectures on Child Psychiatry), Vol. I. Moscow: "Medgiz" Publishing House.

RESEARCH TO PRACTICE IN MENTAL RETARDATION
Biomedical Aspects, Volume III
Edited by Peter Mittler
Copyright 1977 I.A.S.S.M.D.

LYSOSOMAL ENZYME ACTIVITY AND NERVE CELL PATHOLOGY IN THREE LIPIDOSES

E. H. Kolodny and R. S. Williams
Departments of Biochemistry and Neuropathology
The Eunice Kennedy Shriver Center for Mental Retardation, Inc.,
at the Walter E. Fernald State School,
Waltham, Massachusetts 02154, and the Department of Neurology,
Massachusetts General Hospital and Harvard Medical School
Boston, Massachusetts, 02114, United States

Considerable progress has been made within the last decade in establishing the nosologic identity of the cerebral lipidoses. Each has a distinctive clinical presentation and pathological anatomy, and most now have a clearly defined biochemical abnormality. Furthermore, technical refinements such as the Golgi methods, electron microscopy, and subcellular fractionation (Kornguth et al., 1974) allow the neurobiologist to define more precisely the pathophysiology of these diseases at the cellular level. Recent studies from our laboratories on the late infantile forms of G_{M2}-gangliosidosis (TSD) and neuronal ceroid-lipo-fuscinosis (NCL), and on Krabbe's globoid leucodystrophy serve to highlight these principles.

CASE HISTORIES

1. The child with late infantile Tay-Sachs disease, a boy of non-Jewish ancestry, appeared normal until after age one year. Beginning at 15 months, his development slowed, he lost interest in his surroundings, his visual coordination was impaired, and he fell more frequently. At age 22 months he could still walk but showed truncal instability. His head circumference was above the 97th percentile, and an ocular squint, cherry-red maculae, and a mild startle response were present. Four months later he was no longer

Supported in part by Grants HD-05515 and HD 04147 from the USPHS, and by the Joseph P. Kennedy, Jr. Memorial Foundation.

walking or feeding himself and by 35 months he had no speech or eyesight and displayed frequent periods of thrashing in his crib. His EEG showed paroxysmal bursts of high-voltage slowing and polyspikes. Death occurred at age 39 months.

2. A diagnostic cerebral biopsy specimen from a $4\frac{3}{4}$ year-old girl with late infantile neuronal ceroid lipofuscinosis was also studied. Her development was normal until age $3\frac{1}{2}$ years when clumsiness, frequent falls, episodes of staring, and worsening speech articulation were noted. She developed myoclonic jerking and occasional incontinence. At the time of her biopsy, there was microcephaly, a marked intellectual deficit, decreased visual acuity, and increased deep tendon reflexes. She displayed a high amplitude, high frequency irregular tremor of her head, trunk, and extremities, and could not stand or walk unassisted. Her EEG showed irregular high-voltage slow-wave activity with spikes, polyspikes, and atypical spike-wave complexes. A preliminary report of the clinical and pathological features of this case appears elsewhere (Williams, Ferrante, and Caviness, 1976a).

3. The patient with Krabbe's disease was a girl whose signs and symptoms began at age 4 months, and included irritability, vomiting, seizures, poor head control, and abnormal posturing. Her CSF protein was 150 mg% and the EEG showed high voltage slow-waves and scattered sharp activity. Subsequently, she developed microcephalus, progressive tetraparesis, blindness, and recurrent pneumonia. She died at age 39 months.

METHODS

Lysosomal enzyme activity was determined in the serum and leucocytes of each case as described previously (Kolodny and Mumford, 1976; Wenger et al., 1974). The biopsy specimen was fixed in either Golgi solution, buffered glutaraldehyde, or 10% formalin and prepared for Golgi and electron microscopic analysis as well as for routine cell and fiber stains. Autopsy tissue was fixed in 10% formalin before Golgi and routine histological analysis, and in buffered glutaraldehyde for electron microscopic analysis. Procedures for Golgi impregnations are published elsewhere (Williams, Ferrante, and Caviness, 1976b).

RESULTS

A specific diagnosis in each case was obtained during life. Lysosomal enzyme assays revealed a deficiency of hexosaminidase A in the boy with late infantile Tay-Sachs disease (TSD) and of galactocerebrosidase in the girl with Krabbe's disease (Table 1). No reliable enzyme test presently exists for the diagnosis of neuronal ceroid-lipofuscinosis (NCL). Accordingly, this diagnosis was made by morphological study of a cortical biopsy (Duffy, Kornfeld and Suzuki, 1968).

Routine Histology

Routine cell and fiber stains for light microscopy suggested neuronal storage in both TSD and NCL. In TSD, neurons were obviously ballooned with PAS

Table 1. Lysosomal enzyme activity in three lipid storage diseases

| Leucocyte enzyme | Specific Activity[a] | | | |
	Late Infantile Tay-Sachs	Late Infantile Neuronal Ceroid-Lipofuscinosis	Krabbe's Disease	Controls
α-galactosidase	31	42		22–37
β-galactosidase	241	106	114	78–113
galactocerebrosidase			0.0	0.44–1.82
β-glucosidase	7.4	5.2		4.1–12.5
β-glucuronidase	97	94		62–88
α-mannosidase	173	190		116–214
total hexosaminidase	1,088	1,078	1,042	600–1,800
% hexosaminidase A	0%	51.2%	73.6%	55%–75%

[a]Specific activity expressed as nmoles/mg leucocyte protein/hour.

positive material which displaced the nuclei to the periphery. In NCL, by contrast, neurons were only occasionally and mildly distended with faintly PAS positive material. Although the patient was highly symptomatic, her biopsy was obtained relatively early in the course of her disease, and evidence of cell loss and astrogliosis was not found. No diagnostic histologic abnormalities were present in the biopsy specimen under the light microscope, but when these same sections were examined under the fluorescence microscope (500 nm) all cells, glial as well as neuronal, fluoresced bright yellow. In Krabbe's disease, the primary focus of pathology was in the white matter. In the cerebrum, and to a lesser extent in the brain stem and cerebellum, there was striking myelin loss with an astrocytic and histiocytic response. Histiocytes were strongly PAS positive but only weakly positive for neutral lipids. Typical globoid cells were found in areas of more active myelin breakdown. In the most severely involved regions of the corona radiata and centrum semiovale, few intact axons could be found in Bodian stains. The subcortical arcuate fibers, by contrast, contained abundant myelinated axons. The cortical mantel remained normal in thickness, and contained apparently normal numbers of well-developed neurons with intact Nissl substance. The normal laminar architecture of the cortex was preserved, and no astrogliosis was evident in grey matter structures. Cells from Krabbe's disease and TSD, in contrast to those from NCL, were not autofluorescent.

Electron Microscopy

A characteristic ultrastructure distinguishes the inclusion bodies in each case. In TSD, neurons contain concentrically laminated bodies (MCBs) bound by a unit membrane. In NCL, the inclusion bodies consist of membranous curvilinear tubular profiles (CLBs), also bound by a unit membrane. They are found in the cytoplasm of all cells, glial and endothelial, as well as neuronal. In both TSD and NCL, inclusion bodies are confined to the cytoplasm in neurons, and though they occasionally can be found concentrated in the dilated proximal axonal segments of cortical pyramids, they are rarely found more distally in axons or dendrites, or elsewhere in the surrounding neuropil. Inclusions in Krabbe's disease are confined to the cytoplasm of histiocytes (globoid cells), and consist of stacks of tightly packed curved or twisted spicules.

Although the morphology of the inclusion bodies was explicit in all three cases, tissue preservation was too poor in the autopsy cases for detailed analysis of intracytoplasmic organelles or synaptic specializations. In the biopsy specimen, however, the neuropil of the cortex contained abundant axon and dendritic terminals complete with morphologically normal type I and type II synaptic specializations. Unattached spines and axons undergoing "dark degeneration" were not found. However, glial processes with rich glial fibrils were judged to be increased in relative volume. In contrast to the apparently normal synaptic density of the surrounding neuropil, type II synapses were rarely found on the somata or initial segments of pyramidal neurons. The rare type II synapses that could be identified with confidence, however, were normal morphologically. Type II synapses are not abundant on the somata of normal neurons (Cragg, 1976), but impressions of their reduced density in the present case were strengthened by the finding that large areas of the membranes of neural somata and initial segments were occluded by proliferative astrocytic processes.

Golgi Impregnations

The Golgi methods are a selective histological technique that, under favorable conditions, impregnates cellular elements in their entirety with an opaque precipitate of chromate and a heavy metal. It is the only technique currently available that permits the detailed study of individual neurons including their axons and recurrent collaterals, and dendritic arbors with spiny postsynaptic specializations.

Findings in TSD were striking, and confirm the recent observations of Purpura and Suzuki (1976). In our autopsy specimen obtained in the terminal stages of the disease, most neurons had beaded, truncated, spine-poor dendrites indicative of neuronal degeneration (Robertson, 1899; Williams, Ferrante, and Caviness, 1976c). The somata of most neurons were dilated in globular fashion, and some contained anomalous spine-like processes similar to those normally found only peripherally on dendrites. The proximal axon segment of most cortical pyramids also was dilated in fusiform fashion, and in many instances, contained both spine-like processes, and longer filamentous processes that were themselves studded with spine-like structures (Figure 1). These anomalous structures, called "meganeurites" by Purpura and Suzuki (1976), are found on most cortical pyramids, but are rarely encountered on stellate nonpyramidal neurons. They occur at the base of the neuron and are interposed between the initial segment and the typical axon which emerges from them. They are in general larger on the smaller cortical pyramids; in some cases their surface area is two to

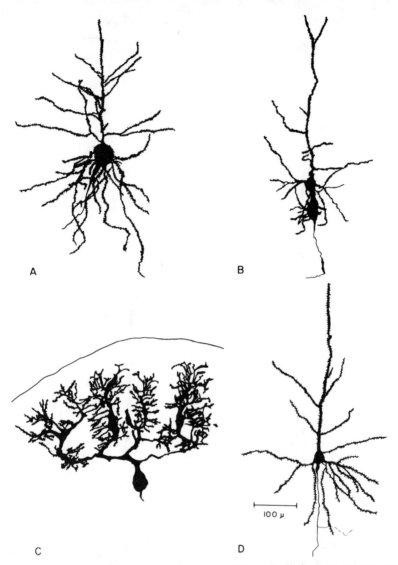

Figure 1. Pyramidal neurons (A and B) and Purkinje cell (C) from an autopsy case of Tay-Sachs disease. The somata of pyramidal cells are swollen and contain numerous anomalous somatic spines. Dendrites are thin with occasional degenerative blebs. Portions of the dendrites in (B) have reduced spine density. There is fusiform (A) to globular (B) expansion of the proximal axon. In (B), anomalous processes with spine-like appendages emerge from the axonal enlargement. An axon of normal caliber emerges from the base of the enlargements, and in (B), contains a degenerative bleb. Purkinje cells (C) characteristically have swollen dendritic processes, especially at the bifurcations of secondary and tertiary branches. Tertiary branchlets are reduced in number and are spine-poor. In contrast to pyramidal cells, enlargements are rarely found on Purkinje cell axons. Illustrated in (D) is a layer III pyramidal neuron from the biopsy specimen of a 4-year-old with late infantile neuronal ceroid-lipofuscinosis. The perikaryon is mildly distended, and there is a fusiform enlargement of the proximal axon segment. Dendrites and spines and the axon that emerges from the enlargement, are morphologically normal (Golgi-rapid preparation, camera lucida drawing).

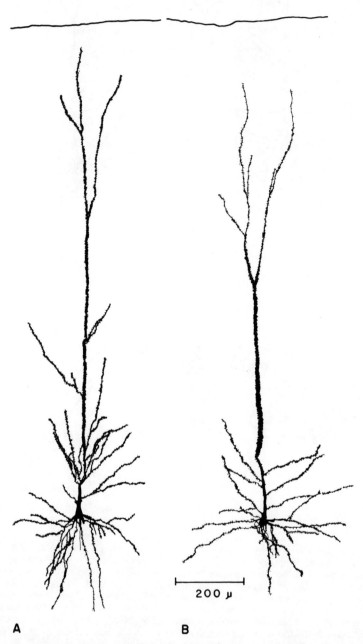

200 μ

A   B

Figure 2. Pyramidal neurons from the precentral gyrus in 3 1/2 year-old Krabbe's disease (A) and 3-year-old normative (B). Dendritic length and branching pattern are comparable. The spine density on the basal dendrites, and oblique branches and terminal arbors of the apical dendrites is also comparable. There is reduced spine density on the mid-portion of the apical shaft in Krabbe's disease (Golgi-rapid preparation, camera lucida drawing).

Figure 3. High power photomicrograph of apical shafts from pyramidal neurons in Figure 2. In Krabbe's disease (A), there are reduced numbers of short stubby spines and a relative predominance of long thin spines (× 2,400).

three times that of the perikaryon. By contrast, they are proportionally smaller in overall surface area on the larger pyramids of layer V. Although found on most neocortical pyramids, they are rarely present on the pyramids of the hippocampus or the granule cells of the dentate fascia, and are not present on Purkinje cells in the cerebellum. Comparable structures are rarely found on dendrites in the cerebral cortex, but Purkinje cell dendrites are often dilated in clubbed or fusiform fashion, especially at bifurcations of secondary and tertiary dendrites (Figure 1.C).

Purpura and Suzuki (1976) had reported neuronal degeneration as the prominant feature in two autopsy cases of juvenile NCL. In our case of late infantile NCL, the biopsy was performed early in the course of the disease, and evidence of neuronal regeneration was not found. Impregnated neurons of all classes had well-developed dendrites, and pyramidal neurons had a normally rich spine investment. The most striking abnormality was a fusiform enlargement of the initial axonal segment of most cortical pyramids as well as some of the multipolar polymorphic neurons of the deepest layers (Figure 1.D). Comparable enlargements were never found on stellate-nonpyramidal neurons. Although these enlargements were similar in location and distribution to those found in TSD, they were never as large, and did not contain spine-like or filamentous processes.

Cortical neurons in Krabbe's disease contained well-developed dendritic arbors that were comparable in their length and branching pattern to age-matched normative controls (Figure 2). Neuronal somata and proximal axons were morphologically normal. Although the dendritic arbors of cortical pyramids appeared well-developed, they were spine-poor relative to normal controls. Reduced spine density was most apparent on the mid-portions of apical shafts of cortical pyramids, where spine density was only 50–80% of normal. Spines of the short stubby type appeared most deficient, and long filamentous spines predominated (Figure 3). Convincing evidence of neural degeneration was not found in Golgi impregnations of Krabbe's disease.

DISCUSSION

Under normal circumstances, the lysosomal enzyme hexosaminidase A is believed to degrade G_{M2}-ganglioside, one of a family of sialoglycolipids found in high concentrations in neurons and synaptic membranes (Derry and Wolfe, 1967). Another lysosomal enzyme, galactocerebrosidase, acts on galactocerebroside, a neutral glycolipid which is an important myelin constituent. Consequently, if hexosaminidase A is deficient, as occurs in Tay-Sachs disease, G_{M2}-ganglioside accumulates causing impairment of nerve cell function. Similarly, in Krabbe's disease, the inability to properly metabolize galactocerebroside because of a deficiency of galactocerebrosidase results in disruption of the myelin membrane and subsequent loss of the afferent and efferent fibers connecting the cerebral cortex with subcortical structures. The underlying enzymatic defect in NCL has not yet been convincingly demonstrated but is presumed to be a disorder in peroxidation causing complex polymers of aminoglycolipids to accumulate within many different types of cells including neurons (Zeman, 1974). Neurons appear to be preferentially vulnerable to the biochemical abnormality, whatever its nature, resulting ultimately in neuronal degeneration.

The accumulation of nondegradeable membranous macromolecular material in the neurons of both TSD and NCL is associated initially with malfunction and ultimately with cell death. The formation of membranous inclusions within neurons may eventually be parasitic with depletion of substances necessary for the formation of normal intracytoplasmic organelles (Zeman, 1974). Additionally, the inclusions appear to be carried into the enlarged proximal axon segments of cortical pyramids. The inclusions may be excluded from the distal segments of axons and dendrites by their absolute size, or by a grating mechanism comparable to that demonstrated for particles of horseradish peroxidase (Holländer, 1975). Pyramidal neurons are projection neurons that characteristically have long axons. Presumably the volume of orthograde and retrograde axoplasmic flow will be higher in these neurons than in local circuit, nonpyramidal neurons which do not demonstrate the enlargements. Conceivably, impaction of inclusions proximal to the axon could lead to disruption of the kinetics of axoplasmic flow resulting in altered hydrolic forces against the walls of the initial segment and perikaryon. The unique physiology of axon and dendrite transport, particularly in projection neurons with long axons, may explain why these cells, more than all other cells in the body, are selectively vulnerable to the ubiquitous inclusions in NCL.

A provocative but less certain observation in NCL is the virtual absence of type II synapses on the somata of cortical pyramids. The validity of this observation is strengthened by the finding that large areas of the perikaryal membrane are occluded by proliferative astrocytic processes. Though the mechanism is not certain, this observation is similar to that of the shedding of axosomatic synapses from anterior horn cells undergoing "axonal reaction" (Grafstein, 1975), or after disruption of the microtubules thought to be necessary for rapid axoplasmic flow (Cull, 1975). Type II synapses are thought to be inhibitory (Palay and Chan-Palay, 1976). Therefore, loss of type II axosomatic synapses early in the course of NCL might explain the diffuse paroxysmal activity of the cortex so characteristic of this and similar cases.

Although the axonal enlargements are similar in location and distribution in NCL and TSD, there are striking differences. Purpura and Suzuki (1976) have pointed out that in Golgi and electron microscopic preparations these enlargements have membrane characteristics more compatible with dendrites than with axon hillock and initial segments. In electron micrographs of their biopsy specimen, they have confirmed that the spine-like processes have morphologically normal type I synapses. There is no precedent for this anomalous membranous and synaptic differentiation in experimental neuropathology, and its pathophysiology with respect to accumulation of G_{M2}-ganglioside is unknown. It is interesting to speculate that this anomalous differentiation may be a manifestation of neuronal plasticity resulting from altered hydrolic forces occurring at a much earlier stage of neuronal development than NCL. Whatever the mechanism of formation, the altered synaptic relationships inherent in the basal position of the "meganeurites" would likely result in neuronal hyperexcitability (Purpura and Suzuki, 1976), consistent with clinical and EEG findings in TSD.

Despite almost total disruption of major extrinsic afferent and projection efferent cortical axons in Krabbe's disease, there is no convincing evidence for neuronal degeneration or loss. Dendritic arbors have developed well beyond their appearance in the neonatal period, and in most respects, are comparable to age-matched controls. These observations are in accord with experimental literature on the isolated cortex of animals (Cajal, 1928; Purpura and Housepian, 1961; Rutledge, Duncan, and Cart, 1972), and suggest that neurons have survived and continued to develop by virtue of the sustaining influence of local intracortical connections. Although dendritic development is comparable to normal development, spine density is less than normal, especially on the apical shafts of cortical pyramids. In the present case, we cannot be sure to what extent this is a result of loss of extrinsic afferents, or is a result of axonotomy of the affected neurons themselves. However, similar changes in spine density have been observed in experimental animals after denervation of the specific thalamic afferents of the visual cortex (Globus and Scheibel, 1967; Valverde, 1968). Although intrinsic disease of neurons has not been demonstrated in Krabbe's disease, the altered synaptic relationships attendant to axonal loss could be expected to result in paroxysmal activity of the cortex as observed in this case, and in experimental animals (Purpura and Housepian, 1961).

CONCLUSION

Recent advances in the neurochemistry of the cerebral lipidoses have disclosed a specific enzyme deficit in most cases, presumably reflecting the direct consequence of a single autosomal mutation. The accumulation of nondegradeable stored substrates in most instances leads to the formation of characteristic (though usually not specific) membranous intracytoplasmic inclusions. The mechanisms by which these membranous inclusions are generated remains largely unknown, but analysis of these cases with high resolution techniques such as the Golgi methods and electron microscopy, has permitted new insights into the pathophysiology of these diseases at the cellular level. In some cases, these methods have allowed us to determine why neurons, even certain classes of neurons, seem to be preferentially vulnerable.

ACKNOWLEDGMENTS

Our sincere appreciation to Mr. Robert Ferrante for preparation of the illustrations, and to Mrs. Dora Paglierani for preparation of the manuscript.

REFERENCES

Cajal, S. R. Y. (1928) Degeneration and Regeneration of the Nervous System. Vol. 2. New York: Hafner (reprinted 1959).

Cragg, B. G. (1976) Ultrastructural features of human cerebral cortex. J. Anat. 121:331.

Cull, R. E. (1975) Rôle of axonal transport in maintaining central synaptic connections. Exp. Brain Res. 24:97.

Derry, D. M., and Wolfe, L. S. (1967) Gangliosides in isolated neurons and glial cells. Science. 158:1450.

Duffy, P. E., Kornfeld, M., and Suzuki, K. (1968) Neurovisceral storage disease with curvilinear bodies. J. Neuropath. Exp. Neurol. 27:351.

Globus, A., and Scheibel, A. B. (1967) Synaptic loci on visual cortical neurons of the rabbit: The specific afferent radiation. Exp. Neurol. 18:116.

Grafstein, B. (1975) The nerve cell body response to axonotomy. Exp. Neurol. 48:32.

Holländer, H. (1975) Observations on cortical neurons labeled with horseradish peroxidase. *In* Advances in Neurology, Vol. 12, Physiology and Pathology of Dendrites, (Ed. G. W. Krutzberg) New York: Raven Press, p. 315.

Kolodny, E. H., and Mumford, R. A. (1976) Human leukocyte acid hydrolases: characterization of eleven lysosomal enzymes and study of reaction conditions for their automated analysis. Clin. Chim. Acta. 70:247.

Kornguth, S., Wannamaker, B., Kolodny, E., Geison, R., Scott, G., and O'Brien, J. F. (1974) Subcellular fractions from Tay-Sachs brains: ganglioside, lipid, and protein composition and hexosaminidase activities. J. Neurol. Sci. 22:383.

Palay, S. L., and Chan-Palay, V. (1976) A guide to synaptic analysis of the neuropil. Cold Spring Harbor Symp. Quant. Biol. 40:1.

Purpura, D. P., and Housepian, E. M. (1961) Morphological and physiological properties of chronically isolated immature cortex. Exp. Neurol. 4:377.

Purpura, D. P., and Suzuki, K. (1976) Distortion of neuronal geometry and formation of aberrant synapses in neuronal storage disease. Brain Res. (in press).

Robertson, W. F. (1899) Normal and pathological histology of the nerve cell. Brain. 22:203.

Rutledge, L. T., Duncan, J., and Cant. N. (1972) Long term status of pyramidal cell axon collaterals and apical dendritic spines in denervated cortex. Brain Res. 41:249.

Valverde, F. (1968) Structural changes in the area striata of the mouse after enucleation. Exp. Brain Res. 5:274.

Wenger, D. A., Sattler, M., Clark, C., and McKelvey, H. (1974) An improved method for the identification of patients and carriers of Krabbe's disease. Clin. Chim. Acta. 56:199.

Williams, R. S., Ferrante, R. J., and Caviness, V. S., Jr. (1976a) The cellular pathology of late infantile neuronal ceroid-lipofuscinosis. (Abstract) J. Neuropath. Exp. Neurol. 35:310A.

Williams, R. S., Ferrante, R. J., and Caviness, V. S., Jr. (1976b) The cellular Golgi analysis pathology of microgyria: A Golgi Analysis. Acta Neuropathol. 36:269.

Williams, R. S., Ferrante, R. J., and Caviness, V. S., Jr. (1976c) The Golgi-rapid method in clinical neuropathology: The morphologic consequences of suboptimal fixation. J. Neuropath. Exp. Neurol. (in press).

Zeaman, W. (1974) Presidential address: Studies in the neuronal ceroid-lipofuscinoses. J. Neuropath. Exp. Neurol. 33:1.

RESEARCH TO PRACTICE IN MENTAL RETARDATION
Biomedical Aspects, Volume III
Edited by Peter Mittler
Copyright 1977 I.A.S.S.M.D.

PROTEIN TOPOGRAPHY IN HUMAN SYNAPSES AND SMOOTH ENDOPLASMIC RETICULUM

S. Kornguth
Neurochemistry Laboratories,
Waisman Center Room 659,
University of Wisconsin,
2605 Marsh Lane,
Madison, Wisconsin 53706,
United States

The protein components of isolated synapses have been investigated for the following reasons: the historical evidence that proteins and glycoproteins frequently participate in processes involving cellular interactions such as synaptogenesis (e.g., antibody production, phage-membrane interactions), the strong evidence that unique antigenic determinants are present in synaptic endings (Wald et al., 1968; Kornguth, 1969; Mickey et al., 1971), and the demonstration that transmitter receptors are enriched in the synaptic region (Bosmann, 1972). A most impressive observation of the previous studies is that the protein compositions of synapses from 1) different species (human, macaque, swine, guinea pig, rat, and mouse) (Banker, Crain, and Cotman, 1972; Grossfeld and Shooter, 1971; Wannamaker and Kornguth, 1972; Jones, Mahler and Moore, 1975), 2) different brain regions, and 3) different stages of ontogeny are similar with respect to molecular weights of the major protein constituents. Additionally, although synapses have unique ultrastructural features, the protein components of the synapse appear to be the same as those of smooth endoplasmic reticulum and microsomes (Wannamaker and Kornguth, 1972; Jones, Mahler, and Moore, 1975) as demonstrated by electrophoresis on several acrylamide gel systems. An exception to this is the observation in Dr. Rapport's laboratory (Korenovsky, Mahadik, and Rapport, 1975) that gradient gel electrophoresis reveals several minor proteins unique to the synaptosome and others unique to smooth endoplasmic reticulum.

The major proteins of the synaptic complexes isolated in CsCl-sucrose gradients (Wannamaker and Kornguth, 1972) and in Ficoll-sucrose gradients

(Banker, Crain, and Cotman, 1972) have molecular weights of 97,000, 53,000, 43,000, and 36,000. These proteins may be single-chain proteins or subunits of multi-chain proteins because sodium dodecyl sulfate and β-mercaptoethanol were in the gels. In our laboratory, it was shown that the major 53,000 molecular weight (MW) protein from human and swine synaptic endings was tubulin (Kornguth and Sunderland, 1975). Banker, Churchill, and Cotman (1974) demonstrated that a protein of similar molecular weight was the major component of isolated postsynaptic densities. The majority of proteins within the synaptic ending remain to be characterized and localized with the synaptic membrane.

One must then ask whether the unique morphology and antigenic properties of the synaptic membrane reflect the existence of unique proteins in this membrane system or if they are attributable to an unusual topographic organization of proteins common to the synapse and other membranes. If the latter hypothesis is correct, then studies on the organization of proteins within the synaptic membrane become important to the understanding of the molecular basis of synapse formation.

Within the past year, Mahler and colleagues (Wang, Crawford, and Mahler, 1975) have demonstrated that the external surface proteins of synaptosomes isolated in Ficoll-sucrose gradients may be distinguished from internal proteins by lactoperoxidase catalyzed iodination. They found that proteins with molecular weights of 145, 118, 100, 66, 50 and 35 K daltons were external surface proteins and those of 205, 185, 92 and 39 K daltons were internal proteins.

This chapter describes the distribution of proteins in the human and swine synaptic ending. Intact synaptic complexes were isolated from swine cerebral cortices and human frontal and occipital lobe cortices by centrifugation in discontinuous sucrose gradients and subsequently in continuous CsCl-sucrose gradients. The purity of swine synaptic endings prepared by this method was shown to be $> 85\%$ and the purity of the human synaptosomes were shown to be $> 57\%$ by electron microscopic analysis (Kornguth, 1974). Two separate preparations of swine synaptic complexes ($\rho1.185$) were radioiodinated by the methods to be described. The human synaptic endings ($\rho1.185$) were obtained from a 21-year-old male that died with a choriocarcinoma. The isolated synaptic complexes were radioiodinated by three different procedures: 1) chloramine T catalysis in the presence of low iodide concentrations (1.0 mCi of carrier free ^{125}I per 500 μg of protein); 2) chloramine T catalysis in the presence of high iodide concentrations (1.0 mCi of ^{125}I mixed with 50 μl of 0.001 M NaI per 500 μg of protein); and 3) lactoperoxidase catalysis in the presence of high iodide concentrations. Experiments with viruses (Montelaro and Rueckert, 1975) indicated that iodination with chloramine T at low iodide concentrations resulted in the selective iodination of external surface proteins. At high iodide concentrations all viral proteins were labeled to a similar extent. By analogy with the viral system, the first procedure labels external surface proteins of the isolated synaptic endings including the cleft zone because the small size of the chloramine T permits penetration of the cleft. The second method randomly labels all the external and internal compartment proteins. The third method selectively labels external surface proteins except for those in the cleft because of the large molecular weight of lactoperoxidase. If the three procedures yield similar labeling patterns, it may be concluded that either there is no asymmetry to the distribution of proteins on the external and internal synaptic membrane surfaces (unlikely in light of Mahler's data (Wang, Crawford, and Mahler, 1975), or that the compartmentation was destroyed during the extensive isolation procedure. If the labeling pattern does indicate an asymmetry of protein distribution, it may be concluded that the isolated synaptic endings retain compartmentation; we can then designate which proteins are in each membrane surface. Additionally, the labeled proteins can be used to facilitate identification of protein peaks after they have been separated by chromatography on ion exchange resins, G-200 Sephadex filtration, and preparative gel electrophoresis.

Tables 1 and 2 report the relative iodination of proteins within the isolated human and swine synaptic ending. It may be observed that there was a marked asymmetry to the distribution of synaptic membrane proteins. A 35,000 to 36,000 MW protein was labeled to a greater extent by chloramine T catalysis

Table 1. Distribution of proteins in synaptic endings from human brain (percent of ^{125}I in each protein band)

Molecular weight	Lactoperoxidase	Chloramine T High I	Chloramine T Low I	Location
29,000	4.78 (±0.40)	5.30 (±0.17)	3.68 (±0.19)	Internal
33,000	5.35 (±0.40)	5.65 (±0.32)	6.44 (±0.14)	Not asymmetrical by lactoperoxidase
36,000	4.69 (±0.05)	5.52 (±0.50)	7.43 (±0.67)	Restricted (out)
39,000	4.63 (±0.03)	5.40 (±0.16)	4.66 (±0.04)	Internal
42,500	9.43 (±0.45)	9.40 (±0.19)	6.70 (±0.01)	Not asymmetrical by lactoperoxidase
46,500	6.50 (±0.12)	6.93 (±0.27)	6.40 (±0.11)	Not asymmetrical
49,500	7.27 (±0.90)	10.88 (±0.83)	9.17 (±0.22)	Internal
54,000	14.89 (±0.10)	12.85 (±0.01)	13.19 (±0.31)	Slight external
61,000	7.77 (±0.13)	6.85 (±0.52)	8.06 (±0.30)	External
66,000	11.99 (±0.18)	9.29 (±0.30)	12.48 (±0.75)	External
75,000	10.79 (±0.24)	10.51 (±0.11)	10.59 (±0.26)	Not asymmetrical
87,000	11.91 (±0.43)	11.43 (±0.90)	11.24 (±0.39)	Not asymmetrical

These data are the averages of two completely separate iodination experiments. The percent of radioactivity in each peak was determined as follows: the counts per minute in each 3 mm zone of peak radioactivity were summed and then the total counts per minute in the 12 peaks were calculated. The counts were peak divided by the total counts in the 12 peaks represent the percentage. The peaks were all calculated from 10% polyacrylamide gels. Proteins were determined to be asymmetrically distributed when the ratio of the low iodide to high iodide percentages was less than 0.85 (the larger of the two percentages must be in the denominator of the ratio).

Table 2. Distribution of proteins in synaptic endings from swine brain (percent of ^{125}I in each protein band)

Molecular weight	Lactoperoxidase	Chloramine T High I	Chloramine T Low I	Location
29,000	4.05 (±0.26)	5.92 (±.10)	4.67 (±.04)	Internal
31,500	5.66 (±0.33)	9.98 (±.67)	4.45 (±.12)	Internal
35,000	7.18 (±0.22)	9.57 (±.29)	10.70 (±.73)	Restricted (out)
38,500	5.48 (±0.26)	6.53 (±.01)	4.74 (±.47)	Internal
42,500	8.98 (±0.56)	7.62 (±.40)	6.20 (±.17)	Out by lactoperoxidase
46,500	6.74 (±0.56)	6.98 (±.43)	6.30(±1.09)	Not asymmetrical
50,000	6.45 (±0.06)	7.32 (±.16)	5.94 (±.21)	Internal
54,000	19.89 (±0.45)	12.39 (±.19)	22.56 (±.20)	External
60,000	8.40 (±0.20)	8.31 (±.54)	8.20 (±.28)	Not asymmetrical
66,000	7.93 (±0.25)	7.80 (±.19)	7.87 (±.32)	Not asymmetrical
75,000	8.64 (±0.17)	8.16 (±.01)	8.17 (±.30)	Not asymmetrical
87,000	9.30 (±0.49)	9.40 (±.71)	10.14(±1.33)	Not asymmetrical

These data are the averages of two completely separate iodination experiments. The percent of radioactivity in each peak was determined as follows: the counts per minute in each 3 mm zone of peak radioactivity were summed and then the total counts per minute in the 12 peaks were calculated. The counts per peak divided by the total counts in the 12 peaks represent the percentage. The peaks were all calculated from 10% polyacrylamide gels. Proteins were determined to be asymmetrically distributed when the ratio of the low iodide to high iodide percentages was less than 0.85 (the larger of the two percentages must be in the denominator of the ratio).

with low iodide than by either lactoperoxidase or chloramine T with high iodide concentrations; therefore, it is a cleft protein in swine and human synapses. The 42 and 54 K dalton proteins of swine synapses were more extensively labeled by lactoperoxidase than by chloramine T and high iodide and were therefore external membrane proteins. The proteins from swine synapses of 29, 31.5,

Table 3. Distribution of proteins in smooth endoplasmic reticulum membranes from human brains (percent of ^{125}I in each protein band)

Molecular weight	Lactoperoxidase	Chloramine T High I	Chloramine T Low I	Location
29,000	4.00	5.35	4.27	Internal
33,000	4.98	6.85	6.56	Internal or restricted
36,000	2.86	5.58	4.18	Internal
39,000	7.60	7.05	6.68	Not asymmetrical
42,500	6.44	10.38	5.45	Internal
46,500	8.53	6.35	8.84	External
49,500	17.03	9.22	13.42	External
54,000	6.89	10.94	8.36	Internal
61,000	10.43	7.51	12.54	External
66,000	9.99	8.17	9.14	Slight external distribution
75,000	9.32	10.32	9.45	Not asymmetrical
87,000	12.24	12.27	11.11	Not asymmetrical

38.5, and 50 are internal. In the human synapses, the 54, 61, and 66 K dalton proteins are external, and the 29, 39, and 49.5 K dalton proteins are internal. Our data indicate that the proteins of the synaptic endings prepared in CsCl-sucrose gradients retain their asymmetric distribution. The prolonged centrifugation in CsCl does not seem to facilitate entry of lactoperoxidase into the synaptic envelops more readily than does the short centrifugation in Ficoll-sucrose gradients used by Mahler.

Because of previous results from our laboratory indicating that the protein composition of smooth endoplasmic reticulum (SER) was essentially identical to that of synaptic membranes (determined by their electrophoresis on acrylamide gels containing 8 M urea and 1% SDS), the topographic distribution of proteins within the SER fraction was determined (Table 3). It may be seen that the 46.5, 49.5, and 61 K dalton proteins are the only ones that appear primarily as external surface components. The 29, 36, 42.5, and 54 K dalton proteins are primarily internal. Although the total protein patterns of synaptic endings and SER are similar (as determined by gel electrophoresis and comparison of labeling with chloramine T and high iodide concentrations) the topographic distribution of proteins within the membranes of these two subcellular compartments is markedly different.

It is of particular interest that the 35,000 MW protein is restricted in human and swine brains because synaptic endings isolated from Tay-Sachs brain samples had a markedly reduced (or absent) content of the 35,000 MW component (Kornguth et al., 1974). It is then imperative to determine whether or not synaptic endings recovered from retardates' brains generally have a depleted level of this 35,000 cleft protein.

SUMMARY

The experiments reported demonstrate that proteins are asymmetrically distributed in the membranes of synaptic endings that were isolated from human and swine brains. Some proteins are primarily on the external surface of these synapses, others are primarily in the internal compartment and a third group appears to be uniformly distributed. A 35–36,000 molecular weight protein is restricted in the synapse. It is of interest with respect to mental retardation that this restricted protein is either absent from or markedly depleted in synapses recovered from Tay-Sachs brains.

REFERENCES

Banker, G., Churchill, L., and Cotman, C. (1974) Proteins of the postsynaptic density. J. Cell. Biol. 63:456.
Banker, G., Crain, B., and Cotman, C. (1972) Molecular weights of the polypeptide chains of synaptic plasma membranes. Brain Res. 42:508.

Bosmann, H. (1972) Acetylcholine receptor. J. Biol. Chem. 247:130.

Grossfeld, R., and Shooter, E. (1971) A study of the changes in protein composition of mouse brain during ontogenic development. J. Neurochem. 18:2265.

Jones, L., Mahler, H., and Moore, W. (1975) Synthesis of membrane protein in slices of rat cerebral cortex. J. Biol. Chem. 250:973.

Korenovsky, A., Mahadik, S., and Rapport, M. (1975) Characterization of rat brain subcellular fractions by electrophoresis of SDS extracts on slab gels. Neurosci. Soc. Abs. 1:603.

Kornguth, S. (1974) The synapse: A perspective from in situ and in vitro studies. *In* Reviews of Neurosciences Vol. 1 (Ed. Ehrenpreis, S., and Kopin, I.) New York: Raven Press, p. 63.

Kornguth, S., Anderson, J., and Scott, G. (1969) Isolation of synaptosomes in a cesium chloride density gradient: Electron microscopic and immunohistochemical studies. J. Neurochem. 16:1017.

Kornguth, S., and Sunderland, E. (1975) Isolation and partial characterization of a tubulin-like protein from human and swine synaptosomal membranes. Biochim. Biophys. Acta. 393:100.

Kornguth, S., Wannamaker, B., Kolodny, E., Geison, R., Scott, G., and O'Brien, J. (1974) Subcellular fractions from Tay-Sachs brains: Ganglioside, lipid and protein composition and hexosaminidase activities. J. Neurol. Sci. 22:383.

Mickey, D., McMillan, P., Appel, S., and Day, E. (1971) The specificity and cross-reactivity of antisynaptosome antibodies as determined by sequential adsorption analysis. J. Immun. 107:1599.

Montelaro, R., and Rueckert, R. (1975) On the use of chloramine T to iodinate specifically the surface proteins of intact enveloped viruses. J. Gen. Virol. 29:127.

Wald, F., Mazzuchelli, A., Lapetina, G., and De Robertis, E. (1968) The effect of antiserum against nerve-ending membranes from cat cerebral cortex on the bioelectrical activity of mollusc neurons. Exp. Neurol. 21:336.

Wang, Y., Crawford, G., and Mahler, H. (1975) Topography of the synaptic plasma membrane. Neurosci. Soc. Abs. 1:618.

Wannamaker, B., and Kornguth, S. (1972) Electrophoretic patterns of proteins from isolated synapses of human and swine brain. Biochim. Biophys. Acta. 303:333.

NEUROPSYCHOLOGICAL ASPECTS

RESEARCH TO PRACTICE IN MENTAL RETARDATION
Biomedical Aspects, Volume III
Edited by Peter Mittler
Copyright 1977 I.A.S.S.M.D.

HEART RATE AND RESPIRATORY RESPONSES DURING VISUAL SEARCH IN NORMAL AND RETARDED CHILDREN

S. W. Porges and M. M. Humphrey
Department of Psychology,
University of Illinois,
Urbana-Champaign, Illinois 61820,
United States

Aside from the common IQ definition of mental retardation, there are many behavioral characteristics that distinguish a retardate from a normal individual. Behaviorally, retardates have slow reaction times (Baumeister and Kellas, 1968), poor inhibitory skills (Denny, 1964; Krupski, 1975), and exhibit an attentional deficit (Zeaman and House, 1963; Leibert and Baumeister, 1973; Krupski, 1975). These characteristics, although quite general, describe a global pattern of behavioral incompetence that distinguishes retardates from normal individuals.

One reason often proposed for the retardate's poor performance in problem-solving tasks is his difficulty in inhibiting responses to irrelevant stimuli (Zeaman and House, 1963; 1967; Furby, 1974). This deficiency may prevent the retardate from attending to relevant, although often less salient, cues in a situation. This inhibitory deficit, actually a deficit in sustaining and focusing attention, may result in the retardate's inability to obtain sufficient information to perform adequately. It is possible that the cumulative effect of this inability might be reflected in deficient cognitive development (c.f., Weisz and Achenbach, 1975).

This chapter will focus on a specific category of inhibitory skills in which the retardate is deficient. This category of behavior is characterized by an inability to sustain attention. One problem in the study of the etiology of pathological attention has been the ambiguity associated with defining the construct of attention. Psychologists often disagree about the definition of attention. Responses associated with attention have ranged from reactions to massive changes in stimulation (such as a startle response) to the active instrumental behavior associated with sustained or focused attention. The notion that there may be different psychological processes associated with the construct of attention is not new. James (1890) distinguished between passive-reflexive and active-voluntary attention. Passive-involuntary attention was always immediate and related only to objects that directly affected the sensory systems. Voluntary attention was associated with the concept of interest or selection and could be directed toward sensory objects or toward ideational as well as represented objects.

In a series of psychophysiological studies, different heart rate response components have been associated with different types of attention (Porges, 1972; Porges et al., 1975). Based on observations from these studies and the use of multivariate statistics such as factor analysis (Cheung, 1973) and discriminant analyses (Walter and Porges, 1976), a two-component model of attention has been postulated that parallels the two categories of attention identified by James. The first component is associated with reactive attention and is indexed by short-latency, directional, heart rate responses to changes in stimulation. This component is generally reflexive in nature, short in direction, and parallels either the orienting reflex or defensive reflex. The second component is associated with sustained or tonic attention and is correlated with a reduction of heart rate variability (the interbeat intervals become more constant) and a generalized inhibition of motor and respiratory activity (either reduced respiratory amplitude or a temporary cessation of breathing). This response persists as long as the subject elects to attend. The present study was designed to assess the ability to sustain attention in normal and retarded subjects. Thus the response system into which the task is attempting to delve shall be characterized by inhibition on a behavioral level of not responding to irrelevant stimuli, and by suppression of heart-rate variability and respiratory activity on a physiological level.

The task was designed to maximize the occurrence of physiological responses associated with sustained attention by requiring only slight motor responses and by maintaining the duration of the task to facilitate the occurrence of sustained responses.

Two similar experiments were performed: one with normal grade-school children and a second with retarded adolescents of approximately the same mental age as the grade-school children. Twenty-nine children (13 males and 16 females) between the ages of 5.9 and 8.8 ($\bar{x}$ = 7.1) participated in Experiment I. All subjects were enrolled in an elementary school in Urbana, Illinois. All children were seen individually for a cognitive assessment and desensitization session. A week later, the sustained visual attention task was given, during which heart rate and respiratory responses were assessed. All data were collected in the spring of the school term. Sixteen adolescent retardates (ten males and six females) between the ages of eight and 26 ($\bar{x}$ = 19) with mental ages between three and eight years ($\bar{x}$ = 5.9) participated in Experiment II. All subjects were residents of the Wheeler School for Exceptional Children, a small private school located in Rankin, Illinois. All subjects were tested in the late summer. The procedures and data quantification for the two studies were identical.

METHOD

All sessions were conducted in a two-room mobile laboratory located on the school grounds. During the first session, the subjects were given a series of tasks designed to assess development of four cognitive skills. They were presented two problems each of numerosity, class inclusion, egocentrism, and conservation of liquids.

During the second session, the subjects participated in a sustained visual attention task while the electrocardiogram (ECG) and respiration were monitored. The ECG-recording sites on the back of the child were cleaned with 70% ethanol before the application of Beckman Bio-potential silver-silver-chloride electrodes that were filled with electrode paste and attached with Beckman adhesive collars. The placement was chosen to reduce the influence of movement artifacts on heart rate. Respiration was monitored using rubber bellows placed around the child's thorax. As the child breathed, the change in pressure produced by the bellows was transduced into voltage by a Grass Model PT5A volumetric pressure transducer and recorded on a Sony Model TC 353D tape recorder with a Vetter Model 3 FM adapter or Hewlett Packard Model 3960 FM tape recorder via a Beckman Type RS dynograph.

After electrodes were attached and respiration bellows secured, the subject (S) was seated in the experimental room of the laboratory, facing a response panel and a $30'' \times 30''$ rear projection screen that was used to present the visual attention task. Immediately before the task, 90 seconds of prebaseline ECG and respiration data were collected. Each display slide contained four cartoon pictures bordered in red, green, yellow, or blue; one in each quadrant of the slide. S was instructed to search for drawings of "Snoopy" hidden in the four pictures on the projected slide. S was to press the "on" button on the response panel to illuminate the colored lights on the panel corresponding to the colors of the borders on the pictures in which Snoopy appeared. If a Snoopy was not in a picture, that picture's corresponding light was to remain off. "Off" buttons also were located on the response panel to allow S to change a choice if desired. S was instructed to press a final "all done" button on the panel when the S felt he had finished searching for all Snoopys. This last response marked the end of the trial that had begun when the slide was displayed. Between the termination and onset of subsequent trials was an intertrial period of 15 or 20 seconds. The task consisted of five warmup trials and 15 test trials.

Each of the 15 test trials was divided into three five-second periods: a pretrial period consisting of five seconds immediately before the slide onset; a second period consisting of the first five seconds after trial onset; and a third period consisting of seconds six through ten after trial onset. ECG and respiration were sampled second-by-second during each of the within-trial periods. Only trials which had a duration of at least ten seconds were used for the data analyses. Since all subjects did not have the same number of trials with a duration of more than ten seconds, second-by-second, mean heart rate, and heart-rate variability during each within-trial period for each subject, collapsed over trials, were used for all analyses of physiological responses. Because of the long response times for the retardates, two additional five-second periods were sampled of on-trial ECG and respiration.

It has been hypothesized that the retardate is capable of inhibiting ongoing activity but that it takes him longer to gain control. To gain additional information regarding this hypothesis, two additional five-second periods of heart rate variability activity were quantified and analyzed.

RESULTS

Recalling the initial hypothesis regarding the relationship between attentional deficit and physiological activity, we might predict that normal subjects would exhibit a suppression of heart rate variability while retardates would not.

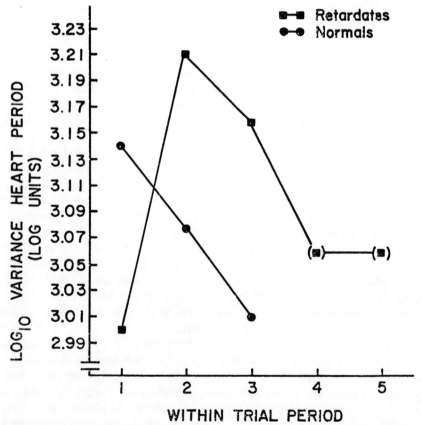

Figure 1. Heart-rate variability during the pretrial (Period 1) and on-task periods for retardates and normals.

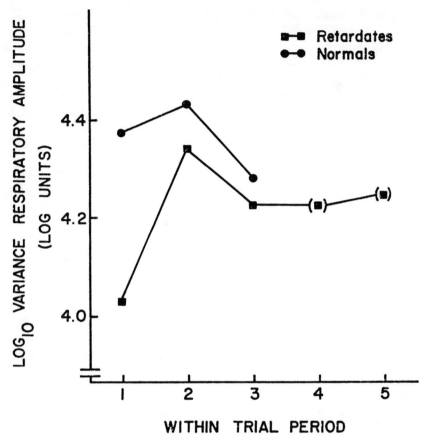

Figure 2. Respiratory amplitude variability during the pretrial (Period 1) and on-task periods for retardates and normals.

Supporting this deduction, there was a main effect of Period for the normal subjects, $F(2,52) = 6.9$, $p < .0.005$. As illustrated in Figure 1, heart rate variability was suppressed as the trial progressed relative to pretrial level. The retarded subjects also exhibited a significant Period effect, $F(2,28) = 3.88$, $p < 0.05$. However, this effect was characterized not by a suppression but by a significant increase in heart rate variability relative to pretrial level.

A second part of the hypothesis linking physiological activity to sustained attention was the hypothesized relationship between respiratory activity and sustained attention. Stated simply, when individuals sustain attention they inhibit motor and respiratory activity. To assess this hypothesis, the mean amplitude and $\log_{10}$ variance of the five-second periods of respiration amplitude sampled every second were analyzed. When the variance is low it reflects smaller changes in the circumference of the chest that should parallel both respiratory and motor inhibition.

For the normal subjects, a main effect of Period was obtained for mean respiration amplitude ($F(2,52) = 6.7, p < 0.005$). The mean amplitude decreased from the pretrial level during the task. Changes in respiratory amplitude variability, although exhibiting a reduction on task, were not statistically significant.

For the retardates, respiratory amplitude variance significantly increased during the task demands ($F(2,29) = 10.9, p < 0.0005$). Note in Figure 2 the contrast in activity between the normals and the retardates; the normals tend to suppress respiratory variability while the retardates show a significant increase that does *not* return to base level during later periods (Period 4 and Period 5) in the trial.

Other physiological measures and behaviors were assessed. The response latency comparison resulted in nonoverlapping distributions. The mean heart rate within each of the five-second periods did not reflect a significant Period effect for the normals or the retardates. When the heart rate response pattern was analyzed in successive one-second windows, there was a significant seconds effect only for the normals. This response was characterized primarily by an acceleration.

DISCUSSION

The findings in this study describing the differences between normals and retardates in the physiological responses associated with sustained attention support the contention that the retardate suffers from an inhibitory skills deficit. This deficit is manifested on more than the obvious behavioral level. The retardate, besides exhibiting slow performance and a low level of cognitive functioning, is defective in the autonomic correlates of sustained attention. These autonomic correlates may be characterized as another level of inhibitory control (suppression of autonomic activity). The normal subjects exhibited a suppression of respiratory activity and heart-rate variability on task while the retardates exhibited increases in respiratory and heart rate variability.

This contrast might reflect the normal subject's ability to demonstrate "inhibition" on task, while the retardate subject not only is unable to inhibit ongoing behavior on task but exhibits a physiological "excitation." There have been hypotheses suggesting that the attentional deficit in the retardate is a problem of response latency, suggesting that the retardate has the capability to sustain attention but that it takes him longer to exhibit it. The present study suggests that even when the trials are prolonged, the retardate exhibits no indication that his physiological activity will be suppressed (see Figures 1 and 2).

SUMMARY

The study investigates the relationship between physiological response patterns and mental competence in retarded and normal children. Physiological evidence is presented that demonstrates that the retarded child responds to task demands with excitatory responses which are incompatible with sustained attention, in contrast to the inhibitory responses characteristic of normals.

REFERENCES

Baumeister, A. A., and Kellas, G. (1968) Reaction time and mental retardation. *In* International Review of Research in Mental Retardation, Vol 3 (Ed. Ellis, N. R.) New York: Academic Press.

Cheung, M. N. (1973) Factor analytic components of the cardiac orienting response. Masters thesis, West Virginia University.

Denny, M. R. (1964) Research in learning performance. *In* Mental Retardation: A Review of Research (Eds. Stevens, H. A., and Heber, R.) Chicago: University of Chicago Press.

Furby, L. (1974) Attentional habituation and mental retardation: A theoretical interpretation of MA and IQ differences in problem solving. Hum. Dev. 17:118.

James, W. (1890) Principles of Psychology. New York: Holt.

Krupski, A. (1975) Heart rate changes during a fixed reaction time task in normal and retarded adult males. Psychophysiology 12:262.

Leibert, A. M., and Baumeister, A. A. (1973) Behavioral variability among retardates, children, and college students. J. Psychol. 83:57.

Porges, S. W. (1972) Heart rate variability and deceleration as indexes of reaction time. J. Exp. Psychol. 92:103.

Porges, S. W., Walter, G. F., Korb, R. J., and Sprague, R. L. (1975) The influences of methylphenidate on heart rate and behavioral measures of attention in hyperactive children. Child Dev. 46:727.

Walter, G. F., and Porges, S. W. (1976) Heart rate and respiratory responses as a function of task difficulty. The use of discriminant analysis in the selection of psychologically sensitive physiological responses. Psychophysiology 13:563.

Weisz, J. R., and Achenbach, T. M. (1975) Effects of IQ and mental age on hypothesis behavior in normal and retarded children. Develop. Psychol. 11:304.

Zeaman, D., and House, B. J. (1963) One programmatic approach to retardation. *In* The Experimental Psychology of Mental Retardation (Ed. Routh, D. K.) Chicago: Aldine.

Zeaman, D., and House, B. J. (1967) The relation of IQ and learning. *In* Learning and Individual Differences (Ed. Gagné, R.) Columbus, Ohio: Charles E. Merrill.

RESEARCH TO PRACTICE IN MENTAL RETARDATION
Biomedical Aspects, Volume III
Edited by Peter Mittler
Copyright 1977 I.A.S.S.M.D.

HABITUATION AND REINSTATEMENT OF SKIN CONDUCTANCE AND HEART RATE RESPONSES IN THE MENTALLY RETARDED

A. C. Bower and D. L. Tate
Rideau Regional Centre,
Smiths Falls, Ontario, Canada

The orienting response (OR) or the "what is it?" response of Pavlov (1927), reflects a very basic reaction to information input from an organism's surroundings. It was proposed by Sokolov (1960) that incoming stimuli leave traces of their characteristics in the central nervous system that result in a neuronal mode. Subsequent stimulus inputs are compared to the information in the model. If the input matches the model closely, no OR results, but if the input is discrepant, an OR occurs.

Developmental psychologists (for example, Lewis and Goldberg, 1969) have found in the OR a useful technique in studying the growth of information processing. For instance, a young child can be shown a visual stimulus a number of times until habituation—perhaps indexed by cardiac deceleration—occurs. Then the stimulus is changed in some aspect. If a large deceleration is evoked, the researcher concludes that the child's information processing system is sensitive to stimulus changes in that category.

A series of studies reported by Luria (1963) suggested that mentally retarded children could be distinguished from nonretarded children on the basis of the OR. Some retarded individuals were shown to have unstable or weak ORs, which if they occurred, extinguished rapidly. These OR deficits were said to relate to attentional problems and poor learning.

In the current study, information processing was examined in retarded groups differing in IQ level and in a nonretarded peer group. Habituation of skin

---

Research supported by Grants 421 and 459 to A. C. Bower from the Ontario Mental Health Foundation.

conductance and heart rate responses to a series of 15 tones were studied. It was expected that IQ level would relate to rate of OR habituation. That is, low IQ subjects would have difficulty forming "models" of the stimulus and hence would take longer to habituate. Also, reinstatement of the OR produced by a change in tone intensity was expected to be poorer in low IQ groups because of "model" development.

METHOD

Subjects

Three groups of twenty-four subjects each were matched on age (range = 18–30 years) and sex. The first group was of average intelligence and consisted of summer students and Centre staff. A second group (low IQ) consisted of retarded persons with a mean IQ of 38 (range = 31–49), and a third group of retarded (high IQ) had a mean IQ of 67 (range = 58–73). None of these subjects had Down's syndrome or epilepsy, and none were taking tranquilizers.

Recording and Procedure

Skin conductance was recorded with chrome-plated electrodes attached to the middle phalanx of the second and fourth fingers of the subject's right hand. Heart rate was obtained from a Nihon Kohden reflecting plethysmograph fastened to the first phalanx of the third finger of the subject's hand. All subjects were tested individually in the EEG laboratory at Rideau Regional Centre. Subjects were informed that they would hear periodic tones and that they should relax and listen to them. After the subjects had been allowed several minutes for adaptation, two series of 16 tones were presented. Half of the subjects in each group heard one-second tones during the first series and ten-second tones during the second series. For the remaining subjects, tone duration was presented in the reverse order. Moreover, half of the subjects in each group heard 15 loud tones followed by a soft tone (65 decibels) during trial 16 in each series. The remaining subjects heard 15 soft tones followed by a loud tone (85 decibels) during the 16th presentation. Therefore, tone duration varied within subjects while tone intensity was varied between subjects. Intervals between tones varied from 28 to 44 seconds. A two-minute rest period separated the two series of tones. (More details on recording and data quantification can be found in Bower and Tate, 1976.)

RESULTS AND DISCUSSION

The 0.01 level of statistical significance was used throughout, unless otherwise noted. Conservative F tests were used with repeated measures.

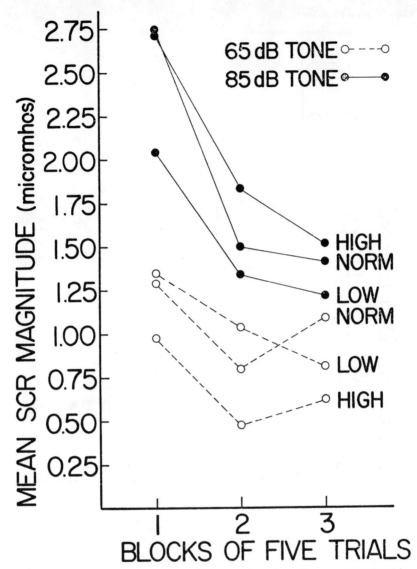

Figure 1. Mean skin conductance response (SCR) magnitude for subject groups by intensity during habituation trials.

OR Habituation

Figure 1 shows the mean skin conductance responses for three blocks of five tones for each of the three subject groups at the two intensity levels—65 and 85 decibels. An analysis of variance (ANOVA) with subject groups, tone intensity, order of tone duration, and sex as between-group factors was conducted on the block means with tone duration and blocks as repeated factors. There were

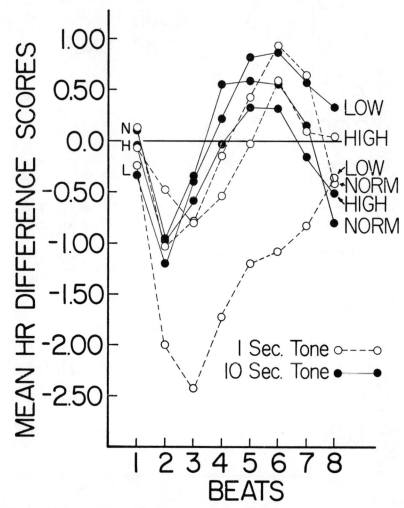

Figure 2. Mean heart rate (HR) difference scores for eight poststimulus beats for subject groups by tone duration.

statistically significant main effects for tone intensity ($F(1/48)$ = 7.97, EMS - 10.58) and blocks ($F(1/48)$ = 31.52, EMS = .76). However, as Figure 1 illustrates, these effects were qualified by an intensity by blocks interaction ($F(1/48)$ = 7.56, EMS = .76). This was caused by the fact that the larger skin conductance responses to loud tones decreased faster over blocks relative to soft tones. The subject groups portrayed in this figure and the following three figures did not differ statistically.

Figure 2 portrays the mean change in heart rate over eight poststimulus beats for each subject group for both stimulus durations—one and ten seconds. One sees the typical heart rate deceleration during early beats followed by an acceleration and then a return to baseline. Heart rate was evaluated by an ANOVA for difference scores utilizing the four previously mentioned between-group factors with blocks, tone duration, and beats as repeated measures. None of the between-group main effects were statistically reliable. Further, heart rate failed to show habituation over blocks of trials. This finding is not unlike the results obtained in previous work (Das and Bower, 1971). The only significant effect shown in Figure 2 was for beats ($F(1/48) = 16.22$, EMS = 6.89). There was a marginal effect for duration ($p < 0.10$) but this could be largely attributed to the large deceleration of the low IQ group. Unlike the skin conductance results, there was no indication that heart rate was influenced by stimulus intensity within the range used.

The skin conductance and heart rate results failed to reveal any differences in OR habituation rates between retarded and nonretarded persons. Thus, the reports of Luria (1963), Baumeister, Spain, and Ellis (1963), and Tizard (1968), which had shown differential habituation rates between retarded and nonretarded persons, were not supported. Rather, the predominant finding of Western research of no habituation difference in relation to IQ was upheld in the current study, although IQ was varied over a wider range than usual. Thus, in terms of Sokolov's (1960) model, it appears that mentally retarded persons as a group develop a neuronal model of a stimulus as rapidly as their nonretarded peers.

Stimulus Change

Figure 3 shows the mean skin conductance magnitudes for tone 15 and 16, that is, the last trial of habituation and the following trial on which the intensity was changed to reinstate the OR. Solid lines indicate that the change was from soft to loud while broken lines indicate that the stimulus change was from loud to soft. An ANOVA with tones 15 and 16 and duration as repeated factors was conducted. There were four between-group factors. Groups did not differ significantly. Far greater conductance occurred to the 16th tone than to the 15th one ($F(1/48) = 37.47$, EMS - 12.45). However, an intensity by tones interaction ($F(1.48) = 30.45$, EMS - 12.45) indicated that the response to the stimulus change was greater when the shift was from soft to loud than for the reverse.

Figure 4 shows the change from prestimulus level for heart rate scores over eight beats for each subject group and for trial 15 and 16. The only significant effect was for tones ($F(1/48) = 16.98$, EMS = 15.56). Examination of the figure clearly shows that deceleration was the predominate feature of heart rate on the 16th trial. It is interesting to note that unlike skin conductance, the direction of stimulus change was not a relevant factor with the heart rate measure.

In regards to stimulus change, it is clear that a change in intensity reinstated both skin conductance and heart rate components of the OR. However, skin conductance increases were only reliably produced by increases in tone inten-

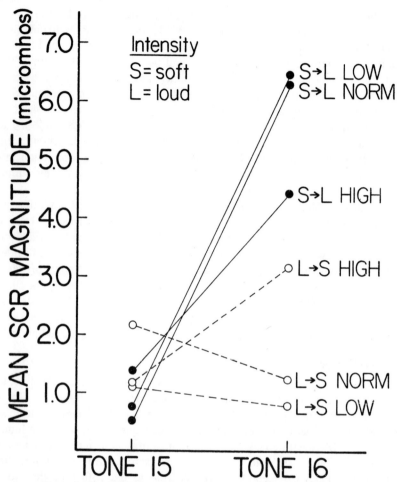

Figure 3. Mean SCR to change in stimulus intensity for each group.

sity. This finding supports the conclusion reached by O'Gorman (1973) in his examination of the effects of stimulus change on the galvanic skin reflex. However, the fact that heart rate was sensitive to both decreases and increases in tone intensity suggests that this measure may reflect cognitive factors additional to those reflected in skin conductance. Certainly the report of Lacey and Lacey (1974) indicates that the acceleration and deceleration components of the heart rate curve can be readily influenced by the task employed.

The failure of the current study to find any subject group differences in OR habituation and reinstatement suggests that differences between retarded and nonretarded persons rarely exist when stimuli are weak or simple in nature. Rather, differences are most likely to occur if tasks requiring active participation

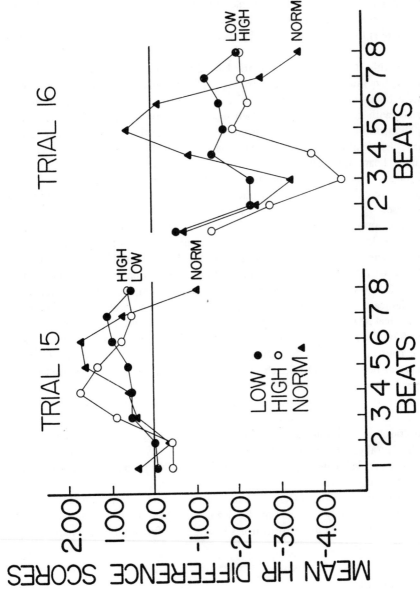

Figure 4. Mean HR difference scores for eight poststimulus beats as a result of stimulus change.

and/or cognitive demands are employed (for example, Siddle and Glenn, 1974; Krupski, 1975; Bower and Tate, 1976). In the Siddle and Glenn study, visual stimuli varying in complexity were used to obtain an interaction between complexity and IQ level. It seems likely that the more complex stimuli produced greater cognitive demands, thus allowing IQ differences to surface. I would like to support this line of argument by describing the Bower and Tate study in some detail.

In this study 16 mentally retarded adolescents with a mental age of nine years, ten months, were compared with two nonretarded groups matched with them on mental and chronological age. All subjects received 20 reaction time trials with music during the four-second preparatory interval and 20 trials without music in a counterbalanced order. The warning signal was a one-second light presentation and the respond signal was a 82-decibel tone. Skin conductance, heart rate, and digital and cephalic pulse amplitude were recorded throughout the reaction time task. Because the music failed as a distractor, all data were collapsed over the distraction condition. The 0.05 level of significance was used.

Our results showed that over trials the reaction times for the retarded subjects deteriorated while those of the nonretarded control groups remained stable. The retarded subjects also became much more variable from trial-to-trial. The heart rate difference scores reflected an acceleration during the preparatory interval followed by maximal deceleration at the moment of the reaction signal (as indicated by Lacey and Lacey, 1974) and then acceleration to baseline. Statistical analyses of the acceleratory component during the preparatory interval found the retarded group to have the smallest change and the chronological age control the largest. Similarily, analyses for degree of deceleration (RS beat subtract beat −2) found the chronological age group to decelerate more than the retarded group but not more than the mental age group. Moreover, skin conductance and cephalic pulse amplitude responses were also smaller than for the retarded subjects. Thus, overall, the retarded subject was seen as debilitated in contrast to intact nonretarded subjects of the same age, both physiologically and behaviourally. We interpreted these differences by suggesting that retarded persons are deficient in processes related to actively mobilizing and maintaining attention in preparation to respond.

One can sense the difference between the passive habituation study and the reaction time study in terms of the degree of subject participation required. To uncover differences in performance and cognitive functioning, the nature of the task can be vital.

REFERENCES

Baumeister, A. A., Spain, C. J., and Ellis, N. R. (1963) A note on normals and retardates. Amer. J. Ment. Defic. 67:23.

Bower, A. C., and Tate, D. L. (1976) Cardiovascular and skin conductance correlates of a fixed-foreperiod reaction time task in retarded and nonretarded youth. Psychophysiology. 13:1.

Das, J. P., and Bower, A. C. (1971) Autonomic components of verbal conditioning. Proc. 2nd Congr., IASSMD, Warsaw, p. 297.

Krupski, A. (1975) Heart rate changes during a fixed reaction time task in normal and retarded adult males. Psychophysiology. 12:262.

Lacey, B. C., and Lacey, J. I. (1974) Studies of heart rate and other bodily processes in sensorimotor behaviour. *In* Cardiovascular Psychophysiology: Current Issues in Response Mechanisms, Biofeedback and Methodology. (Eds. Obrist, P. A., Black, A., Brener, J., and DiCara, L.) Chicago: Aldine Publishing Ltd., p. 538.

Lewis, M., and Goldberg, S. (1969) The acquisition and violation of expectancy: An experimental paradigm. J. Exp. Child Psychol. 7:70.

Luria, A. R. (Ed.) (1963) The Mentally Retarded Child. Oxford: Pergamon Press.

O'Gorman, J. G. (1973) Change in stimulus conditions and the orienting response. Psychophysiology. 10:465.

Pavlov, I. P. (1927) Conditional Reflexes. An Investigation of the Physiological Activity in the Cerebral Cortex. London: Oxford University Press.

Siddle, D. A. T., and Glenn, S. M. (1974) Habituation of the orienting response to simple and complex stimuli. Amer. J. Ment. Defic. 78:688.

Sokolov, E. M. (1960) Neuronal models and the orienting reflex. *In* Central Nervous System and Behaviour. (Ed. Brazier, M. A.) New York: Josiah Macy Foundation.

Tizard, B. (1968) Habituation of EEG and skin potential changes in normal and severely subnormal children. Amer. J. Ment. Defic. 73:34.

RESEARCH TO PRACTICE IN MENTAL RETARDATION
Biomedical Aspects, Volume III
Edited by Peter Mittler
Copyright 1977 I.A.S.S.M.D.

QUESTIONS FOR A PSYCHOPHYSIOLOGY OF COGNITIVE PROCESSES

M. N. Nelson
Illinois Institute for Developmental Disabilities
1640 West Roosevelt Road,
Chicago, Illinois 60608,
United States

Psychophysiological research with retarded children has been conducted in part because of the difficulty in obtaining verbal or behavioral evidence for the operation of various cognitive processes. Even in normal children, it is frequently difficult to obtain unambiguous verbal reports or behavioral responses that can be directly compared with the reports of cooperative normal adults. To the extent that psychophysiological responses may be used in lieu of other responses, then, they may permit comparisons of complex processes that are difficult if not impossible to evaluate using other methods.

My remarks in this chapter deal with three questions or issues which are of crucial importance in research that attempts to use autonomic responses to measure cognitive processes and their development in the retarded. The issues concern: first, the comparative advantage of recording autonomic versus overt behavioral responses; second, the importance of defining the specific cognitive processes being measured; and third, the question of differential sensitivity of various autonomic changes to specific characteristics of cognitive development.

I have tried to illustrate the issues raised above by presenting some data I have collected from severely and profoundly retarded children (Nelson, 1976). The children were 11 years old, while their mean mental age was 1.5 years. There is little these children could do, but they did acquire a discriminated conditioned eyelid response after extended training. Figure 1 shows the results of eight days of differential eyelid conditioning, 50 trials per day. The children were split at the median on the basis of their discrimination between positive and negative conditioned stimuli (CS) on days seven and eight. Those above the median achieved significant differential responding and were called "good conditioners," while those below the median failed to respond differentially and were defined as "poor conditioners." Labeling children as good versus poor conditioners adds no new information, however. The question is whether or not good and

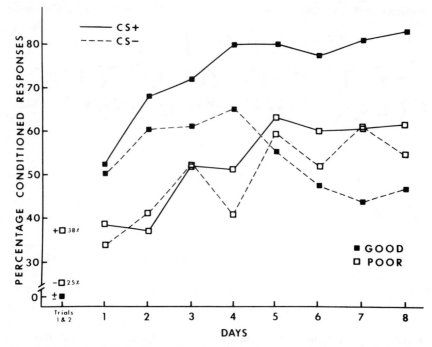

Figure 1. Mean percentage of conditioned eyelid responding to CS+ and CS– for good and poor conditioners (*N* = 8 per group) across eight days of differential conditioning, 50 trials per day.

poor differential conditioners differ in any underlying process important for conditioning. Concomitant recording of heart rate orienting responses suggested they did. Figure 2 shows the heart rate responses of the two groups to the first tone they heard. The Figure shows that good and poor conditioners differed considerably in the strength of their first cardiac deceleration. Only the good conditioners showed a strong, 22 bpm average deceleration, i.e., a strong heart rate orienting response, which is associated with attention in a great number of conditioning studies of normal adults, children, and animals. Poor conditioners, in contrast, responded with a less than 6 bpm deceleration. Seven of eight children in each group showed this powerful relationship between initial orienting response strength and terminal differential eyelid-conditioning performance.

The large initial difference in orienting response strength, shown in Figure 2, persisted throughout most of conditioning, and changed systematically in relation to conditioning performance in good conditioners. In addition, the form of the good conditioners' heart rate response—a short duration deceleration peaking at the second poststimulus second—closely resembled the response form observed in normal adults in a very similar conditioning situation (Putnam, Ross, and Graham, 1974), and suggested that processes of stimulus recognition associated with uncertainty about contingencies might be operating in a manner similar to that observed in normal adults.

Considering just the eyelid data presented in Figure 1, a large difference in responding can be obtained in the absence of knowledge of what processes might be responsible for the difference in conditioned behavior. The heart rate data, collected using a paradigm almost identical to that used in previous

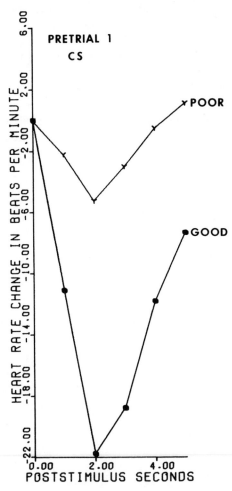

Figure 2. Mean heart rate responding of good and poor conditioners (*N* = 8 per group) during the first CS pretrial presented on Day 1. The abscissa shows sec X sec, computer-weighted heart rate averages, with second "0.00" indicating prestimulus heart rate.

conditioning research with normal adults, were crucial in suggesting that differences in attentional processes apparently discriminate good from poor differential conditioners. In this research, at least, neither autonomic nor overt behavioral data alone would have provided sufficient information about the acquisition of differential responding in severely and profoundly retarded children. The research was fruitful because it was based on extensive parametric research with a variety of subject populations. That is, the relationship between cardiac orienting and differential conditioning performance had already been sharply delineated. Finally, cardiac responding was chosen to index the orienting response instead of skin conductance, respiration, etc., because the cardiac-orienting response has been extensively investigated in a variety of learning situations (Obrist et al., 1974), and has been shown to relate systematically to differential eyelid-conditioning performance (Putnam, Ross, and Graham, 1974).

The research reported in the following chapters first raises some important questions about the equivalence of different autonomic response measures, and then goes on to show how the recording of certain, carefully selected autonomic responses can tell us much about attentive behavior in the retarded in various learning situations.

REFERENCES

Nelson, M. N. (1976) Cardiac correlates of conditioned response formation in severely and profoundly retarded children: Activation of recognition processes is indexed by orienting and is specific to particular conditioning paradigms. Paper presented at the Centennial Convention of the American Association on Mental Deficiency, Chicago, Illinois.

Obrist, P. A., Black, A. H., Brener, J., and DiCara, L. V. (Eds.) (1974) Cardiovascular Psychophysiology. Chicago: Aldine.

Putnam, L. E., Ross, L. E. and Graham, F. K. (1974) Cardiac orienting during "good" and "poor" differential eyelid conditioning. J. Exp. Psychol. 102:563.

RESEARCH TO PRACTICE IN MENTAL RETARDATION
Biomedical Aspects, Volume III
Edited by Peter Mittler
Copyright 1977 I.A.S.S.M.D.

AVERAGED EVOKED POTENTIALS AND HUMAN INTELLIGENCE

R. Halliday and E. Callaway
Langley Porter Neuropsychiatric Institute,
401 Parnassus Avenue,
San Francisco, California 94143, United States

Our understanding of how the brain manages to acquire complex behaviors is still in a primitive stage. Past efforts to unravel the intellectual activities of the central nervous system (CNS) have been plagued by the difficulty of isolating the relevant signals from the ongoing background activity. For example, application of the electroencephalogram (EEG) to the problem of intellectual assessment has not been very productive, and those relationships that have been reported may arise from the fact that both the IQ and the EEG are sensitive to brain damage (Ellingson, 1966).

In the late 1950s and the 1960s the development of electronic and computer technology made it possible to isolate stimulus and task-specific brain responses from the background activity of the EEG. These evoked potentials, or responses, are time-locked to the stimulus that generates them, and research over the past decade has amply demonstrated that the responses are modified by a wide range of cognitive activities and different ability levels.

This chapter selectively reviews some of the relationships that have been reported between performance on complex tasks such as intelligence tests and the averaged evoked potential (AEP). It will suggest some alternative ways of utilizing this technique that may greatly expand our understanding of the brain processes that underlie complex behaviors. Before reviewing the evidence, we have briefly reviewed the underlying rationale of the averaging process and specified a few of the measures that are derived to characterize the AEP.

This research was supported by National Institute of Mental Health Grant MH22149 and also received support from the Office of Naval Research Contract N00014-75-C-0398, NIMH General Research Support Grant FR05550 (Langley Porter Institute), General Research Support Grant FR05521 (Kaiser Foundation Hospital), The Grant Foundation and the Community Service Program Fund of Kaiser Foundation Hospital.

THE AVERAGED EVOKED POTENTIAL

Stimulation of a receptor, e.g., a brief flash of light, evokes a small response on the surface of the scalp. These responses typically range between 5 and 20 microvolts (μv) and are generally buried in the 50–100 μv activity of the EEG. In order to increase the ratio of the single (EP) to the noise (background EEG), one records the EEG at the time of stimulus occurrence for a period of 500–1000 milliseconds (msec) over a number of trials (usually 50–100) and then averages these results for each time point. If a plot of the average amplitude of the response against the time following the stimulus is made, the result is a complex wave form.

Typically, investigators measure the amplitude of prominent components and their latency. However, because each time point represents an average of many observations, one can obtain measures that reflect the variability of these samples.

Figure 1 illustrates a number of features of the AEP, including AEP variability dynamics. The measure of variability with which we are primarily concerned is a gross measure that is normalized to remove the correlations of amplitude across subjects that are caused by differences in amplification or attenuation constants.

The two 100–event visual AEPs labeled AVERAGE show, for two children, the series of typical biphasic amplitude changes found in most averages. In both children, a negative-positive component occurs between 100 and 150 msec. Another negative-positive component between 200 and 400 msec is well-marked in these two children, but this component was not observed in all children. A second feature is seen in the AEPs labeled 1–5. Each of these AEPs is an average based on 20 consecutive EPs drawn from the same sample space as AVERAGE. The individual AEPs in the low-variability child are remarkably similar from average to average and suggest that, whatever neurophysiological processes mediate the EP, they are constant over trials and are fairly represented by AVERAGE. The five component AEPs of the high variability child, in contrast, differ markedly from average to average, and the ensemble of 5 AEPs does not easily fit the average. Finally, one can see that the less variable average has larger amplitude components than the more variable average. The normalized variability measure, SD/norm, has been shown to be inversely related to amplitude. However, this relationship does not necessarily hold for all measures of variability. A detailed discussion of variability-amplitude relationships can be found in Callaway and Halliday (1973).

To summarize, the majority of AEP studies have stressed the speed (latency) or size (amplitude) of various components of the AEP. In addition, measures of stability, or its inverse variability, also have been reported. These three AEP dimensions, however, are not independent and are correlated in complex ways.

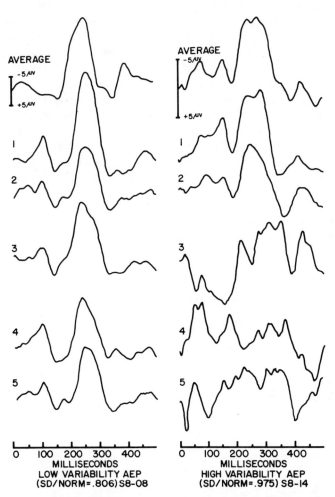

Figure 1. Low and high variability visual AEPs from two hyperactive children. AVERAGE is based on a sample of 100 EPs. The AEPs numbered 1–5 were obtained by dividing these 100 EPs into 5 sets of 20 EPs each. The amplitude of the 6 AEPs for each child is the same. The scale is different, however, for both children. Copyright © 1976, The Society for Psychophysiological Research. Reprinted with permission of the publisher from "Averaged evoked potential predictors of clinical improvement in hyperactive children treated with methylphenidate: An initial study and replication," *Psychophysiology*, 1976, 13:429–440.

AGE-RELATED CHANGES IN AEP

The first requirement for a measure to predict complex human performance is that it improves with age. Measures that do not change with age are not likely to be useful as predictors of complex skill attainment. Two studies have reported dramatic changes in AEP measures with maturation (Callaway and Halliday, 1973: Dustman, Schenkenberg, and Beck, 1976). In general, the AEP becomes more stable (i.e., less variable) with age, and the amplitude of later components increases markedly. Figure 2 shows these age changes in terms of polarity histograms. This measure is analogous to the usual averaging technique, but differs in that the ordinate represents the percent of time the individual EPs are positive or negative. Larger percent values reflect more stable and large amplitude components. As the figure shows, both early and late components become more stable with age, at least from ages 6–15. Changes in amplitude are not, however, always linear. Results from our study and those of Dustman, Schenkenberg, and Beck (1976) show that gross amplitude measures increase until age

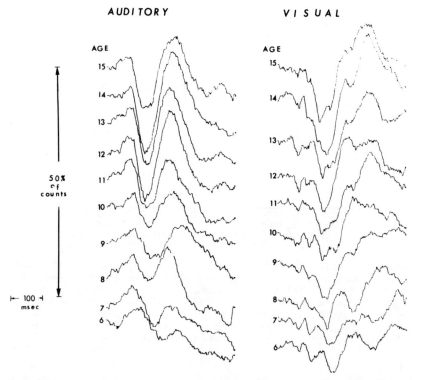

Figure 2. Visual and auditory polarity histograms for 10 groups of children at ages shown. Each histogram is based on data obtained for 12 children. Reprinted from *Electroenceph. Clin. Neurophysiol.* 34:125–133, 1973, with permission.

9, decrease until age 13, and then increase again. What these changes signify in terms of cortical maturation are at present unclear, but one might speculate that those processes which mediate attention may be of importance.

AEPS AND INTELLIGENCE

One of the first studies documenting the relationship between AEPs and intelligence was reported by Chalke and Ertl (1965). Reasoning that more intelligent people may have faster-operating brains, these investigators found that latency of the larger components in the visual AEP (142–374 msec) occurred significantly faster in a group of high IQ subjects when compared with a group in the dull to average range. Subsequently, in a large scale study of 573 school age children, Ertl and Schaffer (1969) reported a median correlation of −0.33 between these same components and psychometric measures of intelligence. Correlations of this same magnitude have also been reported by Shucard and Horn (1972) and by Plum (cited by Callaway, 1975). Additionally, two studies have reported that the latency of late components of the visual AEP is significantly longer in retardates (Down's syndrome) than in normal, age-matched children (Bigum, Dustman, and Beck, 1970; Galbraith, Gliddon, and Busk, 1976).

Considering the diversity of procedures and techniques for defining peaks, these studies supply impressive support for a small but consistent relationship between latency of AEP components and measures of psychometric intelligence. However, there have been studies that failed to find any significant relationship between IQ and AEP latency, and in some cases, a significant but positive correlation has been reported.

A study quoted by Callaway (1975, p. 47) found no relationship between AEP latency and IQ in a large sample of school children. Dustman, Schenkenberg, and Beck (1976) investigated the relationship between visual AEP and intelligence in two different groups of children. In the first group of children (N = 51, $\overline{X}$ IQ = 110) the relationship between latency of the late components and IQ was significant, but the correlations were positive, i.e., brighter children had longer latency AEPs. Moreover, this effect was confined to centrally placed electrodes. In the second study (N = 114, $\overline{X}$ IQ = 88) none of the latency-IQ relationships were significant. Significant correlations with amplitude were reported in the first study, but the amplitude-IQ correlations were limited to occipital leads. The second study did not replicate the amplitude-IQ relationships. Callaway (1975) also reported that while latency and amplitude of the auditory AEP correlated with psychometric intelligence, the correlations were all positive and opposite in sign to their relationships with age, i.e., higher IQ appeared to go with more immature auditory AEPs. Finally, Everhart, China, and Auger (1974) reported a correlation of −0.31 between IQ and scores on a latency-sensitive device marketed by Ertl. Unfortunately, he found the same correlations even when the stimulus lamp was disconnected so that no AEP was produced.

In summary, a number of studies have reported significant negative correlations between psychometric intelligence and latency of the middle and late components of the visual AEP. These relationships are, however, small and not found in all studies. Although technical procedures and electrode sites sampled are not always comparable, these differences by themselves do not account for the observed discrepancies. Dustman, Schenkenberg, and Beck (1976), as we have pointed out, obtained different results for two different samples of children. While one could argue that the observed relationships are the results of sampling error, this hardly seems parsimonious given the consistency of the −0.30 correlation between late components of the visual AEP and psychometric intelligence reported across different studies. One possible explanation for the differences is that the relationship between IQ and AEPs is nonlinear and complexly determined. Thus, one would not anticipate that one or two measures of AEP activity would be sufficient to describe this relationship. In short, one would anticipate that subjects with different ability levels would cluster in different positions along several independent dimensions. This certainly would be more consistent with the complexity of the brain's operation.

MULTI-VARIATE APPROACHES TO IQ/AEP RELATIONSHIPS

In an early publication, Callaway and Stone (1969) reported that a plot of AEP variability versus performance on the Berry Visual Motor Integration Task (VMI) was discontinuous. Good and poor performance on the VMI accompanied low variability. However, high variability AEP, which characterizes younger children, precluded high scores on the VMI. Thus, low variability AEPs were sufficient for the development of good performance but did not guarantee the end result.

Since variability decreases with age, the finding of an empty quadrant for high variability–good VMI performance suggests that the neural mechanisms associated with this task are not yet mature enough for competent expression. In short, there appear to be three groups of children each characterized by a combination of AEP and VMI scores. In view of the complexity of the AEP, it seems reasonable that a multi-variate approach would produce better separation between various ability groups.

Lewis, Rimland, and Callaway (1976) studied visual AEPs in 207 Naval recruits. The sample was divided into low and high ability groups on the basis of their preinduction scores on the Armed Forces Qualification Test (AFQT). The scores of the low ability group corresponded to an IQ range of 87 to 96. Scores in the high ability group corresponded to an IQ range of 113 to 133. Visual EPs were recorded from a number of electrode locations and measures of AEP variance, amplitude, and hemispheric asymmetry computed. The data were then analyzed by a stepwise discriminant program to determine if some combination of measures would objectively discriminate the low and high AFQT groups. Stepwise programs are notorious for their ability to produce classifications difficult to replicate. Hence, the data were subdivided, and the discriminant weights obtained from half of the data applied to the remaining cases. The results can be viewed as erring on the conservative side.

The results showed that the best separation occurred when four AEP variables were entered into the program. However, more information was necessary to classify the low ability group. For example, 69% of the high group were correctly classified by the entry of one variable (AEP variance), whereas only 27% of the low ability group were correctly classified. At the fourth step, the classification accuracy had improved by only 3% for the high ability group, while the low ability group was now discriminated correctly 49% of the time. Thus, the high ability group was more homogeneous than the low ability group. This result is not totally unexpected. There are undoubtedly many variables that underlie poor performance and fewer ways in which good performance can be accomplished.

The implications of this finding for the study of mental retardation are straightforward and consistent with the general philosophy that retardates are not a very homogeneous group. The application of discriminant and clustering techniques to AEP and performance measures could conceivably lead to the identification of groups that are more homogeneous.

Perry et al. (1976) have recently applied multi-variate statistics to visual AEP and IQ data in a group of 5–6 year old normal children ($N = 98$). The results are difficult to interpret, but, in essence, the authors report a canonical correlation of 0.49 between linear composites of AEP variables and subtests of the performance scale of the Wechsler Preschool and Primary Scale of Intelligence (WPPSI). The authors note that should the results hold up on a larger age range of children, the correlation would be substantially increased. But as Perry et al. point out, high AEP/IQ correlations are not necessarily desirable. The utility of the AEP is not in its ability to substitute for IQ tests. Rather, its potential should be applied to solve theoretical and clinical problems that have been refractory to standard assessment schemes.

One current clinical problem that looks particularly well-suited to AEP investigation is the diagnosis and remediation of learning disabilities. Learning disabilities represent a group of children whose academic difficulties are not predicted by their standing on IQ tests. It is somewhat ironic, then, that such tests as the Wechsler Intelligence Scale for Children are used after the fact to draw clinical inferences regarding the nature of a problem that could not be predicted in the first place. It seems obvious from even a cursory inspection of the literature in this area that some other means of assessing these academic problems is badly needed.

John and Thatcher (1977) have developed an extensive neuropsychological battery and are currently investigating differences between several diagnostic groups, including subjects with learning disabilities, and normal children along several AEP and EEG dimensions. Preliminary results are encouraging and suggest that multi-variate statistical techniques may reveal distinct differences between groups that otherwise would not look appreciably different.

The application of clustering and other multi-variate techniques to identify different AEP-performance groups will require a large number of subjects under carefully controlled conditions before the validity of this approach can be assessed. The final section of this chapter examines how the AEP might be applied profitably to current clinical evaluations in child psychiatry.

ASSESSMENT OF ATTENTION AND THE AEP

A major focus in current research is how different cognitive tasks affect the AEP. In general, if a task requires complex processing, the late positive components (300 msec) are increased in amplitude. If, on the other hand, the task is simply to monitor and report an occasional odd event, then the amplitude of the early components (100–200 msec) will be enhanced (Callaway, 1975). These findings suggest that the AEP might be useful in the assessment of attentional disorders.

Attentional problems are a prominent feature of the hyperactive child syndrome. In addition, the clinical symptoms, along with the improvement in these children following a trial of stimulant drugs, suggest that some deficit in CNS functioning may play an important part in maintaining the hyperactive child's poor attentional performance. While the number of studies reporting on the AEP in this population is small, the consistency of the results opens up the possibility that this technique may not only provide a badly needed research tool, but may eventually provide a useful screening device for drug therapy.

Prichep, Sutton, and Hakerem (1976) have reported significant differences in AEP amplitude between age matched normals and hyperactives off-drug (methylphenidate). These differences were, however, obtained only on an attentionally-demanding task with one important exception. Hyperactives showed a significantly larger P300 component under conditions that had low attentional demands. P300 is generally regarded as one of the signals that accompanies some kind of cognitive computing; therefore, the authors concluded that hyperactives show inappropriate attentional responses. The administration of methylphenidate to the hyperactives normalized their AEPs, i.e., abolished the differences between normals and drug-treated hyperactives, while a placebo had no effect. Finally, the authors repeated their procedures twice within each drug condition. No significant session differences were found. Thus, in the absence of effective treatment, intersession reliability was high.

Zambelli et al. (1976) have reported similar results in a group of adolescents who were diagnosed hyperactive as children. AEPs were recorded to binaural clicks presented under instructions to count the number of occasional higher frequency "target" pips presented to one of the ears. Age-matched normals showed significant amplitude differences between attended and nonattended ears. Hyperactives, on the other hand, showed no differences in this respect. Since the overt symptoms of this disorder frequently "disappear" during adolescence, these findings provide a neuropsychological explanation for the academic and social difficulties that hyperactives continue to show even in early adulthood.

While the use of stimulant drugs in the treatment of hyperkinesis continues to be an area of much controversy, controlled studies have demonstrated that *d*-amphetamine and methylphenidate markedly improve a variety of skills in some hyperactive children. The basic question that has remained unanswered since Charles Bradley discovered the therapeutic effect of these drugs in the 1930s is which children will respond to these drugs and why. Conners (1970) reported an increase in the amplitude of certain components of the visual AEP in a group of hyperactives following eight weeks of *d*-amphetamine therapy. Placebo-treated hyperactives, on the other hand, showed an amplitude decrease. His results, along with some preliminary results in our laboratory, led us to explore the possibility that treatment response might be predicted from the AEP. Two studies have been completed, and we have found two AEP markers that differentiate responders from nonresponders (Halliday et al. 1976).

Visual AEPs were recorded on three separate occasions under no-drug, methylphenidate, and placebo in a group of hyperactives before a clinical trial of stimulants. Attention was manipulated within sessions by having the child either look for an occasional dim flash embedded in a series of brighter flashes or simply observe the flashes. The child was then placed on a therapeutic dosage of methylphenidate and his progress evaluated at home and school. Figures 3 and 4 summarize the results. In general, an attentional task enhances AEP amplitude and decreases AEP variability. Thus, one would anticipate that a passive task would lead to a more variable AEP than one involving attentional demands. As Figure 3 shows, when responders were given methylphenidate this expectation held up. However, when this drug was administered to children who subsequently showed few clinical gains, the expected variability relationship between the attentional and passive task was reversed. Thus, nonresponders on stimulants appear to show inappropriate attentional AEPs. Figure 4 shows changes in the middle components (145–200 msec) recorded in the attending condition for the three drug conditions. Methylphenidate increased the amplitude of this component for responders over both the no-drug and placebo conditions. Nonresponders did not show any significant drug effect. The order of sessions was counterbalanced and statistical analysis showed no significant sessions effect. Thus, explanations in terms of adjustment to the laboratory or motivational differences have been ruled out. Moreover, the same pattern of results was observed in two independent studies, suggesting that the results are replicable.

Although these results are encouraging, we have encountered a number of problems that have not been resolved. The principal difficulty is not with the AEP technique but in the evaluation of clinical change. Progress in our sample

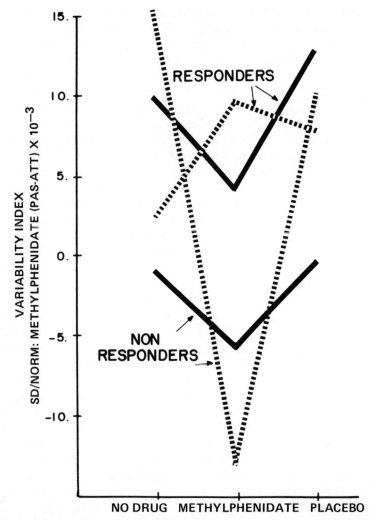

Figure 3. Mean of variability index (Passive Task-Attending Task) for each drug condition. ——— = Placebo session 2, Methylphenidate session 3. −−− = Methylphenidate 2, placebo session 3. Copyright © 1976, The Society For Psychophysiological Research. Reprinted with permission of the publisher from "Averaged evoked potential predictors of clinical improvement in hyperactive children treated with methylphenidate: An initial study and replication," *Psychophysiology,* 1976, 13:429–440.

was independently assessed by the pediatrician. While his judgment was backed up by ratings made by the teacher during a double blind trial with methylphenidate and placebo, the two sets of ratings did not always concur. Improved techniques for objective evaluation are currently being planned, and it is hoped that they will allow us to draw more precise parallels between electrophysiological and behavioral characteristics.

The limits of the AEP technique in the study of attentional processes in development have scarcely been touched. The sophisticated methodology that has been apparent in adult studies over the past few years has only recently begun to be applied to children. In this respect, the studies by Prichep, Sutton, and Hakerem (1976) and Zambelli et al. (1976) clearly show that procedures used with adults can be extended to children with surprisingly good results.

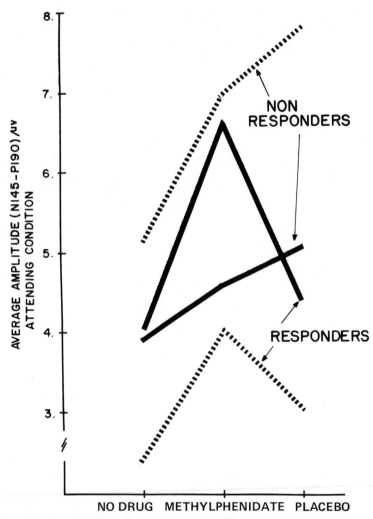

Figure 4. Mean of average amplitude of the N145-P190 component obtained in the attending condition for each drug condition. ———— = Placebo session 2, Methylphenidate session 3. ––– = Methylphenidate session 2, placebo session 3. Copyright © 1976, The Society For Psychophysiological Research. Reprinted with permission of the publisher from "Averaged evoked potential predictors of clinical improvement in hyperactive children treated with methylphenidate: An initial study and replication," *Psychophysiology,* 1976, 13:429–440.

While the importance of the task has been recognized for some time, variation in task difficulty has been a neglected area, at least in children. Recently, Freidman, Vaughn, and Erlenmeyer-Kimlings (1976) have shown that the introduction of a memory component into a standard vigilance procedure increases the amplitude of late components. This finding raises the possibility that the AEP might pinpoint where, in the chain of stimulus and response events, performance begins to degrade. Comparison of different clinical groups has not received much attention. Most of our information about developmental pathologies is relative to age- and IQ-matched normals. What, for example, are the differences between the AEPs of hyperactives with and without academic disabilities as opposed to children with specific learning disabilities minus the hyperactive component, and what are the task parameters that accentuate or alternate these differences?

SUMMARY

The relationship between evoked potentials (EPS) and intelligence is discussed. Data is presented that these relationships exist but are small and generally not normally distributed. The nature of these relationships is discussed, and techniques for unraveling their complexity suggested. The potential usefulness of this approach toward developing a theory relating brain and intelligent behavior is emphasized.

REFERENCES

Bigum, H. B., Dustman, R. E., and Beck, E. C. (1970) Visual and somatosensory evoked potentials from mongoloid and normal children. Electroencephalogr. Clin. Neurophysiol. 28:202.

Callaway, E. (1975) Brain Electrical Potentials and Individual Psychological Differences. New York: Grune & Stratton.

Callaway, E., and Halliday, R. (1973) Evoked potential variability: Effects of age, amplitude and methods of measurement. Electroencephalogr. Clin. Neurophysiol. 34:125.

Callaway, E., and Stone, G. (1969) Evoked response methods for the study of intelligence. Agressologie. 10: Suppl. 535.

Chalke, F., and Ertl, J. (1965) Evoked potentials and intelligence. Life Sci. 4:1319.

Conners, C. (1970) A clinical comparison between magnesium pemoline, dextroamphetamine and placebo in hyperactive children. Paper presented at the Meeting of the American College of Neuropsychopharmacology, San Juan, Puerto Rico, December.

Dustman, R., Schenkenberg, T., and Beck, E. (1976) The development of the evoked response as a diagnostic and evaluative procedure. In Developmental Psychophysiology of Mental Retardation (Ed. Karrer, R.) Springfield, Illinois: Charles C Thomas.

Ellingson, R. (1966) Relationships between EEG and test intelligence: A commentary. Psychol. Bull. 65:91.

Ertl, J., and Schafer, E. (1969) Brain response correlates of psychometric intelligence. Nature. 223:421.

Everhart, J., China, C., and Auger, R. (1974) Measures of EEG and verbal intelligence: An inverse relationship. Physiol. Psychol. 2:374.

Freidman, D., Vaughn, H., and Erlenmeyer-Kimlings, L. (1976) Task-related cortical potentials in children in two kinds of vigilance tasks. Fourth International Congress on Event Slow Potentials of the Brain.

Galbraith, G., Gliddon, J., and Busk, M. (1976) Electrophysiological studies of mental retardation. *In* Developmental Psychophysiology of Mental Retardation (Ed. Karrer, R.) Springfield, Illinois: Charles C Thomas.

Halliday, R., Rosenthal, J., Naylor, H., and Callaway, E. (1976) Averaged evoked potential predictors of clinical improvement in hyperactive children treated with methylphenidate: An initial study and replication. Psychophysiol. 13:429.

John, E. R., and Thatcher, E. R. (1977) Assessment of brain dysfunction in children with learning disabilities. Neuroscience. 2. Hillsdale, New Jersey: Lawrence Erlbaum Associates (in press).

Lewis, G., Rimland, B., and Callaway, E. (1976) Visual evoked potential correlates of aptitude among navy recruits. Unpublished manuscript.

Perry, N. W., McCoy, J. G., Cunningham, W. R., Falgout, J. C., and Street, W. J. (1976) Multivariate visual evoked response correlates of intelligence. Psychophysiol. 13.

Prichep, L., Sutton, S., and Hakerem, G. (1976) Evoked potentials in hyperkinetic and normal children under certainty and uncertainty: A placebo and methylphenidate study. Psychophysiol. 13:419.

Shucard, D., and Horn, J. (1972) Evoked cortical potentials and measurement of human abilities. J. Comp. Physiol. Psychol. 78:59.

Zambelli, A., Stamm, J., Maitinsky, S., and Loiselle, D. (1976) Auditory evoked potentials and selective attention in formerly hyperactive children. Unpublished manuscript.

RESEARCH TO PRACTICE IN MENTAL RETARDATION
Biomedical Aspects, Volume III
Edited by Peter Mittler
Copyright 1977 I.A.S.S.M.D.

AGE-RELATED EEG ALPHA PATTERNS IN MENTALLY RETARDED INDIVIDUALS

G. C. Galbraith and J. B. Gliddon
Neuropsychiatric Institute,
Pacific State Hospital Research Group,
Pomona, California 91766,
United States

Berger (1932) was the first to show that children have a lower alpha frequency than adults. Lindsley (1936), Smith (1937), and Gibbs and Gibbs (1944) then demonstrated a progressive increase in dominant frequency of the resting electroencephalogram (EEG) for the first few months of life through maturity. At the other end of the age continuum, several studies have documented a slowing of the EEG alpha rhythm in normal, aged adults (Obrist, 1954, 1963; Obrist and Busse, 1965). Studies of alpha amplitude have shown that a maximum is reached at 6–9 years (Eeg-Olofson, 1971; Petersen and Eeg-Olofson, 1971).

It is thus apparent that normal development is associated with predictable changes in both EEG frequency and amplitude. Very few studies, however, have reported age-related EEG changes in mentally retarded individuals. Yet, altered patterns in EEG maturation could well be expected in such individuals. Galbraith, Gliddon, and Busk (1975) reported delayed EEG frequency increases in mentally retarded individuals, and suggested that the relative amount of EEG slowing might be used to estimate the degree of central nervous system maturation. This same idea has been formulated for the nonretarded (Matousek et al., 1967).

In the present study we report the results of a computer analysis of scalp EEGs recorded in 229 institutionalized mentally retarded individuals who differed in age and diagnosis. The purpose of this study was to assess central nervous system development and, hopefully, to establish normative values for a

Supported by NICHD Grant No HD-06650 and DHEW, Developmental Disabilities Division, Grant No. 54-P-71020/9.

mentally retarded population against which it might be possible to compare the developmental progress of a single individual.

METHOD

Subjects

EEGs were recorded from a total of 300 residents of Pacific State Hospital, Pomona, California. Results are presented here for a total of 229, because data analyses at the time of this writing are not fully complete. The age range in our sample was from six to 73 years, although only a few subjects were available at the extremes (actual age distributions will be presented in Results). In our sample 80% were male. A number of diagnostic categories were represented, but the largest were: Down's syndrome ($N = 39$), uncertain-structural ($N = 62$), uncertain-functional ($N = 45$), and asphyxia ($N = 29$).

EEG Recording

Grass gold-plated disk electrodes were positioned on the scalp over the following cortical locations according to the international "10–20" system: left occipital (O_1), right occipital (O_2), left central (C_3), and right central (C_4). Linked ear lobes were used as the recording reference in a monopolar derivation. Inter-electrode resistance was always kept below 10,000 ohms. EEG signals were amplified by Tektronix 2A61 differential amplifiers with a bandpass of 1–22 cps (3 dB down).

One experimenter continuously monitored the amplified EEG on a multi-channel oscilloscope. However, input signals to the analog-to-digital converter, which generated a computer-compatible magnetic tape, were obtained from the playback heads of an analog tape recorder. This allowed a time delay of 1.7 sec between the time an artifact appeared on the monitor oscilloscope and the time it appeared as input to the data acquisition system. This time was sufficient to detect obvious artifacts and to generate a delete code on the computer tape. In addition, a second experimenter constantly observed the subject and independently coded periods in which the subject's behavior was inappropriate (e.g., movement, eyeblinks, etc.). Subsequent computer analyses were thus able to delete segments of the record contaminated with artifacts and/or inappropriate behavior.

Procedures

EEG recordings were obtained during quiet resting with eyes-open (EO) and eyes-closed (EC) (a technician held the eye lids closed for those individuals who could not fully cooperate). If possible, two minutes of artifact-free EEG were recorded in each condition. The order of EO and EC was counterbalanced across subjects, although complete data were not obtained from all subjects. In addition, most subjects performed a simple motor task with eyes-open and eyes-closed. Only the resting eyes-closed data are presented here.

The EEG data reported in the present study were analyzed by computer in order to determine spectral intensities for each of the four separate EEG channels (auto-spectra) as well as the six pair-wise combinations of EEG channels (cross-spectra). This analysis yielded quantitative estimates of EEG power in frequency bands ranging from 0–32 cps, with a frequency resolution of 1.0 cps. In addition, cross-spectral combinations were further analyzed to determine linear coherence and phase angle. Coherence (C) is a measure of the overall similarity between two EEG signals, computed at each frequency in the analysis. Coherence is bounded between 0 (no linear relationship) and 1.0 (perfect linear relationship). Phase angle (ϕ) is a measure of the degree to which one signal leads or lags another signal, computed in degrees of angle. Positive ϕ values indicate that the electrode with the larger subscript leads, e.g., positive ϕ in the C_4–O_2 electrode combination would mean that alpha peaks occur in C_4 before O_2, while negative ϕ indicates a reversed relationship between peaking in the two electrodes. In order to assure that reliable values of phase angle were considered, only those values of ϕ associated with $C \geqslant 0.50$ were analyzed.

Spectra were computed for successive 2.56 sec epochs and then averaged over all artifact-free epochs in order to enhance spectral reliability. Only activity in a somewhat widened alpha frequency band (7–14 cps) was considered in the present analysis. The maximum spectral intensity within this frequency band was defined as the dominant alpha frequency. Reported values of spectral intensity, coherence, and phase angle are for this specific frequency, although a weighted mean of alpha frequency was computed by taking into account the spectral intensities on either side of the peak intensity.

RESULTS

Figure 1 presents EEG intensity recorded over the left hemisphere (O_1 and C_3). Data are presented only for the left hemisphere because the results over the right hemisphere were nearly identical. The data are presented in five-year intervals from 5–20 years of age followed by ten-year intervals thereafter, except for the final interval which spans the age range 60–75 years. The number of individuals in each age range is also shown. The results of Figure 1 show a large alpha amplitude in the youngest age range studied (5–9 years), although it must be appreciated that these data are based upon relatively few subjects. In all later age ranges it can be seen that occipital alpha intensity is greater than central alpha intensity. Moreover, there seems to be a consistent increase in alpha intensity that reaches a maximum in the third decade for occipital activity, and a maximum in the fourth decade for central activity, followed by a decline thereafter.

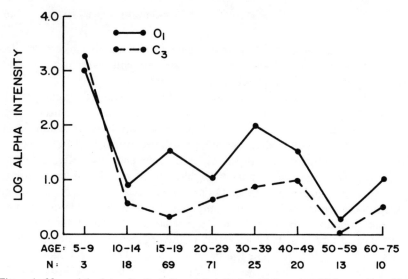

Figure 1. Mean alpha intensity for left occipital (O_1) and left central (C_3) recordings. Units on ordinate are equal to $\log_e (I^2/10\mu V^2)$. Abscissa shows the age groupings and the number of subjects in each age group.

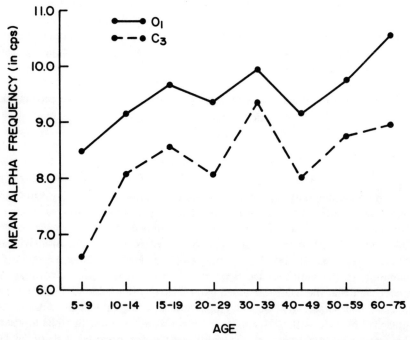

Figure 2. Mean alpha frequency for left occipital (O_1) and left central (C_3) recordings. Ordinate is in cycles per second (cps). Abscissa is the same as Figure 1 (number of subjects not shown).

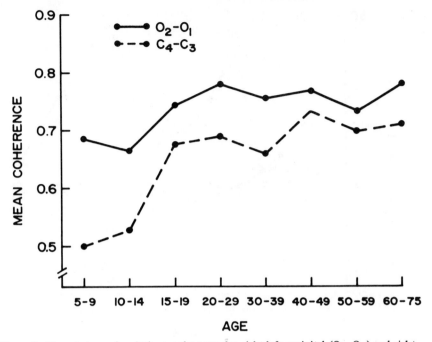

Figure 3. Mean between-hemisphere coherence for right-left occipital (O_2-O_1) and right-left central (C_4-C_3) electrode combinations. Abscissa is the same as Figure 1 (number of subjects not shown).

Figure 2 graphs mean alpha frequency for O_1 and C_3. Although O_1 alpha frequency is consistently faster than C_3 frequency, by as much as 1 cps or more, both recordings show a consistent frequency increase across the entire age range.

Figure 3 presents the mean between-hemisphere coherence. In general, occipital alpha coherence is stable across age, although it does tend to increase from the early years up to the second decade. Central alpha, however, shows a sizeable and steady increase in coherence from about 0.5 in the youngest age group to about 0.7 in the older age groups.

Figure 4 presents the phase angle data. Results are presented for between-hemisphere $(O_2-O_1$ and $C_4-C_3)$ and within-hemisphere $(C_3-O_1$ and $C_4-O_2)$ comparisons. The results show that between-hemisphere phase hovers around 0 degrees, i.e., alpha activity in homologous sites of the two hemispheres is tightly coupled in time. Within-hemisphere phase, which represents an anterior-posterior comparison, is more variable, but predominately positive. Positive ϕ values in this case indicate anterior leading. These results show a definite bimodal peaking, with maxima reached at 15–19 and 40–49 years of age. When the units of degree are converted to actual milliseconds, the 40–49 year data convert to an anterior leading of 9.3 msec.

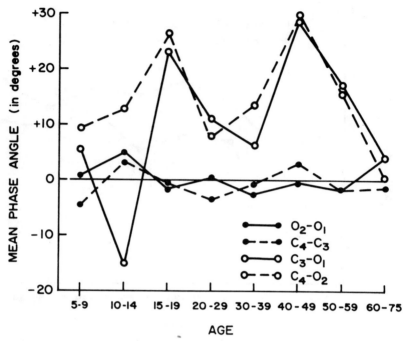

Figure 4. Mean phase angle (in degrees) for alpha recorded from between-hemisphere (*filled circles*) and within-hemisphere (*open circles*) electrode combinations. Positive values on the ordinate indicate that electrodes with larger subscripts lead those with smaller subscripts, e.g., C_4 and O_2 throughout the age range. Abscissa is the same as Figure 1 (number of subjects not shown).

DISCUSSION

The present results indicate consistent developmental trends in the electroencephalogram of mentally retarded individuals. However, these trends appear to differ in some rather striking ways from reported trends in nonretarded individuals. Thus, EEG amplitude showed a secondary peak in the third decade of life in our sample of mentally retarded individuals (Figure 1), while the nonretarded appear to reach their peak amplitude very early (Eeg-Olofson, 1971; Peterson and Eeg-Olofson, 1971). Also, our sample showed a consistent increase in mean frequency over the entire age span (Figure 2). However, nonretarded EEG alpha frequency typically reaches the maximum somewhere in the middle to late teenage years (Lindsley, 1936; Smith, 1937; Gibbs and Gibbs, 1944), then declines in frequency with the onset of senescence (Obrist, 1954; 1963; Obrist and Busse, 1965). In our sample, occipital alpha was consistently faster than central alpha by approximately 1 cps. Yet, previous reports (Brazier, 1968) indicate, in nonretarded children, that central frequencies are faster than occipital frequencies. It should also be noted that our sample of retarded individuals did not reach a normal alpha frequency of 10 cps until well into the adult years. These results suggest a constant, but slow, maturation of the central nervous system in the mentally retarded. Moreover, there is a paradoxical absence of age-related slowing in the EEG during the later decades of life, and possible retarded development of sensorimotor areas as reflected in slower central brain rhythms.

The coherence data (Figure 3) showed a steady increase in central coherence between the two hemispheres. The adult levels of coupling were approximately 0.7, which agrees quite closely with published reports of adult nonretarded individuals (Busk and Galbraith, 1975). These results indicate an increasing degree of coupling in the alpha rhythm recorded from over the left and right sensorimotor areas. Busk and Galbraith (1975) showed that higher levels of EEG coherence were obtained for electrode combinations that reflected known visual-motor anatomical pathways. The present data may, therefore, suggest a steady increase in the functional interaction between the sensorimotor areas of the two hemispheres. Since maturation of the mentally retarded nervous system is associated with increased central frequencies and increased coherence between left-right sensorimotor areas, it would be expected that those individuals with faster frequencies and higher coherence possess greater sensorimotor skills. We are currently investigating this question.

The phase data (Figure 4) indicate a very tight temporal relationship between homologous electrodes over the left and right hemispheres. Although anterior-posterior relationships are more variable with age, the results consistently favor anterior leading (positive ϕ). It is difficult to explain the reduced anterior leading in the middle age range, but it appears that ϕ increases from the earliest age tested up to 15–19 years, and then declines steadily beyond age 40–49 years. It is interesting to note that Darrow and Hicks (1965) reported that anterior leading in nonretarded individuals is associated with conditions of arousal and attention; and Galbraith and Schultz (1976) have shown that anterior leading is associated with a reduced ability to generalize to new temporal relationships in a visual-motor task. Clearly, more work is required before we can fully appreciate the significance of phase relationships in the nervous system of the mentally retarded individual.

In conclusion, our results show definite developmental trends in the electroencephalogram of institutionalized mentally retarded individuals. Development appears to be slower than expected from published reports with nonretarded individuals, and in certain instances there are apparent aberrations in the developmental trends. Because these trends appear to be stable, however, it should be possible in the future to evaluate a given retarded individual, and to assess the relative degree of central nervous system maturation. Evaluations of this type may, it is hoped, provide valuable new information concerning an individual's sensorimotor readiness and his ability to benefit from remedial learning programs.

SUMMARY

The electroencephalogram (EEG) was recorded in 300 mentally retarded individuals differing in age and diagnosis. EEG signals were analyzed by computer in order to quantify patterns of electrical activity recorded 1) from single scalp electrode sites (auto-spectrum), and 2) between pairs of electrode sites (cross-spectrum). The results of these analyses are presented according to differences in age. The possibility of assessing the functional development of the nervous system in a given individual is also discussed.

REFERENCES

Berger, H. (1932) Ueber das Elektrenkephalogramm des Meschen. V. Arch Psychiatr. Nervenkv. 98:231.

Brazier, M. A. B. (1968) The Electrical Activity of the Nervous System: A Textbook for Students. London: Pitman, p. 286.

Busk, J., and Galbraith, G. C. (1975) EEG correlates of visual-motor practice in man. Electroencephalogr. Clin. Neurophysiol. 38:415.

Darrow, C. W., and Hicks, R. G. (1965) Interarea electroencephalographic phase relationships following sensory and ideational stimuli. Psychophysiol. 1:337.

Eeg-Olofsson, O. (1971) The development of the electroencephalogram in normal children and adolescents from the age of 1 through 21 years. Acta Paediat Scand. Suppl. 208:1.

Galbraith, G. C., Gliddon, J. B., and Busk, J. (1975) Electrophysiological studies of mental retardation. In Developmental Psychophysiology of Mental Retardation (Ed. Karrer, R.) Springfield: Charles C Thomas, p. 311.

Galbraith, G. C., and Schultz, W. (1976) EEG correlates of visual-motor rearrangement in man. Paper presented at the Annual Meeting of the American EEG Society, Dearborn, Michigan, September.

Gibbs, F. A., and Gibbs, E. L. (1944) Electroencephalographic changes with age in adolescent and adult control subjects. Trans. Amer. Neurol. Assoc. 70:154.

Lindsley, D. B. (1936) Brain potentials in children and adults. Science. 84:354.

Matoušek, M., Volavka, J., Roubiček, J., and Roth, Z. (1967) EEG frequency analysis related to age in normal adults. Electroencephalogr. Clin. Neurophysiol. 23:162.

Obrist, W. D. (1954) The electroencephalogram of normal aged adults. Electroencephalogr. Clin. Neurophysiol. 6:235.

Obrist, W. D. (1963) The electroencephalogram of healthy aged males. In Human Aging: A Biological and Behavioral Study (Eds. Birren, J. E., Butler, R. N., Greenhouse, S. W., Sokoloff, L., and Yarrow, M. R.) Washington, D.C.: U.S. Government Printing Office, p. 76.

Obrist, W. D., and Busse, E. W. (1965) The electroencephalogram in old age. In Applications of Electroencephalography in Psychiatry: A Symposium (Ed. Wilson, W. W.) Durham: Duke University Press, p. 185.

Petersén, I., and Eeg-Olofsson, O. (1971) The development of the electroencephalogram in normal children from the age of 1 through 15 years. Neuropaediatrie. 2:247.

Smith, J. R. (1937) The electroencephalogram during infancy and childhood. Proc. Soc. Exp. Biol. Med. 36:384.

RESEARCH TO PRACTICE IN MENTAL RETARDATION
Biomedical Aspects, Volume III
Edited by Peter Mittler
Copyright 1977 I.A.S.S.M.D.

EVENT-RELATED POTENTIALS AND RESPONSE INITIATION IN THE RETARDED

R. Karrer and C. Warren
Illinois Institute for Developmental Disabilities,
1640 Roosevelt Road,
Chicago, Illinois 60608,
United States

Various laboratories have found that the retarded individual has a different topography of event-related potentials than equal age normals. These differences in pattern and timing of brain electrical activity are a promising lead to our understanding of brain-behavior relations. To fulfill this promise, patterns and timing of evoked potentials must be firmly related to performance and behavioral state.

Our laboratory has been studying the waveform and topography of the slow electrocortical activity preceding simple movements during development and in the retarded.

Previous research by Vaughan, Costa, and Ritter (1968) and by Deecke, Scheid, and Kornhuber (1969) has shown a specific waveform preceding a voluntary movement in normal adults. Figure 1 shows a slow negative-going trend which precedes the movement by 500–1,000 msec. This negative trend increases sharply at approximately the time of onset of muscle activity. Finally, accompanying the discrete movement there is a large positive-going "rebound."

We expect our research on these movement potentials to tell us something about the organization of motor behavior in the retarded and, ultimately, about the impaired performance of the retarded. In this chapter, we have briefly related two studies of these potentials that precede movement in the retarded. The first study used a simple, voluntarily emitted button press, while the second used a simple reaction time (RT) to a light flash. There was no warning preceding the flash. The response was identical in both tasks (a button press); therefore, the difference between them lay in whether or not the response was externally cued

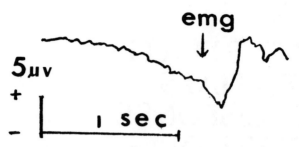

Figure 1. Waveform of activity preceding voluntary movement.

by the subject himself. The details of the studies have been published elsewhere (Karrer et al., 1976a, 1976b).

CUED RESPONDING

Figure 2 shows the activity preceding the cued-response in three samples of normal children, preadolescents and adolescents (age 6–8, 10–13, 16–18, respectively), and in one group of retarded adolescents (age 16–18). The retarded had a mean IQ of 63 and had no organic involvement with the exception of one case of Down's syndrome. It can be seen that there is a developmental trend of greater positive activity preceding and accompanying the muscle activity in the children than in the adolescents. Reaction time also followed an expected developmental trend (RT = 451, 322, 275 msec for children, preadolescents, and

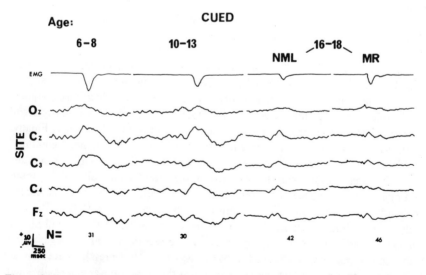

Figure 2. Representative subjects showing activity preceding a cued button press for a developmental sample of normal subjects and for retarded adolescents. Positivity is upwards.

adolescents, respectively). The retarded were comparable in waveform and amplitude to the normal adolescents, but their reaction times were significantly slower (RT = 417 msec).

It is apparent that those processes accompanying cued responding are similar to those of equal age normals. However, the pattern of relations to RT differed in the retarded, as well as developmentally. Activity in the right motor area (lead C_4) was correlated to RT in the adolescents ($r = 0.70$), and frontal activity (lead F_z) was correlated to RT in the preadolescents ($r = 0.66$), but frontal and occipital activity (F and O) were related to RT in the retarded ($r = -0.85$, 0.86, respectively). The normal children had no significant correlations but approached significance in F_z and O_z. Therefore, slower reaction times were accompanied by greater positivity in different areas of each group, and faster RT in the retardates was accompanied by greater frontal positivity.

NONCUED RESPONDING

The activity preceding the noncued task may be seen in Figure 3. Again, there was a developmental trend with positivity preceding muscle activity in the normal children, while the adolescents exhibited the classic, slow, negative-going waveform. The retarded were totally different, exhibiting a slow, positive-going waveform. There was some variability within groups for these waveforms, especially for children and preadolescents. However, as seen in Figure 4, groups differed significantly in the proportion of individuals exhibiting the various

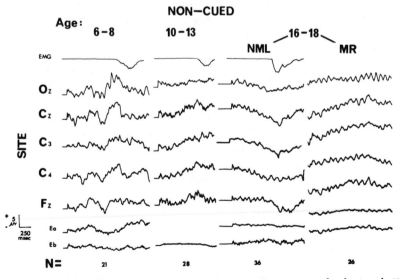

Figure 3. Representative subjects showing activity preceding a noncued voluntary button press for a developmental sample of normal subjects and for retarded adolescents. Positivity is upwards. (N = trials in average)

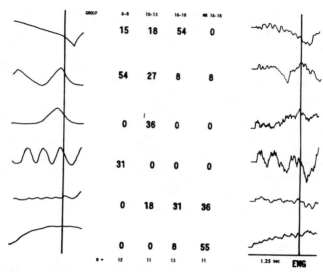

Figure 4. Idealized waveforms (left), representative raw vertex waveforms (right), and the proportion (middle) of subjects, by group, exhibiting each waveform.

waveforms. It also may be seen that there is a development trend in the number of individuals in the different age groups that exhibit the classic negative-going waveform. It is important to note that there is hardly any overlap between the normal and retarded adolescents for waveform.

In order to execute a response efficiently and effectively, it is necessary to inhibit extraneous motor responses that may interfere. Accordingly, we correlated a measure of extraneous responding to the electrocortical activity preceding the button press. Again, there was a different pattern of relationships developmentally and in the retarded. Apparently, positive activity in the right motor area (C_4) accompanies inhibition of irrelevant responding in the normal child ($r = 0.60$) when he is responding with his right hand. The retarded, on the contrary, had correlations indicating that positivity in frontal and occipital leads accompanied inhibition of irrelevant responses. ($r = -0.65$, 0.64 for F_z and O_z, respectively). In fact, the correlation for right motor area (C_4) was opposite in sign but not quite significant ($r = -0.54$ for C_4). The normal adolescent relations were similar to the children but not significant. It should be noted that similar areas were related to RT in the cued-response study (i.e., F_z and O_z for the retarded; C_4 for the normals).

CONCLUSIONS

On the basis of previous studies (Karrer and Ivins, 1976a, 1976b), we have argued that positivity preceding the motor response is related to inhibition of irrelevant motor responding in the child. The monophasic, positive-going waveform of the retarded, however, was unexpected. Deecke, Englitz, and Schmitt (1976) have recently reported similar waveforms in the elderly. It is tempting to conclude that poor performance, whether from retardation, aging, or immaturity, is accompanied by greater positivity (or less negativity) associated with the mobilization of processes to inhibit irrelevant motor activity.

It is particularly intriguing to consider the possibility that the positivity seen in the retarded during voluntary responding may indicate subtle abnormalities in pyramidal motor neurons (Huttenlocher, 1974; Purpura, 1974, 1975). In the retarded, dendritic spines are more primitive and there is a severe reduction in the overall number of spines (Purpura, 1974). The retarded child has a significantly greater number of total cortical synapses (Cragg, 1975); therefore, the data suggest a different, less efficacious synaptic geometry. The positive activity preceding voluntary responding may reflect this altered spatial distribution of synapses.

We have previously found that the retarded exhibited activity similar to that of normals during a forewarned reaction time task even though their reaction times were slower (Karrer and Ivins, 1976a, 1976c). Only the topography of their slow electrocortical activity was different. The present data from the nonwarned, cued-response task show comparable results. It would seem that different processes are involved in responding to an external cue (whether warned or nonwarned) than when voluntarily emitting a response to an intention.

The moderately retarded seem to have processes *similar* to those of normals when responding to a cue (e.g., equal amplitudes and polarity), but these processes seem to be organized differently (e.g., the different topography of activity). This is true whether or not the cue to respond follows a warning signal that allows preparation to respond. The different organization of processes implies that these retarded individuals use different, less effective strategies to perform the tasks (i.e., different topography and poor performance).

On the other hand, activity preceding the voluntarily intended noncued response may indicate *different* processes are mobilized by the retarded and normal adolescents (i.e., different polarity waveforms).

We are pursuing these data in further studies of response organization in the moderately retarded.

SUMMARY

Various laboratories have found that retarded individuals have a different topography of event-related potentials and EEG characteristics, than equal age normals. These differences in pattern and timing of brain electrical activity are a promising lead to our understanding of brain-behavior relations, requiring that they be firmly related to performance and state.

REFERENCES

Cragg, B. G. (1975) The density of synapses and neurons in normal, mentally defective, and aging brains. Brain. 98:81.

Deecke, L., Englitz, H. G., and Schmitt, G. (1976) Age-dependence of the *Bereitschafts* potential. Fourth Conf. on Event Related Slow Potentials of the Brain, Hendersonville, N.C., April. Washington, D.C.: Government Printing Office (in press).

Deecke, L., Scheid, P., and Kornhuber, H. H. (1969) Distribution of readiness potential, pre-motion positivity, and motor potential of the human cerebral cortex preceding voluntary finger movements. Exp. Brain Res. 7:158.

Huttenlocher, P. (1974) Dendritic development in neocortex of children with mental defect and infantile spasms. Neurology. 24:203.

Karrer, R., and Ivins, J. (1976a) Steady potentials accompanying perception and response in mentally retarded and normal children. *In* Developmental Psychophysiology of Mental Retardation (Ed. Karrer, R.) Springfield: Charles C Thomas.

Karrer, R., and Ivins, J. (1976b) Post-warning signal positivity in relation to development, RT performance, and warning signal compounding. *In* The Responsive Brain (Eds. McCallum, W. C., and Knott, J.) Bristol: John Wright.

Karrer, R., and Ivins, J. (1976c) Event-related slow potentials in mental retardates. *In* The Responsive Brain (Eds. McCallum, W. C., and Knott, J.) Bristol: John Wright.

Karrer, R., Warren, C., and Ruth, R. (1976a) Steady potential activity of the brain preceding non-cued and cued movement: Effects of development and mental retardation. Fourth Conf. on Event Related Slow Potentials of the Brain, Henderson, N.C., April. Washington, D.C.: Government Printing Office (in press).

Karrer, R., Warren, C., and Ruth, R. (1976b) Ananalysis of response initiation of the retarded. Paper presented to Amer. Acad. Ment. Retard., Chicago, May.

Purpura, D. P. (1974) Dendritic spine "dysgenesis" and mental retardation. Science. 186:1126.

Purpura, D. P. (1975) Dendritic differentiation in human cerebral cortex: Normal and aberrant developmental patterns. *In* Physiology and Pathology of Dendrites. (Ed. Breutzberg, G. W.) New York: Raven.

Vaughan, H. G., Costa, L. D., and Ritter, W. (1968) Topography of the human motor potential. Electroencephalogr. Clin. Neurophysiol. 25:1.

AUTHOR INDEX

SUBJECT INDEX